Published by the Author

THE JOHN HOPE FRANKLIN SERIES IN
AFRICAN AMERICAN HISTORY AND CULTURE

Waldo E. Martin Jr. and Patricia Sullivan, editors

A complete list of books published in the John Hope Franklin Series in African American History and Culture is available at https://uncpress.org/series/john-hope-franklin-series-african-american-history-culture.

Published by the Author
Self-Publication in Nineteenth-Century African American Literature

Bryan Sinche

The University of North Carolina Press CHAPEL HILL

© 2024 Bryan Sinche
All rights reserved
Set in Merope Basic by Westchester Publishing Services
Manufactured in the United States of America

Complete Cataloging-in-Publication Data for this title is available from the
Library of Congress at https://lccn.loc.gov/2024005615.

ISBN 978-1-4696-7412-4 (cloth: alk. paper)
ISBN 978-1-4696-7413-1 (pbk.: alk. paper)
ISBN 978-1-4696-7414-8 (epub)
ISBN 978-8-8908-8746-7 (pdf)

Cover art courtesy of the American Antiquarian Society.

This book will be made open access within three years of publication thanks to Path to Open, a program developed in partnership between JSTOR, the American Council of Learned Societies (ACLS), the University of Michigan Press, and the University of North Carolina Press to bring about equitable access and impact for the entire scholarly community, including authors, researchers, libraries, and university presses around the world. Learn more at https://about.jstor.org/path-to-open/.

For Melanie

Contents

List of Figures and Tables ix
Acknowledgments xi

Introduction 1

CHAPTER ONE
Not in Giving, but in Buying a Book 37
Self-Publishing and the Supplicant Text

CHAPTER TWO
Independent of the Abolitionists 64
Antislavery Self-Publishing

CHAPTER THREE
He Was Never the Same Man Again 90
Rewriting American History

CHAPTER FOUR
I Sue for Justice to Be Established 118
Self-Publication as Alternate Testimony

CHAPTER FIVE
That This Book May Speak for Me 145
Preachers as Publishers

CHAPTER SIX
A Grand Report in the Way of Selling 173
Publishing for Profit

Coda 196
The Walking Book

Notes 201
Bibliography 229
Index 251

Figures and Tables

FIGURES

I.1 Advertisement for J. W. Burke Printers (1884) 2

I.2 Title page for *The Life of Rev. Robert Anderson* (1892) 6

I.3 Detail from William Grimes's *Life* (1825) 16

I.4A G. W. Offley receipt for printing at Case, Lockwood & Co. (1859) 21

I.4B Cover of *A Narrative of the Life and Labors of the Rev. G. W. Offley* (1859) 22

1.1 Cover of *The Light and the Truth of Slavery*, version three (1840s) 41

1.2 Cover of *The Light and the Truth of Slavery*, version six (1840s) 44

1.3 Flyer in *A Family Redeemed from Bondage* (1851) 59

2.1 "Literary Exhibitions in New York City," *Frederick Douglass' Paper* (1854) 72

2.2 Cover of *Life and Narrative of William J. Anderson*, third edition (1857) 87

3.1 Final page of *Wonderful Eventful Life of Thomas James* (1887) 108

4.1 Cover of *Christ's Millennium* (1811) 124

4.2 Detail from *Christ's Millennium* (1811) and Christopher McPherson's petition to the city of Richmond (1810) 126

5.1 Cover of Elijah Marrs's *Life and History* (1885) 156

5.2 Detail from James Wilkerson's *History* (1861) 168

5.3 *The Midnight Cry* (1859) 169

6.1 Detail from *The Life of Rev. Robert Anderson* (1892) 182

C.1 Portrait of James Mars (1870) 198

TABLES

1.1 Versions of *The Light and [the] Truth of Slavery* 42

3.1 Versions of James Mars's autobiographies 101

3.2 Editions and printings of Jacob Stroyer's autobiographies 111

6.1 Editions of Robert B. Anderson's autobiographies 176

Acknowledgments

Long before I conceived of this project or even heard of most of the authors I write about in this book, numerous scholars did the difficult and often unrecognized work that made future research in African American literature possible. A full accounting of my debts to these scholars would be impossible, but I want to acknowledge Houston Baker, D. Dickson Bruce, Frances Smith Foster, John Hope Franklin, Nathan Huggins, Dorothy Porter, Benjamin Quarles, Marian Starling, and Robert Stepto.

When I was an undergraduate at the University of Michigan, two classes with Kerry Larson made me want to learn more about American literature; Kerry's wit and erudition provided the example that led me toward graduate school at the University of North Carolina. There, I was surrounded by a community of professors and students who fueled my passion for scholarship, two of whom merit special mention: Bill Andrews changed my life by hiring me as his research assistant and teaching me about African American autobiography. He has been a source of wisdom and good advice for more than twenty years, and his influence is evident throughout this book. Philip Gura was an extraordinary mentor who taught me how to be a professor, and his example remains a source of inspiration.

I never would have undertaken this project had I not been a W. E. B. Du-Bois fellow at the Hutchins Center in 2013–14, and I never could have completed it had I not had access to the Harvard University Library since 2014. For her generous assistance over the past decade, I thank Krishna Lewis. For his support over the past two decades and his innumerable contributions to our field, I thank Henry Louis Gates Jr.

Since I began working on this project, many other folks have helped in ways both great and small. In addition to those named above, I have benefited from the advice and support of Susannah Ashton, Tara Bynum, Katy Chiles, Jasmine Nichole Cobb, Lara Langer Cohen, Marcy Dinius, John Ernest, Bridgette Fielder, Eric Gardner, Jim Green, Jennifer Harris, Erica Kitzmiller, Barbara McCaskill, Joycelyn Moody, Edie Quinn, Augusta Rohrbach, Michaël Roy, Jonathan Senchyne, David Whitesell, and Michael Winship. My former students Teresa Dudek-Rolon and Steven Perrone provided crucial research assistance. Jon Daigle, Eric Gardner, Bill Major, Laura

Mielke, Michaël Roy, Melanie Sinche, and Rachel Walker read portions of the manuscript and offered honest criticism that improved the book. Finally, the two readers for the University of North Carolina Press gave detailed and probing critiques that made the final product much better. All these generous colleagues did a lot to save me from myself, but all remaining errors of fact or interpretation are mine.

Librarians at various institutions have been enormously helpful over the course of my work on this book. At the University of Hartford, Randi Ashton-Pritting, Ed Bernstein, and Christy Bird have helped me locate hard-to-find books, pamphlets, and microfilm and have done this work with a kindness that cannot be taken for granted. Thanks also to librarians and staff at the American Antiquarian Society, the Beinecke Library at Yale University, the Bentley Historical Library and William Clements Library at the University of Michigan, the Boston Public Library, the Dolph Briscoe Center for American History (especially Erin Harbour), the Houghton and Widener Libraries at Harvard University, the Huntington Library, the Library Company of Philadelphia (especially Jim Green), the Moorland-Spingarn Library at Howard University (especially Sammie Johnson), the New York Historical Society, the North Carolina State Archives, the Phillips Library at the Peabody Essex Museum, the Schomburg Branch of the New York Public Library, the Small Library at the University of Virginia, the Southern Historical Collection at the University of North Carolina, and the Watkinson Library at Trinity College. Finally, thanks to John Dudek, Michael Everman, Lance Hale, Guylaine Petrin, and Chamere-Poole Warren, all of whom assisted me by locating and scanning court records or other documents.

My work on this book was made possible by various grants of material support that funded research travel and/or course releases. Thanks to Walter Harrison and Belle K. Ribicoff for endowing awards that proved vital to my efforts, to the Faculty Senate at the University of Hartford for awarding me a Coffin Grant, and to the National Endowment for the Humanities, which awarded me a summer stipend. Though the summer stipend proved enormously useful, any views, findings, conclusions, or recommendations expressed in this book do not necessarily reflect those of the National Endowment for the Humanities.

At the University of North Carolina Press, Lucas Church supported this project from the moment he heard about it and helped me navigate the long road to publication. Thanks also to Thomas Bedenbaugh, Valerie Burton, and Liz Orange Lane for their help as the book wended its way through editing and production. I want to especially thank Lindsay Starr and her team for the wonderful cover design; it captures the look of many of the self-published books and pamphlets I examined over the course of my research.

Portions of this book first appeared within chapters in the following collections: *Against a Sharp White Background: Infrastructures of African American Print*, edited by Brigitte Fielder and Jonathan Senchyne and published by the University of Wisconsin Press; *African American Literature in Transition, 1800–1830*, edited by Jasmine Nichole Cobb; and *African American Literature in Transition, 1880–1900*, edited by Caroline Gebhard and Barbara McCaskill, both published by Cambridge University Press. Thanks to the editors and readers of those volumes for their wisdom and guidance, and thanks to both presses for permission to reprint.

At the University of Hartford, I am surrounded by smart, good-natured, and hardworking colleagues. I am grateful for the support of my former chair and current dean, Mark Blackwell, the ready assistance of our departmental administrators Nancy Dudek and Donna Galin, the unwavering encouragement of my department chairs, Robert Logan, T. Stores, and Amanda Walling, and the kindness and wisdom of my colleagues in the Department of English and Modern Languages.

I am fortunate to number several good friends among the University of Hartford faculty with whom I have enjoyed running, gardening, hiking, laughing, and celebrating. Among them, I especially want to thank Jon Daigle, Ben Grossberg, Bill Major, and Dan Williamson, all of whom have made Hartford a happier place to live and work. As my readers probably know, it is hard for English professors to have friends outside the academy since we bore most people, but there are a few folks who have not wandered away just yet. Among them, I especially want to thank Jennifer Daigle, Jennifer Devine, Larry Grady, Ginny Major, Dan Schwab, Eric Smidt, Kurt Spurlock, and Cathy Williamson.

My greatest debts are to my family. My in-laws, Jerry and Lorraine Vigil, have given of themselves for decades, and their support and love have helped to make this work possible. I am also grateful for the kindness, generosity, and good humor of my sister, Laura, and for all my brothers- and sisters-in-law, nieces, nephews, aunts, and uncles. Sheryl and Charlie Sinche, my mom and dad, have been my sturdiest supporters. Over their fifty-plus years of marriage, Mom and Dad have taught me and my family many things, especially the importance of everyday kindness, consideration, attention, and appreciation. I thank them with all my love.

During the decade in which I worked on this book, my sons Charles and Henry grew into giants. These days, I enjoy looking up to them and laughing with them. I invite them to marvel at the direct textual evidence in this book, and I encourage them to use the same in their own writing.

Finally, it would be impossible for me to enumerate the many ways Melanie Sinche has enriched my life since we met thirty years ago, but I love the life we have made together, and she is the principal reason I look forward to the rest of it with joy and excitement.

Published by the Author

Introduction

In the fall of 1890, Rev. Robert Anderson traveled sixty miles from Sandersville, Georgia, to his former hometown of Macon, where he paid a visit to his old Methodist Episcopal colleague, Rev. John W. Burke. Burke owned a printing shop in Macon (see fig. 1.1) where, over his long career, he had produced a weekly magazine for children, several newspapers, government reports, the college catalog for the University of Georgia, church histories, and countless books and pamphlets with titles like *Stray Leaves from the Portfolio of a Methodist Local Preacher* and *Eight Nights with a Reading Club*.[1] Books like *Stray Leaves* were original works by local figures that were typeset and printed at Burke's shop, and it was this part of Burke's business that made him so interesting to the septuagenarian Robert Anderson, a formerly enslaved man who was winding up a decades-long career in the pulpit. In the 1870s and 1880s, Anderson had paid to print two versions of his short autobiography and sold them as he preached all over Georgia; with his ministerial career nearly over, Anderson decided to focus on his authorial career by selling an expanded version of his autobiography. During their meeting in 1890, Anderson paid Burke seventy-five dollars to print the new edition of *The Life of Rev. Robert Anderson* and Burke "agreed to have the books ready for [Anderson] by the time Conference convened in Macon."[2] Anderson's mention of the "Conference" here is important since it indicates that he wanted his book printed before the January 1891 Savannah Annual Conference of the Methodist Episcopal Church. Anderson would be returning to Macon for the meeting, and he wanted to sell his book to old friends, colleagues, and acquaintances.[3] Though the book was not ready until the last day of the conference, Anderson's bookselling efforts in 1891 would prove remarkably successful; by the end of that summer, he had made more than $250, and he would continue selling his self-published books for more than a decade.[4]

This book is about men and women like Rev. Robert Anderson: entrepreneurial Black Americans who paid to print their life stories and circulated those stories themselves. These self-published narratives, many of which have been completely ignored by critics or imagined as lesser versions of canonical slave narratives, are remarkably diverse and creative. At the same

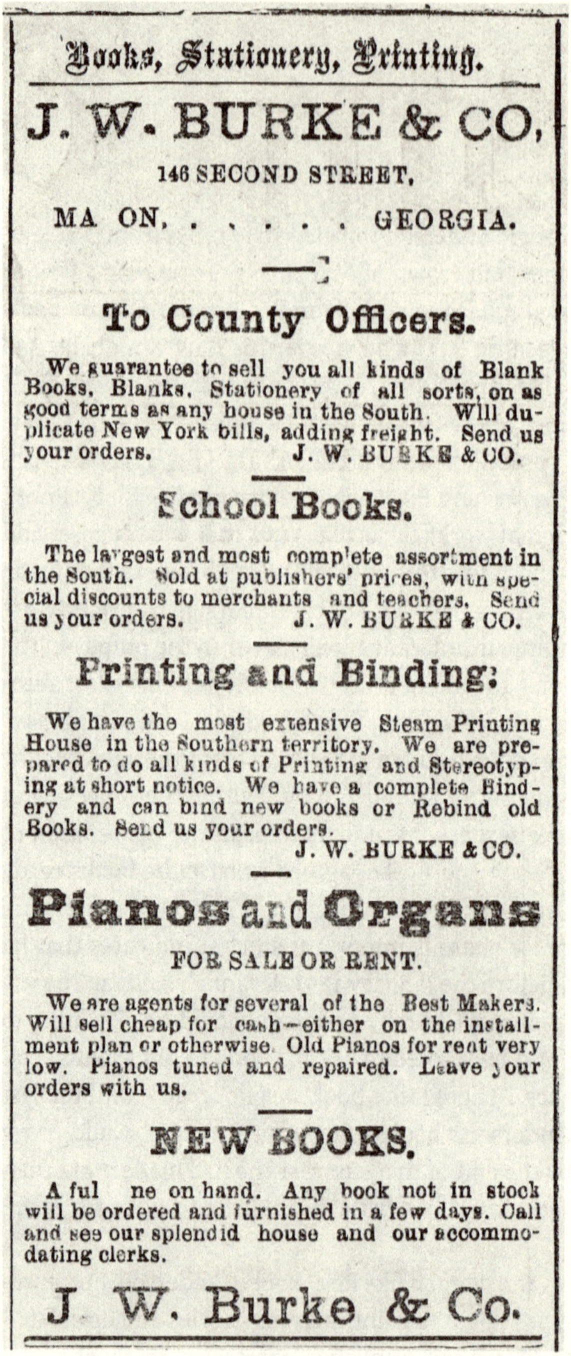

FIGURE I.1
Advertisement for J. W. Burke & Co. Printers from the *Macon Telegraph*, January 15, 1881.

Books, Stationery, Printing.

J. W. BURKE & CO,

146 SECOND STREET,

MA ON, ... GEORGIA.

To County Officers.

We guarantee to sell you all kinds of Blank Books, Blanks, Stationery of all sorts, on as good terms as any house in the South. Will duplicate New York bills, adding freight. Send us your orders. J. W. BURKE & CO.

School Books.

The largest and most complete assortment in the South. Sold at publishers' prices, with special discounts to merchants and teachers. Send us your orders. J. W. BURKE & CO.

Printing and Binding:

We have the most extensive Steam Printing House in the Southern territory. We are prepared to do all kinds of Printing and Stereotyping at short notice. We have a complete Bindery and can bind new books or Rebind old Books. Send us your orders.
J. W. BURKE & CO.

Pianos and Organs

FOR SALE OR RENT.

We are agents for several of the Best Makers. Will sell cheap for cash—either on the installment plan or otherwise. Old Pianos for rent very low. Pianos tuned and repaired. Leave your orders with us.

NEW BOOKS.

A ful ne on hand. Any book not in stock will be ordered and furnished in a few days. Call and see our splendid house and our accommodating clerks.

J. W. Burke & Co.

time, they are quite common. As Elizabeth McHenry opines, "the majority of African American texts that found their way into print in the late nineteenth and early twentieth centuries were produced not by publishers but by printers."[5] In fact, the only thing that may be inaccurate about McHenry's claim is that it is not expansive enough. According to the American Antiquarian Society's (AAS's) Black Self-Publishing website, there were more than 575 books and pamphlets self-published by African American men and women during the nineteenth century.[6] This means that printers, rather than commercial publishers, produced most of the African American writing from the eighteenth century to the Harlem Renaissance. In order to better understand this massive trove of understudied texts, the men and women who produced them, and the material conditions under which they were produced, this book surveys, categorizes, and analyzes self-published first-person narratives from across the nineteenth century. I argue that self-publication was a widespread practice that aspiring authors used to shape their individual circumstances as well as the physical and intellectual spaces they inhabited.

When contemporary scholars think about publishing in the nineteenth-century United States, they probably imagine a professional practice in which (among other things) a manuscript is typeset, printed, bound, distributed, and sold. In a royalty system like the one that came to dominate commercial book production in the nineteenth-century United States and continues to dominate today, this is indeed the role of the publisher.[7] Within that system, an author would submit their manuscript for consideration; if the publisher accepted the manuscript for publication, financial terms would be negotiated. Throughout the nineteenth century, publishers pushed for aggressive terms so they would reap most of the profits from a book's sale. Some well-known authors (like James Fenimore Cooper or Washington Irving) were able to secure a larger percentage of a publisher's profits, but most received 10 percent or less of what a publisher grossed on a particular title.[8] In return for granting a publisher most of the money to be earned, a nineteenth-century author could expect to have his or her work edited, printed, bound, publicized, and then distributed across an increasingly nationalized network.[9] The massive Harper Brothers firm, based in New York, advertised their books in newspapers around the country, though most of those advertisements appeared in the Northeast until later in the nineteenth century.[10] Like the Harpers, other publishers tried to find ways to centralize and nationalize the print market so a single publishing house could dominate large swaths of the country; even so, commercial book publishing would not become a truly nationalized industry until the twentieth century.

While the large publishing houses in New York City became more powerful and influential in the 1800s, the commercial book publishing system remained a small part of the larger print landscape in which newspapers, periodicals, broadsides, advertisements, timetables, visiting cards, invitations, and sheet music were just as ubiquitous as smartphones are today. Books were part of that landscape too, but most Americans would have interacted with newspapers, ephemera, and other forms of "cheap print" far more often than they would have read a bound book published by a firm like Harper's or Ticknor and Fields since most commercially produced books cost fifty cents or more at a time when a laborer only made a dollar per day. For African American readers, periodicals and newspapers were even more important, mostly because of the relatively low cost and geographic reach of such publications.[11] As Eric Gardner argues in *Black Print Unbound*, "the exclusionary practices of 'mainstream' white print culture regularly made the nineteenth-century Black press the best—and often the only—outlet for many Black authors."[12] Gardner's contention is correct insofar as outlets like the *Christian Recorder* or the *A.M.E. Church Review* (among many other periodicals) provided Black authors and letter writers—including some featured in this book—with venues in which their work might reach audiences across the country. What Gardner's assertion misses, though, are the hundreds of men and women who avoided "mainstream" print culture altogether and employed a job printer to publish their work themselves.

Any experienced reader of nineteenth-century African American narratives has seen title pages with phrases like "Published by the Author," "Printed for the Author," or "Published by Himself." The same readers have seen bibliographies with the abbreviation "s.n." in place of a publisher; s.n. comes from the Latin *sine nominee*, meaning "without name," and it suggests the publisher is unnamed. These are the bibliographical hallmarks of self-publication and usually indicate that the publisher and author shared the same name. Self-publishing authors did not need to gain the approval of editors or white-led abolitionist organizations to represent themselves in print. Instead, they embraced what Michaël Roy calls an "artisanal model of publication" by paying a printer and then circulating the broadside, book, or pamphlet they created, usually with the hope of making a profit.[13] Many of these authors probably earned enough to recoup the costs of printing and some made considerably more. The Reverend Robert Anderson would go on to make thousands of dollars as a self-publisher and self-promoter, a level of economic success that sets him apart from most of the men and women in this book. In other ways, though, Anderson is a representative figure since his authorial career highlights several of the defining features of nineteenth-century African American self-publication.

First, Anderson took advantage of the control self-publication offers to produce a book that is unique in terms of both theme and style. Scholars and students alike are accustomed to thinking of nineteenth-century African American life writing in relation to the slave narrative genre, which Frances Smith Foster describes as "a personal account of a life in bondage and the struggle to escape it."[14] The "most impressive feature" of the slave narrative, according to Robert B. Stepto, is the "former slave . . . *remembering* his ordeal in bondage."[15] These two elements are certainly a crucial part of the African American narratives taught and read most frequently, but they are not so crucial to the many narratives by formerly enslaved men and women that skip over, avoid, or deflect the author's personal experience in slavery.[16] Recent work by Teresa Goddu, Michaël Roy, and others has complicated our collective understanding of the slave narrative as a genre by attending to the materiality of African American books and pamphlets. As Goddu puts it, "a material approach to the slave narrative sets the multiplicity of the archive against the monolith of the genre."[17] Goddu's perceptive comment gives us a way to think about Robert Anderson's book (fig. 1.2), which is classed as a "slave narrative" on Documenting the American South but says almost nothing about Anderson's life in bondage.

The title of Anderson's *Life* suggests that the book is a straightforward autobiography, but the subtitles suggest otherwise: "The Young Men's Guide" connects the book to numerous nineteenth-century advice manuals, and "The Brother in White" refers to (often paternalistic) cross-racial alliances in the American South. Anderson indicates that the book also includes biblical history, theology, a remedy for smallpox, and "a series of questions alphabetically arranged." Anderson's claims for his book are more than a bit exaggerated, but his title page suggests a purchaser will get anything and everything out of Anderson's *Life*. Other self-published books include multiple forms or genres (sermons, newspaper stories, images, extracts from other books or pamphlets, letters); several publications are self-consciously "in progress" and appear in multiple editions that update or revise previous versions; many are only nominally autobiographies since they focus less on an entire life story and more on the events or concerns that motivated publication in the first place. All of this is to say that self-publication was, for the most part, an idiosyncratic process in which authors designed their

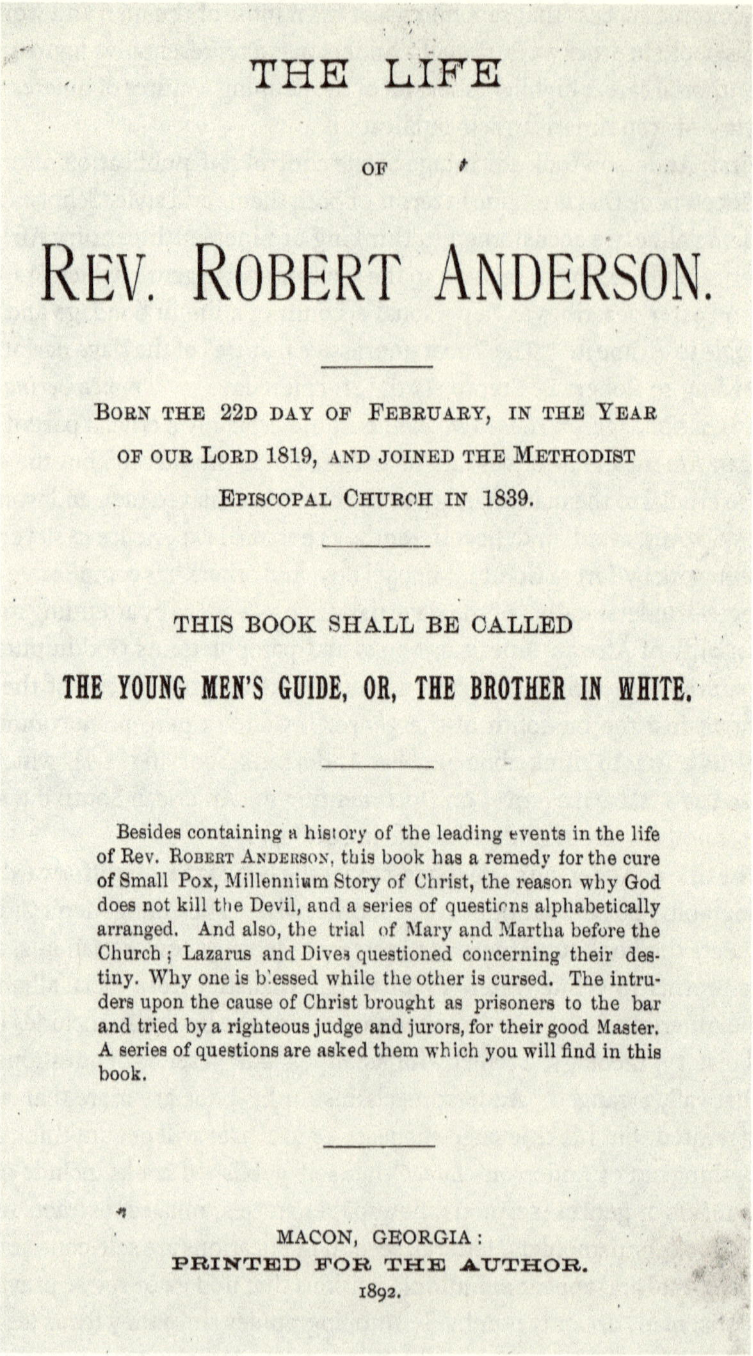

THE LIFE

OF

REV. ROBERT ANDERSON.

BORN THE 22D DAY OF FEBRUARY, IN THE YEAR OF OUR LORD 1819, AND JOINED THE METHODIST EPISCOPAL CHURCH IN 1839.

THIS BOOK SHALL BE CALLED

THE YOUNG MEN'S GUIDE, OR, THE BROTHER IN WHITE.

Besides containing a history of the leading events in the life of Rev. ROBERT ANDERSON, this book has a remedy for the cure of Small Pox, Millennium Story of Christ, the reason why God does not kill the Devil, and a series of questions alphabetically arranged. And also, the trial of Mary and Martha before the Church; Lazarus and Dives questioned concerning their destiny. Why one is blessed while the other is cursed. The intruders upon the cause of Christ brought as prisoners to the bar and tried by a righteous judge and jurors, for their good Master. A series of questions are asked them which you will find in this book.

MACON, GEORGIA:
PRINTED FOR THE AUTHOR.
1892.

FIGURE I.2 Title page of *The Life of Rev. Robert Anderson* (1892). Courtesy of the American Antiquarian Society.

publications depending on their finances, interests, competencies, and needs, and those publications are as diverse as their authors.

Second, Anderson thought of authorship in entrepreneurial terms and prioritized profitability in the ways he designed, printed, and sold his work. This may seem unremarkable since most commercial publishers also prioritize profitability, but self-publication is often imagined in relation to the vanity press; that is, authors only choose self-publication when there is no market for their work. As Anderson and his authorial brethren show, however, self-publishers could capitalize on unique local markets or create brand-new markets that commercial publishers either never imagined or never bothered to access. And, since self-publishers had or established relationships with their purchasers, they enjoyed extraordinary control over marketing and sales. As Michaël Roy notes, Frederick Douglass sold more copies of his self-financed *Narrative* (1845) than his commercially produced *My Bondage and My Freedom* (1855), largely because Douglass took on both the risk and responsibility of selling his first book and did so energetically for several years.[18] A half-century later, Robert Anderson followed Douglass's lead: He met almost all his customers and encouraged them to make purchases; he offered on-the-spot discounts for reluctant buyers; he accepted donations along with his sales that boosted his profit margins. Obviously, selling a book on street corners has some limitations, but it also presents opportunities that do not exist for authors operating within traditional publishing structures.

Third, Anderson understood self-publication to be a timely activity in which his pamphlet or book was designed to meet an immediate economic, social, or political need. Most readers probably think of a book as something that endures over a long period of time, a pattern of thought that has been reinforced by widespread digitization efforts that have made countless nineteenth-century texts available at the click of a button. Some self-publishers certainly hoped their books would endure, but almost all of them wanted to effect some kind of change in a particular place at a particular time. With few exceptions, their publications were designed to be bought, consumed, and *used* rather than bought, stored, and *consulted*. To better understand this distinction, my readers might think about the shelves in their office, study, or library carrel: the books on those shelves often sit unopened for months, years, or even decades. The books—many of them having stood the test of time—signify for visitors as totems of erudition and expertise; they may signify for us as reminders of our own learning and growth; they are objects to which we return when we teach or write, and their significance is measured in decades or centuries. On the other hand, most of the books and pamphlets produced by Black self-publishers were not designed to be examined multiple times or saved for posterity. We might consider the work of self-publishers in relation to contemporary forms like the website, blog, newsletter, or social media post. Most self-published texts were designed and published to address an exigency and—for the most part—were treated as such by their consumers.

Though most of the needs that self-publishers met were practical in nature, there is ample evidence that many self-publishers also enjoyed psychological rewards concomitant with their work. In some cases, those rewards had to do with the work of authorship, as Robert Anderson explains in his 1895 autobiography: "My book, in fact, has made me happy, because I feel that if the white people will read it they will discover that a colored man can write a book, too, just as well as anybody else."[19] There are other kinds of psychological rewards that self-publishers may have reaped as well. Because many of them sold what Roy calls the "itinerant narrative," the work of bookselling was combined with the pleasures and frustrations attending travel.[20] Those pleasures were real though: finding friends and acquaintances on the road, meeting new people through sales, or discovering new places and ways of being. Even aged, infirm, and/or disabled self-publishers seem to have enjoyed aspects of their bookselling lives; for them, the self-published text was both a commodity and a passport.

No matter what kind of rewards they gained, the men and women who created their own books and pamphlets were what Karen Weyler calls "outsider authors;" those who "were marginalized by limitations on their freedom" but who still "grasped the profoundly social nature of print and its power to influence public opinion."[21] As I suggest above, most author-publishers were much closer to their audiences than a large industrial or corporate entity could have been, and those authors were personally invested in their book's success. This audience connection is crucial since, as Timothy Laquintano explains, a self-publisher who is close to his or her audience can focus on "what a book does, or . . . what people do with a book" and on the "systems and practices in which [the book] is situated."[22] Put another way, because self-publishers do not write for mass audiences, they can produce books targeted at a specific group of potential purchasers that will be more likely to circulate within their location and historical moment. And, since nineteenth-century self-publishers usually relied on in-person sales and circulation within a limited geographical and temporal frame, the author could explain the book and set the terms of its purchase instead of relying on the words inside the book to do that crucial work. This is not to say that the words do not matter, but, as Laquintano argues, those words do "not determine the activity in which [the book] is embedded," nor do they always "determine how [a book] will be interpreted, used, or appropriated."[23]

The story of Robert Anderson's bookselling career helps us better understand Laquintano's ideas about the ways books might be used, especially if we consider "use" from the author's point of view. Anderson lived his entire life in the state of Georgia, and he knew how to navigate a social and economic system shaped by white supremacy. Within that system, there were numerous limitations imposed on Black people who wanted to travel by foot or conveyance, something Anderson knew from his long years working as an itinerant minister. When he began selling his *Life*, though, Anderson found that bookselling enabled unfettered mobility. As a former minister selling a book, he had both a reason to travel and a status that allowed him passage on trains and boats for reduced fares. Once he arrived in a new place, Anderson always visited the mayor's office to gain approval for his bookselling mission. On a trip to Athens, Georgia, Anderson met the mayor, who "bought one of [his] books," and "gave [him] leave to sell as many as I could," which meant that Anderson would be unbothered as he moved around town.[24] Similarly, Anderson used his book to gain access to posh hotels and resorts like the Ponce de Leon Hotel in St. Augustine, Florida, which Anderson said was "the finest hotel in the world."[25] What Anderson and many other self-publishers learned is that the very act of bookselling could enable freedom of movement that was atypical for Black Americans. Indeed, bookselling offered self-publishers what Cheryl Fish calls "mobile subjectivity," which she defines as a "subject position . . . that enables its agents to examine and create various constructions of the self and others while moving."[26] For Anderson and so many others, selling offered opportunities that go well beyond disseminating a message.

Because self-published texts are written, marketed, and used in idiosyncratic ways, and because they served as both tools for their author as well as texts for readers, I evaluate them not only by assessing rhetorical markers of complexity like intertextuality, irony, or ambiguity, but also by considering the ways that such texts are connected to their various economic, social, political, legal, and literary contexts. To evaluate self-published texts in this way is to treat publication as what Laquintano calls a "literacy practice" as opposed to a professional practice.[27] Since author-publishers each controlled, at least in part, the ways their words *and* their published form would appear before potential buyers, self-publishing authors were masters of what Jerome

McGann has called the "linguistic code" (the words in a book) and the "bibliographic code" (the size, shape, binding, paper) for their publications.[28] By classifying publication as a "literacy practice," I want to grant the same degree of agency and power to the author-publisher that critics have long granted to the African American men and women who acquired and deployed formal literacy and published their work through commercial or abolitionist-sponsored organizations.[29] For self-published authors, publication was not just something that happened *to* their writings, but a process that was at least partially controlled by the author. This means the words within a publication, the material form of the publication, and even the ways a publication was circulated are all signifying elements through which an author-publisher makes meaning for audiences.

By focusing on the material and the physical in addition to the rhetorical, this book diverges from the seminal work of critics like William L. Andrews, Houston A. Baker, Frances Smith Foster, Henry Louis Gates Jr., and Robert Stepto, all of whom analyze the linguistic codes in Black autobiography and the ways those codes inaugurated a literary tradition extending from the eighteenth into the twentieth century.[30] These critics shaped my understanding of Black autobiography and encouraged my work in the field, but my work is less concerned with either authorial consciousness or the "literariness" of first-person narratives and more concerned with what the books and pamphlets were meant to do for authors and audiences. My analyses foreground the physical and textual elements of publication; the situations in which publication occurred; the markets in which books were circulated, traded, and sold; the economic possibilities associated with book publication; and the social and political effects of bookmaking and bookselling. As I survey and categorize nineteenth-century self-published texts, the majority of which have been ignored or mentioned only in passing by scholars of African American literature, I argue that self-publication was a vital print practice for nineteenth-century African Americans since it gave hundreds of "outsider authors" the chance to create and circulate unique books and pamphlets that revealed the challenges and joys attending life in the United States and imagined new social, political, and economic horizons for Black Americans.

Self-Publication: Format, Finance, and Function

This book concerns itself with African American first-person narratives self-published in North America between 1798 and 1902. I have limited the project to first-person narratives for several reasons. First, by focusing on a single genre, I can highlight the similarities and differences between different texts across a significant temporal expanse. Second, many readers—especially those who have only encountered a few African American autobiographies—view the genre in limited ways. By illuminating the diversity of motives, strategies, and styles in self-published autobiographies, I hope to change that.[31] Finally, many self-published narratives include the stories of their own creation or serve as the keystone of an author's expansive print career, so by centering first-person narratives, I can elaborate a richer story about Black publishing and print culture.

My efforts to locate, read, and contextualize the narratives in this book presented a unique scholarly challenge. Indeed, one reason African American self-publication has failed to attract a great deal of scholarly attention is that—until very recently—we did not know just how common and widespread self-publication was. As McGill and Jacqueline Goldsby explain, this is because most American bibliographies have "failed to reflect the genres of Black writing and the print formats in which Black authors published."[32] Self-publication is a crucial part of the history of African American literature, but, with a few important exceptions, scholars have dismissed self-published books and pamphlets as unimportant or ephemeral. Fortunately, the heroic work of librarians and collectors like Daniel Murray, Dorothy Porter, and Arturo Schomburg preserved many self-published texts, and bibliographies by scholars William L. Andrews and Russell Brignano organized and contextualized many of them that were, in turn, digitized and made widely available. All this work enabled more recent efforts like Goldsby and McGill's Black Bibliography Project (BBP) and the AAS's Black Self-Publishing website.[33]

Because my research began before the BBP or AAS resources became available, I relied on earlier bibliographies by Andrews, Brignano, and Porter and identified more than eighty self-published narratives produced in North America between 1798 and 1902.[34] I read all those narratives and, because their materiality is so important to the discussions that follow, I examined at least one physical copy of each text I discuss (and more than 125 in all). This research led me to discover that there are multiple editions/versions of several self-published texts that have eluded scholars and bibliographers alike.[35] In addition to examining physical copies of the texts, I also pored over printers' records; receipts; letters; journals; court records; newspaper stories; advertisements; census records; church, family, and oral histories; photographs; and maps. As many readers will no doubt understand, it is hard to gather data on many nineteenth-century men and women, especially those whose histories have been ignored or—worse—intentionally excluded or destroyed. This book represents an effort to collect, explain, and evaluate the traces that remain.

As I indicate above in my discussion of Rev. Robert Anderson, there are three specific strands connecting the stories of self-publishers to Black print culture: format, finance, and function. All these strands are relevant to any published writing in any time, but they take on a specific character for Black self-publishers in the nineteenth-century United States. Format describes the size, shape, content, and appearance of self-published Black print and the overlap between these material and textual factors and the authors' goals. Finance refers to the economic considerations that were paramount for authors who had to pay a printer to produce their work and, in most cases, had to recoup their investment through circulation and sales. Finally, function—around which each chapter is organized—refers to the social, political, and/or religious concerns that authors addressed through their publications. In the remainder of the introduction, I treat each of these in turn as I guide readers through the processes of printing, marketing, and sales linked to self-publication.

Format

I begin with the material text and the words within the text, elements of self-publication I group under the banner of "format." My use of this term is indebted to the work of Meredith McGill, who argues that format (rather than form or medium) directs "our attention to the set of choices publishers make in having a work printed, as they keep the field of a book's potential circulation very much in mind. From a publisher's perspective, format is where economic and technological limitations meet cultural expectations."[36] If we combine McGill's insights about a publisher's motivations and goals with D. F. McKenzie's insistence that "the material form of books, the non-verbal elements of the typographic notations within them, the very disposition of space itself, have an expressive function in conveying meaning," we begin to understand the significance of format for self-published authors.[37] While most modern authors do not design their own book cover, select their own paper, or choose the size of their publication, for the unique group of authors I examine in this book, publishers' choices about format are also authorial choices. For those author-publishers, format is not a container in which words are found or something *exterior* to a self-published text; rather, it is a crucial aspect of the text itself and a key to decoding its meanings. As I attend to format in self-published books and pamphlets, I also practice what

McGill calls "a version of book history that can countenance textual evidence, not ignore it or explain it away."[38] Specifically, I examine format for insight into the text of a publication, and I look to textual evidence to explain authorial choices about format and circulation.

With this understanding of format structuring my readings, I focus most especially on two factors. First, there is what McKenzie calls the "material form of books": size, shape, "disposition of space," paper, and binding. In this regard, self-published texts run the gamut: from Major James Wilkerson's massive (fifty-one centimeters by thirty-two centimeters) broadside titled "The Midnight Cry" (1859) to Norvel Blair's tiny (fifteen centimeters) pamphlet (1880), from Henry Parker's eight-page pamphlet (186?) without even a title page to Mifflin Wistar Gibbs's handsome 400-page *Shadow and Light* (1902). Gibbs's book features a blue cloth cover with gold stamped lettering, a photographic portrait of himself above a facsimile signature, and an introduction by Booker T. Washington.[39] These format decisions helped Gibbs convey his economic standing as well as his status as a trailblazing judge and a US ambassador. It is true that Gibbs was a man of considerable means and Parker was a blind man begging for assistance in postwar Ohio, but there are reasons beyond individual economic limitation that each author chose the format he did, and subsequent chapters will explain how a publication's physical properties were closely related to its intended function.

In addition to physical properties, format also encompasses the matter within a publication, that is, the text and its paratexts (title page, copyright, endorsements, etc.).[40] The text itself is particularly interesting in many publications because, as Britt Rusert has argued, early Black writing "routinely culled from and incorporated text drawn from already published works."[41] Most first-person narratives are structured by a timeline that takes readers from an author's birth, through their childhood, and into adulthood, but several self-publishers created variations on this form by eschewing linearity and revealing themselves through a collage of texts and even images. Edmond Kelley uses letters from enslavers to paint a portrait of his family's life; Thomas Smallwood reprints a lost newspaper column to identify himself as an accomplished antislavery gadfly who wrote numerous columns for the *Albany Weekly Patriot*; the Reverend Thomas James employs song lyrics and government documents to celebrate his antislavery labors and his Civil War exploits; perhaps most significantly, Levin Tilmon published the first bibliography of African American writing within a pamphlet of his lectures and sermons. Each of these men created a unique first-person narrative that—in the words of another nineteenth-century self-publisher—"contains multitudes."[42] This meant that a self-published book could serve as a straightforward narrative, a compendium of related writings, an individual literary history, or—in many cases—a combination of all three. There is no one textual format typical for self-publishers, but the diversity of their books and pamphlets is itself representative of what John Ernest calls "the stability of improvisation and adaptability [and] the stability of method over matter" in African American writing.[43] Format varied depending on authors' moment, goals, resources, and unique sensibilities, but most self-published narratives share the same improvisational method that has made them hard to categorize or even think about.

Before an author made decisions about format, he or she would have written or prepared a manuscript and taken it to a job printer. The job printer is not unique to the nineteenth century, but job printing reached its apogee in that century, during which it made up a massive part of the print trades. Even by 1904, the Census Bureau found that job printing made up 30 percent of the total value for the printing industry; by way of comparison, book publishing made up only 11 percent while newspapers made up more than 50 percent.[44] Indeed, almost every small town had at least one printer, and even medium-sized cities had dozens; in many instances, newspapers also offered job printing services. The 1871–72 account book for the job printing shop at the *Salem* (Massachusetts) *Press* is both typical and revealing. Over the course of one year, the shop produced countless items for individuals, businesses, and organizations: mailing labels, railway tickets, show cards, magazines, envelopes, sheet blanks, circulars, forms for the County of Essex, checks, programs, bulletins, posters for a picnic held by the Young Men's Catholic Temperance Society, badges with ribbons for a missionary society, rules of the library for the Salem Athenaeum, library cards, business cards, text on the backs of stereopticon cards, and meal tickets. Most of these jobs were performed for less than five dollars.[45]

Like a modern copy shop—which serves many of the same functions—a job printer operated on a fee-for-service basis, so anyone who could pay the bill could have their printing project completed. As Elizabeth McHenry explains, a belief in the importance of job printing as a resource for aspiring authors led W. E. B. Du Bois to purchase the Ed. L. Simon & Co. printing office in Memphis in 1904. Du Bois hoped that such a shop would support the "production of African American letters."[46] Though he was able to find venues for most of his own writing, Du Bois knew that self-publication had long been a crucial resource for Black men and women, and he believed that a Black-owned print shop would encourage other Black writers and could serve as a key component of what McHenry elsewhere calls the "infrastructure being built to support African American print culture."[47] With one exception, I have not been able to identify any Black printers or shop owners who supported Black self-publication in the nineteenth century, but the white job printers who produced an autobiography or a broadside were not gatekeepers in the way that book publishers would be; they merely took a customer's money and did the work of printing without regard for the content. The customer who paid the bill for that work and went on to distribute whatever was printed became the publisher.[48] Thus, self-publishers leveraged their financial capital within a "white" print infrastructure and thereby used that infrastructure to advance their own goals.

Once a customer brought his or her narrative to a print shop and agreed with the owner on a price for the work, the process of printing a book or pamphlet began. First, the author's text would be "composed," that is, set by hand using movable type. Composition—along with paper—was the costliest part of the printing process and was priced according to 1,000 ems (a measure of type width equal to a capital M or an em dash).[49] A skilled compositor could set 5,000–6,000 ems in a day, and, though such work could become mind-numbing, there was an element of creativity involved. For example, in the 1825 edition of William Grimes's *Life*, the compositor began substituting italicized *I*s for regular *I*s on pages 14–16 of the book, suggesting that he had run out of the letter I. Later in the same book, the compositor substituted the number 1 for the letter I (see fig. 1.3). Since autobiographers use an inordinate number of first-person pronouns and smaller print shops have a finite number of letters for any font, compositors like the one working on Grimes's *Life* had to develop workarounds to complete longer jobs. As the century progressed and type became cheaper to produce and purchase, such problems became less common.

Another factor that influenced the price and speed of composition was the nature of the source document, which was usually a manuscript written by the author or someone close to the author. Authors like William H. Johnson and Bethany Veney dictated their stories to an amanuensis who probably helped with the publication process.[50] Other authors like Leonard Black wrote narratives that "needed considerable correction to fit it for the press" and had that work "performed, gratuitously, by a friend of the author."[51] Similarly, Lunsford Lane mentioned that he was "obliged to employ the services of a friend, in bringing this Narrative into shape for the public eye."[52] These intermediaries may well have offered valuable help with no ulterior motives;

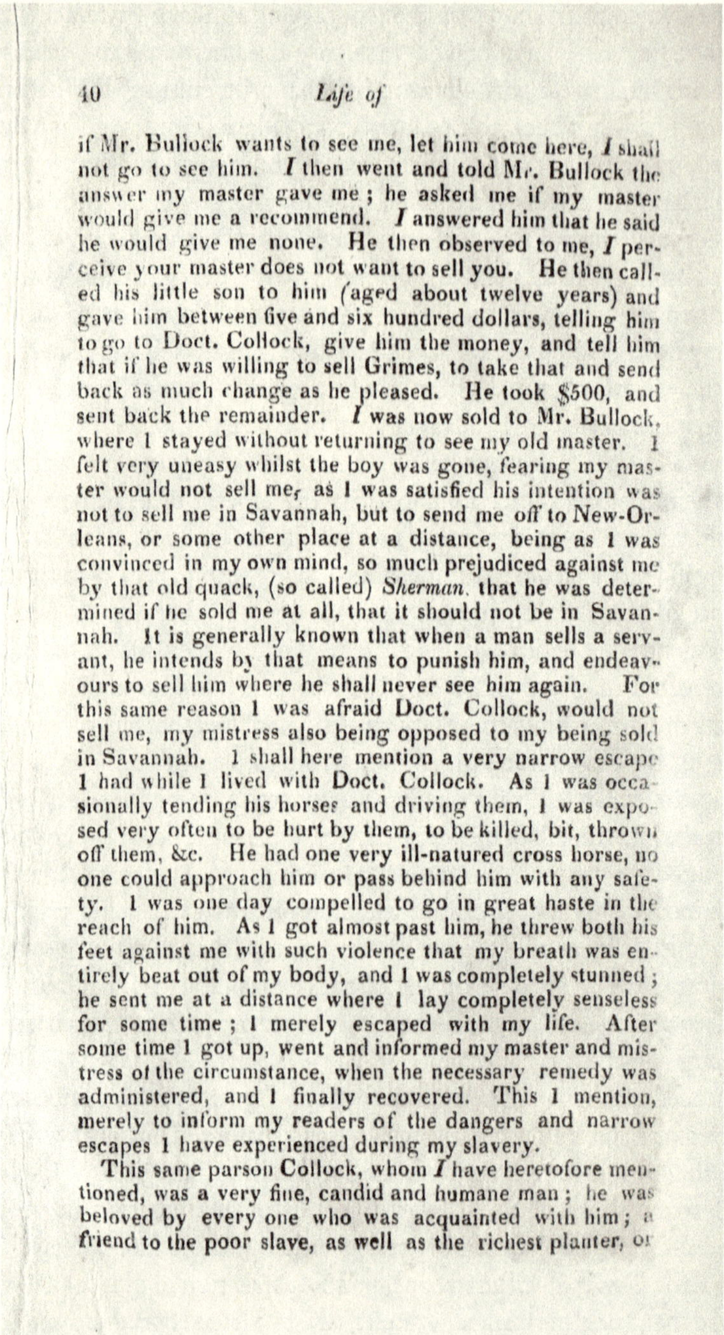

if Mr. Bullock wants to see me, let him come here, *I* shall not go to see him. *I* then went and told Mr. Bullock the answer my master gave me; he asked me if my master would give me a recommend. *I* answered him that he said he would give me none. He then observed to me, *I* perceive your master does not want to sell you. He then called his little son to him (aged about twelve years) and gave him between five and six hundred dollars, telling him to go to Doct. Collock, give him the money, and tell him that if he was willing to sell Grimes, to take that and send back as much change as he pleased. He took $500, and sent back the remainder. *I* was now sold to Mr. Bullock, where 1 stayed without returning to see my old master. 1 felt very uneasy whilst the boy was gone, fearing my master would not sell me, as 1 was satisfied his intention was not to sell me in Savannah, but to send me off to New-Orleans, or some other place at a distance, being as 1 was convinced in my own mind, so much prejudiced against me by that old quack, (so called) *Sherman*, that he was determined if he sold me at all, that it should not be in Savannah. It is generally known that when a man sells a servant, he intends by that means to punish him, and endeavours to sell him where he shall never see him again. For this same reason 1 was afraid Doct. Collock, would not sell me, my mistress also being opposed to my being sold in Savannah. 1 shall here mention a very narrow escape 1 had while 1 lived with Doct. Collock. As 1 was occasionally tending his horses and driving them, 1 was exposed very often to be hurt by them, to be killed, bit, thrown off them, &c. He had one very ill-natured cross horse, no one could approach him or pass behind him with any safety. 1 was one day compelled to go in great haste in the reach of him. As 1 got almost past him, he threw both his feet against me with such violence that my breath was entirely beat out of my body, and 1 was completely stunned; he sent me at a distance where 1 lay completely senseless for some time; 1 merely escaped with my life. After some time 1 got up, went and informed my master and mistress of the circumstance, when the necessary remedy was administered, and 1 finally recovered. This 1 mention, merely to inform my readers of the dangers and narrow escapes 1 have experienced during my slavery.

This same parson Collock, whom *I* have heretofore mentioned, was a very fine, candid and humane man; he was beloved by every one who was acquainted with him; a friend to the poor slave, as well as the richest planter, or

FIGURE 1.3 Detail from page 40 of William Grimes's *Life* (1825). Note the compositor's use of 1 and the italicized *I* in lieu of I. Courtesy of the Library of Congress.

then again, they may have shaped the texts they produced according to their own designs. Irrespective of the motives of amanuenses or the ways that costs and profits were divided when more than one person was involved in producing a manuscript, the process of printing that manuscript would have been no different.

Many self-published narratives combine original writing with previously printed material from the Bible, periodicals, newspapers, and other sources. The reasons authors chose to include reprinted texts are as varied as the publications in which they appear, but there were practical concerns that may have led an author-publisher to embrace the recycling of old print. First, it was between 10 and 20 percent cheaper to set type from a printed text as opposed to a manuscript, and, second, composing from print meant the author him- or herself did not need to write (or rewrite) the narrative.[53] When William Grimes decided to republish his 1825 *Life* in 1855, he "advertised in the public papers" so that he was "enabled to procure a perfect" copy of his publication.[54] And, when he added a new ten-page conclusion to the book prior to republication, he did so by sitting in the composing room of Thomas Stafford's print shop and dictating the text to the printer Samuel H. Harris.[55] In other words, Grimes used a copy of the old book to make the initial setting of the text easier; then he dictated (or verbally outlined) the final pages in the print shop while a compositor listened and set his words in type. Grimes's is the only description of such a process in nineteenth-century African American literature, but—given the nature of many self-published narratives—it may not be unique. At the very least, since many self-publishing authors (and/or their representatives) were having their stories printed at local print shops with employees they may have known by name, they could be directly involved in the processes that brought their words into print.

Once an author knew what he or she wanted to print and decided on the appropriate format for publication, the typeset text would be organized into a "form" that was locked into place, inked, and printed. In the early nineteenth century—and perhaps even until the 1850s in smaller shops—this printing would be done by hand; that is, an individual worker would pull the lever on a hand press and print enough sheets to make up the desired number of copies. Later in the century, most print shops housed steam-powered presses that could produce thousands of sheets in a day. Some short publications like Henry Parker's eight-page pamphlet would have only required half of a full-sized sheet of paper on which eight pages would be printed, and most publications would have required fewer than ten sheets of paper. Once they were printed, the sheets would be folded and stitched together to make a pamphlet. By the 1840s, most commercially produced books would be set by hand only once and then—in a process called stereotyping—the type forms would be transferred to copper plates that could be stored (and reused) for decades. As Michael Winship notes, the stereotype plates for Harriet Beecher Stowe's *Uncle Tom's Cabin* were made in 1852 and reused for more than twenty years and 100,000 copies.[56] James Mars, who had his *Life* printed in Stowe's hometown of Hartford, also had his type transferred to copper plates that he reused for fourteen different printings of his pamphlet. Such a choice was rare, though. Most self-publishers only had their narratives printed once, and it would have been impractical for them to pay for the stereotyping of their work since it nearly doubled the cost of typesetting.[57]

In addition to stereotyping and steam presses, other technological changes in the nineteenth century helped transform printing and publishing: By the 1880s to 1890s, linotype machines (which could cast an entire line of type at once) made typesetting faster and easier, and the typographic quirks that are part of Grimes's 1825 *Life* became a thing of the past. Moreover, paper feeders and sewing machines sped up the processes of printing and stitching even for authors working with small-town job printers or newspaper publishers. Technological change did not just make things faster; it also enabled authors to embrace a different kind of writing and printing. Late nineteenth-century advances in image printing, binding, and stamping made it cheaper for author-publishers like the aforementioned Mifflin Wistar Gibbs to produce longer books with images, ornamented covers, and other elements that had once been beyond their means. Many amateur authors began to favor longer books over the simple pamphlets that dominated self-publishing in the 1820s to 1870s. This is not to say that pamphlets disappeared entirely or that no pre-1870 self-publishers produced books but only to note that technological changes may have brought new options for self-publishing authors and, perhaps, new expectations for their customers.

Though self-published texts appeared in a variety of formats, the most common by far was the pamphlet. What makes something a pamphlet is sometimes hard to pin down, but as Richard Newman, Patrick Rael, and Philip Lapsansky argue in their introduction to *Pamphlets of Protest*, "one might define the pamphlet as something between a broadside and a book."[58] This definition jibes with the 1964 UNESCO "recommendations concerning the international standardization of statistics relating to book production and periodicals," which states that a pamphlet is "at least 5 but not more than 48 pages."[59] By way of contradistinction, Joseph Rezek identifies a book as a "bound codex volume of significant length, heft, and commodity status."[60]

Binding is certainly key to this definition, and research by James N. Green and Michaël Roy indicates that pamphlets were not always thought of as "bound" and certainly not considered to be books. Pamphlets were stitched together, and they could *become* books if bindings were added (usually at another shop), but the pamphlet occupied a sort of textual middle ground: They were cheap to produce, easy to carry and distribute, but difficult to preserve; even so, many certainly enjoyed what Rezek calls "commodity status."[61]

The distinction between books and pamphlets may seem academic, but it is a crucial distinction for twenty-first-century readers who are used to encountering pre-1900 African American writing via a website (like Documenting the American South) or an anthology (like *The Norton Anthology of African American Literature*) in which pamphlets are indistinguishable from any other printed form. In the third edition of the *Norton Anthology*, Douglass's 1845 *Narrative*, which was self-published as a simple but sturdy book, appears the same as Venture Smith's 1798 self-published pamphlet, which looks no different from Olaudah Equiano's 1789 two-volume autobiography, which was published by subscription. In the chronological bibliography of "North American Slave Narratives" at Documenting the American South, Douglass's *Narrative* appears in the "1840–1849" section as one among several narratives and alongside many self-published texts even though it was the bestselling narrative of the decade and one of a few available as a bound book.[62] All of this is to say that anthologies and websites have privileged the "linguistic code" while erasing the "bibliographical code" that nineteenth-century customers would have understood right away. Those readers would distinguish between books and pamphlets, and they would have had different expectations for each.

One of those expectations would have had to do with the time they might expect to spend with the text in question. As Carla Hesse argues, "the book is a slow form of exchange. It is a mode of temporality which conceives of public communication not as action, but rather as reflection upon action. Indeed, the book form serves precisely to defer action, to widen the temporal gap between thought and deed, to create a space for reflection and debate."[63] By its very heft and organization, Hesse suggests, a book signals to potential readers that they will have to spend time with it and consider its contents before using those contents to act in the world. Most Black self-publishers did not conceive of their publications in this way; rather than producing work that would "create a space for reflection," they hoped to spur immediate action. Hesse's understanding of temporality and modes of publication recalls the work of critics like Michael Warner, who (following Jürgen Habermas) imagines an early American public sphere in which print shaped an emergent republican identity. Though Warner is dismissive of the potential for Black participation in a print public sphere, Joanna Brooks notes that Black author-publishers of the late eighteenth century were quite attuned to the political potential of print and used print to develop "Black counterpublics" that privileged "collective incorporation, conscious differentiation, and criticism of dominant political and economic interests."[64] The collective insights of Hesse and Brooks suggest that self-publication was—from 1776 onward—a crucial tool for Black activists seeking to reform US institutions or to develop separate institutions like the African Methodist Episcopal (A.M.E.) Church.[65]

Throughout this book, I pay close attention to the context surrounding publications and the format(s) in which publications appeared, but I do not treat format as determinative. Newman, Rael, and Lapsansky imagine a sturdy link between form and function when they write that "[formerly enslaved] narrators did not enjoy the same editorial freedom as pamphleteers. For example, most slave narratives featured an introduction written by a notable white abolitionist."[66] For Newman and his coeditors, slave narratives were bound books published by white abolitionists, whereas pamphlets were political tracts published by Black activists. This is not at all accurate. Moreover, the principal reason pamphlets offered author-publishers a measure of "editorial freedom" was not because white people were never involved in their production but because pamphlets were inexpensive to print and therefore allowed prospective authors to bypass gatekeepers who offered conditional financial support. During a period in which a day laborer earned about a dollar a day, Jarena Lee paid thirty-eight dollars to print 1,000 copies of *The Life and Religious Experience of Jarena Lee, A Colored Lady* (1839) and Greensbury Washington Offley paid Case, Lockwood & Co. $23.66 to print 1,000 copies of his twenty-four-page pamphlet, *A Narrative of the life and Labors of the Rev. G.W. Offley, A Colored Man, Local Preacher and Missionary* (see fig. 1.4a, 1.4b).[67]

In addition to cost, Lee and Offley may have wanted to publish pamphlets because they are light and easy to transport. Ease of transport was certainly of great importance to Lee, who traveled thousands of miles while she "preached and sold [her] books."[68] And, when she sold out the first 1,000 copies of her pamphlet in 1839, she had another 1,000 copies printed in Cincinnati. Though the printing expense left her "scarce of money," Lee knew that she could make back her investment by selling as she traveled around Ohio

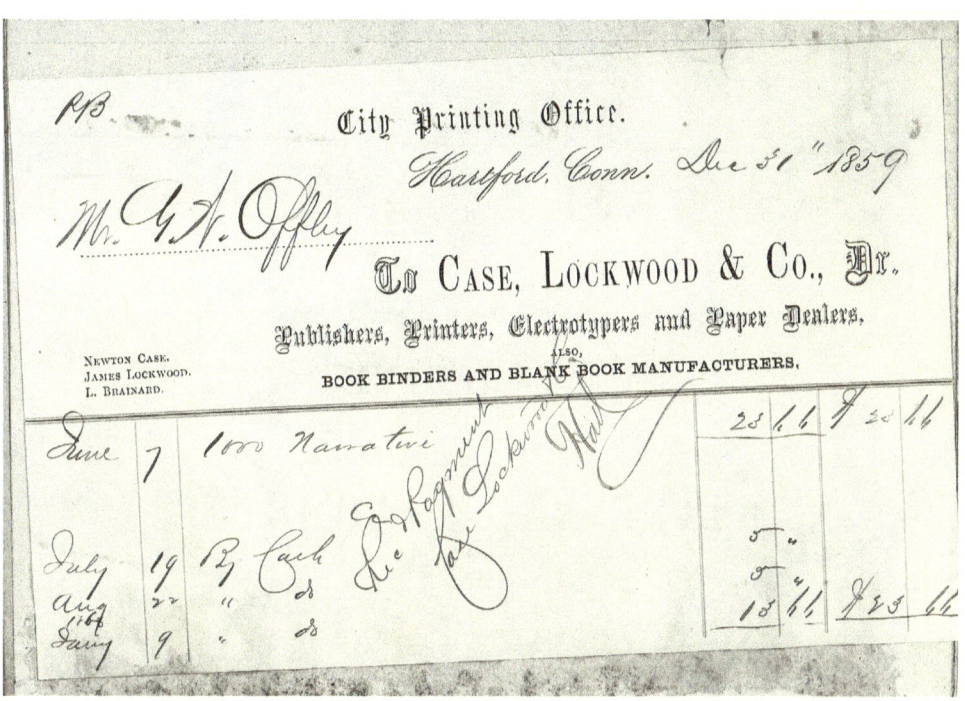

FIGURE 1.4A Receipt from Case, Lockwood, and Co. for printing 1,000 copies of the *Narrative of G. W. Offley*. Courtesy of the American Antiquarian Society.

and back to her Pennsylvania home, and she hawked her pamphlets "at camp meetings, quarterly meetings, [and] in the public streets."[69] Offley's story may have been very much like Lee's, since he sold pamphlets as he traveled around New England raising money to support the construction of Black churches. Indeed, those sales were crucial for Offley since he had made a down payment on printing and needed to sell pamphlets to pay the remainder of his bill. He did so in January of 1860 and then contracted with Case, Lockwood & Co. to print a longer (sixty-page) version of his *Narrative* that he offered for fifteen cents per copy.[70] This story is significant for two reasons: First, it shows how authors could enter the world of print even if they did not have enough money to pay the entire cost up front. Offley paid less than half of the printing cost in advance and settled his bill after selling his pamphlet.[71] Second, based on the price Offley sought for his 1860 *Narrative*, he could have made a 100 percent (or more) profit on the book, which reminds us that cheap print could be valuable for those who produced it. For Lee, Offley, and so many others, self-publication was not only about telling a story but also about selling it.

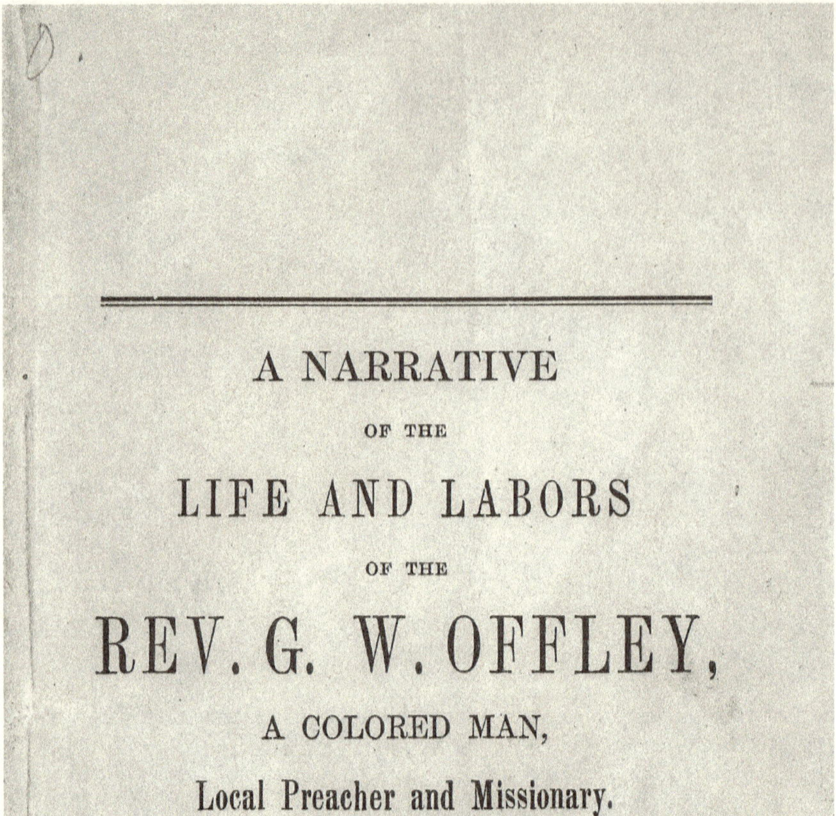

A NARRATIVE

OF THE

LIFE AND LABORS

OF THE

REV. G. W. OFFLEY,

A COLORED MAN,

Local Preacher and Missionary.

FIGURE 1.4B Cover of *A Narrative. . . . of the Rev. G. W. Offley* (1859). Offley paid $23.66 for 1,000 copies of this twenty-four-page pamphlet. Courtesy of the American Antiquarian Society.

Finance

Several critics argue, based on the popularity of a few key texts, that there were ready-made audiences for Black first-person narratives in the nineteenth century.[72] While it is true that, following the publication of Stowe's *Uncle Tom's Cabin* in 1852, books *about* slavery became quite popular, most of the bestselling books treating the subject were fictional works by white authors, and only a few Black authors enjoyed significant commercial success (i.e., selling more than 5,000 copies of a book) on a national scale.[73] So, even though there were many possible markets in which Black-authored texts *might* sell, Black self-publishers almost always tailored their texts for buyers in a particular place and time. My understanding of the various nineteenth-century markets in which Black print circulated is particularly indebted to Leon Jackson's analysis of "authorial economies" and "embedded authorship" in antebellum America. In *The Business of Letters*, Jackson argues that most print circulated within diverse economies that had their own "rules and reciprocities . . . exchange rituals and ethical structures, and even, sometimes, [their] own currencies."[74] One of those currencies, as Karen Weyler explains, was "symbolic and cultural capital."[75] Many nineteenth-century men and women prided themselves on being a published author with a book, pamphlet, or broadside to sell; the publication functioned as a totem of one's intelligence and marker of status. Even though these rewards are not financial, Jackson would still categorize them as currency within a particular authorial economy.

Another feature that Jackson identifies as fundamental to nineteenth-century "authorial economies" is their "embeddedness." An embedded economy is one that functions within a particular social and/or cultural context and "served not simply to convey goods and money from one party to another, but also . . . to create and sustain powerful social bonds."[76] Here we might think about the giving of gifts or donations and the role such actions play beyond the economic exchange itself. In many cases, giving money helps cement social relationships or identify the giver as a member of a certain community. But, by the end of the nineteenth century, Jackson argues, authorial economies became "detached from the dense social worlds of which they were a part" and transactions between authors and customers became "less personal and less trusting, less flexible and less sustained."[77] Authors working within disembedded markets came to rely—as we do today—on "various mediatory individuals and agencies who stood between an author and his or her readers."[78] These mediators are the editors, publishers, distributors, and booksellers who dominated the publishing world during the twentieth century and continue to do so today. With few exceptions, though, such individuals played a minor role in the creation and circulation of pre-1900 Black writing, which means Jackson's revisioning of antebellum literary marketplaces is especially crucial for any understanding of the markets for self-published African American writing *across* the nineteenth century. Even if the publications themselves changed over the course of the 1800s, Black writers working outside traditional literary markets would have continued to employ publishing and distribution strategies common to the antebellum period.

Many readers of nineteenth-century African American literature assume the markets for all Black writing were shaped by political concerns like abolition and civil rights and that Black self-publishers sought to capitalize on those same markets. Several self-publishers did just that, and almost all the authors in this book would have agreed with the political goals of well-known abolitionists and postwar activists. At the same time, most self-publishers thought about their potential customers not just in terms of their political affiliations but also in terms of their locale, their religion, their race, or their social class. And, because those authors published and sold their texts within embedded markets, they could sidestep some of the limitations that have been imagined as a defining feature of the nineteenth-century print landscape. In *Doers of the Word*, for example, Carla Peterson argues that antebellum African American writers could not depend on "a black readership . . . and were consequently obliged . . . to accede to the inevitable constraining presence of a white audience that might be indifferent or even unsympathetic to their needs."[79] This meant, "African American literary production was vastly complicated by the dominant culture's market economy, which sought to regulate the production and dissemination of literary texts."[80] Writing about the period after Reconstruction, D. Dickson Bruce echoes Peterson's analysis and argues that the goal of most Black writers was to "reach a broad, general audience, particularly a white reading public" and were therefore limited in what they could write.[81]

Like Bruce, Peterson imagines the white-dominated literary marketplace as monolithic (i.e., there is simply one "market economy") and views that market as inherently limiting for Black authors; it had to be confronted and surmounted before a truer, more authentic, African American literature could develop. On the one hand, Peterson is correct to note that many white readers were hostile or indifferent to Black authors and that commercial publishers would rarely choose to produce a Black-authored book.[82] But, as

Meredith McGill has argued, "there is no reason why socioeconomic conditions should not be imagined as a potential site of proliferation as well as a principle of thrift."[83] Following McGill, I argue that white publishers' unwillingness to publish Black-authored books led authors to embrace writing strategies and unique methods for circulating and selling their work. I recognize that these unique methods were not panaceas and Black self-publishing does not represent a triumph over white supremacy or racist institutions, nor does self-publishing make up for the disappearance of so many Black writings that were undoubtedly lost, ignored, or destroyed over the course of the nineteenth century. Be that as it may, self-publishing did present economic opportunities for countless Black Americans who, as the saying goes, "made a way out of no way."[84]

The story of an 1890s novel may be useful to illustrate one way self-publishers found readers and buyers within a challenging market without "acceding to . . . [a] constraining presence."[85] In the late 1880s, William Anderson and Walter Stowers, who were two of the five editors of the Detroit *Plaindealer*, wrote a novel titled *Appointed*. The novel was not published until 1894, perhaps because the authors' work at the newspaper occupied all their time or maybe because they tried and failed to find a commercial publisher. When they did finally publish their book, they did so by working with a job printer named Joseph Topping. Their book bore the imprint of the "Detroit Law Printing Co.," but that company never published any other books, and it shared its address with Topping's shop. All of this suggests that the two men paid for the book to be printed and then created a publisher whose name gave their book a kind of legitimacy or status that self-publishing may have lacked.[86] When it came time to sell the book, Anderson and Stowers sent copies to leading intellectuals and activists (Frederick Douglass and Albion Tourgeé received copies) for comment, solicited reviews in several papers, and advertised *Appointed* in the *Cleveland Gazette*, which was a leading Black newspaper of the fin de siècle. Advertisements urged buyers to obtain copies at the *Gazette* office or to send Anderson a dollar in exchange for a copy; the advertisement included Anderson's home address.

Just as they were for Stowers and Anderson, newspaper advertisements and notices were a key tool self-publishers used to market their texts. In 1847, William Hayden traveled from Cincinnati to Boston to sell his *Narrative* and placed a notice of his presence in *The Liberator*; in 1855, Peter Randolph's book was advertised in the same venue. Years later, when Jacob Stroyer or Robert Anderson arrived in a town to sell their books, they visited with newspaper editors and encouraged (or paid) them to place notices or endorsements in a local paper.[87] These notices advertised the author's presence in town rather than simply advertising a book. Major James Wilkerson and Edmond Kelley also attracted attention through newspaper stories, and each man printed broadsides designed for sale and subsequent display in customers' homes.[88] These examples suggest that self-publishing authors were comfortable working with editors and printers and understood that different print formats could work together to advance entrepreneurial or political goals.

Not every self-publisher could afford to place an ad in the newspaper or print a promotional broadside, so some authors relied on other strategies. William Grimes maintained a clothes cleaning and barbering business that may have brought him into contact with potential customers in New Haven and Litchfield, Connecticut. Still others—like Jarena Lee—used public speaking engagements or sermons as the occasions for distributing or selling a text. Finally, many self-publishers sold their books or pamphlets on street corners or even door to door. As future chapters show, self-publishers circulated their books and pamphlets in almost every conceivable situation, though bookstores were probably the least common venue in which one could acquire such an item since bookstores as contemporary readers imagine them did not exist in most nineteenth-century towns. Major cities like New York, Philadelphia, and Boston may have had stores devoted exclusively to book sales, but such sales were almost always restricted to commercially produced books.[89] Some authors may have been able to get their self-published books on display at activist shops like the Anti-Slavery office in Boston or at David Ruggles's bookstore and print shop in New York, but to make any money the author-publisher would either need to get the proprietor to purchase several copies in advance or sell on consignment, which would have required the author to return periodically to collect profits.[90] Neither option was likely to be terribly remunerative, so authors developed modes of circulation and sale unique to their publication and situation.

The unifying factor among most of the circulation methods employed by self-publishers was the personal interaction between seller and buyer. Most contemporary readers never meet the authors of the books we read; the book is selected privately, and our decision to purchase or borrow a book is made as we scan through a website or browse a shelf. Online or in person, readers can examine numerous books and read several pages in all of them before selecting, but these examinations take place without the author nearby pressuring potential readers to approve of the book and to signal that approval by making a purchase. On the other hand, this is exactly the sort of interaction that potential customers would have experienced when they met a self-publishing author. The author might, like Harriet Wilson, have shown testimonials that would signal the quality or truthfulness of the book in question and encourage readers to "lend a helping hand, and assist our sister."[91] Both Henry Parker and the Reverend Thomas James were blind, and they may have used their bodies to generate sympathy that rendered a purchase something akin to charity. Indeed, both the front and back of Parker's pamphlet included the line "Buy this, and you shall have the Prayers of a Blind Man."[92] Newspaper advertisements indicate that authors like Rev. Robert Anderson, Thomas James, and Jacob Stroyer sold their books in the same places repeatedly, and one Connecticut woman remembered that James Mars was "in the habit of stopping at Aunt Mills' hospitable home when he was in [Colebrook, Connecticut]."[93] Mars's repeated stops at a boarding house make sense since he could find new customers there, but the fact that he traveled the same circuit each year suggests that some purchasers were not buying the book to read it but merely to support the person selling it.

The modern analogue for such bookselling arrangements is the traveling canvasser who rings the doorbell, begs a moment of your time, and shares some literature about a pressing problem that can only be remediated through charitable giving. Perhaps my readers have experienced the mix of uncertainty and discomfort that I have felt in these moments. Sometimes I politely decline and close the door; other times, my interest in the canvasser's mission is genuine, and I am moved to donate; most often, I feel that it is easier to hand over some money than to deal with the discomfort I experience during an awkward interaction. For the canvasser, my motivations are likely secondary to the goal of securing a donation; likewise, it did not matter to most self-publishers whether the customer wanted to read the book or just wanted to avoid a further interaction.

Whether selling door to door or at a large, public gathering, the self-publisher could make on-the-spot decisions about pricing their work to achieve more sales. Recall that G. W. Offley added a price (fifteen cents) to the cover of his 1860 pamphlet; a few years later, James Mars did the same thing with several editions of his *Life*, though his price vacillated between twenty and twenty-five cents. Even though these prices appeared on the cover, an author could take whatever he wanted since he controlled every interaction. In fact, in a one-on-one sales encounter, the "cover price" may well have been an opening bid in a negotiation. The author could agree to take less than asked, or the author might take more than the stated price in the form of a donation. Again, this may seem odd to modern readers since they are accustomed to making book purchases in which a book's price is nonnegotiable. In the case of self-publication, though, the publisher was always on hand for the sale and could make immediate adjustments according to perceived demand, the appearance or enthusiasm of a particular customer, or customer requests. The market for self-published Black print was always in flux, but it was at least partially controlled by the author-publisher. It was this control—tenuous as it may have been—that enabled authors as different as Rev. Robert Anderson and Sojourner Truth to profit in the nineteenth-century United States.

Function

Over the past decade, pre-1900 African American literary scholarship has been preoccupied with what has come to be called print culture, though one might argue that print culture has always been central to African American literary history. Indeed, the early twentieth-century professionalization of African American literature and history was enabled by librarians, collectors, and bibliographers like Daniel Murray, I. Garland Penn, Dorothy Porter, and Arturo Schomburg, who gathered, organized, and publicized centuries of Black writing. In the 1950s through the 1970s, pioneering scholars like Houston Baker, Lerone Bennett, Charles Davis, Nathan Huggins, Donald Joyce, Nellie Y. McKay, Benjamin Quarles, and Marian Starling (to name a few) helped to describe and interpret pre-1900 Black writing and bring that writing to wider audiences inside and outside the academy. This work inspired an explosion of anthologies, series, and recovered works edited and contextualized by scholars like William L. Andrews, Frances Smith Foster, Henry Louis Gates Jr., Carla Peterson, and others, which helped create a more expansive canon. This set the stage for the digitization of books, conference proceedings, and newspapers that have further expanded the African American canon and given scholars a better sense of the rich and complex nineteenth-century print landscape. Leading readers through that landscape have been scholars like John Ernest, P. Gabrielle Foreman, Eric Gardner, Elizabeth McHenry, Joycelyn Moody, and Derrick Spires, all of whom have helped bring print culture to the very center of contemporary African Americanist scholarship. The effect of these outstanding recent efforts has been to ensure that African American literature does not become—as John Ernest writes—"a settled story."[94] Echoing Ernest, Joycelyn Moody and Howard Rambsy Jr. insist that, when scholars examine the print legacies created by nineteenth-century African Americans, they can "vitally enrich all examinations of black literature and cultural history by illuminating their origins and contextualizing the involvement of black persons in book and print production."⁹⁵ Moody and Rambsy urge scholars to think about the places where print culture intersects with African American literary and cultural history. This is what I trace by analyzing the function of the self-published text.

The term "function" encompasses both the purpose and effect(s) authors imagined for their publications as well as the ways those publications may have been used by purchasers. Just as I did when I began working on this project, most of my readers probably think of function in straightforward ways and assume an author publishes a book so that people will read it. But author-publishers paid particular attention to the ways customers might value a text and adjusted their products and sales strategies accordingly. For some self-publishers, this meant they developed strategies for selling books to customers who had no intention of reading them; others found ways to sell copies of the same book to the same person again and again; still other authors used the existence of a manuscript version of their narrative to garner food and shelter. These are exceptional cases, and it is certainly true that most self-publishers were seeking readers as well as customers, but consider the savvy involved in creating a product that would be attractive to those customers even if they had no intention of reading!

Beyond highlighting authors' resourcefulness and creativity, I attend to a text's function to demonstrate the diversity of nineteenth-century Black autobiography and to insist that the genre encompasses much more than the slave narrative. Most of the narratives I examine in this book have been identified as slave narratives by Documenting the American South or via other bibliographies, but the texts themselves were published over almost one hundred years and treat a variety of subjects beyond the tragedy of enslavement. Even when authors center the experience of enslavement in their narratives, they do so for reasons that go well beyond giving "nineteenth-century whites . . . a firsthand look at the institution of slavery," which is how William L. Andrews describes the overarching function of the slave narrative in *To Tell a Free Story*.⁹⁶ Andrews goes on to complicate this idea in his book, but there is no doubt that many readers (especially after 1840) expected formerly enslaved narrators to share and somehow verify what they had seen. Self-publishing authors were not entirely exempt from this expectation, but, since they worked outside of commercial and abolitionist print structures, they could create unique publications that transcend generic formulas and expectations.

Many scholars of African American literature know that, as Michaël Roy argues, "the slave narrative has always been a more capacious category than what is assumed when we think of it as a series of separately published works."[97] This book shows that even *among* separately published works, formerly enslaved narrators created a diverse set of texts with varied approaches. Consider, for example, the *Life of James Mars*. While Mars's pamphlet highlights the fact that Mars was enslaved until age twenty-one, it is—first and foremost—a family history written for his sister who was living in Liberia. Mars printed his pamphlet so he could more easily share copies with other members of his family and social circle, and only after he had done so did he realize that he could "sell enough to pay the expenses."[98] I have more to say about Mars in chapter 4, but this brief description of his reasons for publishing recalls Frances Smith Foster's insistence that "positive action" was "a primary factor in creating an African-American print culture."[99] Critics have been wise to follow Foster's lead and to look for Black writing separate from antislavery or other protest movements. While those motivations were important for many authors, focusing only on protest and politics limits our understanding of the field and produces a warped version of African American literature that is largely about white people. James Mars's "slave narrative" was not solely (or even primarily) about white oppression and a Black response; it was about his parents, his siblings, his children, his friends, his church, and his work as an activist and community organizer. Though he had been the victim of monstrous injustice, "positive action" was a key reason he wrote and printed his story.

Another motivation that many publishers pursued quite consciously was what Derrick Spires calls "the work of citizenship," which was constituted through everyday actions even "outside or despite dominant political frameworks."[100] Spires's theorization of citizenship is exciting for many reasons, but I believe his insistence on citizenship as a set of practices (and not a condition of being) is a crucial insight that helps us better understand and appreciate the work of self-publishers like Norvel Blair, Lucy Delaney, and many others. Spires's refiguring of citizenship dovetails with recent work by P. Gabrielle Foreman and the rest of the editorial team at The Colored Conventions Project who have helped contemporary scholars understand the significance of the century-long convention movement to African American life and letters.[101] As Foreman notes, colored conventions privileged "collective writing and organizing" and "advanced collectivity as a way of militating for rights and actualizing community."[102] Though we might assume that self-publication of a single-authored work is the antithesis of collectivity, I would argue that we should take a broader view of the function of those publications and think about them as part of the collective work of citizenship theorized by Spires, Foreman, and others. First, as I noted in the section on format, many self-published texts feature multiple forms and voices, and Osborne Anderson's 1861 pamphlet even includes the record of a colored convention! Second, many self-published texts emerged from and/or responded to the work of religious and political conventions across the century; still other texts were authored by regular convention attendees like James Mars and Thomas James. In other words, the history of self-publication is deeply connected to Black community-building work of the nineteenth century, and we should understand the function of many self-published books as consciously advancing that work.

There is another way in which self-publication can be tied to community formation, and that is through a broad and eclectic reading of the texts themselves. Here, I am thinking of John Ernest's recent call for biographical research on Black lives that might "help us piece together the networks and patterns that emerge when we study people's lives not as abstract and coherent individual stories, or independent tales, but as they were lived, in concert with others."[103] The wisdom of Ernest's ideas appeared over the course of my research, research that continually exposed networks, patterns, and communities that, in turn, revealed something new about nineteenth-century African American writing and those who created it. Throughout this study, then, I try to present historical Black lives not only as a set of documents or dates (e.g., birth certificates, census records, or published texts) but as a collage of texts, actions, relationships, and experiences. Though this aspect of Black community formation was not one that self-publishing authors pursued as individuals, there is no doubt that many of those authors hoped their published words would join a chorus of other voices that their contemporaries would hear and heed. These authors are crucial builders of what Elizabeth McHenry calls the "infrastructure" that supported a growing African American print culture. McHenry's notion of a print infrastructure is composed of "literary projects and people that laid practical and conceptual frameworks for African American literature and the transmission of literary culture."[104] As McHenry explains, these projects and people were not necessarily connected to one another, nor were they always successful (aesthetically, commercially, politically), but their very existence created the conditions for a literature to come.

McHenry's outstanding work directs scholars to consider histories of literary failure or disappearance and to understand those failures as "repositories of knowledge about the literary past."[105] As she notes, histories of textual disappearance help modern readers understand the difference

Introduction 31

between our moment and the moment in which a book or pamphlet first appeared and to comprehend a text's function even when such a function seems incomprehensible. One of the best examples of this kind of research is Kinohi Nishikawa's "history of obsolescence" focused on Herman Gilbert's 1983 novel, *The Negotiations*. Looking back on a novel that appeared, flourished briefly, and then vanished from public consciousness, Nishikawa argues that the "exact textual-contextual conjunctures that made *The Negotiations* popular for a time also explain why it became obsolete when that period expired."[106] As Nishikawa explains, the very things that made a text popular or remunerative in one moment can make the same text unmarketable in another. My mission in this book is to comprehend the contexts in which a self-published text could flourish, an approach that is crucial for books like Rev. Robert Anderson's *Life*, which was published by a formerly enslaved Black minister and sold primarily to rich white "friends" in post-Reconstruction Georgia and Florida. Anderson's book was spectacularly remunerative within the embedded market its author created, but it served a very specific function that depended on historical and social formations that would not persist for long beyond Anderson's lifetime. His book appeared, served its function, and then disappeared again until it was digitized as part of the collection of "North American Slave Narratives" at Documenting the American South.

Telling the stories of literary disappearances and failures expands the map and complicates the timeline of African American literature. And, when scholars attend to that expanded map, they will find, as I have, that white-authored texts and Black-authored texts are more similar than we often imagine, especially in terms of format and function. Just as African American self-publishers penned narratives of religious awakening, commercial success, or Civil War experiences, so too did white Americans who wanted to commemorate their unique experiences for future generations. And, just as women like Harriet Wilson used book publication to seek economic support, countless white authors printed their own stories of suffering and penury and offered those stories in exchange for money.[107] These similarities are sometimes overlooked by scholars of African American literature, who, as Rafia Zafar claims, have not always considered "the possibilities of acculturation and creative engagement" as elements of an African American literary identity.[108] Self-publishing Black writers certainly used genres and forms that were commonplace for nineteenth-century amateur authors. Even as African American writers embraced commonplace forms, though, they did so with the unique experiences, sensibilities, and voice that helped expand their readers' understanding of the Black American experience of discrimination, poverty, war, religion, and the law.

In the chapters that follow, I describe and categorize self-published texts according to their function while paying particular attention to the textual and material elements of various publications (format) and the economic conditions surrounding their production and sale (finance). Organizing chapters based on function is the best way to contextualize the individual efforts of each author and in relationship to other authors. This structure also helps me show that certain kinds of publishing *persisted* across the nineteenth century even as the situation for African American author-publishers changed dramatically. In addition to creating a taxonomy of self-published texts, I have highlighted texts that are either remarkable or representative enough to demand a more in-depth treatment. In these case studies, I employ methods of both the book historian and the literary critic as I show how self-publication worked on a practical level, how author-publishers functioned within various authorial economies, and how those same author-publishers understood and announced the meaning(s) of their efforts.

Among the many familiar and unfamiliar authors whose publications are part of this study, there are some well-known authors who are mentioned only in passing, and their exclusion deserves a word or two of explanation, especially since they self-published some of the urtexts of African American literature: Olaudah Equiano was the first self-publishing entrepreneur, and he parlayed his remarkable story into wealth and widespread acclaim.[109] David Walker, writing forty years later, was hardly an entrepreneur in the economic sense, but, as Timothy Patrick McCarthy argues, "Walker understood the power of an autonomous black print culture . . . better than anyone of his generation."[110] He also had a keen understanding of how to use the technology of print to engage readers and he utilized innovative distribution strategies to attract an audience across the entire Eastern Seaboard.[111] Finally, Sojourner Truth was one of the first Black women to self-publish and market her narrative, and her publication efforts overlapped with a speaking career that spanned decades.[112] Despite the abiding importance of Equiano, Walker, and Truth, this book treats them and their works only briefly. One reason for this choice is that each author already occupies a significant place in African American literary and cultural history and is the subject of extensive scholarly discussion and analysis. The same is true for Henry Bibb, Frederick Douglass, Harriet Jacobs, and Harriet Wilson, who—along with Walt Whitman—were among the most important self-publishers in the years preceding the Civil War. Bibb, Douglass, Equiano, Jacobs, Truth,

Walker, and Wilson loom large in my understanding of African American writing and its traditions, but, for the most part, they are minor figures in this book. As important as these writers were, they are but the most prominent stars in several remarkable constellations, and I want to direct readers to some other stars that have, thus far, been obscured by brighter lights.

Chapter Outline

In chapter 1, I examine what I call the "supplicant text," that is, a publication that announces its author's need for economic support and is offered *in exchange* for that support. Supplicant texts describe the sufferings of the protagonist, insist that those sufferings were largely beyond his or her control, explain how the suffering had led to penury, and beg for the mercy of readers who might remediate the author's need for money. The African American writers who published supplicant texts (Aaron [1843–46], Edmond Kelley [1851], Henry Parker [186?], and Harriet Wilson [1859]) were neither established nor even aspiring authors. Rather, they passed through authorship as they struggled to survive amid a challenging economic landscape. The form(s) their publications take and the rhetorical moves they make shows us that production and circulation was, in many cases, far more important than self-expression.

In chapter 2, I read a series of lesser-known narratives penned by men outside the organized abolition movement. Publications by Levin Tilmon (1853), Thomas Smallwood (1851), and William J. Anderson (1857) certainly capitalize on the demand for antebellum antislavery writings, but they describe unique modes of antislavery labor and civil rights and thereby underscore the myriad ways Black Americans could contribute the cause of freedom. Though the authors' antislavery efforts are perhaps most visible in their self-published narratives, the writers I treat in this chapter use self-publication to catalog other publications (newspaper stories, convention records, court records, sermons, or other books) that document their activism. For these authors, the self-published narrative was the hub within a larger circuit of antislavery writing and activity, and their publications helped broaden the idea of what an antislavery book was supposed to look like and do.

Chapter 3 focuses on narratives by Osborne P. Anderson (1860), Thomas James (1886), James Mars (1864–78), and Jacob Stroyer (1879–1900), all of whom use their life stories to rewrite American history and, in some cases, question the very idea of history. In some ways, this chapter expands on recent scholarly work assessing the rise of African American history and the early efforts of African American historians.[113] At the same time, my readings of these historically minded authors push us toward a new understanding of how "history" is authored, circulated, and used. Even though none of the authors in this chapter presents himself as a historian, each details a personal story that refigures important aspects of American history: abolition, emancipation, slavery, and the Civil War. By insisting on the importance of a Black perspective on American life and history, Anderson, James, Mars, and Stroyer offer their white readers a new understanding of themselves and their cherished mythologies.

The authors I discuss in chapter 4 also used publication to undermine American mythology, though in this case author-publishers lamented the United States' failure to realize the ideal of equal justice under the law. No sooner was the ink dry on the Constitution than men like Christopher McPherson (1811) noted that his legal claims were not taken seriously, so he turned to print to advance those claims in the courts of public opinion. Later in the century, Peter Randolph (1855, 1893), Norvel Blair (1880), and Lucy Delaney (1891) referenced court records that tell a version of their stories and use their own commentary to modify or refract the supposedly authoritative accounts in state and county records. Ultimately, these narratives expose the failure of justice and submit an alternate testimony into the historical record.

In chapter 5, I highlight self-publishing efforts by African American ministers, which make up by far the largest group of self-published texts of the nineteenth century. It can be tempting to imagine that the life writings of religious figures are proxies for institutional viewpoints, but this is a bit simplistic. Indeed, many African American ministers found themselves in conflict with the larger religious organizations with which they identified, and—like the authors of narratives focused on history and law—used their life stories to reimagine the institutions themselves. This is especially true for authors like George White (1810), Jarena Lee (1836–49), and Major James Wilkerson (1859–65). These authors underscore the ways that religious bodies limited membership and maintained power for certain people at the expense of others; they also expose the organizational conflicts that are masked or ignored in institutionally sanctioned histories. Later authors like David Smith (1881) and Elijah Marrs (1885) published narratives in which they looked back on the successes of an earlier generation of African American ministers and missionaries and tried to write their own stories into church lore.

In the concluding chapter, I explore what might be termed the dark side of religious self-publication as I examine the remarkable history of Rev. Robert Anderson, a history I have only begun to sketch in this introduction. Between 1877 and 1891, Anderson worked as an itinerant preacher and sold his book throughout the South (especially in his native Georgia). In 1891, when he was nearly seventy years old, Anderson took up publishing and selling full time, and he sought (and won) the beneficence of rich whites. In turn, he made retrograde political statements, spoke up *for* lynching, and praised former Confederates for their character and political acumen. Anderson published thousands of copies of his book in the last decade of the century, and he sold his book in cities as far afield as Chicago, St. Louis, Boston, and New York. Though his book was little more than a catalog of the journeys he made selling it, whites continued to purchase his book until the first years of the twentieth century, making Anderson one of the most economically successful self-published authors in my study.

Anderson's publishing career, which culminated in the 1890s, overlaps with the rise of both Paul Laurence Dunbar and Charles Chesnutt and the landmark publication of Frances Ellen Watkins Harper's *Iola Leroy* in 1892. There is really no ground for comparison between Anderson and those who are among the finest authors in pre-1900 African American literary history, but Anderson may have sold more copies of his books than any of those authors even though he made his own printing, binding, and distribution arrangements and created all the advertising and publicity for his books, most of which sold south of the Mason–Dixon line. Anderson's story is just one of many in this book that helps expand the range of authors we include in the history of African American literature. Those authors and their unique publications reveal a rich legacy of creativity, entrepreneurship, activism, and community building by ordinary men and women who used print to preserve and circulate extraordinary stories.

CHAPTER ONE

Not in Giving, but in Buying a Book
Self-Publishing and the Supplicant Text

In 1859, the Reverend Noah Davis found himself in a difficult position. Davis, a formerly enslaved man who had purchased his freedom and that of several family members over the years, was entering his tenth year as the pastor of the Saratoga Street Baptist Church in Baltimore. As the nation hurtled toward a war over slavery, Davis faced several personal concerns that all but overwhelmed him. First, there was the matter of his two sons, both of whom were still enslaved in Virginia. Davis had tried for years to raise money to purchase them, but all his efforts had been ineffective, and he was out of dollars and ideas. Second, the Saratoga Street Baptist Church was struggling, as it always had, to pay the bills. This struggle became even greater in the wake of a large building campaign that resulted in a new building for the church and even more financial strain. Facing extraordinary personal suffering and increasing financial pressure, Davis asked himself a question: "Could I not, by making a book, do something to relieve myself and my children?"[1]

The answer to Davis's question is *A Narrative of the Life of Rev. Noah Davis, a Colored Man. Written by Himself, at the Age of Fifty-Four*. The book contains much more than a straightforward narrative, though. It includes Davis's portrait and his reminiscences, sermons preached by Davis and others, pictures of the Saratoga Street Baptist Church, charts documenting membership statistics for the churches in Baltimore, several certificates and testimonials, a rundown of the church budget, and a few advertisements inserted by the printer (Jon Weishampel), who seems to have printed the book for free in exchange for the right to advertise therein. Davis's *Narrative* also shares several similarities with well-known slave narratives circulating in the antebellum literary marketplace: It highlights the narrator's progress from ignorance to knowledge, from faithlessness to Christianity, from slavery to freedom, and from obscurity to local prominence. These similarities aside, there are also several differences, for Davis's *Narrative* offers no strong political messages, eschews extensive descriptions of Davis's enslavement, and, in general, makes very few moral demands on the reader. Davis does not ask that his readers denounce slavery; he does not insist that they embrace the violent tactics used by John Brown in his 1859 raid on Harpers Ferry; he does not ask them to join a movement, a party, or an organization. Davis simply offers a text to local readers and asks for their money in return. Like Harriet Wilson, who would publish *Our Nig* in the same year, Davis was making an explicit bid for charity by asking for assistance "not in giving, but in buying a book."[2]

Davis's and Wilson's books are examples of what I call the supplicant text: a publication that announces its author's need for economic support and is offered in exchange for that support.[3] Supplicant texts described the sufferings of the protagonist, insisted that those sufferings were largely beyond his or her control, explained how the suffering had led to penury, and begged for the mercy of readers who might remediate the author's need for money. When African American authors published supplicant texts, they often told stories that might be read in terms of their antislavery politics, but the key feature of the supplicant text remained the same. It was published because of some admitted financial exigency and sold to remediate that exigency. Because the supplicant text functioned primarily to generate financial gain, authorial worries about narrative and format were secondary or tertiary to the primary concern: Creating a textual product that could be sold for profit.

Selling was never easy, though. As Ann Fabian writes, "exchanges between writing beggars and patronizing readers were complicated" because those exchanges brought many questions to the fore.[4] Did the supplicant need money or something else? Was the supplicant honest? Was the supplicant's need genuine? In most cases, the self-published supplicant text was sold by the supplicant him- or herself, which meant the text, as an item available for purchase, needed to work with the seller's sales pitch in order to generate a sale. This crucial fact puts the materiality of the supplicant text front and center, for both the fact of publication and the item published signified in important ways. A publication for sale showed initiative on the part of the supplicant author, but a buyer still might wonder whether the publication was valuable on its own terms or was a worthless item handed over to mask the true nature of the transaction. We cannot ignore the role that the supplicant him- or herself played in the transaction either, since evidence of bodily suffering or disability could encourage generous purchasers or donors. Once a supplicant text was transferred from author to buyer, the object continued to signify by insisting on the generosity and goodwill of the purchaser. The seller received money, and the buyer obtained a portable advertisement of his own beneficence, not to mention something to be read. This latter aspect of the supplicant text seems least important, though, since many purchasers probably never intended to read whatever they purchased. Therefore, I read supplicant texts not primarily as literary or historical narratives but, first and foremost, as sites where economic transactions might be staged.

Even though concerns over function and finance trumped format for most supplicant authors, financial emergencies drove those authors toward creative innovations. In 1850, Nancy Prince published *A Narrative of the Life and Travels of Mrs. Nancy Prince* as a "means to supply [her] necessities."[5] Her *Narrative* details years of overseas travel with her husband and offers cultural and social insights into life in nineteenth-century Russia. Writing in 1850s Boston, Prince recalled her experience in St. Petersburg, her audience with the emperor, and her observation that, in Russia, "there was no prejudice against color; there were there all casts [sic], and the people of all nations, each in their place."[6] Prince's supplicant text was born of need, but her story is unique among nineteenth-century African American autobiographers. The same can be said of the Reverend Thomas Jones, who published versions of his autobiography in 1850, 1854, 1857, 1862, and 1885. Jones is one of a few narrators to publish a life story before *and* after the Civil War, and, with each new edition, he added testimonials to his book that span more than thirty years. One of those testimonials asks readers to offer Jones assistance in "disposing of his little book, or in securing a collection."[7] For Jones—as for most supplicant authors—a purchase or a "collection" were equally desirable.

In the pages that follow, I highlight the economic goals of supplicant authors and show how those goals drove them to create unique texts they believed were well suited for the situation in which they would be sold. The chapter begins with a detailed analysis of *The Light and the Truth of Slavery*, which was published by an author who claimed to be illiterate and so had numerous amanuenses write his pamphlet for him. The emergence and evolution of this pamphlet shows how supplicant texts could stimulate various charitable responses (food, shelter, assistance, money) and, at the same time, grant the author a sense of purpose. I move on to consider the role of disability in motivating supplication through an examination of Henry Parker's postwar pamphlet, which contains its author's unique life story within a format perfectly suited to Parker's needs and sales strategies. Next, I assess Edmond Kelley's *A Family Redeemed from Bondage*, which positions the supplicant's specific mission alongside the antislavery movement even as it remains insistently personal. Kelley's publishing choices show how supplicant authors considered their own needs and those of their potential customers in shaping a text for the market, and his pamphlet is not so much a life story as it is an explanation of the process of redemption and a brutal exposition of slavery's hypocrisies. Though he may not have intended to break new ground in the antislavery struggle, and though his contributions have garnered little attention over the years, Kelley's use of repurposed texts helps his readers understand the psychological brutality of white supremacy. The last supplicant text I discuss in the chapter is Harriet Wilson's *Our Nig*, which remains a vitally important piece of African American writing. At the same time, it seems to have been a failed supplicant text, mostly, I argue, because its format did not match its intended function.

Aaron Wants You to Buy This Book

The Light and the Truth of Slavery was published by an apparently illiterate and (perhaps) homeless man calling himself Aaron. The pamphlet contains scant and disjointed biographical details along with a mountain of previously printed material; it has no discernible narrative or form and offers nothing in the way of new information or sustained argument concerning slavery in the United States. Because it is part slave narrative, part scrapbook, part diary, and part travelogue, Lara Langer Cohen notes that *The Light and the Truth of Slavery* evinces a "patchwork aesthetic" and is much more like a "commonplace book" than anything else.[8] Cohen's argument accounts for the blend of original writing and clipping or copying that was typical of the commonplace book, a form in which the "reader becomes an author" by making "a book of other people's writing."[9] Of course, Aaron was not a reader, so one wonders how he would have either selected or copied passages from other publications. And, even if we do read *The Light and the Truth of Slavery* as a commonplace book, such a definition does not get us much closer to understanding the mechanics of its creation and distribution, nor would such a definition help us understand its function, which was to serve as an instrument of exchange that facilitated Aaron's career as a peddler. Indeed, the function of the publication is readily apparent in the first lines of the text: "Now reader, Aaron wants you to buy this book."[10] As the text evolved through (at least) six editions and its creator moved around New England searching for succor, shelter, and support, this much remained constant: "Aaron wants you to buy this book." The fact that many people did just what Aaron wanted helps us better understand the unique market for supplicant texts.

Though we cannot be sure when Aaron first decided to create and then publish *The Light and the Truth of Slavery*, the first edition was printed in Worcester sometime in the early 1840s (see fig. 1.1). WorldCat and Documenting the American South give an initial publication date of 1843, and that may be accurate for the first printings, but there are at least six different versions of *The Light and the Truth of Slavery* (see table 1.1), and neither

THE
LIGHT AND THE TRUTH OF SLAVERY.

AARON'S HISTORY.

Reader, here is the picture of the poor, way-faring, degraded Aaron.

There is clear evidence in the life and history of Aaron, that he has been a slave. Aaron cannot read a word. There are very few full blooded blacks at the South that can read a word, Aaron says.

Now reader, Aaron wants you to buy this book. I don't want you to buy it merely to read it through, I want you to buy it and I want you to read it, not for to lay it up in your head, but to lay it up in your heart, and then you will remember the poor way-faring Bondman. The two-thirds of this little book was made up by the poor way-faring degraded Aaron. The Bible says, faith without works is a dead article.

Aaron has a great knowledge of the Bible, but cannot read a word.

FIGURE 1.1 Version Three of *The Light and the Truth of Slavery* (1840s?). Courtesy of the Houghton Library, Harvard University.

TABLE 1.1 Versions of *The Light and [the] Truth of Slavery*

Ver.	Probable Year of Publication	Printed in	Notable Features/Alterations
1	1843	Worcester	No title page image or other images in the text. The forty-page pamphlet includes an "Extract from the history of the Mountain Miller" (drawn from an 1831 tract by William Hallock) that does not appear in subsequent versions. Quotations from the Bible include Galatians 5:19, Revelation 1:12–15, Daniel 7:9, Deuteronomy 23:15–16, Isaiah 33:15, 16, Isaiah 58:5–8, Matthew 7:12, Jeremiah 22:13–15, James 5:1–7, Deuteronomy 15:1–14, and Isaiah 59.
2	1844	Worcester	Includes title page image and three woodcuts, all of which depict scenes in Africa or tropical flora. This is the only version that includes graphics that connect Aaron to Africa. Most of the text of this forty-page version overlaps with the first, but Aaron has added a section on Toussaint L'Overture that begins "friends of the enslaved are continually told that Africans are an inferior race." This section remains in subsequent versions. On page 31, Aaron mentions an incident taking place on May 9, 1844, which means this version could not have been published before that date.
3	1844	Worcester	Title is *The Light and the Truth of Slavery*. Aaron removes all graphics except for the portrait on the title page. Excises the 1,500 words on "The heavenly doctrine of New Jerusalem" that appeared in the first two versions. Adds verses from John 14:1–6. Pamphlet swells to forty-eight pages and includes an excerpt from *The Life of Moses Grandy*.
4	1844	Worcester	Title changes to *The Light and Truth of Slavery*. First page includes a portrait and a short new paragraph on dreams that does not appear in subsequent versions. Aaron also adds most of Isaiah 3 and details on his new residence in

TABLE 1.1 *(continued)*

Ver.	Probable Year of Publication	Printed in	Notable Features/Alterations
			Springfield, which he claims not to own but is saving up to purchase. In later versions these details on Aaron's home in Springfield appear near the end of the pamphlet, but here they are placed in the middle (pages 24–25).
5	1845	Springfield	Version includes a full title page with only a portrait of Aaron and the title of the pamphlet, which is once again *The Light and the Truth of Slavery*. Adds several woodcuts, none of which relate to Africa (as in the second edition). Instead, they are stock images of soldiers, cannons, and ships that relate to criticisms of the United States and the seizure of enslaved people at sea. Aaron adds verses from Genesis 9:25 and Isaiah 5:10, 18, 20.
6	1845	Springfield	The text remains largely the same length as the previous version, but the title has been changed back to *The Light and Truth of Slavery*. The most significant change to this version is Aaron's inclusion of a lengthy excerpt from a book by "Bro. Offley" as well as his alteration of one key detail about his home. Whereas in previous versions Aaron noted that "he wants to try to buy" his home, that sentence is removed in this version.

librarians nor scholars have developed a complete textual and publication history of the pamphlet. That history shows that the text within Aaron's pamphlet changed a great deal during the years he was selling and that he printed at least two later editions in Springfield instead of Worcester. Even so, the physical size, shape, and quality of the publication changed very little. It remained an octavo (twenty-two-centimeter) pamphlet of forty to forty-eight pages with paper covers.

In the two Springfield versions (see fig. 1.2) of the pamphlet, Aaron adds more and more of his life story as a supplicant bookseller traveling around

THE LIGHT AND TRUTH
OF
SLAVERY.

Reader, here is a picture of the poor, way-faring, degraded Aaron.

AARON'S HISTORY.

There is clear evidence in the life and history of Aaron, that he has been a slave. Aaron cannot read. There are very few full blooded blacks at the South that can read a word, Aaron says.

Now reader, Aaron wants you to buy this book. I don't want you to buy it merely to read it through, I want you to buy it and I want you to read it, not to lay it up in your head, but to lay it up in your heart, and then you will remember the poor way-faring Bondman. Two thirds of this book was made up by the poor way-faring degraded Aaron. The Bible says, faith without works is a dead article.

Aaron has a great knowledge of the Bible, but cannot read a word.

1

FIGURE 1.2 Version Six of *The Light and Truth of Slavery* (1840s?). Note especially changes to title, image, and layout. Courtesy of the William L. Clements Library, University of Michigan.

New England. The most remarkable feature of the final Springfield edition is Aaron's inclusion of 2,100 words from the "little book of Bro. Offley's."[11] Based on the text that appears in *The Light and Truth of Slavery*, it seems that the words were written by none other than Greensbury Washington Offley, the African Methodist Episcopal (A.M.E.) minister and church organizer from Hartford who published his own pamphlets in 1844 and again in 1859 and 1860. The words that Offley shared with Aaron, though, are different from those in the pamphlets he published. Offley's presence in Aaron's book indicates that Aaron interacted with other Black authors in New England and suggests that Aaron might have requested *their* stories as he compiled his own story.[12] Indeed, by first adding excerpts from Moses Grandy's *Narrative* and then introducing Offley's story, Aaron seems to position his book as something of an antislavery compendium for politically motivated buyers.

With those potential buyers in mind, Aaron announces the function of his pamphlet on the first page of every edition of *The Light and the Truth of Slavery* in which the author explains that he could not "read a word" and insists, "very few full blooded blacks at the South . . . can read a word."[13] Linking himself with enslaved men and women in the South, Aaron makes his request: "Now reader, Aaron wants you to buy this book. I don't want you to buy it merely to read it through, I want you to buy it and I want you to read it, not for to lay it up in your head, but to lay it up in your heart, and then you will remember the poor way-faring Bondman. The two-thirds of this little book was made up by the poor way-faring degraded Aaron. The Bible says, faith without works is a dead article."[14] Aaron's connection to enslaved Blacks, his "degradation," and his claim of authorship are the things that entitle him to support, and Aaron reminds his readers of the importance of heartfelt religion, which might manifest in charitable works. The pamphlet—structured as it is with a first page like this—would almost certainly have been shown to a prospective buyer as Aaron stood in the doorway of her home or met him on the street.[15] By showing this first page and asking the buyer to read it, Aaron could reveal the subject of the text, verify his own identity through the portrait, establish his need for succor, and encourage the reader to establish his or her Christian credentials by making a purchase. But, for those unwilling to buy, Aaron could offer another way to help: writing.

Since Aaron was illiterate, his pamphlet was penned by others, and he spent a good part of his time traveling through the Northeast looking for people to transfer his spoken words into a manuscript. As such, a significant portion of Aaron's text describes his search for amanuenses and his discussions with those (mostly) anonymous men and women who wrote the book that he could not write himself. Early on, Aaron recalls a group of Universalists in Massachusetts who "wrote considerable for Aaron towards printing in my book, and throwed in and helped me to some money towards getting it printed."[16] Given this mention of printing early in the text, it seems that he always aimed to have his pamphlet published; however, even if the book was never completed, its existence in manuscript or scrapbook form would have helped Aaron gain entrance into the homes of those who might be willing to help him. Though a "poor, degraded wayfarer" might find supplication quite difficult, such a man toting a manuscript that he hoped to complete was a different matter altogether.[17]

As a manuscript, Aaron's pamphlet in the making aided him in his search for charity, as it does when Aaron visits a house "not . . . begging for victuals to eat" but "begging them to write a little for me, being as I could not write a word myself, and it is there they did write a little for me."[18] A few pages later, Aaron recalls that "two angels entertained him very hospitable, made him welcome to stay over the Sabbath with them; merely stopped awhile to ask their wives to write a little, and they insisted on my staying over the Sabbath day."[19] Other kindly amanuenses gave Aaron some victuals as well, and he notes that "sincere christian [sic] people" always treated him "like a brother, but not as a slave, and they let the way-faring Aaron eat when they eat, and don't keep me waiting till they are done eating, and then give me a crust of bread and a piece of old stale meat in the kitchen, the way a great many ministers do in my travels."[20] The people who wrote these lines were themselves helping Aaron, so his spoken words served the dual purposes of praising those who were aiding him and providing a template for future do-gooders.

One such do-gooder who appears in the last Worcester edition as well as the Springfield editions was Jonathan Cossington, a resident of Malden, Massachusetts, who claimed to have written three pages for the pamphlet while Aaron was asleep "in bed . . . our best bed, with clean sheets and plenty of covering."[21] Perhaps unsurprisingly, the text the minster added while Aaron was sleeping has little to do with Aaron himself; instead, it is about Cossington, his religious visions, and his views on preaching to Blacks and whites. Cossington's story is part of Aaron's insofar as he was one of the men who helped the "poor wayfarer," and he serves as an example of what Aaron would have called "true" Christian charity. Another amanuensis hints that writing for Aaron represented a political act against slave power: "Thank God that God is above the devil, and he has kept Aaron's unworthy body out of the hands of his hard task-master. This is what the way-faring Aaron requested me to write. An abolitionist of Leominster."[22] Because these amanuenses insert themselves into the text, they can speak to other, future, amanuenses, and, in the case of "the abolitionist" or Jonathan Cossington, teach other abolitionists how to live their beliefs. Thus, both the manuscript and the printed version of Aaron's story could share the light and truth of antislavery principles as they manifest in concrete terms. If we think about *The Light and the Truth of Slavery* as a record of the author's life in New England, we can see, too, what it was like to depend on charity and to live at the mercy of others. The pamphlet is not simply a supplicant text but also a record of supplication, and those willing to support the supplicant are the heroes of the story. The interplay between charity and supplication in the pamphlet indicates that, even in manuscript form, *The Light and the Truth of Slavery* circulated within a unique market in which writing could be exchanged for anything of value to the author.

Aaron enlisted many people to help him create his publications, and while this collaborative method had many benefits, it affected the author's ability to shape his story into a coherent form. Perhaps that explains why Aaron shares very few details of his past life or enslavement and instead offers bits of scripture, his feelings about those he has solicited for aid, and excerpts from other publications. Ultimately, the history of Aaron's own enslavement is never a significant part of *The Light and the Truth of Slavery*. Therefore, the truth that Aaron communicates emerges from the borrowed and repurposed words that render his pamphlet something like an antislavery scrapbook. Aaron's amanuenses offer stray sentences about his peripatetic life and mentions stops in Virginia, Maryland, Ohio, New Jersey, Connecticut, Rhode Island, Massachusetts, Vermont, and Maine. Giving few dates or names of persons he saw along the way, Aaron makes no effort to connect his many stops in a linear fashion.[23] Aaron's use of recycled material is equally disjointed, for he moves from a description of his own life to a paragraph titled "Slavery a Sin" which he clipped directly from the July 1835 *Anti-Slavery Record*. This paragraph precedes four lines from William Cowper's "Charity" that were reprinted with attribution in the February 1835 *Anti-Slavery Record*. Aaron reprints those same lines without including Cowper's name.[24] These two pieces cut from different sources precede Aaron's further discussion of religion and his own history of supplication.

This strategy of cutting and pasting exemplify a pattern that holds throughout *The Light and the Truth of Slavery*. Whereas Aaron's "light and truth" is a quite personal subject, as is the author's search for light in others who might give him aid, slavery is almost always described in impersonal terms and usually in reprinted material. Moreover, even though Aaron excerpted sections from contemporary writings by Grandy and Offley, most of the antislavery material he reprints was quite dated, coming as it does from volume 1 of the *Anti-Slavery Record* (1835), *The Anti-Slavery Almanac* (1839), and several other sources. The significance of the texts Aaron chose seems to have everything to do with access; that is, he either obtained a copy of certain publications or had them given to him by a sympathetic friend or a printer. Perhaps someone read various stories to him and he pasted them into his manuscript; perhaps Aaron could read printed text and made the selections himself; or perhaps various amanuenses provided Aaron with passages from antislavery texts because they fit the theme of his pamphlet.

Whatever the reason for Aaron's choices, his publication reprints scenes and arguments focused on slaveholder brutality such as a selection from the *Almanac* that cites "Dr. Channing" (William Ellery Channing) as a source on slaves' happiness. In other places, Aaron inserts already-printed stories of atrocities from the *Anti-Slavery Record* such as the tale of a slaveholder who "kept a room apart" dedicated to whipping or the bricklayer who beat a slave until the flesh was "literally pounded to jelly."[25] Though these passages do not tell anything about Aaron's life, they may have recalled his own experience of enslavement, and they certainly reflect a link between supplication and certain kinds of antislavery stories. As his pamphlet makes clear, Aaron had attended antislavery lectures, and he seems to have known many formerly enslaved men and women. These interactions would have convinced him of the link between antislavery protest and charity. Indeed, the single slave narrative he quotes at length attests to this fact, for Moses Grandy's *Narrative* was also a supplicant text. Grandy promised that "Whatever profit may be obtained by the sale of this book, and all donations with which I may be favoured, will be faithfully employed in redeeming my remaining children and relatives from the dreadful condition of slavery."[26] Despite this significant overlap, Aaron makes no connections between Grandy's *Narrative* and his own story; as with Aaron's other borrowed selections, including "Bro. Offley's little book," this one seems to be rooted in access (Grandy's book was published in 1843 and appeared in Massachusetts in 1844) and subject matter (slavery).

The strange format of *The Light and the Truth of Slavery* also shows in Aaron's use of material from the Bible (of which he claims a deep knowledge) and contemporary writing. Aaron sprinkles verses throughout, and he includes the entire text of "A short chapter that the wayfaring Aaron took out of God's holy word" in between snippets from the *Anti-Slavery Almanac* and *The Narra-*

tive of the Life of Moses Grandy without connecting (explicitly or implicitly) any of the text. He also borrows contemporary poetry of the sort that appeared in periodicals and antislavery publications: songs or poems by antislavery mainstays such as Thomas Campbell and William Cowper, Isaac Watts's "Must This Body Die?," and verses from *The Ladies' Literary Cabinet* and *Songs of the Free* (see table 1.1). These insertions may be examples of Aaron's desire to create a supplicant text that was formatted to sell in the antislavery hotbed of New England and so includes personal recollection, descriptions of slavery, songs, and Bible verses. Supplicant texts like Aaron's speak to an awareness of the robust (and growing) market for such texts in the 1840s.[27]

Since Aaron embarked on his yearslong writing and selling journey to support himself, it is fair to ask whether he benefited from this way of life, either materially or otherwise. Answers are hard to figure, but there is no doubt that Aaron's manuscript facilitated his survival on the margins of American society by bringing him closer to sympathetic men and women who helped him produce a text, and the published pamphlet provided further impetus for those same people to purchase and/or support the "wayfaring" author. Even for those not motivated by Aaron's efforts or by a desire to read his pamphlet, Aaron's use of texts created and circulated by antislavery organizations helped him draw on the moral and religious power of the abolition movement and potentially generate sales among politically minded buyers. If some of the men and women he met regarded him as a vagrant, Aaron's ability to compile and publish a pamphlet marked him as a producer in both his own eyes and — quite probably — in the eyes of the law.[28] While soliciting words seems to have been an effective way to solicit charity, assembling those words in a printed pamphlet transformed Aaron into a publisher and a peddler rather than a beggar. He was taking part in an economic ritual rather than simply relying on what Amy Dru Stanley calls the "protection and dependence" characteristic of paternal relationships (including slavery).[29]

Ultimately, Aaron's savvy and skill as a publisher helped him further his commercial goals, and, as he explains near the end of the Springfield editions, "make an honest living."[30] Though he does not draw the connection between his "honest living" and any change in his circumstances, in the Springfield editions Aaron does mention that he "lives in Springfield, a mile and a half from the Connecticut river, in a little red house, one story high, situated upon the 'Hill.'"[31] This house must have been empty most of the time, for he explains that while his "health is very poor, and he is sick two-thirds of the time . . . it is traveling about that keeps him alive."[32] It is hard to imagine how traveling around New England during winter would

Not in Giving, but in Buying a Book 49

help a sick and elderly man stay alive, but if we take Aaron at his word we must imagine that the health benefits were largely psychological.

Though few supplicant authors explicitly announced the psychological rewards of publishing and selling their books or pamphlets, the evidence of those rewards is manifest in almost all of them. Nancy Prince explained that she did not want to depend on friends and so wrote a book "to help [herself]."[33] In the preface to her postwar supplicant text, Mattie J. Jackson wrote that she would use her book sales to "obtain . . . an education, that I may be enabled to do some good in behalf of the elevation of my emancipated brothers and sisters."[34] Writing a few years later, John Quincy Adams insisted that his "little book will help me to do better in the future" and noted that he was "encouraged to persevere."[35] Each of these supplicant authors linked their publication to a hope that they might elevate themselves and their communities. Each of the authors believed in the potential fruit of their authorial labors, but each also believed that the self-published book itself demonstrated something about their character and commitment. This is the unique power of the published supplicant text: it transforms a ritual of dependence into a transaction between equals and thereby elevates the author.

Supplication and Disability

Nancy Prince and Aaron are two of many antebellum authors who describe the infirmities that led them to write and publish supplicant texts. This trend would only accelerate in the postwar period when a host of wounded soldiers wrote and sold narratives describing their service in the Civil War and the injuries that rendered them unable to work.[36] This new kind of supplicant text—which was mainly produced by white veterans—may have made things even harder for Black authors struggling to support themselves by selling their stories. One such author was Henry Parker, who wrote and published his *Autobiography* sometime in the late 1860s. Parker's pamphlet is a brief and direct text that ties the need for support primarily to disability. Though we cannot be sure where and how Parker sold his pamphlet, it seems designed for quick and easy sale on street corners and streetcars, perhaps more as a token exchanged for donations than anything else. In this respect, the format of Parker's publication helped it function as it was intended.

Born into slavery in Virginia in 1835, Henry Parker escaped in 1859 and made his way to Michigan. After three years of exhausting labor in the North, Parker woke one day with his eyes "feeling somewhat heavy and very hot" and then lost his vision entirely.[37] After a few years of ineffective treatments and suffering, Parker moved to Ohio, where he published a brief autobiography that he sold to support himself as he sought the care of an eye doctor. Above the title of his pamphlet appears Parker's plea to buyers: "Buy this, and you shall have the Prayers of a Blind Man." A similar message appears on the back page of the publication: "Accept this, my friends. It is one of the means I have to support myself. Buy this, and you will have the blessings of a BLIND MAN."[38] Whether he showed prospective purchasers the front or the back, Parker's text told them the same thing: that he was blind and in need of assistance.

Inside the slim (nineteen-centimeter) pamphlet, Parker shares his story and plays the notes typical of a supplicant author. He reminds readers of his religious faithfulness, recalls all he had done to support his family, and insists on his history as a diligent and uncomplaining laborer even during difficult times. Parker's descriptions of his labors make him sound almost Herculean, for when he lived in Michigan he "was compelled to get up at four A. M., and feed eighteen head of cattle; and the snow was about two feet deep, and remained on the ground for nine weeks; and, also, fourteen head of horses and one hundred and fifty head of sheep, and had to be preparing wood to run two fires, and this wood had to be prepared from trees that were standing in the woods, two miles from the house."[39] Clearly, Parker wanted his readers to know that he was a beggar because of circumstance and not because he was unwilling to work.

Parker reinforces this point by sharing with readers his experience of racism and discrimination. The already-blind Parker was en route (via train) from his home in Michigan to see Dr. Taliaferro in Cincinnati when a man encouraged his fellow passengers to aid the suffering Parker. One passenger refuses and exclaims "'I would rather see all the G—d—n n—s in hell than to give this darkey one cent, but if it was a white man I would give him five dollars.'" Rather than bemoan this instance of ugliness, Parker engages his audience with a query: "How do you think I felt at this time?" Parker follows up this question with the declaration that despite such encounters he "always found a few good friends."[40] By prompting readers to put themselves in his place and think about both his physical and psychological pain, Parker implies that those readers should consider him their equal, even if many potential customers did not. Moreover, if we consider Parker's sales efforts compared to those of injured white soldiers returning from the Civil War, Parker reminds us that he must deal with the burden of an indifferent or even malevolent public along with his disability. This fact comes to the fore as Parker notes that he was "excluded from the blind asylum on account of my color," and could not hope for either education or support from the state of Ohio. By first personalizing his experience of racism and asking readers to consider his "feelings" in relation to that experience, Parker urges his audience to think about race-based exclusion as both unjust and psychologically damaging.[41]

One thing Parker does not mention in his supplicant text bears mentioning here, for it suggests something about both the personality and persistence of this particular author. In 1865, likely around the time he published his narrative, Parker was refused passage on an omnibus operated by William Baker and Co. in Cincinnati despite offering the full fare for a seat. The refusal was based solely on Parker's color, and after he was denied a ride on the omnibus, Parker was left with no choice but to walk the several miles to his destination. In the wake of this experience, Parker sued the omnibus company in the Cincinnati Superior Court. Judge Bellamy Storer—a former Whig congressman—presided over the case, and he seems to have favored Parker's suit. He refused various requests by the defense and charged the jury to decide only whether Parker was entitled to ride on the omnibus in any seat he might choose. The jury decided in favor of Parker and awarded him thirty-five dollars in damages.[42] Parker's suit against the bus company recalls his experience of discrimination on board the train to Cincinnati. In both instances, Parker uses the galling experience of personal insult and discrimination to create an opportunity to win justice for himself or to win donations from sympathetic readers.

Supplication and Redemption

The texts produced by Henry Parker and Aaron do not prove that self-publication of the supplicant text was effective, but their very existence suggests that outsider authors believed that a published narrative could help them appeal to donors. This is probably why several nineteenth-century African Americans turned to publication to help them redeem themselves or others from slavery. In the United States, Noah Davis, Leonard Black, and Thomas H. Jones self-published texts that blended slave narrative and supplication in order to secure the purchase of one or more children; George Moses Horton's poems were published in *Hope of Liberty* so that he might earn enough money to emigrate to Liberia; in England, authors like Moses Grandy, Moses Roper, and Josiah Henson sold their narratives to purchase family members still enslaved in the United States.[43] Even as far away as New Zealand, John Joseph published his story in an effort to buy his sister out of slavery in the United States. Joseph told his tale to the ominously named amanuensis J. Greedy, who encouraged readers to "purchase one of these little books. It would be but little from each of us, and a great deal to John Joseph."[44]

In these supplicant texts, the author does not admit to destitution or disability but does suggest that slavery has created economic hurdles too lofty for him to clear and calls on his audience to remedy *his* needs as opposed to the needs of the millions of enslaved men and women who were the subject of more generalized abolitionist appeals. The nature of the appeal for redemption spawns a different kind of supplicant text, which—at least in part—probably accounts for the surprising descriptions of American slavery that appear in Edmond Kelley's *A Family Redeemed from Bondage; Being Rev. Edmond Kelley (the Author), His Wife, and Four Children* (1851). Kelley's text begs readers for assistance not by citing atrocities, bodily degradation, or moral monstrosities but by insisting on the psychological pain of separation and the injustice of bondage. These insistences are framed within a religious context and are published with a ready-made audience of antislavery churchgoers in mind. That audience is yet another unique feature of this supplicant text, for Edmond Kelley did not travel with his publication seeking support along the way. Instead, he marketed and sold his pamphlet in his New Bedford home and appealed to his community members as one of them. In doing so, he was able to garner audience feedback on the format of his publication and modify it so it would most effectively serve his financial goals.

Like Aaron's *The Light and the Truth of Slavery*, Kelley's *A Family Redeemed from Bondage* contains only a few of its author's words even though Kelley was literate and *able* to write his story. Even so, his goals were completely different from those of his supplicant predecessor. First, Edmond Kelley was already a self-supporting preacher in the Second Baptist Church in New Bedford, and he had little interest in describing the "truth" of slavery for anyone other than himself and his family. Moreover, because he was writing for an audience in the antislavery hotbed of New Bedford, Edmond Kelley probably assumed his customers would have some knowledge of American slavery and have strong abolitionist sentiments. The buyers he courted did not need to hear that slavery was unjust, nor did they need to be convinced of Kelley's faithfulness or experience of religion; they simply needed to hear the facts of his *particular* experience of injustice. Second, Kelley published his text *after* his family had been redeemed from bondage, so he was trying to recoup a significant debt rather than trying to support himself as he traveled about New England. This made it easier for him to draw on his reputation in New Bedford since he planned to remain in his adopted home after the debt had been discharged; it also allowed him to showcase the family that he had already redeemed.

In the introduction to his nineteen-page quarto (twenty-centimeter) pamphlet, Kelley explains the history of his publishing venture. Initially, he had intended to produce a longer and larger work and circulated subscription flyers for a book in which he would give "all the facts relative to the purchase of my family, including the letters from various churches, provided they did not object to their being published."[45] Apparently, though, Kelley met with "objections to having the letters printed, on account of their having been written in haste."[46] In the wake of those objections, Kelley had to change his plans since he no longer had a book-sized narrative to print or distribute. Moreover, as he notes, the number of subscribers he had managed to enlist was "so small, that to publish an expensive book would tend to involve me deeper in debt than I am at present, ($865.) If a large number should subscribe, the sale of the book will tend to forward the contemplated object; if not, I shall not make anything on the work."[47] Kelley's financial concerns come to the fore in this short note and we see him thinking—almost in real time—about the best way to manage the local market. For whatever reason, Kelley first thought that he should produce a longer book that would, presumably, sell for a high price to subscribers who wanted to support the author and his mission. When he began circulating a prospectus, though, he learned that there was little interest in such a book and that it would cost him more to print than it could make. This meant the publication had to change. Interestingly, Kelley acknowledges that publishing a book was not really that important since he "presume[s that] the friends who subscribed for it, did it merely to forward the object, and not with a view of being compensated to the value of their money."[48]

Here we see quite clearly the rules of the supplicant text: Kelley's prospective buyers never imagined that, in purchasing a book, they would be purchasing something for fair market value. Their intention was to "forward the object" of paying the debt Kelley incurred in buying his family out of bondage. But Kelley *had* promised to sell something rather than just accepting donations, so he felt honor bound to produce a publication. Though they had not planned to do so, the few subscribers to Kelley's project funded the production of a short pamphlet that Kelley used to solicit more donations. What is interesting here is the flexibility of publishing in the nineteenth century. Working with a job printer in Boston, Kelley could make changes to his plan and his text on relatively short notice. For him (and for many others as well), the idea of the "book" was provisional. If a book was what the local market required, then a book would be what he produced. Once those local requirements changed, though, Kelley was not bound to a particular form or quality of publication since his only mission was realize his financial goals. The text is purely instrumental and entirely focused on Kelley's unique situation.

This sets Kelley apart from well-known author-lecturers like Frederick Douglass and Sojourner Truth, who railed against their own enslavement and the American system of slavery. The genius of someone like Douglass lies in his ability to transform the particular into the universal and make his own experience of slavery intelligible and meaningful to diverse audiences who, in turn, worked to end slavery. Kelley, though, had no interest in making his case anything more than his. Indeed, it is the very particularity of his case that gives *A Family Redeemed* its remarkable urgency as it focuses entirely on dates and documentation rather than narration, description, or moralizing. Kelley uses his pamphlet to show his readers exactly how much money he needs and why he needs it. As Kelley explains, "many of the churches and friends, in responding to my petition for assistance, to enable me to redeem my family from slavery, have requested me to furnish them with a sketch of my history," so he gives the people what they want.[49] Kelley seems to understand that this "sketch" is part of a ritual of giving and need not treat his life story in exacting detail. As such, Kelley gives a few sentences about his birth, conversion, marriage, and licensure as a preacher before compiling a lengthy plea built with documents, notices, and letters.

Kelley's use of this material links him to many other formerly enslaved authors who included legal or personal documents in their narratives. In the last chapter of his *Narrative*, Frederick Douglass documents his church-sanctioned marriage to Anna Murray, thereby highlighting his rights as a free man and his embrace of religious rituals denied him when he was enslaved.[50] In *Behind the Scenes*, Elizabeth Keckley includes the text of every legal document related to her emancipation to prove that she had repaid money she had borrowed.[51] Keckley and Douglass wanted to do more than prove something about themselves; they also wanted to prove something about slavery by showing that the system denied such fundamental rights as the ability to marry or the ability to own oneself and one's labor. Similarly, Edmond Kelley uses documents and letters to demonstrate his character and to confirm the legitimacy of his financial need. And, though he describes no atrocities, abuses, or terrors, Kelley manages to reveal one of slavery's most vexing monstrosities: Slaveholders' uses of both emotional and legal justifications for maintaining ownership of other humans. So, as he fulfills his primary goal of securing money to pay the debts he incurred as he tried to reclaim his family from bondage, Kelley also reclaims the meaning of "family" from the proslavery forces that sought to define it.

Edmond Kelley was a Baptist minister, and his use of the verb "redeemed" in the title of his publication suggests that he viewed his quest to secure his family's freedom in religious terms. Like the Israelites "redeemed" from bondage in Egypt, so too was Kelley trying to win the earthly salvation of his wife and four children. Kelley's efforts to redeem his family had a legal and practical dimension as well, and the man against whom he struggled in this contest was James Walker of Columbia, Tennessee, a wealthy man whose brother-in-law was the recently deceased ex-president James K. Polk. Though Walker did not claim to own Kelley himself, he did claim Kelley's wife Parmalee, all of Kelley's children, and Parmalee's mother Dolly. At the time he tried to secure his family's freedom, Kelley was enslaved by the widow Ann White, also of Columbia. When White met with straitened circumstances in 1846, she provided Kelley with a pass that allowed him to leave Tennessee and support himself by preaching. Though the pass allowed Kelley to travel to "any State in the United States," it also required Kelley to return when "called for by [his] owner."[52] Soon after receiving the pass, Kelley made his way to New York before traveling on to Boston and then New Bedford, where he became the pastor of the Second Baptist Church in September 1848. Kelley does not explain why he settled in New Bedford, but the reasons may be easily guessed since that city maintained a significant and vibrant African American community that could support religious and civic institutions like the Second Baptist Church. Moreover, since New Bedford was an important urban center connected to the abolitionist movement, it would have been an ideal place for a fugitive like Kelley to live.[53]

After Kelley moved to Massachusetts, the Concord Baptist Association (CBA) in Concord, Tennessee, made plans to purchase his freedom and collected $77.90 toward that end. Unwilling to wait (or unwilling to accept that he could be purchased at all), Kelley informed the association that he would not return to Tennessee and would live as a free man in Massachusetts. Upon hearing this news, the president of the CBA suggested that the money be diverted to enable the "purchase of [Kelley's] wife and children," but the treasurer of the organization and the chairman of the "Committee on the Correspondence with Edmond Kelley" noted that the money had been donated to purchase Kelley and not his family. He suggested that the $77.90 that had already been collected be appropriated to Union University, a Baptist seminary in Tennessee. After reprinting the letters written by the leaders of the CBA, Kelley breaks into the narrative and directs readers to consider what they have just read: "N.B.—The Committee could not appropriate the money to the purchase of my family, because it was collected to effect my purchase, but could take the same money and apply it to the support of a beneficiary at Union University."[54]

Kelley moves on to describe his further attempts to secure his family's freedom in the form of direct negotiations with their enslaver, James Walker. In response to Kelley's request, Walker responds with a series of letters that are truly remarkable examples of white self-interest masquerading as lordly beneficence. In these letters, Walker eschews the language of law or rules and instead employs affective rhetoric to thwart Kelley's efforts. In his first letter, Walker begins by assessing the market value of the people in question: $2,800. But, as he explains, "No price, however, could be offered by any one that would induce me to permit them to be the slaves or servants of any but my own family. To part with them, with certain knowledge that they were to be free, and their condition bettered, is a matter I might take into consideration."[55] Here we see the conundrum produced by slavery, for Kelley's family is both subject to market valuation and, at the same time, kept from the very market in which they could be valued. This is because, as Walker explains, Kelley's family "in the tie of affection and regard for their comfort and happiness which exists, are not slaves at all. They, if they are colored, stand next in my affections to my own wife and children and children's children." Surely, it was this deep-rooted affection that led Walker to wonder whether Kelley could make freedom "beneficial to them, if I were even voluntarily to emancipate them. This I shall not do, for the simple reason that I believe doing so would not benefit them, if there were no other reason."[56]

Kelley may have decided that simply allowing Walker to explain those "other reasons" for refusing to grant his "servants" freedom would be the most effective way to couch his plea for support, so he reprinted more of the letter: "My family are accustomed to and must have servants. Servants to whom they are attached, and who are truly attached to them, are invaluable. Servants who are raised up in a family, perfectly honest and upright, attached to those who are their owners and protectors, are a necessary part of a family, not conveniently dispensed with." Recall that the person to whom Walker wrote these words was the biological father of the very servants whom Walker claims as "a necessary part of" *his* "family." Perhaps realizing that Kelley's "family" claim was more significant, Walker finally agreed to sell

Kelley's wife and children, upon which men from the Boston Baptist Association tried to negotiate a lower price. And, just when the question of money arises, Walker once again deploys the language of affect: "I have no disposition to reduce the price of Edmond Kelley's wife and children. If I were disposed to sell them as servants here I could get more money for them, and they are daily increasing in value. No consideration would induce me to sell them to remain in slavery."[57] Now an object of affection, then a commodity for sale, Walker values Kelley's family according to the terms that will net him the best bargain. Though he continually cites their value on the open market, Walker denies that he would ever seek to sell them in that market. As historian Walter Johnson explains, such behavior was typical for enslavers who "measure[d their] paternalism in dollars foregone."[58] Except in this case Walker does not forgo those dollars since the open-market price he cites ($2,800) is also the price that Edmond Kelley must pay to redeem his family.

Raising this amount of money would be a great enough chore by itself, and Walker obviously knew this since he complained that if Kelley could not obtain "[the money] without much delay, I wish he would cease writing to them or me, raising in them hopes that cannot be realized."[59] Casting himself in the role of the aggrieved party seeking to protect the feelings of his "servants," Walker insists that he be paid in full, and soon. It is hardly news that an enslaver could be self-congratulatory, self-interested, obstinate, and obtuse. What makes Kelley's pamphlet interesting, though, is that the enslaver gets to speak for himself at such length. There are few published narratives that feature such extensive, unfiltered testimony from an enslaver's pen, and even though Kelley probably adopted this authorial strategy so he could document the facts of his case for donors, the enslaver's words also clarify the confusing blend of affection and avarice that made those donations necessary. Even though Walker's demand for payment found Kelley $865 short of the amount he needed, Kelley took a loan for that remaining amount and, after a month of legal wrangling and waiting, he finally reunited with his family on May 29, 1851.

Because of the loan he had taken, this happy ending was not the ending, for Kelley still needed to repay his debts, and so he began soliciting subscriptions for the book that finally became the pamphlet *A Family Redeemed from Bondage*. As I have shown, the pamphlet is designed to take readers on an emotional journey until the moment of the family's redemption and then leaves the rest up to their generosity. Indeed, in a printed note that remains in one extant copy of the pamphlet, Kelley seems to charge others with the work of helping him distribute his plea (see fig. 1.3). Kelley's note shows that

> My Dear Brother:
>
> You will perceive from an examination of the accompanying Narrative, that in the final struggle to secure the release of my wife and children, I became involved in over eight hundred dollars debt, nearly all of which is now resting upon me, embarrassing my mind and crippling my energies as a Minister of Christ.
>
> I take the liberty of calling your attention at the present time to the fact that some of my notes must very soon be taken up, and the interest, if no more, of others, be paid. I hope that upon an examination of these facts, you will feel constrained to make my case your own, and do something to aid me in this emergency. May I request that you will consider yourself authorized to bring this matter before your people, and other friends of the slave, as soon as may be, and collect what they may feel willing to contribute.
>
> Any sum, great or small, that you may obtain for me, will be thankfully received, and you will please forward the same to me by mail.
>
> If any persons should desire copies of my pamphlet, they may be obtained by addressing a line to me, for whatever price they may please to give for them.
>
> EDMOND KELLEY,
> *Corner of Middle and Cedar Streets, New Bedford, Mass.*

FIGURE 1.3 Flyer in Edmond Kelley's *A Family Redeemed from Bondage* (1851). Courtesy of Phillips Library, Peabody Essex Museum, Rowley, Massachusetts.

circulation of the supplicant texts could be a communal exercise aided by religious or abolitionist groups. The note also reminds us that the price an author received for a supplicant text (or, really, for any self-published text) was partly up to the purchaser.

Though Kelley's note on sales and pricing does not address this directly, it also suggests that redemption was bound up in the same economic structure that undergirds slavery. Like the enslaver James Walker, who sets the monetary value of his "servants" according to his affection for them, purchasers of Kelley's text must also consider how much their feelings are worth. Kelley would not sell his family for any price—this is what it means to claim individuals as family as opposed to family servants—but he does stage an emotional contest for prospective donors and asks them to measure their feelings for his family against those of the enslaver. Kelley pushes his readers to feel enough Christian love to match the affective avarice of James Walker. None of this is meant to suggest that New England abolitionists were really the same as Southern slaveholders, but I do want to insist on the commonplace mingling of economics and emotion in discourse about slavery. A supplicant text like Kelley's indicates that money was the measure of Christian commitment and fellow feeling. Like Aaron, Kelley asks readers to purchase his text not for what it contains but for what the purchase itself represents.

Texts like Kelley's are not unique, but there were likely more items of this sort published than have survived. Many of these short supplicant pamphlets would have lacked what Joanna Brooks identifies as physical "movement" or a connection to "movements," either of which enabled early Black print to flourish and survive.[60] As Kelley's note shows, though, he found a way to generate movement for his publication even if he never left New Bedford. There is another quality we might consider that accounts for the endurance of Kelley's first publication. That other quality is prominence, something Kelley appears to have developed during his life in Massachusetts. In 1864, Kelley (writing as Edmund Kelly) published *Important Questions Adapted to the Use of Sabbath Schools, Bible Classes, and Private Families: Including Many Testimonials North and South*; in the 1870s he published broadsides on politics, on population distribution, and on migration.[61] Each of these broadsides was prefaced with a small portrait of Kelly and each concluded with his stereotyped signature, both of which are signs he had achieved elevated status in New Bedford. That local standing might have encouraged people to save copies of Kelley's earliest publication so they could preserve a reminder of Edmund Kelly's former life as Edmond Kelley: fugitive slave and supplicant author.

Rethinking Harriet Wilson's Supplicant Novel

Harriet Wilson's *Our Nig* (1859) remains one of the most famous self-published texts in the African American canon. Wilson's novel was republished by Henry Louis Gates Jr. in 1983 and has been on syllabi and exam reading lists ever since. This trend has only accelerated since P. Gabrielle Foreman, Eric Gardner, Reginald Pitts, and Barbara White uncovered even more information on Wilson's biography and helped show that the author's life and business career extended well beyond the moment she published her first and only book.[62] Over the past forty years, *Our Nig* has spawned a host of articles, book chapters, and conference panels, and it remains an intriguing text for literary critics. Indeed, Wilson's novel is ready-made for the current generation of African Americanist print culture specialists since it concludes with a description of the author's motives and goals. In the one-page preface she might have shown to prospective buyers, Wilson explains that she wrote *Our Nig* because she was "[d]eserted by kindred" and "disabled by failing health." These exigencies led her to "some experiment" that could "aid [her] in maintaining [herself] and child." Though most purchasers of Wilson's book were white, she appealed to her "colored brethren universally for patronage," suggesting an (apparently unrealized) hope that her book would circulate beyond her New Hampshire hometown. At the conclusion of her story, Wilson renews her plea for support and insists that she has told enough of her story to demand a reader's "sympathy and aid."[63] Like supplicant authors who came before her, Wilson ties sympathy to charity and asks her readers for both.

Scholars who read *Our Nig* today are almost always vexed by the conclusion of Wilson's remarkable novel, for it seems that this heartfelt plea fell on very few receptive ears. *Our Nig* was probably printed only once, and it sold a handful of copies.[64] The novel attracted little attention from the abolitionist press, and it seems to have disappeared as suddenly as it appeared. Looking back on African American literary history and knowing just how special this book is, scholars wonder why Wilson's contemporaries did not take notice of what she had done and turn the book into the sensation it has now become. Why was *Uncle Tom's Cabin* a bestseller and this book all but ignored?

In trying to answer that question, most critics have argued that Wilson's novel failed to make a splash because of the words on its pages. For example, Ellen Pratofiorito insists that antebellum writings on race and slavery needed to fit into certain categories in order to be marketable and that there "were limits on how and what racial matters could be commercially entertained."[65] David Dowling argues along similar lines that Wilson's book was anathema to Northern abolitionists (and therefore received no attention from them) because Wilson unmasked the racial and economic inequalities in the North and located "northern racism precisely in the . . . unfair labor practices that make a mockery of 'freedom' for northern blacks."[66]

These and other astute analyses locate *Our Nig* within already existing literary markets for antislavery or abolitionist writing and show how — in one way or another — Wilson's book did not conform to the standards for those markets.[67] Most of these critics place Wilson's book in context with the mass-produced antislavery publications of the period. Given the way Wilson wrote and published her book, though, this seems suspect. There is little evidence that she imagined *Our Nig* as a novel for the masses, nor is there any suggestion that she tried to secure a different kind of publishing opportunity. Absence of evidence is not evidence of absence, but if Wilson was facing dire financial circumstances in 1858, she would have known that self-publication would allow her to reap whatever profit came from her novel, especially if that publication was partially or wholly subsidized by the printer, George Rand, as Eric Gardner speculates.[68]

Gardner's analysis of the printing and reception history of *Our Nig* demonstrates that very few readers ever held the novel in their hands and indicates those who did tended to be (1) quite young, and (2) close to Wilson's home in Milford, New Hampshire.[69] Though this clustering of readers fits with the idea that *Our Nig* was sold door to door as a supplicant text by Wilson herself, Gardner insists we cannot be certain whether *Our Nig* was "suppressed by part of the abolitionist power structure" or whether it was, indeed, "a book charitably produced for the author's personal distribution."[70] Given that she was writing in the post–*Uncle Tom's Cabin* years, Wilson may have been able to publish her book with a trade publisher, or she could have tried to publish her novel with the support of abolitionists, though, as Michaël Roy has shown, such arrangements were rare in the late 1850s.[71] Though either of these potential strategies could have yielded greater sales for Wilson's book, neither would have guaranteed sales or profits, and there is no evidence to suggest that Wilson sought other forms of production or distribution. This leads me to regard the novel as—first and foremost—a supplicant text. As a supplicant text, it circulated within the same sort of local markets as other supplicant texts and was almost certainly regarded, by readers and abolitionists, in much the same way as those publications.

Though modern readers can see the many differences between *Our Nig* and *The Light and the Truth of Slavery*, one wonders whether rural New England readers (who would have been familiar with book peddlers) would have seen those same differences, at least at the moment of purchase. After all, both texts were sold door to door by an author/solicitor without any formal connection to either an institution or a movement. There was nothing authorizing the solicitor beyond his or her published text and his or her reputation, and each of those texts featured a one-page note that explained what the book was and why it was being sold. Like other supplicant texts (but unlike Aaron's pamphlet), Wilson's book also included appendices speaking to Wilson's history and character and encouraging readers to "assist our sister, not in giving, but in buying a book."[72] Given the hortatory quality of the paratexts and the length of Wilson's novel, it seems that the transaction between seller and buyer would have preceded the reader's enjoyment of the book, and because she sought those buyers in and around her hometown of Milford, she might have imagined that they would already be familiar with her story or at least her connection to the family in the text. For Wilson's customers, a book purchase allowed them to aid a woman they already knew and to whom they wished to demonstrate their sympathy. If this were indeed the case, then Wilson's story aligns with that of many Black writers who passed through authorship to pay their bills.

Even though Wilson may have shared several traits with other supplicant authors, and even though her text may have circulated through the local and face-to-face networks favored by most of those authors, *Our Nig* is, nevertheless, a unique supplicant text in at least two respects. First, Wilson's novel can claim generic difference from most other supplicant texts. Typical supplicant authors sold their stories for money and support, but Wilson seems to be pushing in a somewhat different direction as she tries to sell *a story* for support. Though *Our Nig* may be autobiographical, it is not only a tale of personal suffering but an "attempt" to create something entirely new: a novel about the overlapping experiences of racism and domestic cruelty. Despite Wilson's aesthetic innovation, though, her book seems to have been marketed and sold according to the patterns established by her supplicant forebears. Second, *Our Nig* appeared in a very different format from most supplicant publications. The quarto (twenty-centimeter) book is bound with a simple cover, and it is longer than most other supplicant texts of the period. In other words, it is most definitely a *book* as opposed to a pamphlet.

The combination of Wilson's remarkable "attempt" and an unusual format may have made it hard for her to find purchasers. As I suggest above, as a supplicant Wilson was seeking *buyers* first and *readers* second; however, as an author, she would have been seeking *readers* who were also buyers. Given the ways supplicant texts worked within the marketplace, this disjunction may have posed a problem for one or the other of Wilson's goals. To be sure, Harriet Wilson was neither the first nor the last author to find her aesthetic goals in conflict with her commercial aims. What sets Wilson apart, though, is that this conflict was not played out so much in the pages of the novel she wrote but in the format she chose for her only publication.

CHAPTER TWO

Independent of the Abolitionists
Antislavery Self-Publishing

In *The Slave's Cause*, Manisha Sinha writes that "slave narratives were the movement literature of abolition."[1] From Frederick Douglass's *Narrative* to Sojourner Truth's *Life* to Solomon Northup's *Twelve Years a Slave*, many of the bestselling and enduring texts of the African American autobiographical canon are connected to the political movements supporting the abolition of slavery. And yet, as Michaël Roy explains in *Fugitive Texts*, when we look at the publication histories of "slave narratives," we discover the "heterogeneous nature of what is often perceived as a homogenous whole."[2] Put another way, the "movement literature" that Sinha describes was sometimes disconnected from the movement itself.

Writing in the 1840s, Frederick Douglass and William Wells Brown paid to publish their own narratives and then sold the books themselves at speaking engagements that were sponsored or supported by the Massachusetts Anti-Slavery Society (MASS).[3] Similarly, Sojourner Truth self-published several editions of her narrative and then sold it at speeches and meetings. Truth's speaking tours were sometimes supported by abolitionist organizations, but sometimes were not. Other authors, like Josiah Henson, Northup, Samuel Ringgold Ward, and James W. C. Pennington, had their work promoted by antislavery organizations, but they published their narratives with commercial firms in the United States. And, as Audrey Fisch and many others have shown, numerous Black authors (including Douglass, Brown, and Henson) found lecture audiences, publishers, and readers in England, especially in the 1850s following the passage of the Fugitive Slave Act.[4] These various publishing situations suggest that—even for the most connected and prolific authors—the relationship between antislavery authors and the abolition movement was never settled or static.

Even if abolitionist organizations did not publish or endorse narratives by formerly enslaved authors, they certainly shaped those narratives either directly or indirectly. Direct shaping is evident in Douglass's *Narrative* (1845), in which prefaces by William Lloyd Garrison and Wendell Phillips provide interpretive frames for the book, thereby enclosing Douglass's words within what John Sekora calls a "white envelope."[5] Abolitionists (and abolitionist discourse) shaped Black autobiographies in indirect ways as well. In his 1849 essay titled "Narratives of Fugitive Slaves," Ephraim Peabody, a Massachusetts minister and abolitionist, argued that slave narratives were among the "most remarkable productions of the age" because they provided "pictures of slavery by the slave" and were full of "poetry and romance."[6] Peabody's framing of the slave narrative suggests that, even if an author was not directly sponsored by MASS or another organization, they still had to attend to abolitionists' concerns if they wanted to find willing listeners and purchasers. This is why Dwight McBride argues that abolitionist-sponsored meetings and publications gave a formerly enslaved speaker "the occasion for bearing witness, but to an experience that had already been theorized and prophesied."[7]

Another way the abolitionist movement structured possibilities for Black writers was through the range of symbols and ideas common to its messaging. Robert Fanuzzi argues that the "abolitionists' print culture . . . served as a memory culture, instructing contemporaries in the historic significance of their current struggle and establishing a system of analogies with distant events," especially the American Revolution.[8] In other words, Black writers not only had to "bear witness" to certain truths, they also had to analogize in ways that would resonate with white listeners and readers. In some cases, this meant lionizing the words of men like Thomas Jefferson or Andrew Jackson, both of whom remain troubling representatives of American ideals. As Benjamin Quarles, Leon Litwack, Stephen Hall, and John Ernest have shown (and as I try to elaborate in chapter 3) some Black writers found ways to rethink the historical legacies to which they would pay obeisance, but it could be difficult for abolitionist speakers and authors to simultaneously claim and revise a connection to the founders.[9]

Finally, since abolitionism was a political movement that was influenced by white expectations and demands, McBride insists that white men became "the arbiter not only for what abolitionism is but of who has access" to the category of "abolitionist."[10] As Peabody's essay suggests, formerly enslaved narrators might work with abolitionists and give testimony to support the cause, but they could not shape the movement itself.[11] This is why self-publication was an attractive option: Not because self-publishers could avoid or ignore the structures of thought and feeling that shaped abolitionist discourse, but because self-publishers did not have to mirror that discourse to enter the world of print. Though an independent self-publishing author could not rely on the same networks or publicity as institutionally affiliated authors and speakers, they were also free to critique abolitionist organizations or reimagine the meanings of abolitionist labor and activism.

Into the spaces created by self-publication stepped men like Leonard Black, who was enslaved in Maryland until 1837. In 1847, Black published two versions of his *Life and Sufferings* (one in Providence and one in New Bedford) to rail against slavery and garner money for his education; he published an expanded version of his life story along with several of his sermons four years later.[12] William H. Johnson published his *Narrative* in Worcester in 1847 and bemoaned his own treatment and especially that of enslaved women; he also insisted that "every true Christian, male or female, is an abolitionist."[13] Like Black and Johnson, G. W. Offley had been enslaved in Maryland before moving to New England where he wrote and published two different versions of his autobiography. In his 1860 *Life*, which is more than twice as long as his 1859 edition, Offley explains that even though he never intended to write "an anti-slavery book," he added to his earlier edition because he had "been requested by friends to complete the story of Jane Brown, the slave woman."[14] In all three of these New England narratives, the authors wrestle with the relationship between autobiography and abolition as they try to stake out a unique position for themselves and their stories. By writing in ways that might resonate with antislavery readers but doing so outside the constraints imposed by white-run organizations, self-publishers helped broaden the mantle of abolitionism and foreground Black labor in the antislavery struggle.

Like the convention organizers with whom many of them were allied, self-publishing antislavery writers were practicing what P. Gabrielle Foreman calls "a *parallel politics* actualized in the face of official exclusion."[15] Whereas the conventioneers Foreman describes were taking part in political rituals from which they had been legally excluded, the authors in this chapter were, instead, trying to shape a movement in which they could participate but not fully control. That is, self-publishing authors had their own sense of the best way to advance the antislavery cause, and they tried to pursue their visions while broadening the very idea of what an "anti-slavery book" was supposed to be and do. As such, the distinguishing feature of the self-published anti-slavery book is its format. In books and pamphlets by Offley, Black, and the other authors in this chapter, readers come upon newspaper stories, convention records, court documents, sermons, and bibliographies that could contribute to the antislavery cause.[16] The authors who crafted these unique publications centered the voices and actions of Black men and women who were fighting against slavery and sought to dislodge the narratives that "had already been theorized and prophesied."

In this chapter, I uncover the stories of three self-publishing authors who sought to capitalize on the market for antislavery books while expanding the idea of what such books could look like and do. The chapter begins with an analysis of Levin Tilmon's multiple publications and the role he imagined for literary productivity within the antislavery struggle. As a writer and a pastor in New York City, Tilmon linked himself to well-known abolitionists like Frederick Douglass and James McCune Smith and celebrated the power of print as a tool for combating prejudice and historical ignorance with the hopes that both of those missions might engender political transformations. Writing around the same time as Tilmon, Thomas Smallwood used the publication of his autobiography to fight for a position in the antislavery movement in Canada and to rail against opportunistic and money-hungry abolitionists connected to the Underground Railroad. Smallwood's autobiography is certainly an antislavery book, but it also condemns many of the powerful abolitionists who led the fight against slavery. In this way, it works for the antislavery cause while separating that cause from the abolition movement as such. Like Smallwood, William J. Anderson spent years ferrying fugitives to the North only to find himself threatened by enemies to the south. In the wake of his brief career as a pro-Republican speaker during the 1856 election season and his subsequent arrest in Kentucky, Anderson published three versions of his life story in which he seems to wrestle with the limitations so often imposed on Black speakers and writers within the antislavery movement. Anderson's tangled story reminds us of both the power of Black activists and the limits of self-publication as a political tool.

Levin Tilmon and the Community of Letters

When Levon Tilmon first made his escape to Philadelphia after fleeing an abusive Delaware man to whom he was indentured, his "heart leaped for joy, with the prospects of a home, and of making money."[17] His first stay in Philadelphia would be a short one since he was recaptured only a week later, but after four more years living with a new (and more generous) man who held his indenture, Tilmon secured his freedom and began working for himself in 1829. Soon thereafter, he looked for ways to get ahead in the North. Part of his search took him to new places: Wilmington, Philadelphia, Trenton, and then Philadelphia once again where he worshipped at the African Methodist Episcopal (A.M.E.) Church and was eventually convinced of his salvation. When he published his autobiography in 1853,

Tilmon closed the autobiographical portion of his book with his pronouncement that, at last, he was "a sinner saved by Grace."[18]

This ending suggests that his narrative is a conventional spiritual autobiography in which the subject secures both his temporal and eternal salvation by first escaping from an enslaver and then finding refuge in God, but Tilmon's pamphlet—which he titled the *Brief Miscellaneous Narrative of the More Early Part of the Life of L. Tilmon*—is anything but conventional. As Tilmon indicates in the title, the narrative is focused entirely on the early part of his life, though the autobiographical portion makes up less than half of the book. In the first edition, Tilmon concludes the narration of his life story with his salvation, but then he appends thirty pages of newspaper articles and letters to the editor that he had written during his years as a missionary and traveling preacher who raised money to support the construction of Black churches in New England. These letters and articles extend his life story but do so entirely from the standpoint of Tilmon's public work on behalf of the church. Moreover, some of Tilmon's letters—to Frederick Douglass at *Frederick Douglass's Paper*, George Hogarth at the *A.M.E. Church Magazine*, and to the editors of the *Christian Herald* and the *Roman* (New York) *Citizen*—appear to have been printed in those papers, whereas other letters in the *Narrative* were never printed. Among the miscellaneous documents swelling his book, Tilmon also includes a sermon (presumably one of his own) and Frederick Douglass's "Letter to His Former Master." Through these reprintings, Tilmon's personal history flashes on us at certain moments, but, for the most part, his life story is but one piece of what reads like a scrapbook of Tilmon's writing life. Put another way: his autobiography doubles as a bibliography.

Later in 1853—perhaps after he had amassed enough money to pay for a second printing—Tilmon published the second edition of his *Miscellaneous Narrative*. This edition, like the first, is a small duodecimo (seventeen-centimeter) pamphlet and was printed by at the offices of the Jersey City *Sentinel*, an anti-Democratic paper published by William and Luther Pratt.[19] Beyond the possible political overlap between the editors and Tilmon, there is nothing to indicate why Tilmon chose the *Sentinel*'s printing offices for his project, but perhaps their work on his first edition inspired him to return there. Or, perhaps they kept the type from the first edition standing so Tilmon could print his second edition more easily. Though printers did not usually leave type standing for long, this certainly could have been the case since Tilmon's second edition reprints the entirety of the first with only a single blank page separating the fifty-nine pages of the first edition from the thirty-eight pages that follow. The first ten of those new pages are reprintings that reprise the bibliographical style from the end of the first edition, though the reprintings are from the *New York Tribune* and mention neither Tilmon nor the A.M.E. Church. Thereafter, Tilmon resumes narrating his life, forty-odd pages after the conclusion of his life story from the first edition.

When he returns to the autobiographical portion of his narrative, Tilmon makes almost no mention of the lengthy caesura in his pamphlet but returns to 1830 (where he had left off) and goes on to describe his years of service to the A.M.E. Church as a traveling preacher and missionary charged with raising funds and building churches.[20] In some ways, Tilmon's continuation of his life story returns us to the letters he reprinted in the first version of his book, letters that highlighted the places he had traveled during his years as a minister. As we learn, though, those letters do not tell the whole story, for Tilmon had taken an extended break from his ministerial work starting in 1837. Because he had found himself "much reduced in pecuniary circumstances," he "engaged in the beer business; finding it to be a lucrative pursuit."[21] Later he "followed teaming" and eventually earned a "comfortable living" that enabled him to purchase property in and around Philadelphia.

Skipping over his efforts to realize a more secure economic position, Tilmon moves quickly to discuss his gospel labors in the mid-1840s. In 1844, Tilmon returned to a formal role in the church; he was ordained a deacon by the New York conference in 1845, and he was admitted to "full connection" by the New York conference in 1847. This would have meant that Tilmon was licensed by the church elders to preach in the pulpit as opposed to simply leading prayer meetings or Sunday school classes. Being admitted to "full connection" signaled a minister's ability to preach according to his interpretation of the Bible, and it was the pinnacle of ministerial achievement and trust. By the time Tilmon published his life story six years later, though, he "had been driven" from the church by "oppression and cruel treatment."[22] Curiously, while Tilmon spends much of his book describing or otherwise commemorating his work for the church, he avoids discussing the nature of the "oppression" that drove him from his position. This silence notwithstanding, his decision to publish his book may have been tied to his altered situation since, after he was dismissed from the A.M.E., Tilmon founded the First Colored Congregational Church in 1852. We can assume that Tilmon's decision to publish his book was a way for him to publicize his faith and experience and to help him secure both patronage and a continued pastorage at the brand-new Congregational church.

In between the publication of the two editions of his *Narrative* (both of which appeared in 1853), Tilmon made another effort to enter the print marketplace and to link himself with the emerging African American community of letters in New York City.²³ This effort took the form of a short pamphlet featuring Tilmon's essay titled "The Consequences of One Important Misstep," which Tilmon had printed at Mitchell's Book and Job Office. The print shop was run by William Mitchell, who had been in business since the 1830s and seems to have cared little about his customers' ideology since he had printed both abolitionist and anti-abolitionist pamphlets over the years.²⁴ Tilmon's thirty-six-page octavo (twenty-two-centimeter) pamphlet includes the titular essay, a treatise on the value of the "productive system," and the first bibliography of African American writings published in the United States. Though Tilmon does not mention the bibliography on the cover of his pamphlet (it is mentioned only on the title page), it is easily the most interesting aspect of Tilmon's publication. Numbering only five pages, the bibliography purports to include "A LIST OF AUTOBIOGRAPHIES (COLORED)," but is composed of texts from multiple genres: Phillis Wheatley's poetry, Douglass's "What to the Slave is the Fourth of July," David Walker's *Appeal*, Henry Highland Garnet's "Past and Present Condition . . . ," William Nell's *Services of Colored Americans in the Wars of 1776 and 1812*, R. B. Lewis's *Light and Truth*, Martin Delaney's *Condition, Elevation, Immigration and Destiny* . . . , R. M. Johnson's *Liberia as It Is*, and—interestingly enough—Harriet Beecher Stowe's *Uncle Tom's Cabin*.²⁵ Tilmon also includes autobiographies by Olaudah Equiano, William Wells Brown, Leonard Black, Sojourner Truth, James W. C. Pennington, and Charles Bowles along with his own *Miscellaneous Narrative*.

As his prefatory note to the bibliography makes clear, Tilmon (like the historian William C. Nell and many other author-activists of the antebellum period) believed that the diffusion of knowledge among Black readers could dispel the white supremacist mythology on which the United States is founded. He notes that whereas the achievements of white men are engraved in marble, the "various achievements of colored men can only be traced by his bleaching bones upon the hill summits of the American continent."²⁶ Tilmon imagines that storytelling and other forms of commemoration could begin to change this situation. For him, it was not just the acquisition of literacy by Black people but *literary production* by them that could remedy social and educational deficiencies. His outlook explains his desire to commemorate his own efforts within his various self-published books and pamphlets, and it also explains his championing of literary production in the form of the "Young Men's Literary Productive Society, No. 1," which Tilmon founded and presided over at his church.

Very little information on the society remains, but the group—or its purpose—was significant enough to win the attention of Frederick Douglass, who visited the society on at least two occasions. After his first visit, in the spring of 1853, Douglass editorialized: "I attended an exhibition given by [the members] and could wish that every slaveholder and negro-hater in the land had done the same. There were among those lads many who would shine in any circle of intellectual white boys, it has been my fortune to witness." Douglass went on to wonder why the ministers of the "Zion" and "Bethel Church" did not "copy the very laudable example of Rev. L. Tilman [sic]" and start their own literary societies. Since Tilmon had been dismissed from the A.M.E. Church, Douglass's jibe at the A.M.E. and A.M.E. Zion church leaders must have pleased him.[27]

The Young Men's Literary Productive Society put on several readings and programs, though newspaper accounts grant us only brief glimpses of the events themselves. According to the "Order of Exercises" planned for November 7, 1854 (fig. 2.1), the program included original compositions on "Utility or Society," "Reform," "The Duty of Colored People towards the overthrow of American Slavery," and "Elevation of the African Race."[28] Later that winter, at the February 1855 meeting of the society, Douglass delivered the keynote address at Tilmon's church. After Douglass spoke, James McCune Smith stood up to lobby for donations to support the purchase of new type for *Frederick Douglass's Paper*; and his request yielded over eighty dollars.[29] This anecdote about Douglass, Smith, and Tilmon illustrates the ways that activism, authorship, and entrepreneurship might go hand in hand, and it also demonstrates the degree to which publication could be realized as a communal or community-supported endeavor *outside* the aegis of the white-sponsored abolition movement. Indeed, the communal aspects of literary production seemed to appeal to Tilmon most especially: whether it was writing a "miscellaneous narrative" that featured texts authored by numerous writers, crafting a bibliography of Black authors, or developing a society to encourage literary production, Tilmon was always thinking about himself as part of a group of Black Americans who were using books, pamphlets, and newspapers to push for abolition and equal treatment under the law.

For Tilmon, authorship, community uplift, religious training and worship, education, and economic productivity—pursuits that Derrick Spires labels as "citizenship practices"—all contributed to the project of abolition and civil rights.[30] In his bibliography of Black writings, Tilmon reminds readers of the polyvocal (and long-standing) nature of antislavery and anti-racist

LITERARY EXHIBITIONS IN NEW YORK CITY.

THE MEMBERS of the Young Men's Literary Productive Society, under the auspices of the First Colored American Congregational Church, Sixth St., in the City of New York, of which the Rev. L. Tilmon is Pastor, (the Season having arrived,) propose giving a course of LITERARY EXHIBITIONS, for the mutual benefit of said Church and Society, commencing in said Church on Tuesday evening, at 8 o'clock, Nov. 7, 1854. Come, young men, and join our literary band!

The members intend enlivening their Exhibitions with subjects of the most thrilling interest, and unrivalled eloquence.

Miss ELIZABETH JENNINGS will preside at the Organ.

ORDER OF EXERCISES.
PART I.

1. Overture, By the Choir.
2. Prayer, By Guardian
3. Singing, By the Choir.
4. Reading Articles of the Association.
5. Address "On Reform," E. L. Francis.
6. Singing, By the Choir.
7. Address, "Utility or Society," John Stevens.
8. Address, "American Slavery," J. C. Sanches.
9. Singing, By the Choir.
10. Address, Jas. Anthony.

PART II

1. Singing, By the Choir.
2. Address, "The Duty of Colored People towards the overthrow of American Slavery," John Stevens.
3. Address, Henry Latham.
4. Singing, By the Choir.
5. Address, M. P. Sanders.
6. Address, "Bible," Geo. W Myres.
7. Singing, By the Choir.
8. Address, Albert J. Ewell.
9. Address, "God," Geo. W. Myres.
10. Singing. By the Choir.
11. Address, "Elevation of the African Race," P. S. Ewell.
12. Remarks, By Guardian.
13. Singing, "Old Hundred," at which time the audience is expected to rise.
14. Benediction, By the Pastor.

The avails are to be turned over towards the benefit of the Church and Society.

Tickets of Admission 12-2 cents, to be had at the door on the evening of the Exhibition, and of any of the members of the Society.

Doors open at 7 o'clock.

FIGURE 2.1 "Literary Exhibitions in New York City," for a meeting of the Young Men's Literary Productive Society. *Frederick Douglass's Paper,* November 3, 1854. Courtesy of the American Antiquarian Society.

writing. And, in his *Miscellaneous Narrative,* Tilmon develops a version of his life story that highlights his community-oriented efforts across several decades. Tilmon is a figure who encompasses what Jeannine DeLombard identifies as the "defining characteristics of nineteenth-century black reading and writing: his church-based education, his associational activities, his political activism, his occasional print publication, his involvement in both the black and the mainstream press, and, crucially, his membership in an internally diverse African American reading community."[31] In his embrace and celebration of all of these elements and his attempts to reanimate them in his writing, Tilmon's autobiography is an inclusive document that, by its very nature, resists a conventional form. Even in a book nominally about himself, Tilmon's heroes are the writers, speakers, preachers, and citizens who band together to buttress their social and political power. And, as he expands readers' understanding of both abolitionism and the circle that might include people who wanted to be abolitionists, Tilmon makes a place for himself in the antislavery struggle. Like Tilmon, Thomas Smallwood wanted to define the term "abolitionist" in new ways, but he did so by seeking to exclude those who did not measure up to his own high standards.

Thomas Smallwood Battles the Abolitionists

As evening approached on February 7, 1851, Paola Brown must have been excited, for he was about to deliver the most important speech of his life. Brown was a longtime resident of Hamilton, Canada West (now Ontario), and he worked there as a handyman and town crier. Condescending newspaper reports from the period also claim that Brown was known for his showy dress and his "characteristic African voice."[32] Though we can hold the attitudes in these reports at arm's length, several of them note Brown's fondness for publicity and his desire to be a leader in the Black community of his adopted hometown. And, amid the unprecedented migration of African Americans into Canada after the passage of the Fugitive Slave Act, Brown knew that it was time for him to speak up. So he circulated a petition and had it "signed by the names of 210 citizens." Then, insisting that he "could not refuse" a request to speak signed by so many of his fellow Hamiltonians, Brown promised to "astonish" his audience "by the force and brilliancy of reasoning which he [would] bring to bear on the subject of man's wretchedness."[33]

Brown's big night did not go as he had planned. Soon after Brown began speaking at Hamilton City Hall, a prankster extinguished the lights and, according to a reporter from the Hamilton *Weekly Spectator,* "the lecturer was left in the midst of darkness when the audience retired, tumbling over each other to the door."[34] Brown was undeterred, though. He responded to this initial setback by printing copies of his speech and taking to the streets to sell them. For the professional town crier, selling was probably easy work, and he hawked copies of the *Address Intended to Be Delivered in the City Hall, Hamilton, February 7, 1851, on the Subject of Slavery* in both Hamilton and Toronto. After the disappointment attending his speech, Brown may have hoped that his self-published book would bring him a measure of fame and give him a chance to participate in the abolition movement north of the border.[35] On this score, at least, the timing was especially propitious: Henry Bibb (*The Voice of the Fugitive*) and Samuel Ringgold Ward (*The Provincial Freeman*) began publishing antislavery newspapers in the early 1850s, and organizations comprised of fugitive slaves and local activists were coalescing around opposition to the Fugitive Slave Act and a desire to help those displaced by it.[36] Indeed, the time was right for Paola Brown; it is just that Paola Brown was not counting on Thomas Smallwood.

Thomas Smallwood was born in Maryland in 1801 and was bequeathed to the wife of J. B. Ferguson. Ferguson, who was "no friend of slavery," taught Smallwood how to read and write, and he freed Smallwood at age thirty once he had "work[ed] out" what Ferguson had paid for him. After he left Ferguson, Smallwood and his wife moved to Washington, DC. There, Smallwood worked as a shoemaker and then a laborer in the Washington Navy Yard. Over the course of the 1830s, Smallwood became a more and more ardent abolitionist, and he longed to involve himself in the fight against slavery.[37] He found a way to do just that in 1842 when he met Charles Torrey, a white Congregationalist minister and abolitionist from Massachusetts who resided in a boarding house on 13th Street. Torrey had worked with William Lloyd Garrison and the American Anti-Slavery Society for years, but he left Garrison in 1838 over his denunciation of American churches and his rejection of electoral politics. Torrey believed that abolitionists should try to reform the laws of the United States through political means, and he supported both religious awakening and the Liberty Party in his efforts to spur such a reformation. After breaking with Garrison, Torrey helped form the Massachusetts Abolition Society to advance his views; soon thereafter, he moved to Washington, DC to work as a congressional correspondent for various abolitionist papers. It was through the press that Thomas Smallwood first learned of Charles Torrey, and Smallwood used a personal connection (his wife washed clothes for Torrey's landlady) to initiate a meeting with the daring abolitionist.[38]

For his part, Torrey was closely connected with several men from the Eastern New York Antislavery Society (ENYAS), located in Albany. Counting Abel Brown, Gerrit Smith, and others among his friends, Torrey was well financed and he knew that ENYAS and the Albany Vigilance Committee (formed to protect fugitives in the North from their Southern enslavers) would aid escaped slaves if he could get them to Albany.[39] Moreover, unlike many white abolitionists, Torrey was apparently quite happy to work on equal terms with Black men like Smallwood.[40] This would prove especially important since Smallwood's local knowledge and skin color allowed him to circulate within the African American communities in Washington, DC. Between Torrey's national connections and Smallwood's local connections, the two men made a good team: Between July 1842 and December 1843, they helped nearly one hundred people escape to New York along what came to be called an Underground Railroad. Their productive collaboration ended not in disagreement but in disarray after district authorities foiled an escape attempt in November 1843 that precipitated Smallwood's permanent resettlement in Toronto. A year later, Torrey was captured, tried, and convicted, and he would die in jail in 1846. Despite this unfortunate end to his career as a conductor on the Underground Railroad, Smallwood was enormously (and justly) proud of both his efforts and his accomplishments. Perhaps that is why he was so upset when he read Paola Brown's self-published *Address* in 1851. As he turned the pages of the pamphlet, Smallwood realized that "Brown's *Address* was "a copy, almost verbatim, of a book known as 'Walker's Appeal.'"[41]

Brown's borrowings from the *Appeal* deeply offended Thomas Smallwood since he idolized David Walker, whose *Appeal* combines high-flown and aggressive rhetoric, condemnation of all forms of hypocrisy, and a valorization of action on behalf of the enslaved. For Smallwood, Walker was a model abolitionist and activist , and Smallwood appreciated the fact that—just like his friend Charles Torrey—David Walker was a martyr for the cause. Incensed by what he perceived as Brown's theft of Walker's words, Smallwood wrote and published his sixty-four-page (sixteen-centimeter) pamphlet: *A Narrative of Thomas Smallwood (Coloured Man)*.[42] In the *Narrative*, Smallwood tells his own story to celebrate a particular form of antislavery effort. Railing against impostors, race traitors, money-grubbing American abolitionists, and greedy former slaves, Smallwood orients his pamphlet toward a specific function rather than his own financial gain. Specifically, Smallwood wants to define the true meaning of the term "abolitionist" and insert himself into the historical record as a model of the same.

Like many of the authors I describe in this book, Thomas Smallwood tried to write a narrative that differed from others in terms of both its matter and its manner, which may have been the reason he chose self-publication. Then again, there were no other fugitive slave narratives printed in Canada before Smallwood's, so, even if he did want to publish his pamphlet with a commercial publisher, he would have been hard pressed to demonstrate its potential marketability. Whatever the case, the rhetorical possibilities inherent in self-publication are evident from the beginning of Smallwood's *Narrative*, for his rambling preface is unlike any other in nineteenth-century African American literature. The preface begins with the assertion that "perhaps in no period of the world's history, in the annuals of no ancient clime, in no grand epoch of the past, have any strange events taken place to which the present century may not produce a loftier parallel" and ends with a declaration that Smallwood's pamphlet was "wholly original" as opposed to the item "purporting to be a production of Mr. Paola Brown, of Hamilton."[43] One way Smallwood marks his difference from Brown is by attributing all of the quotations that appear in his preface. Among those Smallwood cites in the first six pages of his publication (before his denunciation of Brown): John Milton, William Shakespeare, William Wordsworth, Napoleon Bonaparte, Samuel Johnson, Robert Burns, Lord Byron, Henry Wadsworth Longfellow, George Thompson, and William Cowper. These citations show us that Smallwood has done his reading and situates the author within a transatlantic literary tradition. This is significant because many slave narratives included white-authored prefaces like the one in Thomas Jones's 1862 book that confirmed the author was "an honest and upright man."[44] Eschewing any endorsements from others, Smallwood uses his preface to document his familiarity with the great writers and thinkers of Western literature. Smallwood's citations also remind readers that he knows the difference between an original and a copy, which helps confirm the originality of the rest of the *Narrative*.[45]

In the second part of his preface, Smallwood reprints—again with attribution—Henry Highland Garnet's introduction to the 1848 edition of Walker's *Appeal*, which includes a sketch of Walker's life. Smallwood insists that Garnet's words would show that Paola Brown was "not honest in putting forth a work like the one in question in his name and as his own production."[46] Though a short biography of David Walker that includes no quotations from the *Appeal* could not *prove* Brown's dishonesty, Smallwood's logic here is clear enough. He wants readers to understand that Walker was a great figure, and Smallwood locates that greatness in Walker's originality and his willingness to speak his own opinion without regard for either personal safety or pecuniary gain. Garnet's sketch furthers Smallwood's mission by explaining that Walker, "like most of reformers [sic] was a poor man—he lived poor, and he died poor," in part because his "hands were always open to contribute to the wants of the fugitive."[47]

In addition to critiquing Paola Brown and lionizing David Walker, Smallwood had other reasons for publishing his pamphlet when he did. The *Narrative* was published in April, which was the same month Frederick Douglass spoke at the brand-new St. Lawrence Hall in Toronto and only months before he served as a delegate to the North American Convention of the Anti-Slavery Society of Canada, which was attended by Henry Bibb, Martin Delany, Josiah Henson, and Israel Campbell (among others).[48] The arrival of committed antislavery warriors in Toronto and other parts of Canada meant that Smallwood had a ready audience for his work, so the spring of 1851 was the perfect time for Smallwood to circulate an autobiography that documented his achievements and provided a rubric for evaluating the achievements of others. With his own vertiginous standards and impressive achievements in mind, he may also have hoped that his *Narrative* would serve as a history of abolition that positioned Smallwood himself close to its center.

In the autobiography itself, Smallwood barely mentions his experiences in slavery and discusses his early life in only two paragraphs. Smallwood moves on to critique less effective, capable, and/or committed abolitionists by focusing on their economic motivations and national prejudices. Again, David Walker's example is instructive. Smallwood believed that, like Walker, true abolitionists needed to reject monetary gain and privilege the plight of the enslaved over everything else, and the *Narrative* confirms that Smallwood had consistently done both. From the beginning, in fact, he insists that he "declined the many opportunities and offers . . . to become a tool in the hands of the enemies of that class of people with whom I am identified." It was this principled stand that "deprived [him] of a considerable portion of this world's wealth."[49] When discussing his rejection of colonizers, he beats the same drum: "I preferred to live in indigent circumstances, and enjoy my morsel with a good conscience, rather than be possessed with wealth and a burning conscience."[50] Despite having little, Smallwood gave much, even though abolitionists and colonizers would, "without a murmur, . . . give their thousands to purchase a few individuals" but "would complain bitterly against Mr. Torry [sic] and myself if they were called upon by us to give a few shillings to those fugitives whom we sent among them."[51]

It was not just that these organized antislavery groups (which Smallwood calls "gangs") were stingy with their time and money, either. Many

Independent of the Abolitionists 77

mainstream abolitionists had denounced the work that Smallwood performed on behalf of the enslaved, going so far as to claim that he and Torrey took an "undue amount of money," a contention that led Smallwood to give a detailed accounting of dollars he spent and received.[52] These precise expense reports within the *Narrative* verify Smallwood's involvement in the escape schemes he describes and, just as important, they suggest a desire to be open and honest about the costs and benefits of antislavery labors. Smallwood's references to money seem intended to gain the trust of his readers, and his precise accounting implies a critique of the profiteering surrounding the abolitionist endeavor.

Such profiteering could take an especially dark cast, too, as Smallwood explains: "I frequently had lots of slaves concealed about in Washington, who had fled to me for safety when they got wind that their masters were about to sell them to the slave traders, and when the united rewards for them would amount to from six to eight hundred, and a thousand dollars." Had Smallwood pursued his own interests at the expense of those he was trying to save, then he could have "made [his] jack." George Lee was one of those who pursued his own goals. Instead of helping Smallwood as he was supposed to, Lee "went about among the slaves collecting money in [Smallwood's] name from them, [before] appropriating it to his own use."[53] It was not only the greed that bothered Smallwood, but the fact that "there was not a coloured man to be found . . . who had the courage to try to do anything" for the enslaved. To really do something for those in need, Smallwood found, one had to be "as independent of the Abolitionists . . . as oil is of water," and to reject all "pecuniary aid" offered by them.[54] The abolitionists, Smallwood insisted, were men who "stand off at a respectful distance, out of harms [sic] way, and like cowardly curs bark at slaveholders."[55] Smallwood seemed to believe that financial benefits accrued in inverse proportion to meaningful antislavery action, and readers come to understand that a rich abolitionist is either corrupt, cowardly, or both. In addition to full-throated critiques of callow opportunists that serve to paint him in a positive light, Smallwood uses his *Narrative* for both self-congratulation and exculpation. These combined strategies render his *Narrative* much more than the story of a single life or of the Underground Railroad; instead, it becomes a history of abolitionism's missteps and flaws, an exposé of all that had gone wrong and a call to align antislavery efforts with certain key principles that Smallwood believed he embodied.

Though Smallwood looms as a larger-than-life character at certain points in his *Narrative*, the man himself receded from public view over the course of the 1850s. All extant information indicates that Smallwood was a successful businessman and civic leader in Toronto well into the 1860s, but, as he comes to the end of his *Narrative*, Smallwood makes no effort to inform readers about his current doings or residence.[56] Thus, it seems that Smallwood published his pamphlet to expose Paola Brown, insert himself into the historical record, and recalibrate the meaning of abolitionism outside of a national or organizational context.

These latter goals come to the fore at the conclusion of his pamphlet. Smallwood closes his *Narrative* with a newspaper article he wrote for the June 29, 1843, *Albany Weekly Patriot* under the pseudonym "Samivel Weller, Jr."[57] As Smallwood explains, the lone article he reprinted was one of many he wrote for the *Tocsin of Liberty* and *Albany Weekly Patriot* in 1842 and 1843, but all the others had been lost since Smallwood was "so beset by the slave hunters before [he] left Washington, [he] was compelled to destroy them, for fear of detection."[58] According to Smallwood, his letters and articles "were a great annoyance to the slaveholders in that section, and they would have been very glad to have got the writer."[59] Though we cannot be sure, Smallwood's lament over not having his old newspaper articles available to reprint may have stemmed from his belief that those writings—like his brave actions—demonstrated the power of his commitment to the antislavery cause and would help him prove that commitment in the pages of his *Narrative*. Whether or not this was the case, there is no doubt that Smallwood's alter ego, the newspaper columnist Sam Weller, was a fierce champion of the antislavery cause and an acerbic critic of slaveholders, politicians, police, abolitionists, and anyone else who demurred from the aggressive antislavery course he charted.

My reading of all extant issues of the *Tocsin of Liberty* and *Albany Weekly Patriot* between 1842 and 1844 has identified eighteen articles published "over the signature of Sam Weller," suggesting that Smallwood was a prolific and energetic columnist. In his very first column from July 1842, Smallwood commented on the text of a runaway slave advertisement posted in Washington, DC.[60] This was a preview of what was to come, too, for Smallwood would use his columns to riff on runaway ads throughout 1842-43. In some of those columns, he taunted the person who placed the ad by sharing information on the men and women he had already ferried off to Canada. Smallwood continued to write as "Sam Weller" for nearly two years. In many of his columns, Smallwood anticipated the technique of Ida B. Wells, who used white newspaper stories as the basis for her crusade against lynching. Wells's *A Red Record* contains numerous statistics and newspaper articles that Wells analyzes through a completely different lens. Through her analysis, Wells shined a light on the capricious violence that terrorized Black Americans. Smallwood's use of runaway advertisements and other writings from white enslavers served a very similar purpose, though the terror Smallwood was exposing was that endemic to slavery.

Though Smallwood's newspaper writings were not self-published, they could only be attributed to Smallwood once he published himself as their author; moreover, his decision to close his *Narrative* by admitting his "regret that [he had] not the manuscripts of the various articles which appeared" and then reprinting his only extant column suggests a hope that the other columns might someday extend (and complete) his self-published autobiography.[61] In this way, Smallwood mirrors the bibliographical impulse on display in Levin Tilmon's work. And, by unmasking himself as "Sam Weller," Thomas Smallwood uses print and his legacy of printedness to confirm both his ability as a writer and his bona fides as an antislavery activist.

The Limits of Self-Publication and the *Narrative of William J. Anderson*

I have argued that self-publication allowed the authors featured in this chapter to address concerns and suggest strategies apart from those associated with the major abolitionist organizations. By using their self-published autobiographies as catalogs of broader authorial and antislavery activities, Tilmon and Smallwood help readers think about abolition outside of an institutional framework. Self-publication is not a panacea, though, as we can see by examining the publishing career of William J. Anderson. Like many of his fellow self-publishers, Anderson used his *Narrative* to tell the story of his own economic rise and antislavery activism, but hostile newspapers in his home state of Indiana made it more difficult for him to tell and sell that story on his own terms. To illustrate the problem Anderson faced, it is helpful to return to the work of Dwight McBride, who uses the term "the theater of abolitionism" to describe an overarching structure that "enables the moment of articulation" by the Black speaker or narrator.[62]

A theater is usually home to scripted performances, and, as McBride explains, the theater of abolitionism was no different, for it required the Black speaking subject to "speak the language that preexists the telling of his or her story."[63] Abolition gave formerly enslaved men and women the occasion to speak and write, but that speech and writing would often be judged according to standards the speaker could not control. William J. Anderson wanted to claim a unique role within the antislavery drama, but he found that he was bound by rhetorical and behavioral codes crafted not only by abolitionists but by the racist writers and politicians aligned with the Indiana Democratic Party. These hostile editors and party leaders created a caricature of Anderson as he spoke on behalf of antislavery candidates in the 1856 gubernatorial and presidential campaign, and their rhetorical assaults against Anderson helped land him in jail. Facing financial hardship in the wake of his arrest, Anderson published three editions of his life story but struggled to find an authorial voice and a published form that could serve his political and economic purposes.

William J. Anderson was born free in Virginia in June 1811, and his mother indentured him to a local slaveholder named Vance. He, in turn, kidnapped Anderson when he was only fifteen years old and sold him to a trader who took him to Natchez, Mississippi; there, Anderson was sold and lived on a plantation just north of Natchez. Anderson escaped after three years but was captured by a duplicitous white man who took him to New Orleans, where he was sold again and returned to Mississippi. Anderson would be sold five more times in Mississippi before he made his escape on board a steamboat in 1836. After being accosted by the captain of the boat—which was bound for Louisville—Anderson jumped into the Ohio River and swam to the Indiana side. He made his way to Madison, Indiana (about fifty miles northeast of Louisville) on July 15, 1836, and he resided there for most of the next thirty years.

In Madison, Anderson was a man on the rise. Indeed, his story aligns with those of other Black autobiographers who became active in business or the church. Soon after his escape, Anderson began working as a laborer and then a mason; he joined the Methodist Episcopal (M.E.) Church, married, and acquired property. He "prospered most wonderfully in earthly acquirements, and while favors were heaped upon me in my temporal affairs, I felt that my spiritual progress was onward and upward." Anderson progressed rapidly within the M.E. Church: He "was promoted to the office of class-leader in the church, and head steward. Two years after this, [he] procured a license to exhort, and in two years more [he] had permission to preach the gospel of Christ." While he was serving in the pulpit, Anderson also worked diligently to assist the enslaved, and he proudly notes that his "two wagons, and carriage, and five horses were always at the command of the liberty-seeking fugitive."[64] Apparently, Anderson's antislavery work led to some conflict within the church since he left the M.E. denomination in 1849 and helped build the first A.M.E. church in Madison.[65] This change in denomination seems not to have had any effect on Anderson's professional ascent or standing: In the 1850 census, Anderson described himself as a "wagoner" and claimed $2,000 in property and assets, which was more than most of his fellow townspeople, Black or white.[66] During the 1850s, Anderson worked as a church agent securing money to build A.M.E. churches, a grocer, and a bookseller. Though he does not say much about his "trade in books," one can imagine this work could have helped him learn more about the literature of the antislavery movement and may have prompted Anderson to tell his own story years after he made his escape. The more likely reason Anderson did not tell his story for many years, though, was because there was no compelling reason to do so. All of that changed in 1856 when he began working as a political surrogate.

By 1856, Indiana politics were in a state of upheaval, just like many other states in the North. In 1854, the Democratic Party had suffered major defeats during congressional elections, and Fusion/Know-Nothing candidates maintained a majority of the seats for the Indiana delegation. The Fusion and Know-Nothing Parties differed in their views toward immigration and other matters, but both were at least somewhat antagonistic toward slavery and fought against its expansion, while the Democratic Party supported the perpetuation of slavery. In 1856, Fusion and Know-Nothing elements in Indiana came together to support the Republican Party, which would nominate its first candidate for president (John C. Fremont) and for governor of Indiana (Oliver P. Morton). The Democrats were anxious to reclaim their congressional majority and triumph in the state and federal elections, and they used the specter of abolition and social equality to turn out votes. It was in this context that Anderson began working as a political speaker and campaign surrogate even though—as an Indiana resident—he could not vote in either state or federal elections. Since the evidence for Anderson's political activism is sparse and since that evidence is horribly racist in its attitude toward Anderson, it is difficult to say what constituencies Anderson sought to motivate, whether Anderson's work was effective, or whether he was operating independently or in conjunction with a candidate (or candidates). All we can really see at this distance is how Anderson was covered by the press, and it is clear from that coverage that he was cast as a threatening figure by racist editors aligned with the Democratic Party.

In the *Terre Haute Wabash Express* from January 1856, Anderson is described as giving a "Colored Revolutionary lecture" in Michigan City.[67] Though the purported transcript of the lecture is rendered entirely in dialect and is obviously meant to ridicule Anderson, it does suggest that Anderson was speaking about Black men who served in the American Revolution—a key feature of his book in progress. A story from the *Goshen Democrat* in July 1856 noted that Anderson gave speeches in Goshen and Elkhart (just southeast of South Bend). The editors of the *Democrat* decried the advent of fusionism, Republicanism, and everything else associated with equal rights and lamented that Anderson was a paid employee of the "fusion party, at $1.50 per day and expenses." According to the *Democrat*, Anderson was committing the grave offense of "advocating the cause of his party, and like his *white* associates, amplifying upon the wrongs of old line policy" (i.e., the Fugitive Slave Law).[68] Another story from the *Democrat* published later in the fall of 1856 mocks Anderson as an "indomitable and renowned gentleman" who boasted of the horse and carriage "which 'Massa Fremont' had offered him as a recompense for his indefatigable labors during the campaign."[69] In an article from the *Vevay Weekly Reveille* (a Know-Nothing paper), the editors referred to him as a "real black buck" and again complained that Anderson was receiving $1.50 per day to canvass the state.[70] The insults did not end with the election, either. In articles and snippets published after the election (in which the Democrats triumphed decisively), Anderson is referred to as a "Colored Stumper" and listed along with Fremont, William Dayton (nominee for vice president), and John D. Defrees (editor and later congressman) as one of the men behind "Disunion."[71]

Anderson's political work is another example of what Spires classifies as "citizenship practices." As Spires explains, Black activists "reject definitions of 'citizen' based on who a person is, a preordained or predefined subject or subjectivity, in favor of definitions grounded in the active engagement in the process of creating and maintaining collectivity."[72] No matter what effects followed from Anderson's speeches, all evidence suggests he was working to create a new political collective. And, in the very act of doing political work, he generated new understandings of the polis in Indiana. At first those new understandings manifested in the language of fear and threat, but by 1860, those understandings had shifted, and the Republicans would win the state quite handily. Even in the absence of the franchise, Anderson performed citizenship by advocating for a political platform that would eventuate in voting rights for Black Americans. He did so at great personal risk to himself and his finances, and there is little doubt that his arrest and detention functioned as retribution for his political endeavors during the preceding year.

On December 12, 1856, Anderson was in Jeffersonville, Indiana (just across the Ohio River from Louisville) when he decided to take a ferry to Louisville where he planned to board the *Telegraph*, a steamboat heading upriver toward Anderson's Madison, Indiana, home. As soon as he boarded the *Telegraph* in Kentucky, Anderson was arrested and informed that "there was a reward offered for [him] up at Carrollton, in Kentucky," and that he was accused of "running off the slaves of a Mr. Guiltners."[73] The story gained traction in the national news (especially among the abolitionist press), and *The Liberator* reported that "Rev. William Anderson, a negro preacher of the Methodist Church North, was captured . . . with a carpet bag failed with incendiary documents."[74] As a Republican-affiliated antislavery lecturer, it comes as no surprise that Anderson might have been toting books, pamphlets, and other materials that advocated for abolition, but toting those materials through Kentucky was decidedly different from carrying them around Indiana. After his arrest, Anderson quickly secured counsel; at his arraignment, no witnesses could offer proof to convict him.[75] Since the judge agreed that "there was something in [Anderson's] carpet bag very antagonistical to slavery," Anderson was held in jail and threatened with a sizable fine, but he was eventually freed and returned to his Indiana home.[76] This is the end of one story but only the beginning of another, for if we consider Anderson's political activism and subsequent arrest in relation to his publication and republication, we can begin to understand both his decision to publish as well as his rapid revisions to the autobiography in the wake of his arrest.

Most of Anderson's first edition seems to have been written before he was arrested, and the slight (seventeen-centimeter) pamphlet was formatted and structured in entirely conventional ways. Perhaps it was imagined as a companion piece to his lectures and intended for sale as he traveled around Indiana giving speeches. In his preface, Anderson sounds a note of gentle self-congratulation, noting that "although they are trampled down, some noble minds rise up and develop themselves to the world, beyond the expectations of many." Anderson concludes his preface in typical abolitionist fashion with a closing ("Yours for the fraternity and the oppressed") and his name.[77] The first edition is fifty-nine pages long and traces Anderson's life from childhood to enslavement to freedom. Like Anderson's later editions, it includes a "Simple and Easy Plan to Abolish Slavery in the United States" and a series of sketches on Black Americans' contributions to the American Revolution that were drawn from books like William C. Nell's *The Colored Patriots of the American Revolution* (1855).[78] The first edition features a simple title page as well, but as Anderson explains at the end of that edition, everything changed on December 12, 1856, when he was arrested and thrown in jail.

A deep-seated cynicism and anger over personal and political failures led Anderson to make significant changes to his pamphlet when he published it for the second and third times later in 1857. When Anderson printed his somewhat longer and larger (nineteen-centimeter) second edition, he added elements that would, as William L. Andrews suggests, "demand the attention of even the most indifferent reader."[79] These included a new title that foregrounds the violent elements of Anderson's life story: LIFE AND NARRATIVE OF WILLIAM J. ANDERSON, Twenty-four Years a Slave; SOLD EIGHT TIMES! IN JAIL SIXTY TIMES!! WHIPPED THREE HUNDRED TIMES!!! OR THE Dark Deeds of American Slavery Revealed. Beyond the changes to the title, Anderson's new title page embraces what Marcy Dinius calls "radical typography" in its use of punctuation and at least six different fonts. As Dinius argues in relation to David Walker's *Appeal*, certain typographical features enabled readers to "hear his rising voice and anger in his text's italics, capitalized words, and multiple exclamation points."[80] The title page of Anderson's *Life* mirrors these same elements, which reinforces its function as a harangue against Anderson's enemies and the system of slavery. And, in his preface, Anderson no longer spoke the lofty language of idealism; instead, he fairly screamed in anger: "After praying to God and asking His blessing to rest upon me and my book, I enter into the task, because I have the blacks and some of the whites to contend with. The blacks I know will be prejudiced against me because I cease to labor as they do."[81] Here, Anderson refers to his work as a lecturer and directs his greatest ire at his Black neighbors even though he was a minister who still lived in Madison. This suggests that Anderson did not plan to sell his book in his hometown, which is probably why he had it printed in Chicago at the offices of the *Daily Tribune*.

In the second paragraph of his new preface, Anderson remains strident in his tone and makes his economic motives very clear: "I have been sold, or changed hands about eight or nine times; I have been in jail about sixty times; I had on irons or handcuffs fifty times; I have been whipped about three or four hundred times. Any persons who do not believe what I say, if they are very desirous of knowing the fact, can see the receipts by paying the stipulated sum of five dollars."[82] In his mention of "receipts," Anderson seems to refer to his scarred back, which he offers to display in return for cash. Though one might read this line as crassly opportunistic, it seems more likely that Anderson was exposing the market in which he was operating. Anderson had tried to speak as a citizen and advocate for political change, but that had not worked; indeed, it had brought him widespread mockery and financial ruin. In response to the indignities he suffered in 1856, Anderson may have modified his book to make it more sensational and therefore more suited for the antebellum "theater of abolitionism" in which Black men and women were constrained to certain roles and identities that did not include "abolitionist."

Independent of the Abolitionists 85

Anderson may have made these changes to improve his sales or, perhaps, to offer an ironic critique of the limitations he faced.

In either case, he made another striking modification when he published a third version of his *Narrative* later in 1857. Anderson's final version maintained the unique typography of the second edition's title page but added a cover with a portrait by John William Orr, a New York engraver whose work appeared in numerous publications throughout the 1850s and 1860s (fig. 2.2).[83] The portrait he added was not a self-portrait but an image that mirrors almost exactly an image from a bowdlerized version of Rev. Thomas H. Jones's autobiography that was published in 1854.[84] There is no way to know why Anderson selected this engraving, but the image appeared on two different pamphlets published during the same decade in cities nearly 1,000 miles apart, so it is likely to have been a stereotyped image that was widely available to printers. And, it would have been one of a few such images that featured a person of color. Anderson's use of a generic portrait that bears no connection to his textual self-presentation highlights a longstanding problem for Black writers searching for positive graphic depictions.[85] Whereas Anderson may have wanted to present himself as a respected preacher or to celebrate his work on the Underground Railroad, he would have found that such graphical depictions were unavailable in the print offices of the *Chicago Daily Tribune*.

Then again, perhaps Anderson embraced the cartoonish image for his new edition since his publishing innovations (his changes to the cover, title page, and the text itself) seem entirely focused on attracting notice within a market in which spectacle and sensationalism—rather than truthfulness—commanded attention. Anderson would have known that, as Lynn Casmier-Paz writes in her analysis of author portraiture in slave narratives, most author portraits provided "evidence of the credibility and truthful authority of slave narratives." He would also have known that his use of what Casmier-Paz calls "playful irony" in the form of a cartoonish cover could generate a "potential problem of misreading" for his narrative.[86] What does it mean, then, that Anderson selected an image that appears almost identical to the comic image on the cover of bowdlerized slave narrative? Perhaps Anderson wanted a visually arresting cover and made do with whatever graphics were available at the *Tribune* print shop. More provocatively, it might also be the case that Anderson deliberately selected a comic image to produce the "playful irony" that Casmier-Paz reads as problematic. Which Anderson were readers to believe was the "real" Anderson: The dedicated minister and Underground Railroad operative or the comic trope who appeared in various

FIGURE 2.2 Cover of the third edition of William J. Anderson's *Narrative* (1857). Courtesy of the American Antiquarian Society.

newspapers throughout the 1856 campaign? Maybe Anderson's use of an ironic image was meant to remind readers that you cannot, in fact, judge a book by its cover.

While Anderson's motives are impossible to divine, his revised text (like his revised cover) certainly makes extensive use of sensationalism and hyperbole. Though the autobiographical sections hew to many of the standard elements readers might expect from slave narratives—a description of how the author learned to read, graphic descriptions of punishments and torture, a harrowing tale of a hairbreadth escape—Anderson's third edition is not so much a linear narrative as it is a compilation that seems directly tied to an anecdotal lecturing style. A few examples of Anderson's method will suffice. Describing his time on a Mississippi plantation, he explains, "It was as common for the widow Hampton to have her men and women stripped by the overseers before her eyes and whipped naked, as it was to eat. She had eight or ten runaways in the woods constantly. She gave us very little to eat, and we had often to steal or take what we had. We were compelled to work nearly all day every Sunday. A great deal of whipping had to be done on Sunday, for offences committed during the week."[87] The rapid movement through various details here (nudity, escape, deprivation, labor, punishment) suggests that Anderson is rehearsing a story his audience may have expected to hear based on the best-known examples of the slave narrative. One can hear echoes of William Wells Brown, especially, in Anderson's descriptions of "the slave-pen at Natchez," "the calaboose whipping room," and the escape attempt of Phill Sharp, who dove into a Mississippi swamp and found himself trapped between an alligator in the water and a panther on shore.[88] These stories seem like corollaries to the lines in the preface in which Anderson promises to show the "receipts" in exchange for money, and he more than owns the transactional nature of his work. Indeed, by foregrounding the theatricality that is a part of that transaction, Anderson forces white readers and viewers to consider their own investments in abolitionism.[89]

There is no evidence that Anderson printed any other editions of his pamphlet after 1857. There are only scattered mentions of Anderson in midwestern papers in the run-up to the Civil War, and the vitriol he engendered as a lecturer during the 1856 campaign seems to have worked against him as he attempted to claim a prominent role as an antislavery laborer.[90] Apart from its political effectiveness, it is also hard to say whether Anderson's pamphlet was successful as a money-making venture. The three separate editions of the book suggest that Anderson circulated several hundred (or more) copies as he lectured into the 1860s, and, depending on the size of the print runs and his success in selling, he could have made quite a bit of money. Or, perhaps the work of bookselling helped him remain in the public consciousness even if it did not prove politically or economically effective. Two stories from the 1865 *Christian Recorder* suggest that Anderson did remain active as a pastor and as a church builder trying to raise money to support the construction of a church in Niles, Michigan (on the Michigan/Indiana border). This kind of work tracks with his past experiences and it makes sense geographically given that Anderson was most active as a speaker in Chicago and Northern Indiana.[91]

Two obituary notices from 1867 give us a bit more insight into Anderson's life after publication. One from the *Indianapolis Herald* that was reprinted in the *Cincinnati Enquirer* notes simply that Anderson was a "well-known and eccentric preacher of the gospel" who died in Madison.[92] This kind of condescending notice was typical for many newspapers of the time, but the fact that the *Herald* (and the *Enquirer*) identify Anderson as well-known suggests he was still moving around Indiana and the Midwest well into his later years. The second, more robust, obituary from Anderson's hometown *Madison Courier* explains that Anderson sold all his property in the wake of his 1856 arrest and quotes briefly from Anderson's *Narrative*. The obituary closes by explaining that Anderson's "later home" was "located at 313 East Fifth Street, next to the African Methodist Episcopal Church."[93] A faithful man and a minister of the gospel for more than twenty years, Anderson closed his life next to the church he helped to build. Anderson's story serves as a powerful indictment of the restrictions placed on Black speakers in the antebellum period, and it highlights both the significance and the limits of self-publishing as a counter to those restrictions.

Though they may not have been as successful as he had hoped, Anderson's publishing forays were but a part of his antislavery efforts. As was also true for both Levin Tilmon and Thomas Smallwood, the self-published autobiography was a piece of a much larger activist agenda that included other pamphlets, newspaper writings, sermons, speeches, and direct action. By using self-publication to catalog and explain these efforts, authors connected their own antislavery work to that of other activists who were abolition's foot soldiers. They also aligned their work with that of a much larger community outside (or in some cases hostile to) major abolitionist organizations. None of this is to deny the significant role those organizations played in fighting for the abolition of slavery, but, as the men featured in this chapter show, we must look beyond those organizations and the publications they produced to broaden the category of "abolitionist" and our understandings of antislavery authorship.

CHAPTER THREE

He Was Never the Same Man Again
Rewriting American History

Long before Carter Woodson helped professionalize the field of African American history in the early twentieth century, authors and activists believed the writing of African American history would fill a void for the countless Americans who lacked accurate knowledge of African Americans and their innumerable contributions to the nation's history. In James W. C. Pennington's *Text Book on the Origins and History . . . of the Colored People* (self-published in 1841) and William Cooper Nell's *Colored Patriots of the American Revolution* (published by Robert Walcutt in 1855), the authors also insisted that published histories could reshape political realities for African Americans in the moment of publication. Elizabeth Rauh Bethel explains that books like Pennington's or Nell's "[fused] particularized memories of the past to a politicized vision of the future," especially for African Americans who were "reaching for a new body of tradition and myth."[1] Bethel's assessment of these early histories and their function mirrors the aspirations of the authors themselves. Looking back to the distant past, Pennington wrote to "unembarrass the origin . . . of the colored people in the different periods," and Nell, writing about the American Revolution, tried to provide "a narration of those military services which are generally conceded as passports to the honorable and lasting notice of Americans."[2] Pennington and Nell offered new understandings of both ancient and modern history so their readers—whom they imagined to be African American—could see themselves as deserving of the national belonging each author sincerely desired. Once Black men and women could claim a history, the thinking goes, they could begin to make economic, political, and social claims on their fellow Americans.[3]

Even if this were true, there were several obstacles standing in the way of men like Nell, William Wells Brown, and Martin Delaney, all of whom published books of African or African American history in the 1850s and 1860s. The first of these obstacles was access to both the primary sources and capital (financial and cultural) that would enable a person to write and publish new versions of American history. The self-publishers whose personal narratives take a historical turn surmounted these problems by using their own lives as the raw material for historical writing and by avoiding the book publishing industry altogether. But the authors who published their life stories were often producing versions of history that were either unrecognized or unwanted by their readers, so they had to suggest new standards of both evidence and value even as they tried to circulate their books. My examination of self-published books that refract American history and historiography draws on the idea suggested by Claire Parfait and others that Black writers "used their marginalized position[s] to look for new sources" that could, in turn, "set the record straight on their role and place in the American society" and "counter negative expectations."[4] As Parfait notes in her case study of *The Black Phalanx*, most nineteenth-century African American historians had to publish their own books since the historical profession was then (as now) overwhelmingly white.[5] The authors I examine in this chapter, though, were neither professional nor amateur historians but rather autobiographers who strove to rewrite an "authorized" American history in some way. As such, each of the authors engages directly with particular stories advanced by white writers or speakers and contradicts those stories based on personal experience.

Examples of such revisionist narratives span the nineteenth century, though most appeared in the years after the Civil War when self-publishers described the experience of enslavement and the long-lasting effects of that experience on both Black and white Americans. Writing more than forty years after his escape from slavery in 1838, James Lindsay Smith noted that while he had learned a great deal while enslaved and had moved on to a position of middle-class comfort in postwar New England, many of the virulent racists in his native Virginia "seem to be marked by the vengeance of the Almighty; they are wasting away like the early dew, for many have nowhere to lay their heads, except among those whom they have abused."[6] In Smith's telling, it is not Union soldiers or radical Republicans who have ruined Virginia but lazy and inept Southerners who cannot fend for themselves, and Smith's juxtaposition of his own economic rise with the declining status of old Virginia is commonplace in postwar autobiographies. For example, in Betheny Veney's 1889 narrative, the author recalls a time with her former enslaver (Mr. McKay) visited Worcester and dined with her. During the meal, McKay inquires about a pair of leather gloves that Veney owned, so she takes him shopping, and "had the pleasure of paying for them, and then presenting them to him."[7] As was true with Smith's description of his return visit to Virginia, Veney's anecdote highlights the persistence of white dependence.

Smith and Veney demonstrate the wisdom of John Ernest's argument regarding autobiographical narratives that showcase "an identity that was itself an argument either for or against political and social oppression."[8] By showing that they, and not their enslavers, were true inheritors of American ideals of self-sufficiency, Smith and Veney make an implicit argument for full political, social, and economic citizenship. This connection between American ideals and full citizenship is a hallmark of the narratives in this chapter. In addition to telling their stories and attesting to Black agency and activity in the United States, each of the authors in this chapter also examines the roots of historical commemoration and the stubbornness of certain historical ideas. By critiquing both the idea of history and the ways in which history was written, the authors unsettle any notion of a singular (read: white) history. Moreover, the authors in this chapter all published multiple editions of their books. This means the work of rewriting American history was also the work of rewriting itself. By publishing various versions in differing lengths and formats, these authors remind us that history itself is always vital and evolving. For the authors in this chapter, Black history was something that could expand and deepen over time, sometimes as new events occurred, sometimes as their books continued to sell and create new demand, and sometimes as old events came rushing back.

All the publications I analyze in this chapter help us understand American history in new ways, but not all of them were conceived with this grand project in mind. Indeed, one of the interesting features of the publications I discuss in this chapter is the evolving relationship between format and function in many of them. Osborne P. Anderson wrote *A Voice from Harper's Ferry* in 1860 and published it the following year. He sold it in the first months after secession when it had a clear political purpose; when the pamphlet was republished thirteen years later, it appeared in a different format and with a completely different function even though the text itself had changed not at all. Though he began writing a few years after Anderson, James Mars published fifteen versions of his *Life* between 1864 and 1878 and updated his text in both significant and insignificant ways during that time. Mars's pamphlet maintained the same external appearance over his fifteen-year authorial career, but its function changed completely over the same period. Moreover—like several other authors in this book—Mars eventually added a price to the cover of his pamphlet so he could better manage its profitability. Like Mars, the Reverend Thomas James eventually added a price to his pamphlet as he sold it in the mid-1880s. Unlike James Mars, though, Rev. James traded on his personal experiences with famous abolitionists and military figures, and he revised his publication to insist on the significance of his contributions to the American cause during the Civil

War. The revisionist impulse on display in the narratives by Mars and James reaches its apotheosis in the series of autobiographies published by the Reverend Jacob Stroyer. In addition to being one of the finest writers I analyze in this book, Stroyer was also one of the most accomplished bookmakers as he added thousands of words to new editions and completely reworked the structure of his narrative. Stroyer also took advantage of new technologies as he revised his publication from a simple pamphlet to bound book. The evolution of Stroyer's life story hints at his success as a bookseller and at his status in his adopted hometown of Salem, Massachusetts.

Beyond All Praise: Osborne P. Anderson and John Brown

Born in Pennsylvania in 1830, Osborne P. Anderson was never enslaved, but he became a committed antislavery activist in the years before the Civil War and eventually participated in John Brown's raid on Harpers Ferry in October of 1859. After the raid, Anderson slipped out of Harpers Ferry—he was one of a few rebels to escape from Virginia without being tried and executed—and made his way to Canada. Just over a year later, Anderson wrote and published a seventy-two-page octavo (nineteen-centimeter) pamphlet titled *A Voice from Harper's Ferry*. The title page indicates that it was "Printed for the Author" in Boston, and contemporary reports attest that the profits would be returned to its author-publisher, but Anderson's self-publication seems to have been a collaborative process. In preparing the book, Anderson was aided by his friend Mary Ann Shadd-Cary, with whom he had worked in Canada West during the 1850s. Before Anderson began working as subscription agent for Shadd-Cary's *Provincial Freeman*, he had also worked as a printer, which—along with Shadd-Cary's input—certainly would have given him a handle on the process of producing a pamphlet like *A Voice from Harper's Ferry*.[9] Shadd-Cary may have helped in other ways too, for when it came time for Anderson offer the book to purchasers, he could have drawn on her editorial assistance as well as her knowledge of abolitionist print and lecture networks that, in turn, helped him garner speaking audiences and sales opportunities.[10]

In fact, even before he published *A Voice*, Anderson was laying the groundwork for the book's ultimate reception. In the spring of 1860, soon after he had fled Harpers Ferry and made his way to Canada, Anderson began speaking at political gatherings. According to the *Weekly Anglo-African*, Anderson gave a lengthy address at Toronto's Terauly Street Baptist Church on April 9, 1860. In his speech he thanked God that he had been spared to "transmit to posterity a truthful history," and concluded by making an "eloquent appeal to the pockets of the audience," before leaving Toronto on April 12.[11] Given his connection with Shadd-Cary, one would imagine that Anderson made more appearances throughout Canada West as he was preparing the text. By January 1, 1861, Anderson had published his pamphlet and was promoting it in Boston where, according to the *Anglo-African*, abolitionists and fellow travelers gathered at the 12th Baptist Church to "express approbation and render aid."[12] At the gathering, William C. Nell described the "interest manifested by several anti-slavery friends in Boston for Mr. Anderson, and which had been remitted in the publication" of Anderson's book.[13] Nell himself reported on the same meeting in the *Liberator* and wrote that Anderson's friends hoped the book would "obtain a wide circulation, both as a means of imparting the only authentic information of these memorable scenes, and of assisting the author, who . . . now happened to be in need."[14] Nell also noted that, even though Anderson had left Boston, the book could be "obtained at the anti-slavery office for 15 cents each, or $10 a hundred."[15] The very mention of bulk purchasing here reminds us that the pamphlet was light and easy to mail or distribute. It also indicates how Nell (and, presumably, Anderson) hoped the book might be used: Purchasers could buy up a hundred or more copies and distribute them so that Northern citizens could read about Anderson's bravery and willingness to fight for his rights.[16] In January 1861, with the Civil War about to begin, political propaganda of this sort was extremely valuable to antislavery activists.

Later in the winter, Anderson made his way to Rochester, New York, where, according to *Douglass' Monthly*, he "disposed of quite a number of his books." Though Anderson would not stay long in Rochester, his "pamphlet . . . sold for 20 cents" and could be purchased at "Hall's News Depot."[17] By the autumn of 1861, Anderson was back in his native Pennsylvania where he participated in a meeting of the state antislavery society held at West Chester.[18] This would have been another opportunity for Anderson to tell and sell his story. Those sales were certainly important to Anderson since he was still, in many quarters, a wanted man; as such, he could hardly feel safe settling down almost anywhere in the United States. In fact, during an 1860 July 4th memorial service for John Brown in Palmyra, New York, that Anderson attended, a group of abolitionists pledged to use all necessary force to defend Anderson should any Democrats be lurking among the assembly. All of this is to say that while Anderson survived the raid on Harpers Ferry, he did not immediately return to a "normal" life. That meant that—at least in the early 1860s—he would have been particularly dependent on the kindness of antislavery "friends."[19] By 1862, with the Civil War raging and John Brown's exploits no longer central to the abolition movement, Anderson's pamphlet was still being advertised in the *National Anti-Slavery Standard* (indeed, it is listed as a "Tract Published By The . . . Society") as available for sale at "Anti-Slavery Offices" in New York, Philadelphia, and Boston. This edition of Anderson's pamphlet was priced at fifteen cents, though it may or may not have been the same edition as the one he had published in Boston. After 1862, Anderson disappears from the public record until his death from tuberculosis on December 18, 1872.

When he published his book in January 1861, Anderson was seeking material support and making a bid to preserve for posterity the importance of John Brown and his raid on Harpers Ferry. In his preface, Anderson explains that he published to "save from oblivion the facts connected with one of the most important movements" of the antebellum period. This "saving" was not a tell all, for Anderson was unwilling to "expose . . . to public view" John Brown's plans; instead, Anderson insisted, he wanted to correct the historical record, canonize John Brown, and clarify the role of African Americans who assisted with Brown's raid.[20] As with many African American writers whose narratives sought to rewrite history, Anderson insists on the primacy of first-person experience as a means of knowing. Documentary evidence is far less valuable to Anderson than the testimony of his own eyes and memory, and Anderson is careful to point out that certain "facts" had been promulgated for the express purpose of rewriting history in a way that would favor white judicial and military power.

In order to attack the institutionalism that buttressed racism and slavery, Anderson begins by linking Brown to other rebels and insurrectionists like Nat Turner, Gabriel Prosser, and Denmark Vesey, and, at the same time, setting Brown apart for his use of modern tools (the telegraph and railway) and "conventions" and "meetings governed by . . . elaborate regulations."[21] These distinctions allow Anderson to claim that "insurrection has its progressive side, and has been elevated by John Brown from the skulking, fearing cabal, when in the hands of a brave but despairing few, to the highly organized, formidable, and . . . indispensable institution for the security of freedom, when guided by intelligence."[22] Brown shunned the "skulking" so often associated with insurrectionists and embraced both a new *manner* as well as a new *matter* for rebellion against the state; indeed, in Anderson's reading, the Harpers Ferry raiders were in the social and political vanguard. As if to emphasize this feature of Brown's story, Anderson reprinted the minutes of John Brown's Constitutional Convention in Chatham, Canada. These minutes (which include mention of a new constitution ratified by all the attendees) direct readers to consider an alternative model of governance and leadership in which Black and white men could engage on equal terms. With obvious pride, Anderson dismissed the "slaveholding logic" that cast the rebels as nothing but "renegade whites and insolent blacks," arguing instead that by "aggregating their grievances, summing up their deep-seated hostility to a system to which every precept of morality, every tie of relationship, is a perpetual protest, the men in Convention, and the many who could not conveniently attend at the time, were not a handful to be despised."[23] Far from being a band of "renegades" or "insolents," the insurrectionists were principled, civilized, modern men who embraced causes and methods that set them both above and apart from slaveholding Americans.

Within Brown's group, Anderson could detect "no milk and water sentimentality—no offensive contempt for the negro," but instead found "moral, mental, physical, [and] social harmony."[24] In other words, the precepts advanced in the constitution were manifest in the behavior of the rebels themselves; this link between beliefs and actions, between thought and deed, is what sets Brown apart from other antislavery crusaders (something Thomas Smallwood would have celebrated as well). At least for Osborne Anderson, Brown's antislavery family, in which "no ghost of a distinction found space to enter," seems to serve as a model for a larger political body that might emerge from the tumult of Civil War.[25] At the same time, he seems to realize that Brown's actions were but the first effort in what would be a lengthy process since "few ultimately successful movements were predicated on the issue of the first bold stroke, and so it is with the institution of slavery."[26] Referencing both Bunker Hill and the Battle of Hastings as preliminary attempts that augured future triumph, Anderson positions the raid at Harpers Ferry as a crucial moment in history not for what it accomplished but for what it suggests.

In addition to creating a portrait of John Brown and his group of rebels, Anderson wanted to write himself and African Americans into a triumphant history of the Harpers Ferry raid. In a concluding chapter titled "The Behavior of the Slaves," Anderson lamented slaveholders' "studied attempt to enforce the belief that the slaves were cowardly, and that they were really more in favor of Virginia masters and slavery, than of their freedom."[27] Citing his own experiences as well as the numbers of enslaved Blacks "in the fight" who "suffered martyrdom afterwards," Anderson insists on the willingness of African American men and women to fight against "the institution."[28] Though the enslaved who fought alongside John Brown remained—for the most part—unnamed, Anderson asserted that their conduct was "beyond all praise" and thereby wrote African American heroism into the history of the Harpers Ferry raid.[29] The success of this particular intervention or, indeed, of Anderson's intervention more generally, is hard to judge, at least from the perspective of the 1860s. But Anderson's decision to publish as he did helped lay the groundwork for subsequent revisions, and this is, in many ways, the most significant aspect of the narratives cum histories I examine in this chapter. Though Anderson could not reshape public opinion in the moment, he could enter his testimony into a historical record that — in the fullness of time — could find a place for voices like his. In this way, his historiographical endeavors realized the eventual victory that he identified with John Brown's raid, another "ultimately successful movement" whose success was still awaiting consummation in 1861.

Osborne P. Anderson's story has a curious coda that brings his publication into another realm altogether — that of the supplicant text. Even during Anderson's life, his book was billed as a means of support for its struggling author, but that support made sense given the context in which the text was produced and sold, and Anderson does not embed his own financial need into the text itself, as do the supplicant authors I discuss in chapter 1. This is what makes the afterlife of *A Voice from Harper's Ferry* so strange; the book was republished in 1873 — after Anderson's death — as a supplicant text meant to support Anderson's aging father. This version of the book, which was subtitled "Life and Death of the Last John Brown Hero," appeared in a completely different format as a quarto-sized (twenty-four-centimeter) twenty-four-page pamphlet edited by J. D. Enos and published in Washington, DC.[30]

In his brief preface, Enos wrote that the book was "offered to the public for the benefit of the aged and infirm father of our hero" and claimed that he had "assumed in [Vincent Anderson's] behalf, at considerable expense, the great responsibility of reproducing this work to aid necessities' age."[31] At the close of the preface, Enos directed the book "to those who have felt the stings of slavery and others who have sympathized with our struggling race."[32] Given what we know of supplicant texts, it is strange that a book with such a specific purpose (the support of a local figure) was published so far from Anderson's Pennsylvania home, but this speaks to the enduring legacy of John Brown and his raid, especially at the high-water mark of Reconstruction in the early 1870s. Since the book was published in January 1873, perhaps Enos was hoping to capitalize on the rush of Republican office seekers and pro-Grant inauguration crowds that would be coming to the city in the months ahead. Whatever his goals and whatever the outcomes, Vincent Anderson may have received some benefit since he was not admitted to the Chester County Poorhouse until January of 1879; he died only a few weeks later at the age of 74.[33]

The story of Anderson's publication and Enos's republication reminds us that a published text is never a fixed object produced and circulated for a single purpose. When it first appeared, Anderson's *A Voice from Harper's Ferry* served as a powerful testimony against racist public opinion, and the book served a political purpose in the runup to the Civil War. The book also served as a lifeline for an author-publisher who desperately needed economic support. Twelve years later, with the war over, Anderson dead, and John Brown's place in history further cemented, the book became a memorial to Brown *and* Anderson, though it remained a potential lifeline for a man in need of assistance. As Michaël Roy explains, this kind of "(para)textual instability" is a hallmark of African American autobiographies that changed due to shifts in "publishing circumstances."[34] This kind of transformation over time mirrors the story of James Mars, who published multiple versions of his narrative between 1864 and 1878 and, in the process, transformed the meaning of both his publication and his life story.

History in Motion: The *Life* of James Mars

By his own account, James Mars was born in 1790. As a young man, he lived in Canaan, Connecticut, a small town in the northwest corner of the state. Mars's mother had been enslaved in Virginia before moving to Connecticut, and she remained enslaved at his birth; this meant that Mars was also enslaved, even in New England. Connecticut had passed a gradual emancipation law in 1784 that mandated Mars be freed by age twenty-five, but he negotiated with his enslaver to secure his freedom at age twenty-one.[35] He eventually moved to nearby Norfolk, Connecticut, and stayed there throughout the 1820s. In Hartford for most of the 1830s and 1840s, Mars was a member of the Talcott Street Congregational Church and a supporter of both temperance and abolition. He, along with the church pastor James W. C. Pennington, helped support the African American school in Hartford throughout the 1830s and early 1840s, and Mars was active in pursuing civil rights reforms. Mars filed a writ of habeas corpus in Connecticut state court to help an enslaved Georgia woman escape from her owner; he also served as chair of an 1840 convention in Hartford calling for a national convention for African Americans.[36] On several occasions, Mars submitted petitions to the Connecticut Assembly requesting that Black residents be granted the franchise; his petitions always stalled in committee.[37]

After years of activism in Connecticut, Mars moved to Pittsfield, Massachusetts, in 1846, apparently so he could more easily support his large family. In Pittsfield, he became a deacon in the Second Congregational Church and worked as a farmer, and he continued to advocate for the rights of Black Americans. At the 1847 National Convention of Colored People in Troy, New York, Mars was one of many delegates to call for the establishment of a national press and he served on the committee that reported back to the convention that "we need a Printing Press, because a printing press is the vehicle of thought—is a ruler of opinions."[38] Mars, like his fellow committee members, hoped the press would be a "full and complete establishment, wholly controlled by colored men" and that the press would produce "a weekly periodical and a quarterly periodical edited as well as printed by colored men."[39] Though this press never came to fruition, Mars's enthusiastic support for the idea hints at his faith in the power of print and his belief in the importance of Black control over the printed record.

After the 1847 conference, Mars disappears from the public record, and his years in Pittsfield were difficult ones: His wife died in 1850 and his children gradually moved away. By 1864, Mars was seventy-four years old, and he was known in the areas around Norfolk and Pittsfield as a source of information on the early history of Western Massachusetts and northwestern Connecticut. As I note in the introduction, Mars wrote out the story of his life to satisfy his sister's calls for his reminiscences and then found himself besieged by other requests for those reminiscences. Because it was too much work to copy his story by hand, Mars decided to have his octavo (nineteen-centimeter) pamphlet printed at the massive Hartford printing company Case, Lockwood, & Co. which had also printed G. W. Offley's 1859 and 1860 pamphlets. Mars's first editions were probably circulated to those who had asked for them, and he continued to work as a farmer into his mid-seventies, but sales soon became his primary concern.

Before publishing his second edition (heretofore misidentified as the first due in part to Mars's own numbering of his editions), he secured an endorsement from the Pittsfield minister Jon Todd (an endorsement he would update in 1868). By the time he published his third edition in 1865, the seventy-six-year-old Mars claimed that his "joints [were] stiff with old age and hard labor" and that "finding so ready a sale for [his] pamphlets, [he] was induced" to sell books to get a living.⁴⁰ Beginning with his fifth edition, Mars included the following language near the end of each book:

> The question is sometimes asked me if I have not any means of support. The fact is, I have nothing but what I have saved within the last three years. I have spent a portion of that time with my book about the country. I am now in my seventy-ninth year of age, I cannot labor but little, and finding the public have a desire to know something of what slavery was in the State of Connecticut, in its time, and how long since it was at an end, in what year it was done away, and believing that I have stated the facts, many are willing to purchase the book to satisfy themselves as to slavery in Connecticut.⁴¹

These textual changes seem particularly meaningful since they indicate a slight alteration in Mars's bookselling strategy. By shifting his reason for selling books from one rationale (a desire to defray costs) to another (an inability to labor) to still another (sharing a little-known story about slavery in Connecticut), Mars positions himself outside of the supplicant tradition and locates his book firmly within the realm of history. No longer is the autobiography a pamphlet meant to secure donations (a dime here, a dollar there as with the first text) but instead a history with a fixed purpose. As one would expect of a historical text, Mars added to his concluding paragraphs on several occasions and always made sure to change his age in those paragraphs so the book seemed up to date. Moreover, as the years went on, Mars began printing the price on the cover his *Life*, a move that reinforces my reading of the book's evolution into a kind of local history with a fixed value. Mars's book was initially priced at twenty-five cents, though he removed the price from his eighth and tenth editions and dropped the price to twenty cents for his twelfth and thirteenth editions before returning it to twenty-five cents for the final printing of the thirteenth edition (see table 3.1). No matter what Mars's price may have been, it is impossible to know how much money he would have taken from customers. What is more interesting than the price of the book, from my perspective, is the fact that Mars included a price *on* his book; clearly, he thought that including a price was useful or he would not have made this modification. Either it helped him sell his book for more money, it made marketing the book easier, or it made Mars himself feel more confident in his occupation.

TABLE 3.1 Versions of James Mars's autobiographies

All versions published in Hartford at Case and Lockwood. Version numbers correspond to the numbers chosen by Mars himself that are included on each title page. I use the term "version" here to note that Mars stereotyped his book and simply made small modifications to the plates over the years rather than having a new edition typeset and printed. Every version of Mars's *Life* is an octavo sized (nineteen-centimeter) pamphlet.

Version	Year	Where to Find It	Notable Features/Alterations
1	1864	Moorland-Spingarn Library	Thirty-two pages. No endorsement.
1a*	1864	Connecticut Historical Society	Adds endorsement from minister Jon Todd that appears on the reverse of the title page. This is otherwise indistinguishable from version 1, but both are identified as the first edition by Mars and by library catalogers.
2	1865	Watkinson Library (Trinity College)	Adds a three-page appendix that answers questions posed by his readers regarding his life after enslavement, his family, and his role in helping a woman identified as Nancy gain her freedom from a Georgia enslaver named Bullock.
3	1866	Library of Congress	Unchanged but for Mars updating his age and the year (as he does for each reprinting).
4	1867	Documenting the American South	Adds a short paragraph on his son's Civil War service and his death.
5	1867	American Antiquarian Society	Adds a paragraph explaining that the book is his "only means of support" and laments that he cannot vote in the state of Connecticut.
6*	1868	Connecticut Historical Society	First version to include a price (twenty-five cents) on the cover.

(continued)

TABLE 3.1 (continued)

Version	Year	Where to Find It	Notable Features/Alterations
			Mars adds a final sentence explaining that he could vote in the most recent presidential election in Massachusetts but still could not have done so in Connecticut.
7	1869	Connecticut Historical Society	Updates the date (but not the text) of the endorsement from Jon Todd. The price of this version remains twenty-five cents. In some versions the price appears at the top of the cover; in others, the price is at the bottom.
8*	1869	Connecticut Historical Society	Removes the price from the cover.
9	1870	Dolph Briscoe History Center (University of Texas at Austin)	Mars returns a price (twenty-five cents) to the cover and adds a brief note dated September 1870 celebrating the fact that Mars can now vote in Connecticut (because the Fifteenth Amendment had been ratified).
10	1871	University of Virginia	Mars removes the price from the cover.
11	1872	Brown University	No textual changes.
12	1874	American Antiquarian Society	No textual changes, but there is once again a price (twenty cents) on the cover.
13a	1878	American Antiquarian Society	Price increases to twenty-five cents. Mars identifies this as the thirteenth edition even though it was printed two years later than the "other" thirteenth edition and offered for a different price.

*Text available online via subscription or public access website.

Despite Mars's decision to put the price of his book on its cover, we have precious little information on who bought Mars's book.[42] Even so, we can gauge its significance as a historical text by seeing how newspapers regarded the story Mars told and what was most interesting about that story. In 1879, in the wake of the Pension Act, which granted payment of a pension in arrears to the families of deceased Civil War soldiers, Mars filed a pension claim on behalf of his son, who had died in battle. Mars may have used his *Life* to substantiate that claim, or perhaps he (or someone he knew) shared copies of the book with newspaper editors so they could press the pension claim on his behalf. Whatever the mechanics, there is no denying that newspapers began retelling Mars's story during the summer of 1879. In June, the *Lowell* (Massachusetts) *Daily Citizen* noted that Mars was "the only person living who was born and sold into slavery in Connecticut," mirroring the language of Mars's autobiography.[43] In August, several papers around the country reprinted a story on Mars and his successful pension application, and other papers crafted their own version of Mars's remarkable tale.

Again and again, it is Mars's status as a "Connecticut slave" that seems to make his story noteworthy; and, in the description of Mars's story reprinted most frequently,[44] his *Life* is mentioned only in passing and with marked condescension: "Some years ago he wrote an autobiography in pamphlet form, to which Dr. John Todd prefixed an introductory note showing the old man's good character and truthfulness. The work is not precisely as Addison would have done it, but is, after all, a better adaptation of style to subject than Samuel Johnson would have given us. It is remarkably free from large words, and is a refreshing example of idiomatic English simplicity."[45] Mars's notable record of civil rights activism in Connecticut and Massachusetts disappears here as the aging pensioner is turned into a comic trope.[46] At the same time, these news stories do celebrate Mars's significance as a historical figure and, by referencing his status as a formerly enslaved man "born and sold in Connecticut," helped remind readers of the geographic and historical reach of slavery. Just as was the case for Osborne Anderson's narrative, we see the purpose and effect of Mars's pamphlet shifting as the text evolved and as the author-publisher's needs changed. Indeed, each subsequent printing of Mars's story seems to have signified in a new way even if the words themselves did not change at all. In this way, especially, Mars's story shares a great deal in common with that of his contemporary, the Reverend Thomas James, who used self-publication to celebrate his own work as an abolitionist and civil rights leader.

Reclaiming History in the *Wonderful Eventful Life of Rev. Thomas James*

In 1840, the Reverend Thomas James of Rochester, New York, was thirty-six years old. The formerly enslaved man had been an African Methodist Episcopal (A.M.E.) Zion minister for seven years, and he was becoming a key player in the burgeoning abolition movement. James had only lately moved back to his hometown after serving as a minister in New Bedford, where, according to his own recollections, he had licensed Frederick Douglass as a preacher in the church.[47] After returning to Rochester, James signed on to a call for a state convention of "Colored Citizens" in Albany, and he both attended the convention and led the convention in prayer on its final morning.[48] At the convention, James was appointed to the committee on expenditures, which was just another sign that he was poised to make meaningful and sustained contributions to the abolition of slavery along with fellow convention attendees like Alexander Crummell, Henry Highland Garnet, Jermaine Loguen, and Charles B. Ray, who would serve as speakers, ministers, writers, and editors throughout the antebellum era and into the 1870s. After 1840, though, James's name all but disappeared from the historical record. He does not appear on the roll of subsequent New York "Colored Conventions" in the 1840s, and he appears only rarely in newspaper stories, public petitions, church conference proceedings, or even church histories.

The only time Thomas James made much of a stir at all was in 1859, when Frederick Douglass denounced him by name in the pages of his newspaper. This denunciation is so peculiar as to merit reprinting in full:

> In our travels, as well as by letter, we have been often inquired of about Mr. James and his daughter, who are out giving lectures on slavery, and also giving concerts. Hailing from Rochester as they do, and being of the same complexion with ourselves, we are supposed to know all about them, and hence are called upon in the manner stated. To prevent further inquiries, we wish it distinctly understood that Mr. James does not pursue his present vocation with our recommendation. While we know nothing against his morals, we are free to say that his negligence, and want of neatness in his person and dress, counteract any good he might otherwise accomplish. If cleanliness is next to godliness, Mr. James is far from that next, and we think he makes an unfortunate impression for his race wherever he goes.[49]

Based on the frustrated tone Douglass presents at the beginning of the paragraph, it seems clear that Thomas James was trading on his relationship with Douglass as he pursued a career as a singer and/or antislavery lecturer. It also seems clear enough that James was overstating the extent of that relationship, or, at the very least, its importance to Douglass himself. What is most striking about this snippet, though, is Douglass's pointed (and personal) insult about James's hygiene and cleanliness. Douglass was very conscious of himself as a public figure, and he took great pains to present himself in the best possible manner. It is strange, though, that another man's failure to do so would engender such disdain. Perhaps Thomas James's "negligence" was more significant and more damning than Douglass was willing to say.

A few months later, Douglass was back to criticizing James in the pages of his paper, this time with a more menacing tone: "Letters received from our friends . . . make it necessary for us to say that [Rev. Thomas James] has no right to represent himself as being in any way connected with us or our paper, or to claim any endorsement from us, or to use our name in any way to secure the confidence of anti-slavery people in this state, or out of it." Though Douglass had previously steered clear of denouncing James's morals, this time he hope that readers would "avert from us all inquiries as to his manners or morals."[50] It may have been that James was behaving in embarrassing or immoral ways and Douglass wanted to dissociate himself from that behavior once and for all. Even if that were not that case, Douglass clearly wanted to dissociate himself from James's lecturing (and money-making) efforts on behalf of the cause. One could imagine that Douglass's anti-endorsement would have sounded the death knell for James's abolitionist ambitions, and, indeed, James would disappear from public view once again until the end of the Civil War.

In 1865, as the war neared its conclusion, James was working in Kentucky where he was laboring for "freed and refugee blacks," visiting "the prisons of that commonwealth," and freeing all "colored persons found confined without charge of crime."[51] James worked with General Burbridge and General Palmer, both of whom oversaw refugee camps in and around Louisville during the war.[52] Based on his own reports, James's labors in Louisville were Herculean, and he was under near-constant threat of death at the hands of "rebel sympathizers."[53] In 1868, after five years in the South, James returned to his ministerial work, first as a missionary agent for the A.M.E. Zion church and then as a "missionary preacher" in Ohio.[54] His last pastoral call was in in the Lockport (New York) A.M.E. Zion church during the

1880s; he served there until his eyesight failed, which forced him to seek other means of support. The first thing James tried was lecturing, which he took up in order to "raise money to pay for an operation upon his eyes."[55] Presumably, James was somewhat successful in this endeavor since he wrote and published his *Life of Rev. Thomas James, By Himself* in 1886; this gave him another opportunity to garner financial support as a performer within what Dwight McBride calls "the theater of abolitionism."[56] Though McBride locates that "theater" in the antebellum period and imagines its audience as *primarily* white, the postbellum theater consisted of both white and Black audiences and made somewhat different demands on its performers. The nature of those demands becomes clearer as we examine James's life story in the wake of his publication.

Soon after he produced the first edition of his twenty-four-page octavo (twenty-three-centimeter) pamphlet at the *Rochester Post-Express* Printing Company in 1886, James made his way to New York City for the state conference of the A.M.E. Zion church.[57] While there, James announced his "partial blindness" due to cataracts and hawked his just-published pamphlet as a means of garnering support (the hope for surgery does not appear in any other news stories). Excerpts from the pamphlet were printed in a lengthy *New York Freeman* article titled "An Anti-Slavery Veteran," which indicated that James's *Life* could be ordered at the *Freeman* offices "at twenty-five cents a copy" or could be obtained directly by mail.[58] The *Freeman* was a Black newspaper based in New York City and edited by T. Thomas Fortune, and Fortune was sympathetic to James based on his long career of civil rights activism. So, even though Fortune's paper did not print James's pamphlet, Fortune helped support him by offering copies for sale at his offices, which allowed James to access the New York City market. This post-publication media blitz seems to have brought James some attention in the years following the publication of his book. Having been appointed a "missionary at large" by the 1886 A.M.E. conference, James went on to lecture in churches around the Northeast, including the Bethel Church in Wilkes-Barre, Pennsylvania, where he spoke in July 1886.[59] By September, James was back in Rochester, where he was appointed to replace the late Samuel Porter as trustee of funds that had been bequeathed to support the "education of colored children" in Rochester.[60] While in Rochester, he published a second version of his pamphlet.

This series of newspaper notices tells us at least two things about James. First, he was traveling and lecturing in support of his publication and was probably doing so with the approval of the church. His status as a "missionary at-large" granted him access to church audiences around the Northeast, and he—like so many of his self-publishing brethren—lectured and sold pamphlets to receptive audiences. Second, though James was never a prime mover in the abolition or civil rights movements, he did have a story to tell and sell, and he parlayed his history into a bit of local and even national renown. The fact that James was appointed a trustee for funds to support Black education suggests his status as an important citizen in Rochester seems to have grown since the publication of his *Life*. Even as he passed eighty years of age, James was still playing a role in the "theater" and was reminding the next generation of his (and others') past glories. As a speaker to mixed audiences, James, like the former abolitionists Julie Roy Jeffrey discusses in *Abolitionists Remember*, wanted his listeners to know that Blacks were "the engine of their own liberation."[61] In his lectures and in his *Life*, James insisted on his own agency in the antislavery fight and on the relevance of that work to the struggles ahead. James highlights the importance of those continuing struggles as he closes his pamphlet by acknowledging the "cold current of neglect which seems to have chilled against us even the enlightened and religious classes of the communities among which we live, but of which we cannot call ourselves a part."[62]

After publishing a new version of his book in 1887, this one titled *Wonderful Eventful Life of Rev. Thomas James*, James continued to attend church conventions and civil rights meetings, both of which provided venues for him to sell books and burnish his reputation. In addition to adding "wonderful" and "eventful" to his title, James modified his last edition slightly by including two "liberty minstrel" songs that he recalled with fondness and a letter authored by General John Palmer during the Civil War (see fig. 3.1). This notice is the final page of James's final autobiography, and it bears some examination in that context. In Palmer's letter, dated July 8, 1865, James is identified as a military police officer in charge of the "Home for the Colored Refugees" and Palmer claims that James's authority should be regarded as "only subordinate to the Headquarters of the Department."[63] Just like a testimonial appearing in the preface of an antebellum slave narrative, this notice highlights James's influence within a national organization and shines the reflected light of state power onto James himself. Not only does Palmer's notice help confirm the veracity of James's life story, it also reinforces his standing as a proud citizen and a friend to the formerly enslaved men and women he spent years trying to help. Though—perhaps because of his conflict with Frederick Douglass—he had disappeared from public view in the prewar years, Thomas James had spent most of his life working

24

HEADQUARTERS DEPARTMENT OF KENTUCKY.

LOUISVILLE, KENTUCKY, July 8th, 1865.

Rev. Thomas James, now of the Military Police of this Department, is hereby continued in charge of the HOME FOR THE COLORED REFUGEES, in the City of Louisville. His authority to manage the same, subject to the following and such other rules as may hereafter be prescribed, is to be regarded as only subordinate to the Headquarters of the Department.

RULES.

1. Said Thomas James will have charge of the Home and of all the property and furniture therein, and of all the property which may be committed to his care by freed men and women.

2. He will receive into the House only such persons as need temporary assistance; will give all such whatever advice or assistance in finding homes and employment that may be in his power. He will superintend contracts they may make for employment or service, and encourage all to industry and good conduct.

3. No guards or other persons will be allowed to enter said house without his permission.

4. Said James is authorized and directed to establish a Sabbath and Day School in connection with said house, and to make and enforce proper rules for the government of said schools.

5. He will make such rules for the government of the house and the conduct of the inmates as he may deem proper with reference to police, and will read his rules every Sabbath day once to the occupants of the house.

6. Said Thomas James will keep a record of the number of men women and children received into the house each day, No. Sick, No. Deaths, No. discharged and No. remaining over, and such other facts as will give a correct view of his operations.

JOHN M. PALMER,

Maj. General Commanding.

FIGURE 3.1 Final page of *Wonderful Eventful Life of Thomas James* (1887). Courtesy of the Library of Congress.

to make America safer and freer for his fellow Black citizens. By including Palmer's letter on the last page of his pamphlet, James reminds his readers of the trust he had earned and of the hard work he had done.

After James's death in April 1891, T. Thomas Fortune recalled seeing James at the Rochester meeting of the nascent Afro American League and praised "the venerable look, the earnestness and the pathetic voice of the grand old man as he stood upon the floor of the convention and exhorted the young men of the race to gird on the armor of war and go forth to victory."[64] Fortune celebrated James as "one of the old wheel horses of the past," and identified him with the heroic labors of the Henry Highland Garnet/Frederick Douglass/Martin Delany generation. This sort of lionization by association is a common theme of the obituaries for James, which appeared in papers around the country.[65] In most of those death notices, James is not so much praised for what he accomplished himself but for his connection to more famous men whose work shaped the destiny of millions of Black Americans. His late-in-life autobiography likely helped him mold public opinion regarding his contributions to important political movements before and after the Civil War. Thomas James was many things, but—as the *New York Tribune* acknowledged at his death—at the very least he "was an active Abolitionist" and an agent in charge of his own destiny.[66]

Thomas James's fellow northeasterner Jacob Stroyer wrote his life stories around the same time as James, but Stroyer's work has a different temporal and geographic focus. Stroyer's autobiography appeared at a moment when white authors like Joel Chandler Harris and Thomas Nelson Page were creating a sanitized version of Southern history, and Stroyer responded to calls from his readers to expand his personal story by creating a book about the enslavement of the Southern Black community. Stroyer's book does more than present the stories of the men and women he knew; it also recasts the very meaning of history for his (mostly) white audience.

Writing Community History in *My Life in the South*

Jacob Stroyer was born in South Carolina in 1849, and he worked as a carpenter, field hand, hostler, and jockey for his enslaver, Col. M. R. Singleton. Stroyer learned to read during his (forced) service for the Confederate army, and though he was returned to Singleton's plantation until the war was almost over, Stroyer eventually secured his freedom and moved north where he educated himself at Worcester Academy. He then became an exhorter in the A.M.E. church and, finally, a minister at the Colored Mission in Salem,

Massachusetts.[67] In 1879, his first year as a minister in Salem, Stroyer published *Sketches of My Life in the South, Part I* at the offices of the *Salem Press*; he paid to print a second edition of the same text the following year. Stroyer divided his first editions into three parts: The first two sections were entirely autobiographical, and the last section contained a series of sketches (some personal, some not) relating to slavery. In 1885, Stroyer published a considerably revised and expanded version of his book titled *My Life in the South*, which he printed at the *Salem Observer* print shop. For this third edition, he combined the two autobiographical sections into one and doubled the length of the "Sketches" section. Stroyer's sale of his books helped to fund his continued education at Wilbraham (Massachusetts) Academy, Talladega (Alabama) Theological Seminary, and, eventually, Oberlin (Ohio) Seminary. Just before and after he completed his education at Oberlin (1889, 1890, 1891), Stroyer reprinted the 1885 version with only minor changes (see table 3.2); once again, he sold these up and down the East Coast.

By the time he wrote his final edition of *My Life in the South* in 1898, Stroyer was nearly fifty years old and was an established religious and civic leader in Salem. The 1898 edition includes all the previously published matter from the 1885 edition along with a lengthy new section describing Stroyer's experiences during the Civil War. The last publication is different in other ways too: Stroyer took advantage of the technological changes that made it easier to self-publish an elegant book.[68] The 1898 *My Life in the South* is not a bulky pamphlet but a book bound in boards with a stamped cover. It features a photographic image of Stroyer on the page facing the title page along with a facsimile signature. Everything about the book speaks to Stroyer's economic and social standing as a man who had truly risen "up from slavery." We cannot be sure how long Stroyer sold his final autobiography either locally or in other towns, but he would continue to publish his work until at least 1904, when he produced a pamphlet containing his sermon, "The Diligent and the Slothful." Stroyer died in Salem on February 7, 1908, at the age of fifty-nine.[69]

Like many postwar autobiographers, Stroyer used his book to earn money for his education, and he was supported in this endeavor by the white power structure in Salem. The first pages of his books include testimonials—four in the 1879 edition and two more in the 1885 edition—from important men in his town. In the 1885 edition, Stroyer follows these testimonials with a preface in which he thanks his readers for the "very liberal manner in which they have appreciated his efforts" and notes that the

TABLE 3.2 Editions and printings of Jacob Stroyer's autobiographies

Edition	Year	Words	Notable Features
1a*	1879	13,000	Titled *Sketches of My Life in the South* and printed at the offices of the *Salem Press*.
			Stroyer donated copies of this edition to both the Worcester Public Library and the American Antiquarian Society. The book is a duodecimo (sixteen-centimeter) pamphlet of fifty-one pages.
1b	1880	13,000	Stroyer adds an additional preface in which he thanks buyers for the "liberal manner in which they have appreciated his efforts."
2a*	1885	23,000	Titled *My Life in the South* and printed at the *Salem Observer* Book and Job Print.
			This edition adds three new endorsements as well as a completely revised preface.
			In the second section of the book, Stroyer adds four new sketches.
			This and all subsequent editions are octavo (nineteen-centimeter) books bound in boards as opposed to paper. Version 2 is eighty-three pages.
2b	1889	23,000	Titled *My Life in the South* and printed at the *Salem Observer* Book and Job Print. Text Identical to version 2a.
2c*	1890	23,000	Titled *My Life in the South* and printed at the *Salem Observer* Book and Job Print. Text identical to version 2a.
			Includes a head and shoulders engraving of Stroyer on the verso of the title page.
2d	1891	23,000	Titled *My Life in the South* and printed at the *Salem Observer* Book and Job Print. Identical to version 2a.

(continued)

TABLE 3.2 *(continued)*

Edition	Year	Words	Notable Features
3*	1898	30,000	Titled *My Life in the South* and printed at Newcomb and Gauss Print Shop, which was a new name for the former *Salem Observer* Book and Job Print.
			This edition adds four new endorsements, a completely revised preface, and includes a frontispiece with a photo of Stroyer and a facsimile signature that reads "Compliments of the author—Jacob Stroyer."
			Pagination changes a bit in this edition, the text of parts 1 and 2 is almost identical to the second edition. Stroyer removed the concluding paragraph of his second edition and added chapter 3, which is entirely new and includes a history of Stroyer's service in the Civil War.
			The edition is one hundred pages long.

*Text available online via subscription or public access website.

"unexpected favor which the work has met at the hands of those interested in the author and his object, has constrained him to offer . . . a third edition."[70] The word "constrained" might be read ironically here, but Stroyer closes his narrative by insisting, "I make no complaint against those who held me in slavery."[71] Stroyer was apparently too concerned with his progress in the present to dwell on the difficulties of the past; even so, Stroyer's book focuses almost entirely on the experience of enslavement.[72] Given that his experience in slavery is not a source of public complaint, it seems odd that Stroyer returns to the past again and again. It may be, though, that Stroyer intended to write one kind of book and found that his writing led him to reconsider an African American past that, as William Faulkner writes, was "not even past."[73]

Understanding Stroyer's sophisticated engagement with history requires us to look carefully at the testimonials that precede the 1885 edition of *My Life in the South*. Like most white-authored letters in Black autobiographies, the testimonials confirm that Stroyer was "competent . . . trustworthy . . . earnest, devoted, and faithful" and indicate that his bookselling efforts were deserving of "encouragement and support" or "generous assistance."[74] The white endorsers say something more, though. E. S. Atwood writes that "old and bitter wrongs of American Slavery" had "happily passed away forever."[75] E. C. Bolles notes, "the time [had] come when . . . slavery [could] be studied historically, without passion."[76] Finally, Salem mayor Arthur Huntington wrote that slavery maintained "simply an historical interest," at least for him.[77] In spite of these claims by the white men supporting him, Stroyer asks that we see things differently. The time of slavery has passed, he seems to say, but the past has lasting effects, and his unique understanding of those effects drives him to sell a new version of his book so he might "fit himself . . . for labor among his needy brethren in the South."[78] What Stroyer was trying to do in his 1885 edition was to push back against the view that history was something one could move beyond or look on with cool dispassion. Indeed, by highlighting the physical and psychological brutality of enslavement, Stroyer attempts to revise the meaning of history itself; moreover, his book shows that what some people regarded with "simply an historical interest" was, for others, the source of pain that would never dissipate.

As he revises the very idea of history, Stroyer joins a host of African American writers from both the prewar and postwar periods who used what P. Gabrielle Foreman calls "histotextuality," that is, "a method for interpreting sophisticated historicized tropes in narratives whose meaning has previously been thought to be produced by relying on the texts' putatively singular or seemingly impoverished mimetic referent."[79] For Stroyer, the historical narrative he was reinterpreting was rooted in what John Ernest calls "the conventions of reading and of understanding that white readers would bring to narratives of African American life."[80] Stroyer's white readers might have assumed a shared understanding of the idea of history as something "simple," or, to use Foreman's phrase, "putatively singular." For those readers, the history of slavery and national upheaval signified in ways that reinforced narratives of Northern, white virtuousness. The attestations in Stroyer's book also suggest that such readers embraced an uncomplicated idea of history itself as a temporal region to which past events were consigned and then considered as abstractions. From this point of view, the North won the war; the slaves had been freed; good had triumphed; America had been redeemed.

Stroyer rejects this simplistic formulation in the form he chooses for his book, which moves readers from the wholly personal autobiography of chapter 1 to the occasionally autobiographical chapter 2, titled "Sketches." This move accomplishes two things. First, by creating a tapestry of voices and experiences, it denies the possibility of single, authoritative versions of history. Second, as he depicts himself alongside a range of men and women in his sketches, Stroyer situates his own story within a larger African American community. Put another way, the move from his life in chapter 1 to the lives of many enslaved people in chapter 2 transforms the autobiography from *My Life in the South* to Our Life In the South, from, as John Ernest might say, "the individual experience of oppression" to something approaching "collective self-definition."[81] Functioning almost like a West African griot who narrates a communal history, Stroyer rewrites his own story and the larger history of slavery in order to revise the very notion of the historical as it applies to African Americans. He wants readers to understand that the term "history" encompasses more than a series of past events; it also encompasses the lingering emotional and physical traces a community must confront in the present.

Stroyer's revisions for the 1885 edition encompass three different strategies he uses to rework the notion of history for African Americans. The first of these strategies appears on the first page of *My Life in the South*, in which Stroyer changes the first line of his story from "I was born" to "My father was born." Stroyer explains that his father William was born in Sierra Leone and forcibly removed to the United States as a child. In his description of his birth and parentage, Stroyer pays special attention to names: He notes the names of his African grandparents and his fourteen brothers and sisters. Later in the text he includes the names of his uncle Esau and his mother Chloe. Though he had not used any of these names in the 1879 edition (the only people named were his father along with several enslavers and their associates), Stroyer uses his first page to insist on a family identity, an identity that transcended continents and conditions. The act of cataloging names represents what Eric Gardner calls the "archival impulse" in narratives about slavery.[82] Stroyer's archive memorializes the members of his family and enters them into a historical record despite the erasures so common within slavery. It also creates a family history that extends beyond Stroyer himself.

Following his list of names on the first page, Stroyer develops his second strategy, this one focused on complicating the "moonlight and magnolias" view of Southern history popularized in the plantation fictions of the 1870s and 1880s.[83] Stroyer begins with a section titled "Sand-Hill Days" set at his enslaver's "summer seat" where Stroyer and other children were removed during the summer months when their enslaved parents were too busy working to tend to their children. In the sandhills, as many as 150 children were supervised by "three or four" older women and fed nothing but mush six days a week.[84] In a section titled "The Story of Gilbert," Stroyer recalls that the youngest children at the "summer seat" were frequently whipped by a teenager named Gilbert who "used to strip his little fellow Negroes while in the woods, and whip them two or three times a week, so that their backs were all scarred."[85] Stroyer escapes Gilbert and his torments, though there were others: he also recalls the painful experience of having his "unruly wool" combed by another child in preparation for their enslaver's visit.[86] This was an occasional torment to be sure, but it occupies its place in Stroyer's memories alongside "The Story of Gilbert" and "Sand-Hill Days." At the end of these three sketches, Stroyer notes that his "sand-hill days were very pleasant, outside of the seldom changed diet . . . the treatment of Gilbert, and the attempt to straighten out our unruly wools."[87] Attentive readers might note that Stroyer never discusses any of the "pleasant" aspects of his "sand-hill days"; they might also wonder about the "pleasantness" of forced separation, malnutrition, and physical abuse, which seem to be the only memories Stroyer has retained from childhood.

Stroyer's third strategy for undoing the idea of the "simply historical" can be traced throughout the book, though it appears most obviously in the second ("Sketches") chapter of *My Life in the South*. As I indicate above, this chapter is not organized chronologically nor is it focused exclusively on Stroyer's personal experience. Through his sketches, though, Stroyer insists that—like his bodily scars—the psychological wounds of enslavement remained with him long after the "yoke was taken from [his] neck."[88] The first sketch in chapter 2 is titled "The Sale of My Two Sisters," wherein Stroyer recalls the forced departure of his sisters on board a train bound for Louisiana. When the train started moving, he notes, "the colored people cried out with one voice as though the heavens and earth were coming together."[89] The sketch concludes with a haunting reminder of why those cries were so powerful: "from that time to the present I have neither seen nor heard from my two sisters, nor any of those who left Clarkson depot on that memorable day."[90] In his final sentence, Stroyer insists that some losses were permanent and beyond remedy, something he does with chilling regularity in the final sentences of several of his sketches: "he was never the same man again," "Monday was never heard from again," "Poor Jim was not there to forgive him," "Josh died at last, away from home . . . having heard of freedom but not living to enjoy it."[91] These final sentences insist on loss without resolution or salvation. Nothing mitigates the sting of death; nothing restores the connections that have been severed. The sketches make it clear that something has been broken, something that could not be set right ever again. Moreover, the parade of characters in those sketches indicates that the shared experience of this loss was widespread.

By insisting that slavery was an open wound that could never be healed, Stroyer runs against the grain of the postwar writers who looked back on slavery with nostalgic longing or dispassion. History is not a series of events that occurred but a set of human experiences, and those experiences cannot be offloaded into a memory bank any more than a scar can be wiped away. The experiences of tenuousness, contingency, and loss that permeate the "Sketches" shape human consciousness in ways uninitiated readers can barely grasp. Though Stroyer does not *say* this about history, one can locate this idea in his authorial revisions, revisions that participate in a kind of unintentional archaeology: As he digs up more material from his memories to present for the readers who have "constrained him" to produce his book, he shows those readers that the past is a complicated place, and when we dredge up old stories, we dredge up other things — like feelings — along with them. This effect is uniquely tied to Stroyer's self-publishing efforts since his contact with the book buyers who asked him to produce new editions generated a deeper look at the past.

Given his view of history and its lingering effects, Stroyer's stated desire to work "among [his] more unfortunate brethren in the South" makes all the sense in the world.[92] Like William Wells Brown in *My Southern Home* (1880), Stroyer returns to his Southern past to make a claim for present-day reform; in Stroyer's case, that claim seems to have been quite successful, at least if we account for the number of editions Stroyer produced and sold.[93] Newspapers from St. Albans (Vermont) to Cleveland to New Haven mention Stroyer's presence in town and his desire to sell *My Life in the South*.[94] According to the *Worcester Daily Spy*, Stroyer "offer[ed] the book in person," and numerous papers (and the note of Othneil Gager, who purchased the book on October 7, 1885, and recorded the price on the title page) set the price of *My Life in the South* at twenty-five cents.[95] As the editors of the *Cleveland Gazette* suggested, this was a small price to pay so one could enjoy the "satisfaction of knowing that they are assisting a worthy young man to be a preacher and teacher among the ignorant freemen of the South."[96] The transaction for buyers seems clear enough in these notices — money for self-satisfaction and/or knowledge — and none of the brief reviews suggest that readers would be surprised by what they found in Stroyer's book. Even so, Stroyer's decision to publish a book that highlights the emotional costs of enslavement and the extraordinary burden of traumatic experience allows him to show that African Americans had a history that was neither "simple" nor "passed away forever."

When Stroyer published his final edition in 1898, he added four new endorsements and returned once again to an untold portion of his history: his years of forced service to the Confederate army during the Civil War. Unsurprisingly, Stroyer's Civil War experience was of a piece with the rest of his experience in the South, and his work in Charleston Harbor and Fort Sumter throughout 1863–65 was both difficult and dangerous. He recalls that many enslaved men were killed during bombardment of the fort, but perhaps the most galling memory is of a man who was murdered by his enslaver for no reason at all. Looking back more than thirty years, Stroyer remembers that "the Confederates failed to lay the hand of justice upon the officer" who committed the murder, and Stroyer's own "vague ideas of moral justice" led him to wait "a short time for some token of Divine vengeance, but . . . [he] found that no such token as [he] desired existed."[97] Stroyer published his final edition in 1898, two years after *Plessy v. Ferguson* codified segregation as the law of the land. Even though he had left the Confederacy more than thirty years before, Stroyer's hope for "moral justice" was never realized, either in the pages of autobiography or in the country where he lived, and he used his autobiography to remind his readers of this damning fact again, and again, and again. In this respect he is very much like the authors in chapter 4, all of whom offer their self-published narratives as testaments to the lack of moral or any other kind of justice in the nineteenth-century United States.

CHAPTER FOUR

I Sue for Justice to Be Established
Self-Publication as Alternate Testimony

In 1953, Leo Marx published a response to recent essays by Lionel Trilling and T. S. Eliot concerning Mark Twain's *Adventures of Huckleberry Finn*. In his essay, Marx noted widespread scholarly disagreement over the ending of Twain's novel, the twelve chapters in which Huck and Tom Sawyer force Jim to endure any number of tortures and calamities as they try to "free" him. Marx—like many critics before and since—loathes the ending since it turns "the most serious motive in the novel, Jim's yearning for freedom" into an "object of nonsense."[1] Marx's primary concern with the ending is not what it says about Jim or the United States but what it says about Huck, who seemed to have "grown in stature throughout the journey" but—based on his actions in the final chapters—turns out not to have grown much after all.[2] Marx's essay spawned a flood of critical responses debating the ending of *Huckleberry Finn*, only some of which address what I believe to be the real point of the novel's final chapters: Jim is already free when he reaches the Phelps farm, but no one tells him.[3] In other words, Twain's novel shows that Jim's "yearning for freedom" was very much an "object of nonsense" all along since even legal emancipation (Jim had been freed by his enslaver, Miss Watson) did not guarantee that he would be granted any of the freedoms he sought. No matter what futures he may have imagined on the raft he shared with Huck, and no matter what the law said, Jim was trapped within a system in which he was always subject to white supremacy, even if that white supremacy appeared in the form of two teenaged boys. As several other critics have noted, it is no surprise that Twain's novel was published in 1885 as the horrors of the post-Reconstruction era confirmed the difference between legal writ and lived experience for Black Americans.[4]

The story in *Huckleberry Finn* is not unique. Indeed, the United States' failure to deliver justice to Black Americans has been a defining feature of several masterworks of American literature, and, as historians from John Hope Franklin to Leon Litwack to Nathan Huggins to John Ernest to Nikole Hannah-Jones have shown, the struggle for justice in its fullest sense has been a constitutive element of African American politics and identity since 1619.[5] Across the nineteenth century, millions of Black Americans fought as both activists and soldiers to enjoy the rights concomitant with full political citizenship. Among those rights were many of those associated with the justice system: the right to equal treatment before the law, the right to make and enforce contracts, and the right to trial by a jury of one's peers. Before the Civil War securing even some of those rights was a monumental task, and after the Civil War and the passage of the Reconstruction amendments, basic rights were still not guaranteed to Black Americans either in letter or spirit. As a result, Black men and women used whatever platforms they could find to argue for both statutory and practical changes to a system that—far from enforcing the values that were supposedly central to the United States—often seemed to undermine those values.[6] In this chapter, I focus on Black writers' struggles to find justice within the American judicial system and their use of self-publication to present what I call "alternate testimony." Such testimony enables Black authors to contrast their own stories with those preserved in state-authored court and legislative records. In some cases, authors believed their alternate testimonies might allow for immediate remediation or encourage institutional change; in all cases—much like the historians I discuss in chapter 3—the authors featured in this chapter knew that telling and preserving their own stories was a way of keeping alive truths that had been ignored, elided, or denied for centuries.

The temporal elements of this struggle were crucial because laws, which define rules and guidelines for behavior in a particular time and place, have a unique durability. In fact, as Robert M. Cover explains, laws project "an imagined future upon reality."[7] When a judge (and/or a jury) renders an opinion, he wants to indicate that the meaning of a particular idea or action is to be understood in the same way forever after, and deference to judicial precedent helps ensure the permanence of one judge's idea long after the judge has died. In practical terms, this means justice-seeking Americans could only combat legalized discrimination over decades (not years) and across the country (not just in one place) as they sought to project a very different future on their present realities. This was true for self-publishers as well, most of whom understood their legal struggles to be both immediate and durational; these writers were, as Bryan Wagner argues, considering not only the "laws on the books, but in a profound sense, they were also referring to a law that had not arrived, a law whose history was still being written, a law still to come."[8]

The significance of the "law still to come" is on display in early self-published autobiographies by Venture Smith (1798) and Boyrereau Brinch (1818), both of which demonstrate that the rhetoric in America's founding documents was already proving to be hollow. Smith, whose 1798 *Narrative* documents decades of hard work and economic gain in the face of monstrous hardship, closes his narrative with the story of a trumped-up lawsuit brought against him by a wealthy white ship captain. Rather than go to court—where he knew he would lose—Smith paid the ten pounds the captain was demanding. His only recourse was to publish his story and sell it in coastal Connecticut with the hopes his fellow residents would take his side even if the law did not. One can almost hear the anger in Smith's voice as he considers the deeper implications of his experience: "Such a proceeding as this, committed on a defenceless stranger . . . without any foundation in reason or justice, whatever it may be called in a christian [sic] land, would in my native country have been branded as a crime equal to highway robbery."[9] Smith may have been one of the first autobiographers to publish such a lament, but he would hardly be the last. When he published his own story two decades later, Boyrereau Brinch (also known as Jeffrey Brace) described his legal struggles with a "respectable widow" in New England and wondered "what Lawyer would undertake the cause of an old African Negro."[10] Brinch, like Smith, used his narrative to contrast the practice of justice in his native Africa with the injustices besetting Black Americans in the United States.

By the middle decades of the century, the legal situation for African Americans had changed very little, a fact made clear in narratives like *The Narrative of Lunsford Lane* (1842) and *Memoirs of Elleanor Eldridge* (1838).[11] In the latter autobiography, the eponymous narrator suffers at the hands of an unscrupulous sheriff who ignores his own legal obligations simply because Eldridge *"was a laboring colored woman."*[12] Even though Eldridge was a free woman living in New England, she found, like Brinch and Smith before her, that the judicial system was stacked against her in ways that prevented her receiving a fair hearing in court. By simply noting and naming the injustice, all three narrators helped their readers identify the problem of racial discrimination in courts of law. Indeed, as Eldridge's amanuensis writes, "if a *white woman* had been the subject of such wrongs, the whole town—nay, the whole country, would have been indignant, [and] the story would have flown upon the wings of the wind to the most remote borders of our land."[13] Faced with unequal treatment in court and the silence of the press, Brinch, Eldridge, and Smith used self-published narratives to testify to their own experiences and shape public opinion. In this regard, self-publishers helped lead abolitionists who, as Jeannine Marie DeLombard has argued, shared examples of legal injustice to triumph in the "court of public opinion."[14] Though public opinion did not necessarily influence the decisions of judges or juries, it did change the nature of public discussion and debate, and it spurred changes in political alignment and voting that hastened the end of slavery.

In addition to influencing public debate, Black writers could also shape a "law still to come" by rewriting the "official" narratives emanating from powerful men and institutions. This revisionary impulse is especially evident in the proliferation of legal language in antebellum narratives, newspaper stories, and other documents that demonstrate the cultural and social effects of the law. One famous example is *David Walker's Appeal*, which consists of a preamble and four "Articles" that, as Timothy Patrick McCarthy explains, signify on the "formal innovations of American written law."[15] Expanding on McCarthy's arguments in relation to Black print culture and abolitionism, DeLombard argues that "juridical rhetoric" employed by abolitionists highlights the "transformative political potential of popular legal consciousness."[16] And, as DeLombard notes in "Slave Narratives and US Legal History," when Black writers used "the language of law," they could present themselves as "model black protocitizens."[17] As many postwar narratives demonstrate, this rhetorical pose would continue even after the passage of the Thirteenth, Fourteenth, and Fifteenth Amendments.

This chapter examines four self-published narratives published across the nineteenth century, all of which highlight the failure of local and state courts to guarantee the rights of Black Americans. In response to those failures, each author published an "alternate testimony" in which he or she presented a new perspective on both the case(s) at hand and the true nature of justice. Because all these authors were focused on righting wrongs, their publishing stories are very different from supplicant or historically minded authors. Specifically, these authors prioritized function over anything else, and there is scant evidence of sales journeys, speaking engagements, or any other strategy for circulating and selling these texts, all of which were published in only one or two editions. The format of the narratives is in keeping with the utilitarian nature of the publications themselves. Most authors presenting alternate testimony produced short pamphlets that would have been inexpensive to produce and easy to give away or sell for pennies.

For Christopher McPherson, writing in 1811, self-publication functioned as a method for sharing his petition to the Virginia assembly and seeking to gain public support for his complaints against the racist city and state governments that harassed him beginning in 1810. It also represented a claim of extraordinary power that could counter the earthly forces arrayed against him. Peter Randolph was, like Christopher McPherson, born a slave in

Virginia. He wrote his own life story in 1855 and showed how greedy and designing white leaders used the justice system to stymie social and economic progress for Black people and even to subvert the will of white enslavers. Like McPherson, Randolph wanted to arouse the anger of his readers just as much as he wanted justice for himself. After the war, men like Randolph prospered, as did Norvel Blair, who found that his white Republican friends in Illinois were unwilling to let him prosper too much. And so, in the runup to the 1880 elections, Blair shared his own testimony to sway public opinion against the dishonest leaders who had swindled him. Writing at the end of the century, Lucy Delaney told a story from the time before the war when she (and her mother) won their freedom in a Missouri courtroom. Delaney likely published her autobiography in 1891 as white supremacists cemented their control over the South, and her life story reminds readers that even though slavery had been abolished, its legacy continued to limit the horizons for Black Americans trying to imagine an alternate future. In this respect, Delaney's book resonates with a book written by another Missourian a few years earlier.

Making God's Book: Christopher McPherson, Alias Pherson, Son of Christ

According to his narrative, Christopher McPherson was born in 1763 to an enslaved mother and brought up by David Ross, a wealthy Virginia planter. In part because of his father (a white businessman who asked Ross to look after McPherson) and in part because of his native abilities, McPherson obtained employment that was both remunerative and engaging: He served as a clerk to "the Commercial Agent for the State of Virginia" and for a general at the siege of Yorktown.[18] After the Revolutionary War he continued as a clerk at Ross's Elk Horn Store in Petersburg, Virginia. McPherson obtained his freedom in 1792, but he continued to work for Ross until February 15, 1799, when he was converted to Christianity. Though McPherson provides few details, his conversion seems to have engendered a dispute that led him to leave David Ross's employ and initiate a suit against Ross's son. After his suit was resolved, and after he received commands from the Holy Spirit, McPherson began walking the streets of "Richmond, Williamsburg, Norfolk, and Portsmouth" and announcing the imminent approach of "Christ's Millennium." Soon thereafter, the Holy Spirit commanded McPherson to visit Philadelphia and "deliver a message from Omnipotence" to President John Adams.[19] The president received the message, but he was not moved to action, and McPherson returned home. A decade later, McPherson would reemerge on the public stage convinced that he was the "true, real-established, and declared representative of Christ Jesus the Lord of Glory, in the actual stead of himself."[20]

As one would expect, McPherson's remarkable claim was met with some skepticism, but, as one might also expect, men who make such claims are hard to deter. And so, McPherson turned to publishing to communicate his story, his goals, and his unique vision. What makes McPherson particularly interesting as a publisher is that his pamphlet (see fig. 4.1) is a typeset version of a part of the petition he filed in Virginia in 1810 in an effort to overturn a particularly odious ordinance (see fig. 4.2).[21] As part of that petition, McPherson included a history of his life along with several testimonials, and when he published his pamphlet, he tried to manipulate print so it would carry the authority of the documents he filed with the court. To do this, McPherson included in his book all manner of seals, certificates, verifications, testimonials, charts, and letters. Moreover, the book had the express imprimatur of William Mumford, who was "Keeper of the Rolls for the Commonwealth of Virginia." Mumford verified that the contents of the book had been deposited in his office and that the book reproduced official records. By using a state official to verify and authorize his publication, McPherson appropriated state power to himself in his print campaign against the leaders of the very same state. McPherson's bold appropriation represents a form of alternate testimony that attempts to stymie legal proscription by invoking an equivalent or even greater power.

Modern readers may be surprised that a man like Christopher McPherson could find audiences with famous and powerful men whose esteem helped him make his case, but this is at least partially explained by McPherson's years of working in the capital city and for the Virginia legislature. When he decided to publish his story, McPherson leveraged his contacts by listing many of them in his lawsuit and his book. Both the records of his lawsuit and the published narrative contain lists of men who employed him as a clerk or in other capacities, men who "had heard a very favorable report" of his "talents and integrity," men who were "acquainted with Christopher McPherson," and men who "[believed] him to deserve the reputation and character" McPherson himself touted.[22] These long lists include William Hening (a member of the House of Delegates) and William Wirt (clerk, judge, and eventually attorney general of the United States).[23] And, since he was personally acquainted with presidents past and present, McPherson could insist, "Throughout the whole course of my life, I have been considered by my

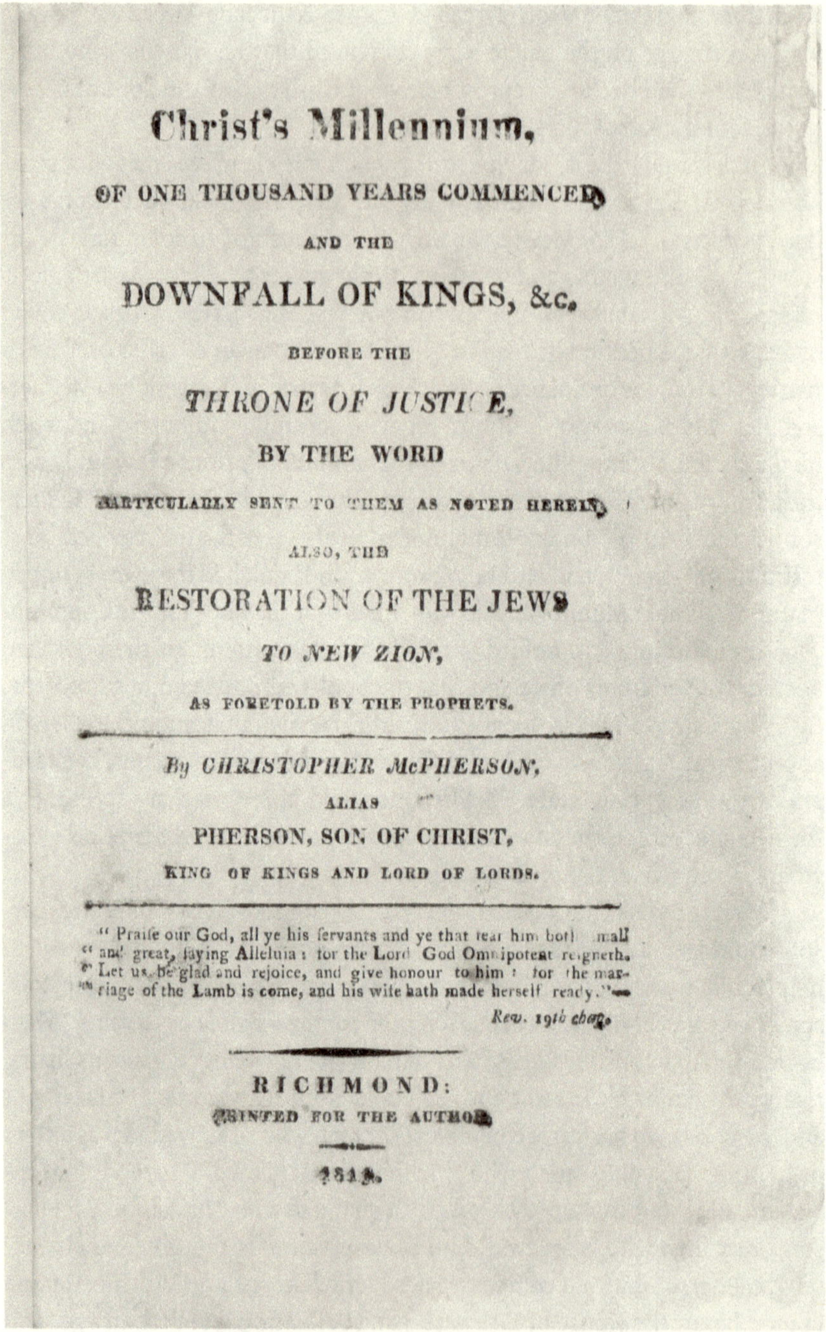

Christ's Millennium,

OF ONE THOUSAND YEARS COMMENCED,

AND THE

DOWNFALL OF KINGS, &c.

BEFORE THE

THRONE OF JUSTICE,

BY THE WORD

PARTICULARLY SENT TO THEM AS NOTED HEREIN;

ALSO, THE

RESTORATION OF THE JEWS

TO NEW ZION,

AS FORETOLD BY THE PROPHETS.

By CHRISTOPHER McPHERSON,

ALIAS

PHERSON, SON OF CHRIST,

KING OF KINGS AND LORD OF LORDS.

" Praise our God, all ye his servants and ye that fear him both small and great, saying Alleluia: for the Lord God Omnipotent reigneth. Let us be glad and rejoice, and give honour to him: for the marriage of the Lamb is come, and his wife hath made herself ready."—
Rev. 19th chap.

RICHMOND:

PRINTED FOR THE AUTHOR.

1811.

FIGURE 4.1 Cover of *Christ's Millennium* (1811). Courtesy of the Huntington Library.

numerous white acquaintances as one of their number, and they have uniformly treated me as such."[24]

Whether McPherson is referring to his skin color or his status when he says he is regarded as "one of their number" is unclear, but his use of certificates and testimonials vouching for his equality to the white men around him resonates with many later African American writers' use of certificates and authorizations attesting to their honesty and trustworthiness. Unlike many later authors, McPherson does not include those authorizations at the beginning of his narrative but places them within the body of his publication, a pamphlet in which McPherson celebrates his business acumen and mathematical abilities. For example, McPherson claims that as the clerk of the Chancery Court he "received the enormous wages, of from 23 shillings to four dollars per diem, which was thought to be judiciously paid by the best officers." As one would expect from such an employee, McPherson "accomplished in about three days . . . two weeks labor."[25] McPherson's decision to spotlight himself through the reflected light of white power is disconcerting for modern readers, but the effect of McPherson's narration is to set him apart from his peers; he is both called by the Holy Spirit and blessed by God with extraordinary talents and character traits, and if Jesus did appoint a formerly enslaved man as his representative on earth, it would make sense that he would be a man such as McPherson.

The problem for McPherson is that he *was* a formerly enslaved man living in Virginia, and it was hard for him to transcend the social and economic limitations the white planter aristocracy had placed on him. As talented as he was, and as comfortably as he fraternized with white men of standing, McPherson would never be treated as an equal, let alone a "Potentate."[26] In 1810, this tension manifested in a series of conflicts with what can only be called the establishment in the Old Dominion. First, McPherson submitted a petition to the city of Richmond "praying for a new burying ground" for "people of colour." In what was probably a coincidence, on the same day, there was passed an "Ordinance restricting free people of colour from using hired carriages." McPherson sent letters protesting this decision and submitted a petition for reconsideration in which he argued that the new ordinance deprived "him of rights to which he is entitled under the laws and constitution of this commonwealth," but the petition "lost in the [Virginia General] Assembly by a majority of three."[27] During the meeting at which his petition was presented, McPherson also submitted a copy of his 1800 message to President Adams; this, too, was ignored.

(21)

(COPY.)

RICHMOND, April 6th, 1810.

I do hereby certify, that the writings on the nine pages preceding this, are true Copies of the original documents filed in my office.

WM. MUMFORD, *Keeper of the Rolls,*
for the Commonwealth of Virginia.

(COPY.)

RICHMOND, Monday, 10th Dec. 1810.

Christoper McPherson, to the Honorable the Committee for Courts of Justice, of the General Assembly of the old dominion and State of Virginia.

I beg leave to introduce myself to you, as being that very express personage, who is set forth in the Revelations of St. John the Divine, in the 11th & 16th verses of the 19th chapter, & the first verse of the 20th chapter. To the truth of this assertion, I take my Almighty God to witness, and he will prove the same, if you require it of him.

I have the happiness to announce to you, and to the world, that the glorious Millennium was planted on this earth, on the 15th day of February, in the year of our Lord 1799.

Omnipotence, out of his great goodness and peculiar distinction towards you, desires me to inform you, that now, it is his wish, that the first acts of his reign on earth, shall emanate from you; and that you are to enact laws, founded upon the pure and sacred principles of truth and justice, reason and religion, peace & harmony and love and unity, which no doubt will be crowned, with faith and power and glory.

John Adams late President of the United States, and the Senate of the same, failed to pay the attention which was due to His most Gracious Message, as is contained in the inclosed address. Our Almighty and Most Glorious Father, therefore, now delegates that message to you; and after mature deliberation, he wishes you to make a solemn and

FIGURE 4.2A&B Detail from McPherson's legislative petition filed in Richmond, Virginia, in 1810 (left). Note the identical text in *Christ's Millennium* (right). Petition image is courtesy of the Library of Virginia. Pamphlet image is courtesy of the Huntington Library.

(Copy)

Richmond Monday the 10.th of December 10

Christopher MacPherson To The Honorable — The Committee for Courts of Justice of the General Assembly of the old Dominion and State of Virginia —

I beg leave to introduce myself to you, as being that very express personage, who is set forth in the Revelations of Saint John the Divine, in the 11.th and 16.th verses of the 19.th Chapter, and the first verse of the 20.th Chapter. — To the truth of this assertion, I take my Almighty God to witness; and He will prove the same, if you require it of Him. —

I have the happiness to announce to you and to the World, that the Glorious Millennium was <u>planted</u> on this Earth, on the 15.th day of February in the year of our Lord 1799 —

Omnipotence, out of His great goodness and peculiar distinction towards you, desires me to inform you, that Now, it is His wish, that the first Acts of His Reign on Earth, shall emanate from you; and that you are to enact Laws, founded upon the pure and sacred principles of Truth & Justice — Reason & Religion, Peace & Harmony and Love & Unity — which no doubt, will be crowned by Faith and Power and Glory —

John Adams late President of the United States & the Senate of the same, failed to pay the attention which was due to His most Gracious Message — as is contained in the inclosed Address. — Our Almighty and most Glorious Father therefore, now, delegates that Message to you — and after mature deliberation, He wishes you to make a Solemn and Earnest prayer for His Almighty Will to be forthwith done: and He will to your perfect satisfaction, that Moment, confirm this Embassy — Inclosed are documents respecting this business, agreeable to the list stated. —

I am Gentlemen;
Your friend & Servant
Pherson son of Christ
alias
Fierce son of Christ

McPherson's inability to get what he deemed a fair hearing from the city, state, or national government seems to have driven him to take further action. In 1811, McPherson founded a "night school, chiefly for free male adults of colour" and, in newspaper advertisements, recommended the founding of "similar institutions throughout the nation."[28] No longer ignored, McPherson now found himself under threat. First, the *Virginia Argus* suppressed his advertisements; then, the "Sergeant of the city . . . served [McPherson] with a summons to appear before the Court of Hustings" since he had made himself a "nuisance" by publishing advertisements in support of night schools.[29] Clearly, McPherson was trying to open opportunities for himself and for other free Blacks; just as clearly, the city fathers in Richmond were not going to let him do that. In May 1811, McPherson gave those fathers the pretext they needed when he and his wife got into an argument and a neighbor called the constable. Both McPherson and his wife spent the night in jail, and—though they were cleared in court—McPherson had been humiliated. Convinced that "in the State of Virginia, a man of colour . . . had but a slender change of success in going to law with weighty officers of the land," McPherson staged a demonstration by "singing, dancing, &c. and walking the streets . . . as to draw the attention of influential characters, who being induced to ask me the cause, might, on hearing my complaint, have formed some plan towards palliating my grievances."[30] After he was again "taken up" by law enforcement, McPherson explained that he was "ill-treated" and that he had a "new name, Pherson son of Christ, King of King and Lord of Lords, and prevailed on them to read the 19th chapter of Revelations, which contains my appointment." This landed McPherson in the lunatic hospital in Williamsburg.[31]

Though McPherson had committed no crime at all, and though he remained a tax-paying property owner and a trusted clerk, his initial request for something approaching equality for free Black men and women seems to have initiated a series of high-stakes confrontations that led to his imprisonment on trumped-up charges. What makes McPherson such a compelling character is that he responded to the machinations of powerful Virginians by crafting a narrative persona that was even more powerful than his tormentors. In his self-published pamphlet, McPherson becomes not just a man aggrieved but the physical embodiment of God's grievances against a racist legal system. I quote—at some length—his remarkable justification for publishing:

> I now most particularly call the attention of the public to this grand point: that I sue not for the justice that is due me in my private and

individual character, as a citizen of these United States, under certain restrictions, as in that case I should scarcely have made any stir in the affair at all; but I sue for justice to be established, and to be rendered to the Great Creator Almighty God, thro' his embassador [sic] Pherson, son of Christ, King of Kings and Lord of Lords, and the amount of damage is fixed to satisfy the insult and injury offered the dignified personage represented, on a ratio similar to an indignity offered through an embassador [sic], by one potentate of the earth to another.[32]

McPherson the "potentate" asks for damages of 10,000 times $10 million against James Drew M'Caw, for damages of $20,000 against the master of police, for damages of $50,000 against Dr. John Adams (a member of the court who called McPherson a lunatic), and for damages of $100,000 against every magistrate in the city of Richmond.[33]

It is easy to side with Dr. John Adams and dismiss McPherson as a lunatic, but the fact remains that he was dismissed from the Virginia state asylum in Williamsburg after only three weeks and one examination by doctors there; so, if McPherson were actually a lunatic, he could certainly pretend to be sane. Perhaps McPherson's "insanity" was not physiological or psychological but social since it was only in Richmond, his home, that he was pronounced insane. The nature of his insanity appears to have been his own self-conception as a free and equal citizen of the United States. In other words, what Adams deemed McPherson's "lunacy" was, at bottom, his desire to be treated like a human being. In response to a racially motivated and unjust imprisonment, McPherson styles himself a "potentate," that is, a powerful man who cannot be imprisoned and who deserves the same respect enjoyed by the rulers of the earth. Whether or not McPherson believed in his appointment as God's representative (and all indications are that he believed just that), his rhetorical maneuver here is a perfect response to those who employed the levers of white power to restrict him. Rather than trying to master those same levers, McPherson invokes a power than sits above the apparatus of the state and then appoints himself the earthly representative of *that* power.

McPherson's publication bears all the markings of its intended function. It is a slim octavo pamphlet of which only one copy remains, and the pamphlet was probably meant to circulate within Richmond so McPherson could more widely share his petition to the city leaders who mistreated him. Like that petition, McPherson's pamphlet seems to have done nothing to change the author's earthly circumstances. In fact, those circumstances declined precipitously over the course of the 1810s leading up to his death in 1818. After his petition and lawsuit failed, McPherson removed to New York, though he did not stay there for long. By 1815, he was back in Richmond where he sold some of his land for use as a burial ground and then accepted money from people wishing to purchase plots on the land he had already sold.[34] McPherson's wife died in 1816, and his financial slide continued—McPherson sold more and more of his land to pay his mounting debts.[35] McPherson died in January 1818, leaving only a few properties in Richmond and Henrico County and hundreds of dollars in unpaid taxes.[36]

There is an interesting coda to McPherson's story that brings his tale up to 1855, the year a man named Christopher McPherson Smith (presumably a descendant) republished McPherson's book at the job office of the Lynchburg *Virginian*, titling it *A Short History of the Life of Christopher McPherson*. Other than the new title and the indication that the new printing was the "Second Edition," the text of the new version is an exact copy of the first.[37] Smith gives no explanation for why he would have reprinted the book, what he hoped to achieve by doing so, or who may have wanted to read it. Occam's razor suggests that Christopher McPherson Smith found his ancestor's book and wanted to preserve it for himself and for future generations, though we cannot discount the possibility that a book like McPherson's—with its blend of complaint and prophecy—was well suited to the moment. As Virginians would learn in a few years, if the state did not heed the claims of Black Americans, then God certainly would.

Peter Randolph and the Power of Interpretation

Around the time Christopher McPherson Smith republished *A Short History*, a thirty-year-old freeman named Peter Randolph published *Sketches of Slave Life* at a print shop in Boston. Randolph's first edition is a short (thirty-six-page) octavo (nineteen-centimeter) pamphlet containing a mostly impersonal history that focuses primarily on the atrocities and horrors Randolph witnessed and heard about that occurred on Virginia plantations. Randolph's first publication was produced with the intention of "increas[ing] sympathy" for the enslaved and "effecting the emancipation of the millions of [Randolph's] afflicted brethren" and was promoted by Daniel Haskill in the *Boston Daily Transcript*.[38] Haskill's support, along with advertisements in *The Liberator*, helped create "great demand" for Randolph's pamphlet.[39] Great demand translated into significant sales, and, a few months after he published his first edition, Randolph published a much longer (eighty-two-page) second edition featuring an endorsement from the white abolitionist Samuel May Jr.[40] After a long career in the ministry, Randolph would publish an expanded autobiography in 1893 titled *From Slave Cabin to the Pulpit*, which—forecasting Booker T. Washington's autobiography a few years later—focuses on Randolph's education and subsequent professional rise. It was in his early editions, though, that Randolph seems most exercised over the uneven application of American justice and most focused on undoing the iron law of white supremacy.

Even though it was written to offer alternate testimony that might advance political reforms, Randolph's first edition of *Sketches of Slave Life* mirrors Jacob Stroyer's use of the sketch nearly thirty years later. In his sketches describing life for the enslaved, Randolph creates space between his own memories and the more generalized story of slavery that could be used for political purposes. For example, in his first edition Randolph describes the work of the "colored drivers" who "are not over the slaves because they wish it, but are made so against their will . . . They bear the angry tones of the slaveholder's voice, admonishing them that if they refuse to whip, they must take it themselves."[41] Near the end of the pamphlet, readers come to understand why Randolph has introduced the work of the "colored driver" as he explains that his father was forced to work as a driver on the nearby Harrison plantation: "I used to think very hard of my father, and that he was a very cruel man; but when I knew that he could not help himself, I could not but alter my views and feelings in regard to his conduct. I was ten years old when he died."[42] As a young man, Randolph may have feared and despised his father, but—writing as an adult—he has come to understand that his feelings were probably misplaced and that his real loathing should have been directed at the system that forced his father to act as he did. Randolph does not address this family history near the beginning of his book, perhaps because that history (like his own feelings toward his father) was too hard to face. By the end of the first edition of *Sketches*, though, Randolph moves from his role as observer/historian to a participant and connects his personal history with the history of American slavery.

Given this emergence at the end of the first edition, perhaps it is no surprise that Randolph's personal story moves to the fore in the second edition, an edition that bears hallmarks of abolitionists' influence in terms of its structure and focus though it remained an octavo pamphlet with paper covers. First, there is the extensive "Note to the preface" authored by Samuel May that tells the story of the sixty-six "Edloe Slaves" who arrived in Boston in 1847 and began their lives as free men and women. In his note, May says very little about Randolph, but he does celebrate the fact the men and women who arrived in Boston with Randolph in 1847 proved themselves capable, honest, and hardworking. As May explains, "they have used their liberty . . . justly and . . . well."[43] May's commendations precede Randolph's discussion of his early life and religious salvation, his brother, and his parents. All the sketches from the first edition of the book remain in the second, but those sketches follow Randolph's personal history. The combined effects of May's note and Randolph's revisions make the second edition of *Sketches* more typical of the texts we have come to know as slave narratives, but the book features crucial additions that draw attention to what Katherine Clay Bassard calls the "legal complications of freedom for African American subjects."[44] Those additions include his enslaver's will and the legal actions and interpretations that both consigned and (eventually) freed Randolph and the other men and women enslaved on the Edloe plantation in Virginia's Prince George County. In his use and analysis of these legal documents and court decisions, Randolph positions himself not only as a literate and emancipated freeman but as an early practitioner of the legal analyst tradition in African American autobiography.

As Randolph explains, the will in question belonged to Carter Edloe, a wealthy plantation owner who, apparently, had deep reservations about holding slaves. This did not keep him from claiming eighty-one people as his property, but it did keep him from church, since he believed Christianity was incompatible with slavery. Moreover, in his will, Edloe asserted, "I desire that my estate shall be kept together and cultivated to the best advantage. . . . to raise a sufficient sum to pay for the transportation of my Slaves to any Free State or Colony which they may prefer, and give to each Slave Fifty Dollars on their departure, either in money or in other articles which may suit them better; but should any of my slaves prefer going immediately, they can do so, but they are not to be furnished with money."[45] Because this was the second clause in the will (following the first in which Edloe directed that his debts should be discharged but before he directed the disposition of the remainder of his estate), it stands to reason that he intended to manumit and compensate the enslaved men and women as soon as sufficient funds permitted it.

In further clauses, Edloe directed money to his nieces and bequeathed $8,000 to an enslaved woman (Harriet Barber) and her children, all of whom were almost certainly also Edloe's children.[46] As Harriet Barber, Philip Randolph, and the other men and women on the Edloe plantation learned, though, there were many powerful people in Virginia who would not countenance antislavery action, even by a dead man. Carter Edloe wrote his will in 1838 and died in 1844, but his appointed executor (John Seldon) refused to honor the terms of the document and spent years conspiring with other lawyers to keep the enslaved on the Edloe lands. What he was not counting on, it seems, was Peter Randolph, who saw a copy of the will six months after Edloe's death and—finding that literacy could indeed set him free—set out to locate someone who would help the enslaved secure their inheritance.[47] This tangled and complex legal history is not the escape story we usually find in slave narratives, but neither is the escape the story of just one person: As Randolph explains, the proper interpretation and execution of the law guaranteed freedom for the sixty-six men and women who would come to be known as the "Edloe Slaves."

Perhaps it is no surprise that Randolph emphasized the connection between law and freedom since he published his second edition soon after Anthony Burns returned to Boston.[48] Anthony Burns was enslaved in Virginia before making his escape in February 1854. His enslaver, Charles Suttle, tracked him to Boston and had him arrested. After a series of demonstrations and a violent confrontation between abolitionists and the Boston police who were holding the fugitive in jail, Burns's case went to court, and Commissioner Edward G. Loring decided that—according to the terms of the Fugitive Slave Act—Burns had to be handed over to his enslaver. Burns returned to Virginia in late May, and he remained enslaved until early 1855 when Rev. Leonard Grimes led a successful campaign (largely funded by Black Bostonians) to purchase Burns's freedom.[49] Burns returned to Boston in March 1855 and spoke at Tremont Temple and other sites in the city before enrolling in Oberlin College later in 1855.

Burns's capture and subsequent re-enslavement in a case decided by a Massachusetts commissioner led James Freeman Clarke to remark that "Massachusetts has been placed . . . at the feet of Virginia" since the laws of the South held sway even in the North.[50] This certainly represents the dark side of American law. But the Burns case would have been instructive for Randolph: If the rule of law were enforced independent of public will—as it clearly had been in Boston—then unscrupulous local officials could not subvert legal guarantees. Put another way, Virginia law might reign supreme in Boston, but that meant it had to reign in Virginia too. Perhaps Peter Randolph had the primacy of Virginia law in mind as he wrote the second edition of *Sketches*, an edition in which he reprinted the entirety of Edloe's will as well as the pronouncements of the county clerks that dictated the actions of the executor. He also included a lengthy gloss on the documents and an explanation of their import.

It is this reprinting and subsequent interpretation of legal texts that allowed Randolph to submit his alternate testimony to the court of public opinion. Writing about the will, Randolph notes that, even though the document gave clear instructions, the executor interpreted Edloe's words to mean that the enslaved "were to stay on the plantation and work there until we had earned [enough] money ourselves."[51] To combat this unjust action, Randolph hired a lawyer named James L. Scarborough who learned that Edloe's estate was valued at $32,000; this should have enabled Randolph and the other freed people to leave the plantation immediately. Instead of obtaining justice, though, Scarborough took a series of payments from the corrupt executor and thereby delayed the case for years. Randolph explains, "when we found out the deception he had practiced . . . we felt very wretched indeed—sure that we had no friend left, and should never get our freedom, but were cruelly robbed of what was our own, not only by right, but as an especial gift."[52] As both the reader and interpreter of Edloe's will, Randolph understands his rights and his desserts, but since he could not act within a corrupt system, he remained unable to claim the freedom that was his. Ultimately, a magistrate named William B. Harrison helped Randolph and the other enslaved men and women after "three years and thirty-five days in unlawful bondage," but each person received only $14.96 instead of the fifty dollars they were promised.

Randolph's narrative helps establish the inadequacy of legal arguments surrounding slavery. Randolph can both read and interpret legal documents that confirm his status as a free man, but knowing the law does not guarantee proper application of that law since the slave power corrupts everything. Even when a Black man was legally entitled to invoke the language of law and argue that contract—and not status—should determine how he was treated, he found that the status relationships inherited from slavery persisted in freedom.[53] For this reason, Randolph cannot simply interpret the will correctly and accept his inheritance; instead, he must argue for a shared sense of justice among both Black and white readers of the texts, for only when white men like William B. Harrison agree with his understanding of the law could Randolph and the rest of the enslaved on Edloe's plantation hope to secure their freedom. What is at issue in Randolph's book, then, is not only the law itself but the extent to which the law would be accepted by the white Americans who claimed to value it. As Peter Randolph certainly knew, a freedom subject to white approval is really no freedom at all.

There is also a more practical way in which the law is connected to Randolph's first two publications. In January 1855, several years after the Edloe slaves arrived in Boston, Randolph signed a deposition testifying to his experience and demanding the payment (at long last) of the fifty dollars that was promised him and the other enslaved men and women on the Edloe plantation. A Virginia lawyer argued Randolph's case, and a Virginia court found in his favor, which brought Randolph and the other surviving members of the Edloe slave community $58.55 each. A few weeks after this decision was handed down in May 1855, Randolph published the first edition of *Sketches of Slave Life*, perhaps—as Bassard speculates—with the long overdue money he received from the estate of Carter Edloe.[54]

Legal Rhetoric in *Book for the People!*

In the runup to the 1880 election, an Illinois farmer named Norvel Blair took the train twenty-six miles from the depot in Morris, Illinois, up to Joliet. He sought out the offices of the only Democratic newspaper in town—the brand-new *Joliet Record*—and he printed his thirty-two-page duodecimo (fifteen-centimeter) pamphlet titled *Book for the People! To Be Read by All Voters, Black and White, with Thrilling Events of the Life of Norvel Blair, of Grundy County, State of Illinois*.[55] The pamphlet was bound in paper and featured an engraving of Blair on the frontispiece; given its size, quality, and raison d'être, it probably sold cheaply if it sold at all, and, as far as we know, Blair never printed another pamphlet. There are few extant copies in libraries and archives today, and there is no reason to believe the text had a geographic reach beyond Blair's neighbors in Grundy and Will Counties nor a temporal reach beyond the November 1880 elections. All indications are that Blair's pamphlet was supposed to function within a particular moment: He used self-publication to testify to his character, indict the American justice system, and encourage other Black people to support the Democratic Party in the 1880 elections. Self-publication could not deconstruct a racist judicial system or drive nefarious Republicans from power, but Blair's use of his pamphlet to launch an explicit attack on the system and the men who ran it represents an act of enormous faith in himself and in the possibilities inherent in full political citizenship.

Norvel Blair's *Book for the People!* is not a typical autobiography but more like a plea, which indicates the urgency of Blair's political and legal appeal. Blair spends less than a paragraph detailing his birth, parentage, and life in slavery before moving on to address his extensive concerns with local politics and a raft of lawsuits in which he was involved.[56] According to the brief autobiographical portion of the narrative, Blair was born in Tennessee in 1825 and was held by four different enslavers during his life. He does not mention when or how he acquired his freedom but given that he moved to St. Louis in 1863 and then on to Illinois later the same year, he was probably freed by the Union army. After working as a laborer and a tenant farmer, Blair bought property in Grundy County where he lived with his wife and (eventually) six children. In 1870, Blair and his family were living in in Wauponsee Township, which lay just south of the Illinois River and the Grundy County seat of Morris.[57] By 1880, Blair had moved a couple of miles west to Norman Township, where he was one of one hundred people of color in a locality that numbered 4,000 men, women, and children. Blair was also one of the (if not *the*) most prosperous Black residents in Grundy County, which may have been the reason prominent whites targeted him again and again.[58]

This is mostly speculation, though, since Blair spends very little time exploring the deeper reasons for his misfortune; he is much more interested in explaining the misfortunes themselves and shaping readers' understanding of them. So, over the first twelve pages of his narrative, Blair describes his regrettable decision to sign several promissory notes, bonds, and mortgages at the prompting of various Republican lawyers in town. At the time Blair was being manipulated, he could "neither read nor write," and he trusted in the good will of the Republicans who claimed to be the "the great friend of the colored man."[59] This trust led him to follow the advice of Republican lawyer John N. Reading, who urged Blair to sign over his property to Lyman B. Ray (Reading's son-in-law) so Blair could avoid "the judgment note that [he] had no knowledge of and never gave."[60] Despite some early defeats in court, Blair "confided in Mr. Reading and . . . gave him control of all [his] property, believing [Reading] to be an honest, fair, and good man."[61] With the help of his son Benjamin, Blair eventually realized he was being defrauded, but by that point he was already named in several lawsuits, and he would be named in several more over the course of the 1870s. Despite his many protestations and courtroom testimonies, there was nothing Blair could do to stem the tide, and so he settled on two new strategies to present his side of the story.

Blair's first strategy was to file suit himself, which he did in 1876.[62] As the case wended its way through the courts (eventually reaching the Illinois Supreme Court), Blair pursued his second strategy: publication. Insisting that he wanted "to give the truth, and nothing but the truth," he declared,

"I publish this book, and do it at my own expense, and pay for it with the money myself, boys, and girls and old wife earned this summer, and by the help of the good Lord we will work and get more, and then I will write another book. But I am not done with this, and will give more facts."[63] Blair's insistence on giving "nothing but the truth" and then "more facts" hints at the testimonial impulse that drove him to write and publish in the first place and the function he imagined for his pamphlet: it was a tool to influence public opinion, if not the opinion of a jury. Also significant here is Blair's stated desire to publish again, as if doing so would emphasize the rightness of his claims or the justness of his cause. In his belief that publication could be both a way of proving his point and marking his status, Blair reminds us of the non-remunerative values of publication. For him, it was worth producing "at [his] own expense" to claim what Karen Weyler calls the "symbolic capital" attending authorship and publication.[64]

Another way Blair accrues the "symbolic capital" of knowledge is through his use of legal rhetoric throughout his pamphlet. At one point in his narrative he echoes Roger B. Taney when he wonders whether "the colored man has any rights to be respected by the courts," and then insists that Reading never "paid me back a cent, because I being a colored man I had no rights that the law, in his opinion, was bound to respect."[65] These remarkable lines suggest Blair was closely attuned to the words he heard in court or the words he had heard in preparation for writing his book, and he wanted to make his argument within the same legal frameworks (and with the same legal language) that had so damaged his material prospects. By doing so, Blair replicates the techniques of authorial predecessors like Frederick Douglass who, as Jeannine DeLombard argues, "directed legal discourse to [his] own rhetorical . . . ends."[66] Blair leverages a very specific kind of legal rhetoric as he insists on the importance of "giving facts," as he notes that he gave a "plain statement of facts," "nothing but facts," "the whole facts," or "PLAIN AND HONEST FACTS."[67] He also asks that Democrats aid him in the "circulation of . . . facts" in advance of the 1880 election.[68]

Since Blair conceived of his book as a portable alternate testimony to counteract the lies of men like Reading and Ray, it is not surprising that he used endorsements to help make his case, though it should be noted these endorsements function as further evidence for Blair's honesty and sobriety rather than authorizations of his right to speak. Blair claims that some of the "very best men in Morris, Grundy county" find him honest in his business dealings and, crucially, able to "fulfill any contracts he may make."[69] The "very best men" who serve as character witnesses for Blair implicitly endorse his "statement of facts" about mortgages, bonds, and notes. Blair's final witness—a traveling performer named Daniel Carpenter—serves an entirely different purpose, since he speaks to Blair's humanity and community orientation:

> I hereby certify that I lived and ate off rotten coons in the bottom on Judge Redding's farm, and did it because no one would give me a day's work only Norvel Blair. I am in Morris to day and will be back very soon and tell more about Judge Reading.
>
> Dan'l E, Carpenter.
> Witness Wm. G. Miller.
> Sept. 7, 1680 [sic]
>
> I got the above from the poor boy Carpenter, who ate the rotten coons to keep from starving, and when I found out his condition I gave him work. He is traveling with Van Amberg's show and will soon be in Morris to stand up and tell the facts in person. The colored race are no longer going to eat the putrified [sic] flesh of horses and coon.[70]

Blair's use of Carpenter's testimony helps him underscore two crucial points. First, Judge Reading really was the kind of heartless Republican monster that Blair believed him to be; second, Blair was the kind of man who looked after others and not just himself. This second point matters because it reinforces Blair's claims to a communal concern when he opines, "the only hope of the colored race is by and through the Democratic party."[71]

Blair's pamphlet allows him to become his own lawyer and crafts a quasi-courtroom testimony from a different point of view. His several references to the court records that tell his story (or a version of it) lend further credence to Eric Gardner's claim that "case files might be read both within and against an expanded sense of the slave narrative tradition."[72] Blair may have believed that his own testimony could modify or refract the supposedly authoritative accounts in the county records; perhaps that is why he writes, "I leave you, dear reader, to judge" and then refers to "the records of Grundy County, Illinois."[73] Blair wanted his testimony to be read alongside or in addition to the extant records, and he wanted these combined testimonies to inform a new judgment. The truth, Blair seems to say, can only be discerned if all relevant voices are heard; by evaluating multiple stories, readers could get closer to an elusive (or deliberately obscured) truth.

Like many of the narratives in this study, Blair's *Book for the People!* helps its author rewrite an authorized or accepted history and enter his own voice into an otherwise unreliable record. Blair's book carries with it an awareness of the limitations inherent in the world in which it was produced, but it also testifies to Blair's belief that those limitations could fall away under the rule of law. In 1880, Blair saw no difference between being "a Southern slave" and "the slave of a Northern Republican," and while he bemoans the fact that "they said we were freemen, but only freemen so long as they can vote us and get our labor for nothing," he retained the hope that he would be a "freeman in the highest sense."[74] Blair insisted that Blacks "had rights under the laws as made by the Republican party, and if we stand firm for the maintainance [sic] of them we will have a perfect freedom."[75] Full citizenship included voting, the confidence that "he and his wife and children can get justice," and his ability to speak in public by having "a book printed to defend himself, wife and children from Republicans," something that was not possible in Morris since Republicans had "the money to buy up and subsadise [sic] the press, that I have been taught to believe could not be bought."[76] At the ballot box, in the courtroom, and in the public sphere, Blair wanted to be treated like a citizen; he knew, though, that he could not effect change by himself, so he wrote a *Book for the People!* to motivate the political actions that could help him realize his goals. Proclaiming, "We have the voting power," he asked his fellow African Americans to "exercise it for our own and our children's future good."[77] In 1880, Blair still finds himself imagining the "law still to come" and hoping that the franchise would enable his children to live under such a law.

Even before he published his book, Blair's strident calls for justice and his denunciations of leading Republicans in Grundy County led to all manner of trouble for him and his family. Blair's house was riddled with bullets, his stock was driven off, and his sons were held up at gunpoint. Blair publicized and decried these acts of terrorism and vandalism, but they seem to have had their desired effect. Blair left Illinois and moved to Fairbanks Township in Sully County, South Dakota, in 1884, where he lived on a farm near the Missouri River with his wife and four of his children. As they had in Grundy County, the family prospered; the 1916 County Land Ownership map shows nine separate plots of land owned by members of the Blair family.[78] Norvel Blair died at the age of ninety-one on October 7, 1916, and his family would remain in Sully County for years.[79] In addition to these living monuments, his book and the associated court records remain as testaments to his indomitability in the face of injustice.

Lucy Delaney Relitigates Slavery

Lucy Delaney published her autobiography more than a decade after Norvel Blair published his narrative, but her story was just as concerned with the past as it was with the present. Indeed, Delaney's narrative looks back to 1844, when Delaney won her freedom in a Missouri courtroom. By the time Delaney published her book, the Civil War and Reconstruction had come to an end, her parents had died, and she was approaching the end of her long life. There was no obvious reason for Delaney to write or publish her story, and she explained that she chose to do so only because "many of my friends have urged me to give a short sketch of my varied life."[80] The conventionality of this apology does not make it false, but it does give one pause, especially since Delaney's narrative, titled *From the Darkness Cometh the Light, or, Struggles for Freedom*, does not discuss the "varied" nature of Delaney's life but, instead, focuses on the years she was enslaved. Why, after four-plus decades, did Delaney commemorate her story? Was it a desire to enter her tale into the historical record? Did she, as Eric Gardner argues, want to instruct a new generation of Missouri women about the sacrifices and separations endemic to slavery?[81] Did Delaney want to comment on the political situation in the postwar United States? Or did she—like Venture Smith before her and Louis Hughes after her—want to celebrate her successes and her membership in the solid Black middle class of her St. Louis home? There is no reason to believe there is only one answer to these questions, but Delaney's historical focus and her intense interest in courtroom actions suggest that she intended her narrative as a commentary on justice (both divine and mundane) and a reflection on Black Americans' likelihood of receiving justice from God if not, finally, from the United States.

Few critics have done more than mention Delaney's book, but those who have pursue three different avenues. Hazel Carby, P. Gabrielle Foreman, and Frances Smith Foster connect Delaney to African American literature of the 1890s, especially fiction by writers like Frances E. W. Harper and Pauline E. Hopkins.[82] As Foreman notes, Delaney's self-portrait finds a literary descendant in the character of Lucille Delaney in Harper's *Iola Leroy*, published soon after *From the Darkness Cometh the Light*. While it is doubtful that Harper ever read Delaney's autobiography, it is hard to ignore the "models of maternal courageousness and determination" on display in both books.[83] Lindon Barrett offers another way to think about Delaney's work, specifically as it reflects certain tropes common to antebellum slave narratives, especially what he calls the "scene of writing." In *From the Darkness Cometh the Light*, that scene takes place not in a garret or in the enslaver's house but in the courtroom where readers witness "the dynamics of language, literacy, and interpretation as they bear on African American 'subjectivity.'"[84]

Eric Gardner and Lea VanderVelde approach Delaney's narrative by illuminating the contexts around her freedom suit and the publication of her book in the early 1890s.[85] Gardner, especially, maintains that we must look beyond Delaney's autobiography to understand the story of her life. With this approach in mind, Gardner discusses Delaney's membership in various St. Louis social and religious groups and argues convincingly that Delaney published her book at the behest of her friends in religious and neo-Masonic organizations and sold or distributed it to those friends.[86] This certainly tracks with the appearance of Delaney's book, which is a small octavo (seventeen-centimeter) volume printed at the publishing office of J. T. Smith; the book is bound in boards with a gold-stamped cover.[87] Like Jacob Stroyer's 1898 book and M. W. Gibbs's 1902 autobiography, Delaney's book features an author portrait and facsimile signature as well. In appearance and heft, *From the Darkness Cometh the Light* is nothing like the simple pamphlets produced by McPherson, Randolph, and Blair. Delaney was self-consciously writing a *book* and orienting her publication toward posterity.

The time lapse between the events she describes and the moment of publication underscores the different audience and function Delaney imagined for her book. Because almost fifty years passed from the moment Delaney won her freedom in court to the time she began writing, her narrative demonstrates how her own understanding of the law evolved over a half century. This is a point Foreman makes when she notes that freedom suits were rarely prosecuted effectively in the antebellum period but that legal challenges to discrimination were more frequent and (somewhat) more effective in the post-Reconstruction era when Delaney published her book. Foreman argues that readers of *From the Darkness Cometh the Light* should shift their focus from the "trial of slavery to the trial of legal appeals in the 1890s" to understand "Delaney's judicial foregrounding."[88] Indeed, when we follow Foreman's prescription, we better understand the function of Delaney's publication.

In that publication, the thirteen-year-old girl who was the subject of a freedom suit in 1844 sits in a courtroom for the very first time, and she is horrified as her enslaver's attorney "talked so bitterly against me and against my being in possession of my liberty that I was trembling, as if with ague, for I certainly thought everybody must believe him."[89] Looking back years later, Delaney realizes that her feelings were born of the fact that she had never "heard anyone plead before, [and] I was very much alarmed, although I knew in my heart that every word he uttered was a lie!"[90] Given that she casts the younger version of herself as naive, we can assume that years of life in the United States have shown Delaney that the language of pleading (and perhaps the language of law more generally) is a language of lies. When Lucy's attorney, Edward Bates, takes the floor and delivers his closing arguments, he reassures his client as he speaks the truth, but the implication in this set piece is clear: the courtroom is not a venue where truth emerges as much as it is a place where versions of the truth are debated. Just as many of the authors in this chapter learned, the law is neither absolute nor inflexible but contingent. Delaney's personal "struggle for freedom" is decided within the realm of this contingency, and mastering those contingencies is the essence of that struggle.

Such mastery was hard for a Black woman to achieve, though, and as she looks back on her childhood experience, Delaney underlines the extent of her powerlessness over what Barrett calls the "determining technologies of legal discourse."[91] On the morning her verdict was read, Delaney felt "helpless" and "dazed, as if [she] were no longer [herself]." She remembers having an out-of-body experience in which she "seemed to be another person—an on looker—and in my heart dwelt a pity for the poor, lonely girl, with downcast face, sitting on the bench apart from anyone else in that noisy room."[92] Delaney's recollection emphasizes the extremity of her situation, a situation the older woman can only fully grasp as she becomes the "on looker" at her own trial. As she looks back, Delaney sees that her younger self was completely alone and lacking in power or agency; she is unable to shape the circumstances of her own life and must depend on the white men around her to either plead for her (or not), and to decide in her favor (or not). As Lindon Barrett writes, in the courtroom scenes of her autobiography, Delaney unveils her inability to claim a stable, self-constructed identity when "the 'constitutional' issue of [her] identity already has been settled without [her] participation or consent."[93] Though the case was settled without Delaney's participation, the young woman did win her freedom in court; at the same time, her freedom is only revealed to readers following Delaney's description of the psychological trauma she experienced while wondering what would become of her. It is that trauma that remains years later, and it could only remind Delaney that her status (and perhaps, as Barrett argues, her identity) were determined by others. To live as a Black woman in the United States is to struggle not only for freedom from enslavement and subjugation but to struggle for the freedom to define oneself. Within a court of law, such self-definition was *always* impossible for Delaney; and, even within the pages of her narrative, Delaney seems bound by certain conventions (the apology for writing, the paean to the "great man," Edward Bates) that are tied to oppressive structures.[94]

This is not to say, as Lea VanderVelde does, that Delaney "buys into legal language and legality, even when that very law reinforces the horrible and unjust institution of slavery."[95] Nor is it to agree with Eric Gardner's claim that *From the Darkness Cometh the Light* "resists slavery on every level" since the book was written a quarter-century after slavery ended.[96] Instead, I want to situate Delaney's book within the century-long discourse concerning law and its application to Black Americans. First, we should acknowledge, with VanderVelde, that Delaney's primary complaint in her narrative is not with the law itself (that is, she is not decrying the statutes that permit slavery) but with its application in her case. At the same time, I see no evidence that Delaney "buys into" legal language in her narrative. Instead, she seems to understand that legal language is, itself, part of the problem. Like so many things in the United States, it is defined and controlled almost entirely by whites and deployed for the purposes of advancing white supremacy. Even as a young girl who was simultaneously plaintiff and onlooker at her very first trial, Delaney understood this fact about the law, and nothing in the fifty years between that trial and her publication of *From the Darkness Cometh the Light* seems to have changed that understanding.

Insofar as Delaney recognizes the profound limitations of American law, her book certainly strikes a resistant chord. This is not the only chord she plays, though. Delaney's commemoration of different civic and religious organizations and her own role in them helps readers envision alternate forms of connection and affiliation that could potentially empower and protect Black Americans even if the justice system could not. Among those groups for Delaney were the Methodist Episcopal Church, the Robert Gould Shaw Woman's Relief Corps, and the Siloam Court; in some of those organizations she held leadership positions as "president," "matron," or "Most Ancient Matron." After sketching the work she did in those organizations, Delaney asks, rhetorically, "And what better can we do than to live for others?"[97] As a wife, a mother, a daughter, and a member of religious and civic organizations, Delaney had, indeed, lived for others, a fact she celebrates and presents as a model.[98] In her concluding sentences, Delaney indicates that her book has helped answer one more rhetorical question: "Can the negro race succeed, proportionately, as well as the whites, if given the same chance and an equal start?"[99] Delaney believes her story answers her question in the affirmative. The key is that some powerful institution guaranteed and protected the "equal start" that Delaney lacked.

Equality would prove a bridge too far as long as the law remained subject to manipulations that never failed to buttress white supremacy.[100] Just as Mark Twain showed in *Adventures of Huckleberry Finn*, this problem did not admit of any solution, but Delaney gestures toward civic and religious organizations as sources of power that might help Black Americans face down the forces arrayed against them. Perhaps even more important than the organizations themselves was the willingness to fight demonstrated by army veterans to whom she dedicates her book. During Reconstruction, US Army troops helped ensure that justice would prevail in the South, and in her dedication, Delaney celebrates the army's "friendship as displayed towards the colored race."[101] The army is only an extension of the government that deploys it, though, so we might read Delaney's dedication as her way of acknowledging that the United States had—at best—an uneven history of protecting the rights of its Black citizens. As her narrative shows, only when the state demonstrated its "friendship" by passing just laws and enforcing them without prejudice would Black Americans have "the same chance and an equal start." Here, again, Delany reveals the different temporal horizon she imagines for her book as she looks toward a future when all Americans would enjoy equal protection under the law.

Around the time Delaney published her book, Peter Randolph was part of a group of Bostonians bemoaning the fact that the United States government still refused to protect its Black citizens even as those citizens were terrorized and murdered by lynch mobs. At the end of a meeting in June 1892, Randolph's Boston group passed a resolution that expressed frustrations lurking just below the surface in Delaney's book: "[T]he government of the United States is unable to protect its own citizens within its borders. We therefore appeal to the heart and conscience of the great republic, who finds ready sympathy for Ireland, Russia, and Germany, that it will extend protection to its own."[102] A lot had changed over the course of the nineteenth century; as Delaney and Randolph could see, though, America's hypocrisy had not. As was the case in 1811, Black authors looked to the law with extraordinary hopefulness even as they knew that its history was "still being written."[103]

CHAPTER FIVE

That This Book May Speak for Me
Preachers as Publishers

In 1804, a forty-year-old formerly enslaved man named George White attended a camp meeting in New York. After the meeting, White found himself feeling a "glow of heavenly joy," and he later experienced a dream vision in which he was called by God to preach the gospel. But, when White announced his intentions to his "Christian brethren," one of them—presumably a white man—replied by saying, "If you are going to preach, I will quit."[1] This experience would be representative for George White, who struggled to climb each rung of the church hierarchy. White's goal—from the moment of his dream onward—was to obtain a license to preach. Doing so would place White in a position of power since a licensed preacher was entitled not only to read, teach, or exhort but also to interpret the Bible. To obtain a license, White had to prove to other ministers that he was capable of reading and understanding the Bible and using that understanding to preach effectively.

George White was denied licensure no less than six times, but he was finally ordained in the Methodist Episcopal (M.E.) Church of New York, a fact he would celebrate in his 1810 self-published narrative. As William L. Andrews notes, White's autobiography presents him as a man of surpassing "aspiration and will" who wanted to realize his personal goals within an institutional structure.[2] In fact, White's *Life* is not so much about his religious awakening as it is about his ability to translate that awakening into a position of power in the M.E. Church. And, when he moved from the Methodist Church to the African Methodist Episcopal (A.M.E.) Church in 1816, White joined with other Black men who came to represent one of the most powerful institutions in African American life before and after the Civil War.[3]

White's story of a move from exclusion to inclusion aligns with the larger history of the Black church. Contemporary historians have emphasized that the Black church offered a space in which men and women could realize spiritual and social fulfillment outside the racist institutions so common in the United States. Historians have also highlighted the community-building power of the church and the impact of religious organizations on the political and economic lives of African Americans. Eddie Glaude Jr. writes that the "church stood . . . as a kind of institutional organization of the community's resources and a kind of ideological and cultural common ground for everyday interaction or association among antebellum blacks," indicating that the church was the place where diverse groups of Black men and women could meet and unite around what John Ernest calls a "common spiritual quest."[4] For Glaude, that quest "helped to construct a collective identity" for antebellum African Americans.[5] In the nurturing and supportive space of the church, Black collective identity had a chance to grow and flourish, and in the writings that emerged from church members and leaders, that collective identity found powerful expression. Indeed, Katherine Clay Bassard insists that antebellum African American religious writing reveals the foundations of "African American notions of community or 'peoplehood.'"[6] In most cases, the collective identity forged through shared religious belief was activist in nature, and it helped mobilize African Americans against the depredations of a racist government.[7] There are numerous autobiographical examples that reveal the symbiosis between faith, politics, and an emergent "African American" identity, perhaps the most famous being Richard Allen's description of the founding of Mother Bethel and the A.M.E. church.[8]

I begin by focusing on religious community and collective identity because this chapter investigates the intersection of (and sometimes, the tension between) communal and individual goals in the self-published autobiographies of African American religious leaders.

The archive of such autobiographies is enormous: Over the course of the 1800s, more than thirty self-published narratives were authored by men or women who identified themselves as preachers, deacons, Sunday school teachers, exhorters, or other religious officials in the Baptist, Methodist, M.E., A.M.E., and A.M.E. Zion churches. Several of the authors I have already discussed in this book identified themselves as ministers of the gospel. But, whereas ministers like Edmond Kelley and Noah Davis published to get their families out of slavery and Jacob Stroyer and Thomas James published to raise money and rewrite American history, the narratives in this chapter function as institutional histories for individual churches and denominations. More than this, if one were to read and analyze the dozens of individual narratives, one would have the outlines of an institutional history for the Black church in the United States. Though such a project would make a book in itself, in this chapter I consider four narratives that showcase two strands of that institutional history.

One strand is composed of church builders and boosters, the men and women who constructed buildings, grew congregations, spread the gospel as missionaries, and preached at churches, camp meetings, and revivals.

Among this number, we can include men like Baptist minister Jeremiah Asher. Asher published two versions of his autobiography and hoped his work would "encourage many who, without education, may be called to the work of the Gospel ministry," within the Baptist Church.[9] Writing in 1875, Charles Thompson published an autobiographical pamphlet and addressed "the members of the United Brethren Church, white as well as colored," from whom he looked for "help in the sale and circulation of my work."[10] Likewise, two women—Julia Foote and Amanda Smith—published narratives that demonstrate the growing role of women in the Black church and the enthusiastic support of their male colleagues. Foote's autobiography, *A Brand Plucked from the Fire*, was prefaced by Thomas K. Doty, the publisher of the *Christian Harvester* and a prolific author of religious tracts in his own right.[11] Amanda Smith, who styled herself "The Colored Evangelist," worked as a missionary across the globe, and her narrative was introduced by Methodist bishop William Thoburn.[12]

For most of these institutionally affiliated authors, the text's function was usually paramount, and, since that function was directed toward future generations of readers who might wonder about the early history of a denomination or church, format was also important. Hence, most of their self-published narratives are bulky, bound books with embellishments (author portraits, gold-stamped covers) that would have cost more to produce and, potentially, commanded higher prices. Typical of this kind of publication is Amanda Smith's *Autobiography*, which is a large octavo volume (twenty-one centimeters) that is 500 pages long and includes a gold-stamped engraving of the author on the cover. Though we cannot be sure, books like Amanda Smith's may have been designed in this way so they were more likely to circulate among church leaders or donors. Or, perhaps the book (and others like it) was designed to be given as a gift.

The books published by Elijah Marrs and David Smith have some of the same formatting elements Amanda Smith employs. Though the books are shorter, both are sturdy, bound books with thick paper and wide margins. Both Marrs and David Smith produced books with stamped covers and gilt lettering on the cover and/or spine (see fig. 5.1). As these authors commemorated their own contributions or versions of institutional histories through impressive books, they also cited their bona fides within existing church structures rather than seeking to expand or remake those structures. David Smith and Marrs are especially relevant because they employ some of the same strategies used by other authors featured in this book. First, each of the authors connects himself to another self-publication tradition even as he celebrates his own religious experiences: David Smith uses some of the marketing strategies common to supplicant authors and Elijah Marrs styles himself as both a historian and a historiographer. Second, both authors situate their books within a broader print landscape that also includes published sermons, newspaper stories, church histories, and convention records. By amplifying their own stories and the many sources in which those stories appear, David Smith and Marrs reinforce the community-making power of African American religious institutions and African American print.

The books published by David Smith and Marrs suggest that the life writing of religious leaders served as a proxy for institutional viewpoints. William L. Andrews warns, though, that an individual undertaking "the act of narrating . . . may be seen as vying with official, institutional rhetoric . . . for the attention of the reader."[13] This is certainly true for the second strand of narratives I examine in this chapter: those that highlight tensions between a narrator and a church hierarchy. While it is true that the tension between an individual narrator and the organization of which he or she is a member is hardly unique to religious narratives, the presence of that tension in African American autobiographies underscores the degree to which the idea of "community" was itself a work in progress for nineteenth-century African American author-publishers. Because they were often printed and sold without the endorsement of a church's leaders or the sanction of a church's press, self-published religious narratives could outline the intragroup tensions and arguments that typify seemingly monolithic institutions.

In this respect, George White's story is representative of the many narratives that critiqued religious organizations or their leaders. Another former A.M.E. minister, the Reverend Daniel Peterson, published his narrative in 1854. In the book, he branded the A.M.E. church a "backsliding sister," denounced Frederick Douglass, and begged his readers to emigrate to Liberia.[14] Peterson and White may not have agreed on politics, but they were hardly alone in criticizing the A.M.E. Church, as we can see in the narratives of Jarena Lee and Major James Wilkerson. For her part, Lee fought against gender proscriptions in the A.M.E. Church and tried to make it a more diverse and inclusive organization during decades of preaching and bookselling. Major James Wilkerson was a denominational booster for part of his career, but following a period of debility and recuperation, he found himself ostracized from the A.M.E. Church and commenced a lengthy print war against the A.M.E. hierarchy. Narratives by Lee and Wilkerson underscore the degree to which dissent was always a part of organizational life. Compared to the pro-institutional books, critical narratives are fewer in number and designed with a completely different function and audience in mind, which affected authors' decisions about format and finance. Those critiquing the church hierarchy could not rely on friendly advertisements in newspapers like the *Christian Recorder*, nor could they always find book-buying audiences in churches and Sunday schools. Therefore, Lee and Wilkerson published inexpensive pamphlets and broadsides and sold them where and how they could.

Expanding Church History

Writing in 1872, the Reverend Thomas W. Henry wrote in his *Autobiography* that the A.M.E. Church had "outstripped the enemy" and was "second to none." Henry said he was proud to tell his story and he did so to "gratify the desires of some of [his] most intimate friends, as well as to the African Methodist Episcopal Bishops, Elders, and the membership composing this Church."[15] Henry, like so many of his fellow ministers looking back on the early years of the church, wrote to "give a faint idea, to the younger clergy of this day," just how difficult it had been to transform the A.M.E. Church into the vital and powerful force it had become.[16] Even so, in Henry's language, one can sense the anxiety of a man whose contributions were very much in danger of being forgotten or ignored as the church grew, prospered, and lost touch with its early history. Thomas Henry's *Autobiography*, published when he was nearly eighty years old, is one of dozens published by former ministers or exhorters from the A.M.E., Colored Methodist Episcopal (C.M.E.), M.E., and/or Baptist Churches in the years after the Civil War. Some, like Robert B. Anderson (about whom much more will be said in the next chapter) told their stories to support themselves in their declining years; others, like Elisha Green and Elijah Marrs, seem to have wanted to include themselves in a history that was often written from the perspective of church leaders. In all these cases, the churchmen-turned-authors claimed a position of influence with a religious organization, but most still believed—and had reason to believe—they were writing as outsiders.

This is not to conflate the obstacles faced by staunch institutionalists with those faced by those writing from outside the church hierarchy but rather to highlight the rhetorical poses common to self-publishers and to consider why well-connected ministers would write outside the aegis of the church publishing houses. Perhaps it makes sense to consider the self-published autobiographies of institutional men and women as productions from what Eric Gardner has called "unexpected places;" that is, geographic locations outside the massive publishing centers in the Northeast. Gardner's formulation is useful in another way, too, for he argues that many Black authors considered "their physical *and* metaphysical places as part of not just the United States, not just the black nation with the nation, and not just, say, St. Louis or San Francisco, but all of these and other 'locations.'"[17] In other words, the institutional men who self-published their life stories may have been trying to place themselves and their communities within an expanding denominational and national map; they were also trying to place their contributions to their denomination and their race within a longer and larger historical record. Many of these men must have hoped, with David Smith, that "when my body sleeps in the silent grave and my spirit is at rest . . . this book may speak for me."[18]

David Smith was born in 1784 to an enslaved mother in Baltimore County, Maryland, and sold to a man named John Burnibue soon thereafter. Despite living with a Catholic family and being forced to attend Catholic services, Smith "inclined . . . toward the Methodists" and thereby incurred the wrath of his enslaver and his family.[19] Fortunately for Smith, a Methodist woman named Matilda White used her lottery winnings to purchase Smith; she immediately manumitted him, and he began his life as a freeman at twelve years of age. From the beginning, Smith demonstrated a strong commitment to religion and a desire for leadership roles in the church. As a teenage member of the Sharp and Light Street Churches in Baltimore, he asked for and was granted "a permit to hold prayer-meetings in private houses."[20] Within a few more years, Smith earned an exhorter's license, which—as George White learned—was the highest rank to which a Black man might aspire in the Methodist Episcopal Church of 1800. Once Smith became an exhorter in the Baltimore churches, he steadily gained influence among congregants and among his fellow religious leaders, and, when several east coast congregations within the M.E. church separated and formed the A.M.E. Church in 1816, Smith became a licensed minister of the gospel and a church leader.

Smith's career in the A.M.E. Church was marked by remarkable successes in fundraising and founding churches; by his own account, he helped found congregations in over a dozen locations, and he preferred the work of establishing new churches to the work of pastoring established congregations. So it was that Smith labored in Maryland, Washington, DC, Pennsylvania, Ohio, Kentucky, and Michigan during his career, and so it was that he came to be a well-known and influential figure in the church. Given his long-standing association with the A.M.E. Church, Smith was also something of a living history of the denomination. He had been present at the founding of the A.M.E. in 1816, a key part of the A.M.E.'s westward expansion in the 1830s and 1840s, and a crucial figure in the establishment of Wilberforce University in the 1860s. By the time he published his second autobiography in 1881, he was living in Xenia, Ohio, just a mile or so from the Wilberforce campus, and he appended Daniel Payne's history of the university to the end of his narrative. This choice, along with the nature of Smith's history and narrative, make the autobiography something of an institutional biography. Instead of writing a story of rebellion against authority (as in the cases of Jarena Lee and Major James Wilkerson), Smith chooses to highlight what powerful religious organizations had accomplished and how those accomplishments had improved the lives of African American men and women.

Given the institutional focus of the autobiography and Smith's pride in highlighting the existence of the A.M.E. book concern and the *Christian Recorder* (which he called the "the exponent and battle-axe of the race, exposing corruption in Church and State and defending the Christian manhood of the race"), one wonders why he chose to self-publish his *Biography*.[21] Perhaps Smith's decision to self-publish had something to do with the fact that an earlier attempt at publishing an autobiography had failed. In his preface, Smith explains that "Just before the civil war I undertook the task of having my life published. I had it all prepared for the press and placed in the hands of a white brother to have it published. This dear brother was then in the M. E. Book Concern at Cincinnati, and when I heard from him, he informed me the manuscript was misplaced."[22] It is interesting that Smith was going to publish his book with the M.E. book concern, and it is also interesting that he entrusted his book to a "white brother," though Smith worked effectively with many white ministers over the course of his career. In any case, Smith's book finally emerged from a joint venture between himself and the Reverend John Coleman, who was stationed in Xenia in 1880. After hearing Smith speak at the Ohio annual conference, Coleman asked Smith to share his story for publication. Smith "carefully considered the matter, and finally concluded I would publish my biography if [Coleman] would assist me in its preparation. He agreed and inside of four months I present this imperfect little book."[23]

Smith's preface and the printing office he chose to produce his "little book," which was a small octavo (eighteen-centimeter) volume bound in boards, indicate that his self-publication may have been financed or at least coordinated by Coleman or by men connected to Wilberforce University. The *Biography* was printed at the *Xenia Gazette*, a newspaper office that printed pamphlets like the *Wilberforce Annual* and *The Biennial Catalogue of Wilberforce*

University, which suggests there may have been some link between the *Gazette* and the university. At the same time, the *Life* appears to be the only autobiography printed at the *Gazette* office, which also printed local histories and articles of incorporation; so, despite its proximity to Wilberforce, the *Gazette* seems not to have functioned as the house organ of the university or the church. Nevertheless, the powers that be at the A.M.E. Church appeared to welcome the publication of Smith's book when it was published in the spring of 1881. In a notice in the *Christian Recorder*, the editors indicate their "surprise" at receiving Smith's "well-written autobiography," and offer praise to both Smith and the book before noting that that "the venerable father's memory has . . . played him false in regard to [certain] matters, but the real merit of the book is such as to make us prefer to overlook them."[24] No other notices of Smith's book would appear in the *Recorder* in 1881, but in 1882, Smith (or someone connected to him) placed advertisements in the paper on no fewer than fourteen occasions. Each advertisement read, "The Biography of the Rev. David Smith or Father Smith who is the oldest traveling preacher in the A.M.E. Church, is completed, comprising his Christian labors for 80 years, and his connection with the Church from her organization until now. Copies can be had by sending $1.00 post paid. Address Rev. David Smith, Glass Box 182, Xenia, Ohio."[25] Smith, like many of the authors in this book, was using a direct marketing strategy, though his advanced age made it impossible for him to travel around the country selling his books. So, he used the *Christian Recorder* and the goodwill of its readers to locate purchasers. Since Smith's advertisements ran for months and since those advertisements did not appear until 1882, we can at least surmise that his books did not sell out quickly, if they sold out at all.

Beyond the questions about Smith's marketing and sales remain the questions about Smith's decision to self-publish his autobiography. One can certainly speculate about Smith's need for financial support in his later years, but there remains a disconnect between the institutional history presented in his book and the mode of publication Smith ultimately embraced. Rather than view that disconnect as evidence of tension between Smith and the church or as evidence of some failure on the part of one or the other, we should instead look to that disconnect to better understand the extraordinary limitations faced by Smith and the church he loved. Even a venerable minister whose one-hundredth birthday party was to be advertised in the *Recorder* could not secure publication with the A.M.E. book concern because profitability was so uncertain. As Eric Gardner has shown, profit — even economic sustainability — was always at issue for the *Recorder* and for the A.M.E. book concern.[26] The concern simply could not afford to take chances on something like Smith's book, which was written by a Black minister for Black readers and therefore depended on a buying public with demonstrably limited resources. Given these limitations and given that he hoped "when my body sleeps in the silent grave and my spirit is at rest, I trust this book may speak for me," Smith did what he could to ensure his book and the church's history would last.[27] First, he advertised his book nationally so readers around the country could have a chance to obtain it. And he appended Payne's history of Wilberforce University so the book would bear the marks of an "official" institutional history that might endure beyond the life of its author. These authorial choices turn Smith's self-publishing venture into something of a hybrid, that is, an institutionally sanctioned self-published text. Such a text could potentially enjoy wider circulation and stand a far greater chance of survival since it might interest readers who were curious either about Smith's life or the history of the denomination.

In addition to employing both a format and a marketing strategy that would help him reach Black churchgoers, Smith's *Biography* works thematically to remind his readers of the power, unity, and endurance of the A.M.E. church. Though the book itself is short on explicit lessons, Smith implicitly favors the development of community capital and real estate as vital ingredients in the success of the church. In fact, as Smith tells it, one of his first jobs in the newly established A.M.E. Church was within the Harrisburg circuit, where he collected "the means to buy lots and build churches, which I did there very successfully, and soon were seen the temples of God lifting their towering heads nearly all over the circuit."[28] Later, when he took up the work of starting a church in Washington, DC, and secured a property for the congregation, Smith found that his first meeting was threatened by "the colored people of the M.E. Church" who sent constables to prevent the congregation from meeting. Smith, though, was ready; he showed the constables a "lease for the ground and a receipt for the money we had paid for the school-house" and "they left the premises, and did not arrest me as the enemies of the A. M. E. Church had intended."[29] When faced with a similar situation in Little Washington, Pennsylvania, Smith called on fellow Masons and used the Masonic temple for meetings; soon thereafter, Smith obtained $900 and used the money to purchase land for a church. This process repeats itself as Smith founded churches in Brownsville, Pennsylvania; New Albany and Jeffersonville, Kentucky; Hartford and Bridgeport, Connecticut; Allegheny, Pennsylvania; and Xenia, Ohio. These buildings and congregations are lasting memorials to the efforts of David Smith and others like him who built the A.M.E. Church.

Along with his paeans to building, which have an obvious metaphorical cast in the *Biography*, Smith also insists on the importance of documentation. In doing so, Smith makes a series of claims about the significance of his own publication and its role in preserving the foundations of the institution he had helped to construct. Like the issue of obtaining real estate, the problem of documentation was present at the founding of the church. As he explains, "the Secretaryship, seemed to be the most difficult position" to fill in the early conference meetings "because there were so few men of color who could write sufficiently well as to keep correct minutes."[30] By the time of his book's publication, Smith might have counted himself among those "few men of color" who could keep a correct record of church history. He recalls, too, his first sermon at the A.M.E. Church in Washington, DC, during which he preached on "John iv: 29: 'Come see a man that told me all things that I ever did. Is not this Christ?' The text is so familiar to the people, even to this day, when I visit that great city, Washington, the subject and text is a traditional talk."[31] Though this might be stretching the point a bit, Smith does seem to align himself with Christ in that he is able to tell "all things" regarding the history of the church and its development. At the very least, he reminds readers of the importance of the "teller" within the religious community. As such a teller, Smith concludes his *Biography* with a metaphor linking him to the many churches he had built: "Now, at the close of nearly a century of years, I stand, as it were, up in the dome of African Methodism."[32]

As a longtime pastor and religious leader, Elijah Marrs certainly merits discussion alongside David Smith. At the same time, as a former sergeant in the Twelfth US Colored Artillery, Marrs is an important chronicler of the Civil War and of African American troops' contribution to the Union cause, so we might also read him as a historian. As if this were not enough, Marrs was a longtime schoolteacher and the first president of the Normal and Theological Institute (later State University and now Simmons College), so he also speaks to the challenges attending postwar education and institutional development. While Marrs resists easy categorization, the diversity of his accomplishments means that Marrs's life intersected with the public record in many ways, and, like so many of his fellow self-publishers, Marrs enmeshes his autobiography within a larger story told in newspapers, magazines, convention minutes, and government documents. By including dozens of extratextual references—dropped like so many breadcrumbs throughout his book—Marrs directs readers to consider his widespread influence and his abiding importance to African American life in Kentucky. Though he claimed that his *Life and History of the Rev. Elijah P. Marrs First Pastor of Beargrass Baptist Church, and Author* was not a work of "merit, but a book somewhat of value in a historical point of view," Marrs's use of the word "author" in his title betrays the false modesty in his preface. Marrs knew that he—like his life—was special, and he wanted to celebrate and commemorate his accomplishments so he could shape his legacy. Perhaps that is why he chose the sentence "We are only remembered for what we have done" as one of the epigraphs for the handsome octavo (twenty-three-centimeter) book, which he published at the job printing offices of Bradley and Gilbert in Louisville, Kentucky, in 1885 (fig. 5.1).[33]

Marrs's *Life and History* begins with his birth to an enslaved mother in 1840; along with his discussion of his enslavement, Marrs also notes that he learned to read at a young age because his enslaver "wanted all of the boys to learn how to read the Bible."[34] Marrs was obviously a quick study and an extremely intelligent young man, and he soon became an intellectual leader among the enslaved people in his neighborhood. During the war, Marrs would "read the newspapers as I would bring them from the post-office" and keep others "well posted as to the prevailing news." He also served as a messenger for the "colored soldiers who . . . sent their letters to their wives, sons, and daughters addressed to [Marrs's] care."[35] Once he enlisted in the army in 1864, Marrs was often employed as a writer for his fellow soldiers who would surround him "waiting [their] turn to have a letter written home."[36] From the start, then, Marrs is a messenger, a man who gives voice to others and who shares the news (both temporal and eternal) with his friends and neighbors.

Marrs's *Life and History* explores his Civil War service in detail and describes his participation in several skirmishes and minor conflicts during his two years in the army. Mostly, though, Marrs's history of the Civil War is devoted to memorializing the "the part our soldiers took" in the war and noting his own work as a leader both within the army and among the African American men and women who relied on the troops for assistance.[37] As a sergeant, Marrs was especially helpful to "the wives and families of men who had gone into war" who were in need of protection since "their former masters [had] driven them from their homes"; these women and children "looked to [Marrs] as if [he] were their Saviour."[38] As he does when he describes his willingness to read the papers or write letters for others, Marrs presents himself as a helpful servant whose manifest gifts obligate him to help others.

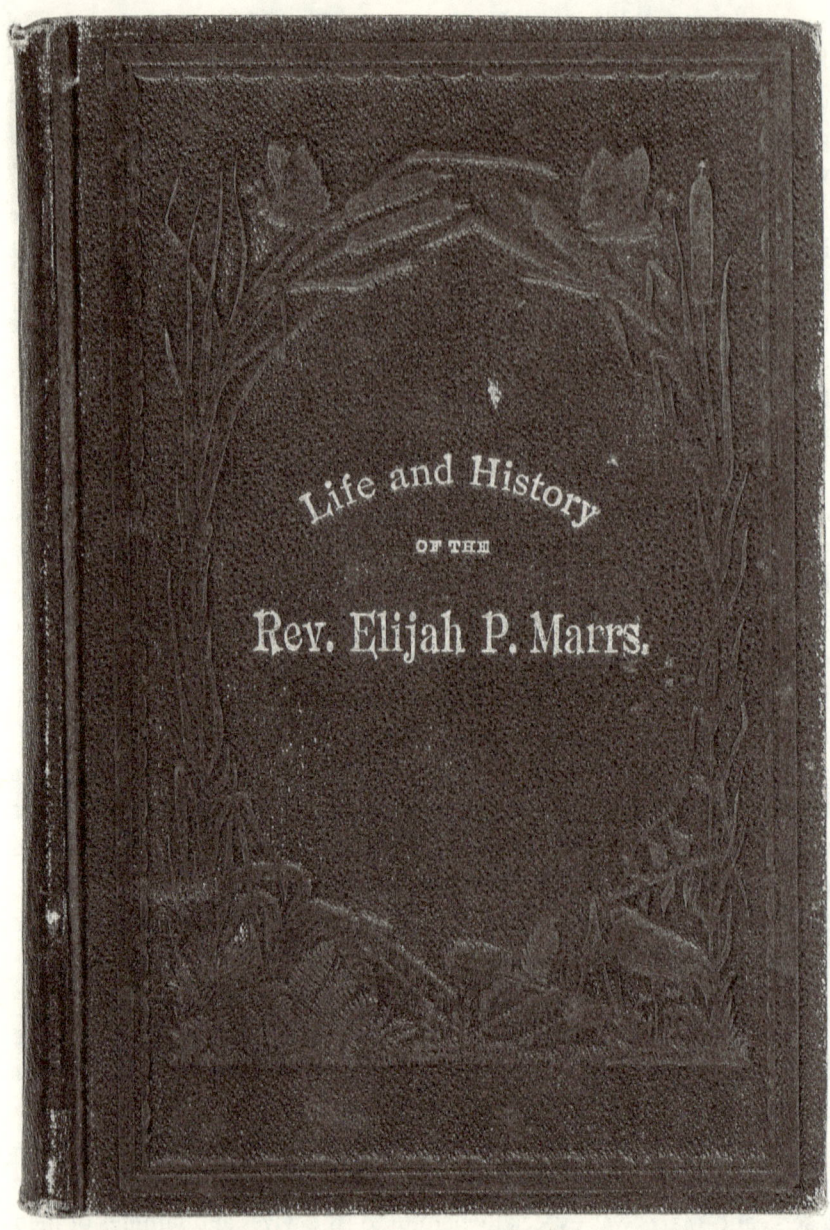

FIGURE 5.1 Cover of Elijah Marrs's *Life and History* (1885). Note the stamped cover and gilt lettering. Courtesy of the American Antiquarian Society.

After the war, Marrs turned to service of other kinds: as a schoolteacher in several towns in Kentucky, as secretary of the Loyal League (an anti–Ku Klux Klan group), as the president of the Republican club of Oldham County, and, eventually, as the founding president of Kentucky Baptist Seminary, the first African American college in the state. As his narrative moves toward its conclusion, Marrs begins to share more and more of his accomplishments, and to verify (or expand on) those accomplishments, he reprints numerous letters and newspaper stories. For example, when describing his success on the state examination for teachers, Marrs quotes the *American Baptist*: "'All over the State white teachers are failing and the colored ones passing. Nothing will keep the black man back. He will pass.'" Letting the *American Baptist* speak for him, Marrs follows up with a bit of modesty admitting that the "flattering compliment was almost too much for me to bear."[39]

Whereas many African American autobiographies include testimonials and certificates as paratexts, Marrs incorporates those same documents in his narrative, suggesting that his late-in-life achievements vouch for his truthfulness concerning his life before he became a public figure. Or, perhaps Marrs wanted to remind his readers of how much he had done as he felt his own achievements being eclipsed by those of other men. Describing his work with the Normal and Theological Institute, he muses "not much is said in favor of its founder now, but . . . if you search the record closely, you will find that E. P. Marrs has saved the life of the Educational Cause of the Baptist Church of this State."[40] Marrs's use of capital letters is particularly interesting in this context; he memorializes his own contributions by imagining a new institution (the "Educational Cause") that he both served and saved. More than this, Marrs insists on the importance of a "record" and provides his readers with some clues as to how that record might be searched. Indeed, Marrs lists or reprints the names of friends and parishioners, contemporaneous news reports (from the *New York Witness, American Baptist, American Citizen,* and *Monthly Magazine*), documents (county and state licenses, legislative records) and conference proceedings (Baptist General Association meetings from 1873 to 1884, the Republican National Convention in 1876, the Kentucky State Convention in 1882, and the National Convention of Colored Men in 1883). For Marrs, the citation of publicly available texts serves to locate the author's book within a broader discursive field of which the author is already a part. Book publication becomes *one among many* public rhetorical gestures and expands on (or, perhaps, modifies) those extant gestures. Self-published autobiographies like Marrs's can be read as keys to decoding the diffuse catalog of speeches, letters, and records in which they are situated. The narrative is not necessarily the most important text nor the one "true" text; rather, it is the text that outlines a lifetime of contributions.

Among those contributions, Marrs's most significant work was within the Baptist Church. He was ordained as a minister in 1874 and soon thereafter attended the Baptist College at Nashville so he could "make a more thorough study of the Bible, and . . . become better acquainted with the cardinal doctrines of the Baptist denomination."[41] Urging his readers to understand the twinned obligations of self-improvement and service, Marrs explains that after he attended college, he "felt . . . more able to preach than . . . before. The people thought that since I had been to college I was not very far from being perfect. My manner was more refined and my delivery was much improved."[42] Perhaps realizing how his "perfection" might have been received by readers, Marrs quickly adds, "I tried . . . to . . . let [the people] see I felt myself no better than they were."[43] After occupying several different pulpits during the first part of his career, he was eventually called to the Beargrass Baptist Church in Louisville in 1880; Marrs would continue to serve as the pastor at Beargrass and as the treasurer of the General Association of Colored Baptists until his death in 1910.[44]

Reading through Marrs's *Life and History*, one glimpses a striver very much like the relentless and indefatigable Booker T. Washington, another man who was born to an enslaved mother, worked diligently to educate himself, and went on to lead an educational institution in which he took enormous pride. Like Washington, Marrs favored institutional solutions to social and economic problems: he supported schools, churches, organizations like the United Brothers of Friendship (UBF), and vigilance societies like the Loyal League. These biographical details mirror certain strategies of self-representation as well. Marrs presents himself as a gifted young man who demonstrates a capacity for leadership even at a young age; and, like Washington, Marrs uses the press to sing his praises while, on occasion, sublimating himself. Given Marrs's deep institutional commitments and his remarkable accomplishments, it remains surprising that he self-published his book with a job printer. Though he claimed that his publication "brought him considerable revenue," it seems to have been printed in only one edition, and there is little evidence beyond Marrs's own assertion that the book enjoyed a wide readership.[45] It may be that Marrs's inability to find a publisher is another example of the well-known limitations that impacted so many African Americans, though it is also true that many white and Black ministers before and after Marrs self-published their life stories.

Even if Marrs never tried to locate a publisher for his book, his choice of a printer is an interesting one since it connects the project of printing to the communitarian focus of Marrs's *Life and History*. Marrs may have selected the printers Bradley & Gilbert because they employed William Butcher, a Black pressman who worked at the firm for over thirty-five years and seems to have been one of the few Black printers in the entire city.[46] In fact, according to William H. Gibson, who wrote a history of the United Brothers of Friendship (a Black benevolent society in Louisville), "much of the knowledge [Bradley & Gilbert] acquired of the printing business was obtained under the tutelage of Mr. Butcher."[47] If Marrs did select the firm of Bradley & Gilbert for this reason, he was also charting a course for his UBF lodge brother William H. Gibson, who would choose the same printer when he penned his history of the United Brothers of Friendship years later. There were more than twenty job printing firms in Louisville during the 1880s and 1890s, so we can assume the two men were choosing to patronize businesses that had some connection to the Black community in their hometown.[48] By doing so, both men show how self-publication could potentially enrich even those African Americans who were not authors themselves.

Battles for Acceptance: Jarena Lee's Autobiographies

When George White published his narrative in 1810, he documented a multiyear battle for acceptance in the M.E. Church. Like White, Jarena Lee spent years trying to gain institutional sanction for her preaching; whereas White had to convince church leaders that *he* was capable of reading and interpreting the Bible, Lee had to convince A.M.E. leaders that any woman could understand and proclaim God's word from the pulpit. As such, in the first edition of *The Life and Religious Experience of Jarena Lee*, the preacher-cum-author plays the role of a religious entrepreneur seeking to spread both the good news and the idea that women could share that good news with a congregation. As she confronted institutional gender proscriptions, Lee, like White, used the dream vision as evidence of God's favor for her mission. In fact, near the conclusion of her 1836 *Life*, Lee seems to realize how important dreams have been to her religious growth and her narrative, and she offers readers an explanation for the outsize influence of these deeply personal religious experiences. Comparing herself to a blind or deaf person whose other senses are more acute, Lee notes that since she "never had more than three months schooling," she "watched more closely the operations of the Spirit, and have in consequence been lead thereby."[49] Those "operations," manifest in a series of dream visions that shape and guide Lee as she grows in her faith; in fact, Lee describes no fewer than nine dreams and visions in her twenty-four-page *Life*.

As is typical of a spiritual autobiography, Lee's first vision is the one that leads her to conversion, and she experiences that vision in church as Richard Allen began his sermon. Lee explains that, immediately after Allen spoke, "there appeared to *my* view, in the centre of the heart *one* sin . . . at this discovery I said, *Lord* I forgive *every* creature. That instance, it appeared to me, as if a garment . . . split at the crown of my head, and was stripped away from me . . . when the Glory of God seemed to cover me in its stead."[50] The intensity of this vision accords with those of other narrators who commemorate their conversions, but what stands out as well is Lee's use of pronouns (my, me, I) that highlight the individual nature of religious experience. The vision and its meaning belong entirely to her, and she would continue to see and interpret visions in the years to come: a vision of the gulf of hell over which she stood balanced, a "form of fire," a shepherd and his sheep, and Jesus on the cross.[51] Of particular importance among these visions is the one she experiences after she asks the "Lord . . . if he had called [her] to preach." Almost immediately, "there appeared to [her] view the form and figure of a pulpit, with a Bible lying thereon, the back of which was presented to me as plainly as if it had been a literal fact."[52] Her dreams leave her, as Frances Smith Foster insists, with a "strong conviction of her own authority."[53] Lee uses dream visions to explain her personal ambitions and desires and to justify those desires for readers and for church leaders. This would have been a particularly effective rhetorical strategy for someone in Lee's position since, as Eileen Razzari Elrod argues, a dreamer who announces her divine authorization becomes "an observer of the divine action occurring in her own body"; thereafter, she can "assert her authority by . . . continuing, ironically, to deemphasize her own agency."[54] In Lee's case, deemphasizing her own agency and insisting on divine authorization allowed her to justify her radical break with tradition and church leadership.[55]

Lee drives home this point when she describes her meeting with Richard Allen in the days after she envisioned the pulpit and Bible. Citing her dream, Lee tells Allen that "[she] felt it [her] *duty* to preach the gospel."[56] Responding to Lee's conviction, Allen permits her to work as an exhorter but demurs when she presses him about occupying a pulpit. Even though Allen had dealt with unreasonable discrimination himself, he seems to have regarded the dissolution of the gender barrier a bridge too far. Lee sees the hypocrisy of his position, though, and she offers a general statement that Allen and other church leaders might have used themselves in somewhat different circumstances: "O how careful we ought to be, lest through our by-laws of church government and discipline, we bring into disrepute even the word of life."[57] Lee understands the tension between institutional legitimacy (or the perception thereof) and true, Christian equality, and she demands that institutions founded on the latter preserve their commitment to the word. By narrating a dream vision in which the word itself was presented to her, Lee confirms that God has given her the right to speak from the pulpit concerning the Bible; it is a *man* and not the Lord who has restricted Lee.

Eventually, Richard Allen would become one of Lee's strongest supporters, and he encouraged her to use her gifts as a preacher until the end of his life. Lee's gospel labors required her to travel throughout the free states and Canada West (Ontario); in the 1820s, she regularly journeyed over a thousand miles in a single year. Because her focus was always on extending the reach of the gospel, Lee may have been particularly driven to "print a book," and she "had some friends to encourage" her as well. But after Lee first published the slight octavo version (nineteen centimeters) of her *Life* in 1836, she was at a loss for how to "dispose of" it because she feared selling the book would "appear . . . too much like merchandize." Soon thereafter, she met "Bishop Allen's widow who bought one." Just as the Reverend Allen had supported Lee in her preaching, his widow supported her in her publishing. This dual sanction seemed to remove Lee's fears about selling, and, as she notes, within four months she was able to pay "sixty dollars . . . for the expenses" (presumably the cost of setting, printing, and stitching the pamphlet).[58]

In the merger of proselytizing and publishing, Lee blazed a trail that other A.M.E. ministers would follow in the years to come, but, despite her effectiveness as both a preacher and bookseller, Lee never won the kind of institutional support she deserved. After Allen's death in 1831, male A.M.E. leaders marginalized Lee more and more, and they refused to sponsor the 1839 republication of her 1836 pamphlet. Indeed, Lee recalled her financial difficulties in the wake of spending thirty-eight dollars to print 1,000 copies of her pamphlet in 1839. Perhaps Lee was willing to endure those difficulties because she believed in the effectiveness of her autobiography as a religious tool and because "from the smallness of [the] pamphlet," she could not "go through with the whole of my journal . . . which, if the Lord be willing, may at some future day be published."[59] In 1836 and 1839, then, Lee was still hoping she would be able to print and sell her lengthy journal, but she did not yet have the financial resources to do so. Lee may have believed that by self-publishing and demonstrating the salability of her work, she could inspire the church to subsidize future publications. Or she may have hoped that continued book sales would help her make enough money to pay for those publications herself.

If Lee hoped for the church's assistance, those hopes were misplaced. As Daniel Payne wrote in his *History of the African Methodist Episcopal Church*, the men of the A.M.E. book committee agreed that "The manuscript of Sister Jarena Lee has been written in such a manner that it is impossible to decipher much of the meaning contained in it."[60] Whatever its faults—a meandering and somewhat repetitive style, for example—Lee's *Journal* is anything but opaque. It seems clear enough that the men of the book concern just did not want to publish the journal and refused to do so. In response, Lee—once again—published her own story. The 1849 *Religious Experience and Journal of Mrs. Jarena Lee* remained an octavo pamphlet, but it contains all but the two concluding paragraphs of Lee's 1836 *Life* and appends nearly seventy pages of new material describing her preaching and bookselling career. Lee's decision to self-publish at significant cost with uncertain economic rewards must be understood as what Foster calls a "consciously political act" rooted in defiance of man-made institutions.[61]

This is not to say that "much of the meaning" of Lee's 1849 pamphlet is, itself, the defiance of those institutions. Lee remained a passionate supporter of both Christian faith and the A.M.E. Church itself, and she wanted to further the work of Christ and the church by selling her books. Even so, I want to attend particularly to the act of selling, not because it represents an attempt at crass "merchandize" or self-enrichment, but because Lee's willingness (and ability) to profit by her own pen highlights the differences between an individual self-publisher and the A.M.E. book concern, which, as Daniel Payne would write years later, was "always in debt and unable to pay."[62] Lee was what Michaël Roy calls an "itinerant author," who was deeply committed to the project of making and marketing her work. As Lee writes, she "preached and sold my books, and paid my own way," which reminds us that her motivations were both religious and personal.[63] Put another way, one of the reasons Lee's books sold widely was because her life was structured around the combined work of preaching and bookselling. A large publisher could never put the same energy into marketing a book that Lee herself could provide, and it is this energy that helped her "[gain] many hundreds of dollars for the connexion."[64] Lee's autobiographies are not institutional histories of the sort produced by the book concern but the personal history of a faithful woman on a physical and spiritual journey. So, even though her narratives always lacked an explicit institutional sanction, that may have been one reason they sold so well.

A Dangerous Man: Major James Wilkerson Attacks the A.M.E. Church

Like Jarena Lee, Major James Wilkerson would experience a life-changing supernatural encounter, though his encounter seems to have ruined a once-promising ministerial career. According to his various autobiographical writings, Major James Wilkerson was born in Virginia around 1810 and was of the "Bengal Anglo-Saxon and Powhatan blood." Wilkerson boasted that he was "the grandson of the Col Wilkerson that fought with General Gates at the Battle of Saratoga."[65] As it turns out, though, that may not have been much to celebrate. Writing about Col. Wilkinson in 1889, Theodore Roosevelt explained that he was a traitor who "had no conscience and no scruples [and] had not the slightest idea of the meaning of the word honor."[66] Whether or not Major James Wilkerson was truly related to the infamous colonel, the younger man was certainly enslaved from birth, and after he converted to Christianity in 1831, he was sold and taken deeper into the South to New Orleans. Though being taken south at this time was undoubtedly a terrible fate for most enslaved men, Wilkerson was comparatively fortunate. Prized for his literacy, which he had gained with the help of a Virginia Quaker named Lucy Harris, Wilkerson was purchased by the New Orleans merchant and businessman Richard Clague, who, in 1833, left for England to marry an African American woman.[67] Before he left, Clague told those he enslaved that they could work during his absence to earn the money to purchase themselves.

Wilkerson was a talented and energetic young man, and he welcomed this opportunity. He worked "at several printing presses . . . the Argus, Evening Courier, Louisianan, True American, and others," and he eventually earned enough money to purchase his freedom when Clague returned in 1835.[68] Wilkerson left New Orleans in June 1835 and visited his mother in Virginia; thereafter, he began moving about the country and preaching in the Methodist Episcopal Church. In 1838, Wilkerson attended the A.M.E. conference in Cincinnati; he joined the church during the conference and accepted a position as a missionary that took him "throughout the West, yea, and even in the South, say as far down as New Orleans, the writer's old and esteemed home."[69] These were early days for the A.M.E. Church in the west, and Wilkerson moved into leadership positions with some rapidity; in 1840, he was appointed to a circuit in the Indiana Conference under Elder David Smith. Benjamin T. Tanner, who had seen Wilkerson preach in Indiana, remembered Wilkerson's "extensive reading" and "acquaintance with human nature." As he recalled, Wilkerson "preached mostly by comparison, and would often make use of some circumstance in his slave life to illustrate the condition of the sinner."[70]

Though Wilkerson does not mention it in his memoirs, he also served as a community and quasi-military leader amid rampant anti-Black violence in Cincinnati in 1841. According to John Mercer Langston, who was an eyewitness to the violence long before he served in Congress or wrote his life's history, Wilkerson was appointed the leader for Black Cincinnatians when they found themselves under assault from whites. Langston wrote of Wilkerson, "never did man exhibit on the field of danger greater coolness, skill and bravery, than this champion of his people's cause. A negro himself, he fought in self-defence, and to maintain his own rights as well as those of the people whom he led."[71] Wilkerson must have enjoyed a bit of renown in the wake of his efforts in Cincinnati, and perhaps that renown enabled him to work more effectively as a missionary and fundraiser for the church in and around Ohio. Or perhaps Wilkerson's experience as a fundraiser for the Indianapolis A.M.E. congregation in 1842 made him a natural choice for the work. Whatever the reason, when the Ohio Conference of the A.M.E. Church voted in 1845 to establish an "institution of a high order" named Union Seminary, they appointed Wilkerson to gather funds to support the institution and—according to a church historian—promised to pay him "one third of all he might collect."[72] In the meantime, the seminary, which also included a home for orphans and retired ministers, functioned in a basement of the Columbus A.M.E. chapel.

Wilkerson was a diligent laborer on behalf of the seminary. He spent years raising funds from white and Black supporters, and he obtained many in-kind contributions of books and materials as well. Wilkerson insisted it was difficult to raise money in the 1840s because "there were so many imposters out upon the good patience of the public, some to purchase wife and children."[73] As a Black man soliciting donations, Wilkerson had to distinguish himself from "imposters," which he did by obtaining recommendations from the governor of Ohio and other political leaders. This seemed not to have made a significant difference, though, and by 1849 Wilkerson found that—his solicitations of materials notwithstanding—because he had collected almost no money, the conference could not pay him any cash and offered him only one-third of the books he had collected. Since Wilkerson "did not care to accept either books or materials" as payment, he chose to "go ahead, and at the next ensuing Conference, to have a final settlement."[74] By this, Wilkerson seems to have meant that he wanted to work for one more year and then collect all his earnings in 1850.

The next year was a year of crisis for Wilkerson: With his mission and need for money both at the front of his mind, he left his family to travel the road in search of donations. Soon, though, he found himself nearing the breaking point with his health failing, his faith waning, and his confidence in his fundraising abilities shattered. On December 27, 1849, as Wilkerson was traveling from Albany to Boston, he remembered that "a most terrific shock smote him upon the crown of his head." Wilkerson felt that it was a "stroke of death," but it was, instead, a visitation by Satan himself.[75] In the decisive battle with the devil, Wilkerson prevailed, but the battle left him scarred and broken. After the battle, he had "a shattered nervous system of the brain, going continually with a shave head, with a white spot of hair, in attest of the severe neuralgia in the head."[76] All of this suggests that Wilkerson may well have had a *literal* stroke and that his failing condition throughout the 1850s was really a case of physical and mental disability. As he reports in his *History*, when he was traveling around New England in 1850, "the mental powers of the writer were somewhat impaired, and it was necessary that he should keep as quiet as possible through this trying period of his journey through life."[77] Further corroboration of Wilkerson's health crisis can be seen in a notice from the July 17, 1850, *Western Christian Advocate* explaining that the leaders of the A.M.E. church were seeking "information concerning their seminary agent, Rev. M. J. Wilkerson. The last communication received of him was in November last [i.e., 1849] and he was expected subsequently to be in Michigan. It is thought that some misfortune has befallen him."[78] A couple of weeks later, at the 1850 Ohio annual conference, Wilkerson was nowhere to be found. During the Tuesday, August 6 session, Rev. John Mifflin Brown—the principal of Union Seminary—proposed a resolution sympathizing with Wilkerson's wife. Later (after he commented on the helpfulness of his assistant, a twenty-five-year-old Frances Ellen Watkins), Brown insisted on the "importance of . . . appointing another Agent to fill the place of Rev. M. J. Wilkerson, who has left us in a mysterious manner."[79] The nature of Brown's comments suggests the elders of the church were certainly concerned about Wilkerson's well-being, but they were also concerned about the whereabouts of the money he was supposed to be collecting.

Writing years later in his autobiography, Wilkerson indicated that his condition in the early 1850s was such that a physician noted "the disordered state of [Wilkerson's] brain," and claimed that "it was absolutely necessary that [the patient] should retire to some remote place on the sea coast, where he might be benefitted by the salt water."[80] Wilkerson must have heeded this advice since the October 1850 *Western Christian Advocate* notes that he had just arrived in Jamaica, and the May 1851 *Madison Daily Banner* indicates he had just returned from "Jamaica and other distant countries by way of New Orleans."[81] According to the notice in the *Banner* (printed on three successive days), Wilkerson planned to lecture at the A.M.E. Church in Madison, Indiana, where, he indicated, "something will be said about Liberia."[82] At this point, one can imagine why the church elders were beginning to treat Wilkerson with a bit of wariness: After years of working as a fundraiser and delivering no money, he had disappeared without a trace and gone to Jamaica for the winter only to return and begin lecturing.

One year later, in August 1852, Wilkerson attended the Ohio annual conference of the A.M.E., which was held in Cincinnati. He managed to deliver the opening prayer on one day of the conference, but the minutes from the meeting make it clear that Wilkerson was still suffering. On the morning of August 13, the members of the conference passed a resolution noting that "the mind of our beloved brother, M. J. Wilkerson, from causes unknown to us, has become impaired, so much so, that he cannot labor in the Itinerancy, nor attend to his domestic affairs, and claims of his family." By the afternoon, the conference had raised $21.15 and trusted Rev. A. R. Green to manage the money and bring Wilkerson's wife from Philadelphia to Columbus, Ohio, so she could be reunited with her husband.[83] This act of generosity suggests the brethren maintained some goodwill toward Wilkerson. At the same time, the conference appropriated money for Wilkerson's family (and not Wilkerson himself) and insisted another minister manage the money and make transportation arrangements. Obviously, generosity was mixed with a degree of skepticism.

There is no explanation—either in Wilkerson's book or in the print record—of how the family managed to survive once they were reunited in Ohio, but Wilkerson was not wholly idle, and he redirected his fundraising energies to other pursuits. In 1850 Wilkerson helped establish the Educational Orphan Institute and began raising money on behalf of "widows and orphans"; he claimed to have raised over $1,400 in cash, secured land valued at more than $2,000, and supplied more than $4,000 worth of books.[84] One can imagine that Wilkerson's repeated absences from home (a fact he laments on several occasions in his *History*) led him to embrace the cause of the disadvantaged widows and orphans. At the same time, readers will sense Wilkerson's feelings of guilt and regret as he insists his work as a fundraiser left his family alone and made him into "a husband to the widow, and a father to the fatherless."[85] This guilt must have been added to the lingering anguish he felt as he realized that Union Seminary would never exist in the form he had long imagined and worked to realize. The seminary was plagued by a lack of resources and a lack of interest among the A.M.E. leadership, and by the 1855 the leaders had decided to move their long-hoped-for institution to a tract of land just outside of Xenia, Ohio. Wilberforce University—a collaboration of the A.M.E. Church and M.E. Church—opened its doors in 1856, and this left Union Seminary in a state of limbo.

After more than a decade of enervating labor on behalf of an institution that would never open, Wilkerson had every reason to feel a sense of loss, emptiness, and even resentment, which is certainly one of the reasons he committed to self-publishing as an economic venture in the late 1850s. Wilkerson had spent his adult years working as a printer, preacher, and fundraiser, and he knew that print (especially combined with exhortation) could be a powerful impetus to charitable giving. So Wilkerson combined his talent with words with his talent for selling and began hawking pamphlets, images, and ephemera as he traveled around the United States. In his *History* (1861), Wilkerson claims to have printed and sold thousands of copies of his own lithograph, as well as "pamphlets . . . alphabets . . . and epistles and addresses" for over $3500 (see fig. 5.2). He is proud to note that he "duly ministered unto his own wants, as in the case of the apostle Paul, in the last several years of his travelling to and fro through the United States, say from 5000 to 10,000 miles per year, going about, as in the case of his Lord, doing good. Yea, he having of the above sum faithfully divided about $3,300 in cash among the poor widows and orphans."[86]

Wilkerson's recording of his sales successes indicates he understood publishing as an entrepreneurial activity necessitated by the penury he suffered in the service of the church, and his "disordered brain" and disordered prose recall the work of other wandering authors who sold their likenesses along with their stories as they tried to stay alive on the margins of American society. At the same time, Wilkerson spent more than a decade traveling about as a fundraiser, and his money-making was directed at more than just self-sufficiency. Given his success in soliciting charitable donations through print offerings, Wilkerson's turn to autobiography in the late 1850s may have been motivated by something besides his desire to raise money for widows, orphans, and himself.

But in the next place, how is the writer to be supported whilst in this feeble state of body and mind? answer, rather than depend upon said Conference for support, he had struck off and sold of

His own Lithograph,	3500, at 40 cents each,		$1400
Lithograph of B. L.	2500, at 25	do.	625
G. Epistles,	4000, at 12	do.	480
Pamphlets,	4000, at 12	do.	480
Alphabets,	2000, at 15	do.	300
Epistles and Addresses	3000, at 10	do.	300
		Total Amount	$3585

FIGURE 5.2 Detail from Wilkerson's *History* (1861) showing a list of publications sold and amounts earned. Courtesy of the American Antiquarian Society.

I believe that Wilkerson's two broadsides (1859, 1865) and his octavo (twenty-two-centimeter) pamphlet autobiography titled *Wilkerson's History* (1861) were part of a campaign he waged against the A.M.E. Church and its leadership. Though the *History* is the longest of those publications, the first text in that campaign was Wilkerson's 3,000-word broadside, *The Midnight Cry* (1859), which devotes equal time to Wilkerson's story and to speculation on the year of Christ's return to earth (see fig. 5.3). The autobiographical portions of the broadside describe Wilkerson's enslavement, his conversion to Christianity, his purchase of his freedom from Richard Clague, and his peripatetic life as a missionary and minister of the gospel. Wilkerson's broadside raises several questions too: First, there is the matter of where and how it was printed and distributed. Though the sheet explains that it was printed by a William Quinn, a Philadelphia card and job printer, it carries a newspaper-like masthead indicating that *The Midnight Cry* emanated from New Orleans, perhaps indicating the special connection Wilkerson felt with the city where he purchased his freedom.[87] Second, there is the matter of just whom Wilkerson's *Cry* was supposed to address and what that address was supposed to accomplish. One might assume that Wilkerson wanted to sell copies of the broadside, but textual evidence from his *History* suggests otherwise: two years after he published his broadside, he explained that "he has

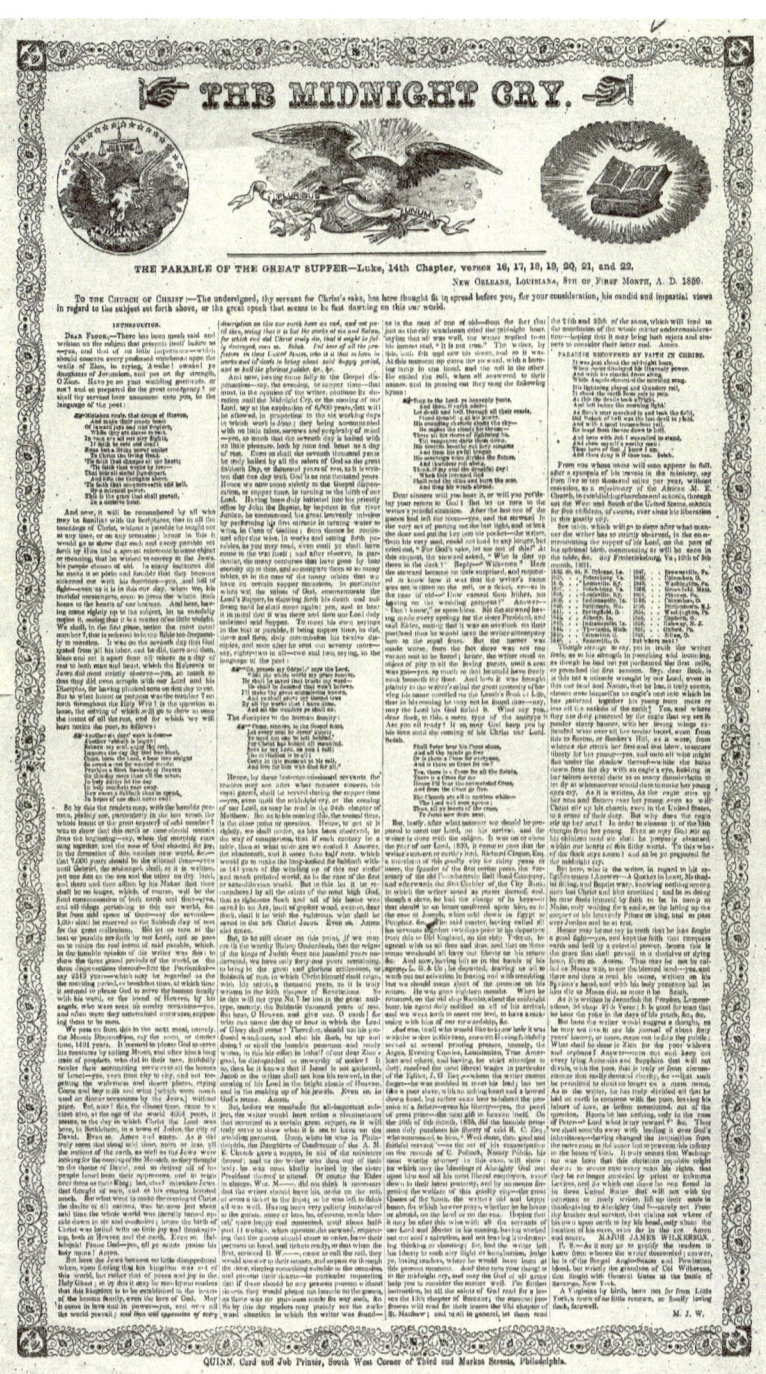

FIGURE 5.3 Wilkerson's self-published autobiographical broadside titled *The Midnight Cry* (1859). Courtesy of the American Antiquarian Society.

nothing . . . but a few copies of his Midnight Cry, that he disposes of in going around."[88] Notably, too, the broadside does not appear on the list of remunerative publications (fig. 5.3) that Wilkerson included in the History. This leads me to believe that The Midnight Cry was distributed gratis to warn people of the impending return of Christ and—more practically—to let people know that Wilkerson was working on a longer version of his life story, which would appear in print two years later.

Wilkerson's decision to publish his life story on the heels of The Midnight Cry was almost certainly driven by two factors. First, as I have suggested, Wilkerson wanted to capitalize on the print market he had been priming over the past few years as he circulated his engravings, religious literature, and The Midnight Cry. As he notes in his broadside, he was working on his "journal of about forty years' history," and he may have returned to former patrons with copies of the History.[89] Second, I believe Wilkerson published his History in 1861 as a response to questions about the appropriation of the funds he had raised for the church. At the twelfth quadrennial general conference meeting in Pittsburgh in 1860, the Reverend J. M. Brown asked the committee on education to "inquire and report whether there is any truth in the report put and continued in circulation, by M. J. Wilkerson, that some six hundred dollars, of money collected by him for the benefit of [Union] Seminary, has been improperly used."[90] In 1860, when he made this damning report, Wilkerson was sick, poor, and worn out in service; little wonder, then, that he was despondent over what he believed to be the misappropriation of $600. Was Wilkerson's complaint legitimate? Did it emerge from his frustration over spending years of his life traveling without adequate compensation? Or was he looking for an easy payday?

The investigatory committee assigned to evaluate Wilkerson's complaints reviewed the minutes of the Ohio Conference for 1856 and 1857 and determined that the funds had not been improperly used, but when we understand the context in which Wilkerson's first two publications appeared (immediately preceding and following the 1860 A.M.E. conference at which he made his complaint), we can imagine that Wilkerson's decision to self-publish was his method of announcing his side of a story that was either muted or ignored within the official records of the church.[91] Indeed, Wilkerson forecasts his sense of himself as an outsider in The Midnight Cry when he recalls being left out of a dinner for church leaders in Philadelphia; this sort of exclusion—which seems to be class-based—particularly rankled a preacher who had spent his life traveling to support others while his peers were "engaged in securing of farms, houses and lots, for themselves."[92] To Wilkerson, A.M.E. ministers seemed a self-interested group, and he consistently lamented both their personal greed and their lack of charity as he contrasted their actions with his.

This brings us back to the *History*, which Wilkerson pointedly directs to "THE CHRISTIAN COMMUNITY, AND THE PUBLIC IN GENERAL" as he identifies himself as a missionary for the Union Seminary and not a representative of the A.M.E. Church.[93] In fact, in both *The Midnight Cry* and the *History*, Wilkerson repeatedly aligns himself with the Quakers, several of whom came to his aid when he was ill. It seems that after being ignored and/or rejected in the 1850s and then being denied what he thought was a fair hearing in 1860, Wilkerson abandoned the A.M.E. Church altogether. Not only did he begin identifying himself as a Quaker, he also went about the country "abusing" the bishops of the A.M.E. Church and "circulating the most slanderous falsehoods" against the church hierarchy, suggesting that they still owed him $600.[94] At the 1864 A.M.E. general conference in Philadelphia, Dr. William Revels lamented these actions and insisted that Wilkerson had not been wronged. Revels claimed that Wilkerson was "unworth[y]" and a "mischievous and dangerous man;" Revels also asked that Wilkerson be "wholly discountenanced by our preachers and people" and have his bad character published in the "Christian Recorder and Anglo-African."[95] Wilkerson no longer occupied a pulpit at this point, so he was not drawing a salary, but Revels probably wanted to make sure the "mischievous" Wilkerson did not collect money from unsuspecting congregants (something he may have been doing as far back as 1851 when he lectured in Madison, Indiana).

Wilkerson's dismissal did not slow him down much. By 1865, Wilkerson had located a new audience among Indigenous people, including the Shinnecock on Eastern Long Island. To support this new ministry, Wilkerson printed a brand-new broadside titled *The Midnight Cry & Millennium Dawn*. The new publication featured none of the material from the original but instead included three songs that Wilkerson claimed to have sung in the "Royal Air" of Eastern Long Island.[96] Two years later, Wilkerson was still on the move representing himself as a Quaker ministering to Indigenous groups on both sides of the Mississippi River.[97] He may have visited the Powhatan tribe during his visit to Virginia in 1867, and a *Times-Picayune* report from later that year suggests that Wilkerson was also ministering to southern freedmen.[98]

Interestingly, after the 1867 report in the *Times-Picayune*, Wilkerson found his way back to the A.M.E. Church and he appears—almost as a ghostly presence—in letters published in the *Christian Recorder*.[99] While one might read this as a sign that he had formally rejoined the church, it is more likely that Wilkerson simply traded on his history and his friendships in order to find friendly audiences and perhaps a bit of financial support. In February 1874, he was in Savannah where he preached at the Sunday service in Henry McNeal Turner's church. Turner explained that Wilkerson was "taking his last tour through the United States, descanting upon the labors of Bishop Quinn, and trying (as he terms it) to funeralize the devil."[100] Turner alludes to Wilkerson's condition in his letter, noting that the aged minister "was represented to me as a man of odd eccentricities, and special idiosyncrasies, which made him a peculiar genius" and that it seemed he had "been reading the Arabian Nights, and were trying to imitate them." These suggestions aside, Turner insists that he "found [Wilkerson] to be as natural as other men." The tenor of Turner's letter indicates that, by 1874, Wilkerson was respected as a figure of historical importance and a living connection to the heroes of the past. When Wilkerson had been slandering the A.M.E. Church and its leaders, he had been a "dangerous man," but a decade later, those slanders were forgotten, and Wilkerson was—once again—an eccentric who could be humored or even lauded. This trend continued after his death in 1881 when a woman named Julia Roberts wrote a letter for the *Christian Recorder* in which she sought to raise funds for a memorial to Wilkerson. The memorial would celebrate "one among the pioneers of the A.M.E. connection."[101] Roberts's letter, like the church histories published in the 1880s and 1890s, demonstrates a willingness to grant Wilkerson a place of respect as an important figure in the early years of the Western A.M.E. Church and leave his more troublesome years out of the official record.[102] Wilkerson's story would expose ruptures, disagreements, and—perhaps—malfeasance, so the story remained untold, except in Wilkerson's own publications.

The books authored by preachers, missionaries, and exhorters are by far the most extensive and diverse form of self-publication in the nineteenth century, and they circulated in a variety of ways: They were sold or handed out in churches and at camp meetings, offered through the mail, and hawked on street corners in exchange for donations. Because the religious autobiography was so commonplace, it was particularly attractive to itinerant booksellers like Jarena Lee. A minister selling her story was someone more likely to be trusted and respected by citizens and authorities, and this was no small concern for a Black woman traveling alone in the antebellum United States. At the same time, the very conditions that made selling easier for a religious autobiographer could be exploited by men like Major James Wilkerson, and, as I suggest in the final chapter, the Rev. Robert Anderson.

CHAPTER SIX

A Grand Report in the Way of Selling
Publishing for Profit

Self-publishers brought a variety of motivations to their work; almost always, one of those motivations was economic. Most authors wrote and published so that they could capitalize within the localized print markets typical of the nineteenth-century United States. Whether those markets were composed of reform-oriented donors in Edmond Kelley's New Bedford, abolitionists in Levin Tilmon's New York, or uplift-minded supporters in Jacob Stroyer's Salem, each author-publisher tailored his or her book to meet the demands of a moment and an audience. This is not to diminish the goals and commitments of people like Kelley, Tilmon, and Stroyer; for each of them the economic motive coexisted with deeply held beliefs or pressing needs. In fact, the sale of most self-published books *depended* on those deeply held beliefs and needs since books by amateur authors were, as Ann Fabian reminds us, "insistently personal, both in their content and in the way they were marketed."[1] Self-publishers wanted to speak up for their books and explain their motivations, and the interactions between an author and potential customers allowed authors to do both. At the same time, localized print markets structured around interactions between an author and potential readers created opportunities that designing salespeople could exploit by telling customers what they wanted to hear.

Among African American self-publishers, there are several who seem to have placed profit before (or alongside) principle. Some—like Moses Roper or Henry Box Brown—made so much money as speakers and booksellers that they continued speaking and selling even after their initial reasons for doing so had been satisfied.[2] In 1840, after Roper had escaped from Georgia, moved to England, and authored his narrative, his former patron Thomas Price denounced him for ignoring his stated intention to get an education and, instead, pursuing a "permanent system of genteel begging."[3] Henry Box Brown spent decades on stage following his dramatic escape from his Virginia enslaver and his subsequent removal to England. Though Brown began his career by reliving his escape on stage and presenting a panorama entitled *The Mirror of Slavery*, efforts that were clearly linked to abolitionist goals (if not to abolitionist organizations), he went on to become a costumed actor and a magician who was, perhaps, "performing for his own mischievous pleasure and profit."[4] Postbellum authors like William O'Neill, Allen Parker, and Harry Smith wrote and sold books that traded heavily on myths and images drawn from "plantation fiction" of the sort authored by those like Joel Chandler Harris and Thomas Nelson Page. Though the autobiographers' stories may have been accurate, they seem to have been willing to make stylistic compromises to find readers in the marketplace.[5]

Some authors went well beyond making compromises and moved into outright fraud and deception. Lewis Charlton wrote and published the first edition of the *Sketch of the Life of Mr. Lewis Charlton, and Reminiscences of Slavery* in 1879 with the help of Edward Everett Brown. In his narrative, which was published in Portland, Maine, Charlton (who lived in Maryland) insisted that he was selling his book to help "colored youth to obtain an education."[6] Though he may have been sincere when he began soliciting donations for a school back in Maryland, by the time Charlton published his *Sketch* he had been from Baltimore, to Pennsylvania, to Boston and then Maine without ever returning home. His subsequent adventures would take him to Quebec and then New Brunswick (where he published another edition of his life story) and finally to England. In 1886, after he had been gone on his never-ending sales trip for more than seven years, his wife finally secured a divorce by citing her abandonment. Charlton would remain in England until his death in 1888.[7] Charlton's remarkable story reminds us that the unique markets for books in the nineteenth century remained—by their very nature—susceptible to manipulation by author-publishers, especially those who were willing to travel.

Among all the postwar compromisers and charlatans, no publisher was as designing or as successful as the Reverend Robert B. Anderson, who made a career out of selling to wealthy white Southerners who embraced the racist status quo. Robert B. Anderson did not create white supremacism, of course, but his economic rise paralleled and was, in part, enabled by waves of anti-Black legislation and violence in the American South during the post-Reconstruction period. Examples of this activity are, sadly, too numerous to count, but a few will make the point: In 1887, the Louisiana National Guard massacred thirty Black laborers striking for better wages and working conditions on the sugar plantations near Thibodaux. In March 1892, following a dispute at the Black-owned People's Grocery in Memphis, three Black men were lynched while being held in police custody. In November 1898, the virulent racist Alfred Waddell helped manufacture a riot that claimed the lives of 300 Black residents in Wilmington, North Carolina, and decimated the vibrant Black middle class in the city. In the wake of the riot he engendered,

Waddell had himself installed as mayor. These atrocities—and many more besides—are examples of white Southerners lashing out at Black citizens who sought economic power that let them live outside the paternalistic frameworks handed down from slavery. Black economic independence threatened white power, and, conversely, economic dependence ensured that no Black citizens rose above a certain station.[8] Amid the retrenchment that marked Southern politics in the post-Reconstruction period, Booker T. Washington used his platform at Tuskegee Institute to fight for expanded economic opportunities for Black Southerners, but Washington's program—for all its successes—did little to alter the political dynamic in the region.[9]

It was within this fraught social, political, and economic environment that the Reverend Robert B. Anderson found his niche. Enslaved at birth in 1819, Robert B. Anderson purchased his freedom in 1851. He turned fifty-eight on February 22, 1877. That birthday would prove to be a special one for Anderson, for it was on that day that he "consented to seat [himself] and write a history of [his] life."[10] These birthday writing sessions would become a ritual, and nearly every year thereafter, Anderson seated himself to write out the story of the year he just lived; he began selling that story in a pamphlet he circulated while he was working as a preacher and traveling from town to town in his native Georgia. After selling out his first edition, which was published between 1877 and 1881, Anderson published a second in 1882. This edition was significantly longer than the first and it detailed more of Anderson's history in and out of slavery as well as his growing frustration with the leadership of the African Methodist Episcopal (A.M.E.) Church, which he had joined in 1866 and would leave in 1882. Though no copies of Anderson's first or second edition are known to survive today, the text of the first two editions of *The Life* appears in subsequent editions of his book, including the heavily revised third edition, which Anderson published in 1891 (see table 6.1).

That third edition was printed by J. W. Burke of Macon, Georgia, and swelled to twice its previous length.[11] This edition was a large octavo volume (twenty-three centimeters) in paper covers, which included a list of prominent buyers who purchased the *previous* editions of *The Life*. The third edition must have sold well, for Anderson listed over 800 buyers of the book in the preface to his fourth edition, two versions of which he published in 1892. The hardcover fourth edition remained a large octavo and was again printed by J. W. Burke in at least two print runs; sales of the book precipitated and funded Anderson's travels to the North and West. The story of some of those travels makes up the body of Anderson's fifth autobiography, *The Anderson Surpriser*, which includes a list of over 600 purchasers on its first sixteen

TABLE 6.1 Robert B. Anderson's autobiographies

Edition	Year	Printer Location	Words	Notable Features
1	1879	?	7,000	Anderson describes his first publication as a pamphlet; it was written beginning in 1877 and published before 1879. Included in all of Anderson's subsequent publications except *The Anderson Surpriser*.
2	1882	Atlanta	30,000	This version adds 23,000 words to version 1; published as a pamphlet just before Anderson left the A.M.E. Church in 1882.
3	1891	Macon	68,000	This longer edition begins with Anderson leaving the A.M.E. Church at the end of 1883 and describes his life up to 1890. Wrapped in a paper cover. Twenty-three centimeters. Includes a list of famous Georgians recommending Anderson's book but no extensive list of "friends" who purchased previous editions.
4a*	1892	Macon	80,000	This 151-page book includes all the third edition and adds approximately 12,000 words describing Anderson's bookselling trips to June 1891. Bound in boards with a stamped cover and gilt lettering. Twenty-three centimeters. First version to include a list of "friends" who bought the previous version of the book.

TABLE 6.1 (*continued*)

Edition	Year	Printer Location	Words	Notable Features
4b*	1892	Macon	100,000	This 192-page book extends version 4a with more information about Anderson's life and bookselling trips up to August 1892. Bound in boards with a stamped cover and gilt lettering. Twenty-three centimeters.
				Includes the same list of "friends" as version 4a.
5*	1895	Macon	53,000	Titled *The Anderson Surpriser*, this is a completely new book that tells the story of Anderson's bookselling trips in 1893–94. Bound in boards with a stamped cover and gilt lettering. Twenty-three centimeters.
				Includes a new list of "friends" who bought versions 4 and 4a.
6*	1900	Atlanta	115,000	This is an expanded edition of version 4b with a new introduction titled "The Anderson Trumpet." Also includes a closing section titled "The Origin of the White Man" that originally appeared in *The Anderson Surpriser*. Bound in boards with a stamped cover and gilt lettering. Twenty-four centimeters.
				Includes a new list of "friends," presumably those who bought version 5.

*Text available online via subscription or public access website.

pages. Like the fourth edition, the *Surpriser* was printed in Macon by J. W. Burke, bound in boards, and adorned with an engraving of Anderson and a photograph of his family on the frontispiece.

By the time he published his final edition in 1900, Anderson had been selling his books full time for nearly a decade, and he sought out a new printer to help him produce and distribute them. That is why Anderson published the final version of *The Life of Rev. Robert Anderson* at Foote & Davies, an Atlanta printer with one of the largest operations in Georgia. According to the printers, who inserted a short note at the beginning of the book, Anderson's newest publication was "about to be introduced into the colored schools." The printers stood to benefit from this, of course, but they also insisted that the "inculcation into the minds and hearts of the pupils of the principles which have governed his life can not fail to raise the race to a higher plane and minimize, if not altogether eliminate, the difficulties of the 'race problem.'"[12] The very fact that Anderson was talked about in such terms is remarkable for a man who had been an enslaved laborer, a drayman, a whitewasher, and a preacher turned out of both the A.M.E. and Methodist Episcopal (M.E.) Churches. What "principles" had governed his life, and how could they eliminate the "race problem" that so vexed the American South? In reality, the principles the publisher references were indistinguishable from those promoted by white supremacists. By all appearances, Anderson was a deeply cynical man who used his position as a minister to exploit congregants and then used his position as a formerly enslaved man to exploit a market for white supremacy in the post-Reconstruction South. If Anderson did these things for any reason but to make money, that reason remains opaque; if Anderson ever had qualms about what he did, those qualms remain hidden.

What is amazing about Anderson is not his cynicism, but just how profitable his cynicism turned out to be. For over a decade, the septuagenarian Anderson supported himself and his family by selling a self-published autobiography in almost every state east of the Mississippi River. In purely economic terms, his accomplishment dwarfs that of every other author in this book. In fact, Anderson represents a limit case for self-publishing since he demonstrates what an author-publisher might accomplish if he or she committed him- or herself only to selling aggressively within a particular market. Anderson produced a book that is about its own processes of production and door-to-door distribution in the post-Reconstruction South. As his book evolved over the last twenty years of its author's life, Anderson learned that the key to making money as an author was not producing a true story or even a compelling story. Indeed, the story seems not to have mattered at all; what mattered instead was the model of Black deference and economic dependence that Anderson projected in his writing and personal interactions.

The Life in the Beginning

The first edition of Anderson's *Life* is quite short and probably circulated in pamphlet form in cities and towns of Bibb and Washington Counties in central Georgia.[13] *The Life* sketched an outline of Anderson's first fifty-odd years, years that saw him rise in the world despite his enslavement and pervasive anti-Black racism. In fact, Anderson paints white Southerners in a flattering light as he notes that his former enslaver required little work of him, allowed him to hire his time, and refused to separate Anderson from his wife.[14] Working as a painter in Macon throughout the 1840s, Anderson made enough to purchase his wife for $500 and himself for $1,000 (in 1846 and 1851, respectively). At the end of the 1840s, he began working as a Sunday school leader and exhorter in the Methodist Episcopal Church, and he was finally called to be a minster in the A.M.E. Church in 1866. Since his ministerial labors required him to move from church to church and town to town, Anderson had to leave Macon for long periods of time, and he imagined his *Life* as a "memorial" for the people of his hometown, "both white and colored."[15]

In this brief "memorial," Anderson shares two important lessons that would serve him well in his career as an author, publisher, and bookseller. The first of these lessons came to him in 1839, when the still enslaved and just married Anderson took up the "business of whitewashing." For his first job, he chose a house that was "very much exposed" and therefore "noticed by all;" widespread notice turned into consistent work, and before long Anderson "began to get up a little as a whitewasher."[16] Like Ben Franklin trundling his wheelbarrow through the streets on a Sunday, Anderson cultivated a reputation for himself through thoughtful "exposure," and he eventually amassed thousands of dollars in cash and property.

As the years went on, Anderson seems to have learned that hard work and publicity were but pieces of a complicated economic puzzle, and he began to cultivate relationships with whites who could assist him. As an agent for the A.M.E. Church in the 1860s, Anderson traveled around Georgia raising money to build churches or fund improvements to existing churches. In the years immediately following the Civil War, Anderson found support from Black men and women wanting, and so he "turned to the white citizens."[17] Among whites, Anderson met with "kindness of feeling from every one," and he would go on to obtain donations and loans from whites to fund the building of his house, an A.M.E. Church, and a moneymaking rail excursion from Macon to Griffin.[18] Though Anderson sought sympathy and friendship among other Blacks, he found that "white friends" were far more likely to offer him substantial material support. As William L. Andrews notes, the term "friends" has a very particular meaning within the crucible of Southern race relations. Before emancipation, "white Southern 'friends'" were often sources of "protection and benefaction" for the enslaved, especially those who "rose into the higher echelons of slavery."[19] Anderson had certainly been in these "higher echelons" economically while he was enslaved; and, long after the Civil War, Anderson found that currying favor with Southern "friends" was still a useful strategy. Perhaps this is why Anderson began whitewashing or altogether avoiding the history of slavery in most of his publications. To obtain support from the people most able to give it, Anderson needed to write the book those people most wanted to see published and market it in ways that reinforced his audience's assumptions about race.

When he produced the second edition of *The Life* in 1882, a lot had changed for Anderson. First, the A.M.E. leadership had removed him from a single pulpit and appointed him to a position in the Fulton County circuit. This required him to travel throughout the county (usually by foot) to supply the pulpit at various smaller churches, which was an arduous duty for an aging man. Moreover, to earn money Anderson was forced to take up a collection for himself at each church he visited, and he "found out that my churches were so poor that, if I did not look out for myself, it would not be long before I'd have to give up the house that I had rented for myself and family, because it appeared as if the members were either too poor or unwilling to do their duty."[20] Anderson rightly assumed that he was given this difficult assignment because the church leaders wanted to drive him out, and he would leave the A.M.E. Church after the publication of his second edition. Even before he left the church, Anderson found that could make more money selling his pamphlet than he could preaching in the small churches throughout Fulton County. While he was still a circuit preacher, he "started with [his] books" and sold them in "Griffin, Forsyth, Macon, Americus, Fort Valley, Columbus, Hawkinsville, Clinton, Warrenton, Washington, Athens, Greensboro, Madison, Marietta, Cartersville, Cassville, and also in Augusta."[21] The second edition (which generated all of these sales) is far longer than the first edition of *The Life*. First, it features a title that concludes with "THIS BOOK SHALL BE CALLED THE YOUNG MEN'S GUIDE, OR, THE BROTHER

IN WHITE." This version of *The Life* is a hodgepodge of nineteenth-century texts: autobiography, religious treatise, medical manual, advice book, and paean to the "brother in white." The 1882 edition also mentions some of Anderson's "friends" who had purchased Anderson's pamphlet, and this list would appear (in a significantly expanded form) in Anderson's fourth, fifth, and sixth editions (see fig. 6.1). Unlike subscribers, whose contributions fund the eventual publication of a text, Anderson's "friends" funded *him*, and they supported the publication of future editions of *The Life* that would allow the aging minister to continue his work as an author.

Even though Anderson's title makes several promises that he fails to keep, the second edition does feature an expanded "history of the leading events in the life" of Anderson himself. The book delves more deeply into the story of his enslavement, his family life, and his work with the A.M.E. Church. Like many formerly enslaved authors, Anderson begins his life story with a whipping scene, one that did not appear in the first edition. This whipping is not delivered by a cruel enslaver, though, but by Anderson's grandmother, who tied him "by the hands and [whipped] him severely several times" because he could not remember the Lord's Prayer. This is Anderson's only mention of violence within slavery, and he excuses the whipping because it served its purpose. The first paragraph ends with Anderson remembering he "slept happy that night, because I had learned the Lord's Prayer."[22] Lurking behind this story of a childhood punishment is an idea that would inform much of Anderson's life and work: the ends justify the means.

Anderson's remarkable first paragraph is but one reversal of expectations in the second edition of *The Life*, wherein the narrator pledges to fight for his enslaver, suffers a gunshot wound at the hands of a rogue Federal soldier, bemoans the dishonesty of his Black congregants, and calls for God's blessings on the recently departed Alexander Stephens (the former vice president of the Confederacy). It is almost as if Anderson intentionally dismantled the characterizations that dominate most narratives of enslavement: Confederates and white authorities prove to be friends, whereas grandmothers, church members, and Union soldiers prove dangerous. While Anderson is neither uniformly negative toward his family and Black churchgoers nor entirely sympathetic toward moneyed whites, the pattern generally holds. This pattern served him well, too, and he quotes a notice from a West Point (Georgia) paper that describes his book as "withal exceedingly conservative and free from politics" and therefore meriting patronage.[23] There is no way to know Anderson's true feelings concerning race relations or politics, but he

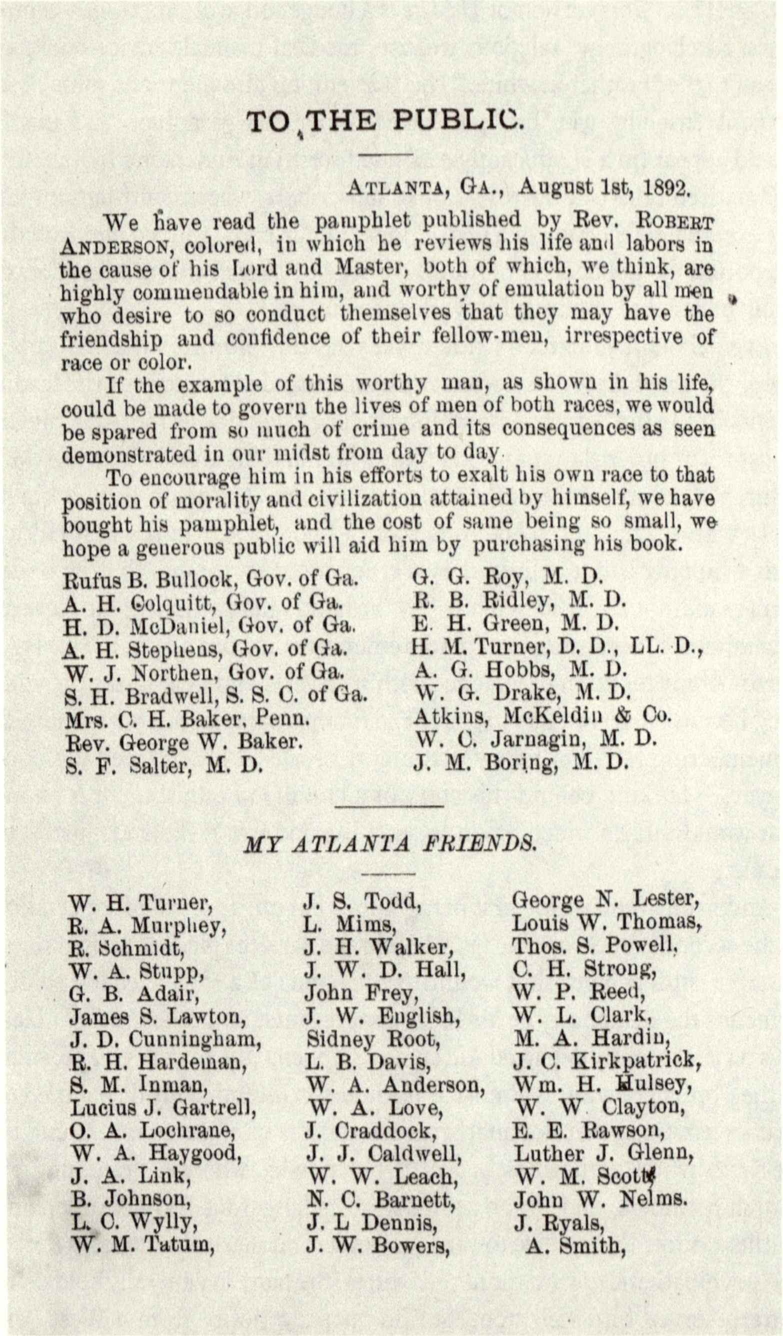

TO THE PUBLIC.

ATLANTA, GA., August 1st, 1892.

We have read the pamphlet published by Rev. ROBERT ANDERSON, colored, in which he reviews his life and labors in the cause of his Lord and Master, both of which, we think, are highly commendable in him, and worthy of emulation by all men who desire to so conduct themselves that they may have the friendship and confidence of their fellow-men, irrespective of race or color.

If the example of this worthy man, as shown in his life, could be made to govern the lives of men of both races, we would be spared from so much of crime and its consequences as seen demonstrated in our midst from day to day.

To encourage him in his efforts to exalt his own race to that position of morality and civilization attained by himself, we have bought his pamphlet, and the cost of same being so small, we hope a generous public will aid him by purchasing his book.

Rufus B. Bullock, Gov. of Ga.
A. H. Colquitt, Gov. of Ga.
H. D. McDaniel, Gov. of Ga.
A. H. Stephens, Gov. of Ga.
W. J. Northen, Gov. of Ga.
S. H. Bradwell, S. S. C. of Ga.
Mrs. C. H. Baker, Penn.
Rev. George W. Baker.
S. F. Salter, M. D.

G. G. Roy, M. D.
R. B. Ridley, M. D.
E. H. Green, M. D.
H. M. Turner, D. D., LL. D.,
A. G. Hobbs, M. D.
W. G. Drake, M. D.
Atkins, McKeldin & Co.
W. C. Jarnagin, M. D.
J. M. Boring, M. D.

MY ATLANTA FRIENDS.

W. H. Turner,
R. A. Murphey,
R. Schmidt,
W. A. Stupp,
G. B. Adair,
James S. Lawton,
J. D. Cunningham,
R. H. Hardeman,
S. M. Inman,
Lucius J. Gartrell,
O. A. Lochrane,
W. A. Haygood,
J. A. Link,
B. Johnson,
L. C. Wylly,
W. M. Tatum,

J. S. Todd,
L. Mims,
J. H. Walker,
J. W. D. Hall,
John Frey,
J. W. English,
Sidney Root,
L. B. Davis,
W. A. Anderson,
W. A. Love,
J. Craddock,
J. J. Caldwell,
W. W. Leach,
N. C. Barnett,
J. L Dennis,
J. W. Bowers,

George N. Lester,
Louis W. Thomas,
Thos. S. Powell,
C. H. Strong,
W. P. Reed,
W. L. Clark,
M. A. Hardin,
J. C. Kirkpatrick,
Wm. H. Hulsey,
W. W. Clayton,
E. E. Rawson,
Luther J. Glenn,
W. M. Scott,
John W. Nelms.
J. Ryals,
A. Smith,

FIGURE 6.1 Detail from *The Life of Rev. Robert Anderson* (1892) showing a list of well-known supporters and the beginning of Anderson's seventeen-page list of "friends" who purchased the previous edition. Courtesy of the American Antiquarian Society.

was happy to project an image of religious and political conservatism to serve his economic mission.

Anderson's work as a bookseller did not go unnoticed by his former colleagues in the A.M.E. Church. In 1884, as Anderson was busy selling his second edition, A.M.E. pastor W. A. Pierce of Quitman, Georgia, wrote into the *Christian Recorder*. He noted that Anderson was "traveling through Georgia passing as a minister of the A.M.E. Church selling a pamphlet worth about ten cents for one dollar, pretending that it contains a history of his life and wonderful remedies for curing diseases. It is a humbug in every particular." As Pierce notes, Anderson had left the A.M.E. Church years before and had returned to the M.E. Church, but Anderson was claiming to be affiliated with the A.M.E. If we take the rest of his career as a guide, Anderson was probably claiming to belong to whatever church would benefit him at a particular moment, but there is no way to be sure about that. Beneath Pierce's letter in the *Recorder* was a note from Dr. Wesley J. Gaines (who would be elected A.M.E. bishop the next year). Gaines confirmed that "Robert Anderson is not a member of the A.M.E. Church and he has been suspended by the Methodist Episcopal Church for falsehoods."[24]

These notices indicate that Anderson was already a thorn in the side of both the A.M.E. and M.E. Churches, and they also show how hard it was to deal with a problematic figure like Anderson. After all, how many people in Georgia read the notice in the *Recorder* that week? How many would remember the notice six or ten years later? How much would such a denunciation affect Anderson's work, especially since he was willing to keep moving around the state and (eventually) around the country to sell his book? In the late nineteenth century, someone peddling a "humbug" only needed to stay in motion to keep ahead of those who might expose him, and Anderson was happy to keep traveling if it was profitable.

The Life Evolves

In the decade following the 1884 *Recorder* notice, Anderson would stay on the move and hone his methods, but even in the 1882 version of his book, he shows how most of his life was about the work of selling the most recent version of his *Life*. Perhaps so he could give readers a sense of that work and its frustrations, Anderson recounts dialogues between himself and prospective customers. Twenty-six of these dialogues (one for every letter of the alphabet) appear in the book, and they reveal "the various excuses of the various persons that have and have not purchased [Anderson's] books."[25] Though there are a few extensive discussions among the twenty-six, most of them are direct and to the point, as with Mr. E:

> "I have a recommendation I would like you to read, if you have the time. I see, though, you are very busy."
>
> "If I had the time I would do so; but excuse me, for I am very busy."[26]

Using formal dialogue, Anderson recalls the excuses of the men and women who claim to be too busy, too ill, too poor, or too disinterested to purchase his book. The addition of story upon story and excuse upon excuse shows how much time and energy Anderson gave to his bookselling efforts and reveals how frequently he met with disappointment and rejection. Because the dialogues are not specific to any individual or any single day, they stand in for the interactions of almost any of the days on which Anderson was "selling his books." His repeated walks around each town and endless journeys around the state meet with the same responses wherever he goes.

Anderson met with success as well, and he interweaves stories of success among the excuses and avoidances. Perhaps unsurprisingly, the dialogues describing success are longer and more personal than the others, suggesting that Anderson could make a sale if he had the chance to talk with his customers. For example, when he meets Mr. W., he tells the story of his self-education to show his initiative:

> "I bought a copy-book in the days of slavery from Mr. Boardman, in the City of Macon. It was called the Self-Penman, and I had that book when I was sent out to serve the churches. I spread that book before me and learned to write. But, when sent to Hawkinsville, I went to school to Dr. Oakland, when I could get the chance, and, in that way, learned a little grammar. I would have had a full education, but the doctor had to move in the country out of town, and therefore I lost my teacher."
>
> "Well," said Mr. W., "you learned enough to write your book."
>
> "Yes, sir."
>
> "Well, I will take one."[27]

Ten of the twenty-six prospective customers buy his book, and he persuades some of them by forgiving men who attacked him or rejecting the political activism practiced by certain A.M.E. ministers. In each case, Anderson makes the discussion personal rather than political, and even when he does not make a sale, Anderson insists that it is "his business to be obliging."[28] As I have indicated above, Anderson's "obliging" manner manifests not only in his affect as a salesman but also in the political outlook of the text itself.

In addition to being "obliging," Anderson also took pains to portray himself as scrupulously honest, especially around matters of money. For example, Anderson describes an incident in 1840 when he was accused of stealing a man's purse and was "tried" and acquitted by the pastor of his church. The rhetorical significance of this episode proving his honesty becomes apparent at the end of the third edition when we learn that Anderson appointed himself a "missionary agent" and, as such, traveled around Georgia collecting money under the aegis of the M.E. Church (even though he had apparently been suspended for "falsehoods" back in 1883). The bishop of the M.E. Church approved of Anderson's plan but wondered "what [Anderson] was going to do with the money." The bishop's curiosity was not unfounded, for even though Anderson presented sixty dollars to the church at the 1890 annual conference, he also notes that he *collected* well over $400.[29] In other words, Anderson used his affiliation with the church to appropriate about $340 to himself for "expenses and debts."[30] Perhaps this is why, at the 1891 conference, the membership voted that Anderson should not collect any more money as a "missionary agent," especially given that Anderson bought his wife an "organ and a sewing machine" with the money he collected before he delivered forty dollars to the church.[31]

The minutes for the Savannah conference for both 1890 and 1891 confirm that Anderson presented sixty dollars and then forty dollars to the church, but they also show that Anderson's brethren were surprised both times he brought money to the meeting. This suggests that no one in the church leadership ever actually appointed Anderson a missionary agent, and, in 1891, the brethren passed a resolution explicitly noting that Anderson was "not authorized . . . to solicit contributions for its superannuated ministers." Another resolution went further, stating, "we urgently and emphatically request him to desist from any further work of this kind for any cause whatever, in which the interest of the M.E. Church is concerned."[32] What is interesting about these resolutions is that, at the same 1891 conference, Anderson was voted a thirty dollar stipend as a "superannuated minister."[33] In other words, Anderson still had his "character passed" by the leaders of the M.E. Church and was compensated along with other retired ministers, but he was forbidden from fundraising to support himself and other aged clergy.[34] Ironically, the M.E. leadership was willing to countenance and support Anderson if—and only if—he was willing to *stop* working as a missionary agent; on the other hand, if Anderson insisted on "working" for the church, then the church wanted nothing to do with him.

Anderson was many things, but he was certainly no fool, and he was ready for the next step in his career. So, he resigned his position and insisted that he was pleased to be relieved of the burdensome job he had created for himself.

Since his "book would be out in a short time," following the 1891 conference, Anderson knew that he "would be able to sell them without putting my brethren to any trouble at all, so far as collecting money for them was concerned."[35] Clearly, Anderson believed that bookselling would perform the same economic function as his work as an agent. In the years to come, Anderson would keep walking the streets of American towns and cities, and his book, like his church affiliation, would give him an entrée with prospective donors.

As Anderson had hoped, the third edition of *The Life* came out on the last day of the annual conference (February 2, 1891), and Anderson began selling the book at the same conference at which he had been censured by his fellow ministers![36] Looking back the next year, he recalled being "happy in doing so, because I meet with so many warm-hearted friends wherever I go, thanks be unto God for it. I am not now required to carry any money to Conference to be talked about, and have my feelings wounded, as they have been many a time."[37] No longer the victim of distrustful churchmen, Anderson celebrates his new occupation and goes on to document how much money he made by circulating his book to buyers. As he explains, book sales were only part of his program, for many "first-class" whites gave him five, two, or one dollar(s) even if they did not take a book. By his own calculations, Anderson made seventy dollars in "Augusta and vicinity," sixty dollars in Savannah, forty-two dollars in Macon, and five dollars for "books and gifts" in the little town of Forsyth.[38] Within a few months, Anderson made at least as much as he made as a traveling missionary, and he got to keep it all.

This was what Anderson had been waiting for all along. Until 1891, when he published the third edition of his book, Anderson had been a preacher and missionary agent who also sold books. The year 1891 marked a turning point, for after he stopped working for the M.E. Church, Anderson became an author and bookseller who occasionally preached. In 1892, Anderson visited J. W. Burke once again, this time with the intention of expanding and improving his book for its fourth edition (see table 6.1). At that meeting, Anderson told Burke that he wanted "a good stiff or 'hard-back' cover, with the name of the book printed thereon in gilt (gold) letters. I wanted a nice and attractive cover, so that I would not be ashamed to show it to my friends while going over the country."[39] Anderson made a down payment of one-hundred dollars with the understanding that the final price would depend on the cost of the binding and stamping he had requested. Just as Anderson intended, the two different versions of the fourth edition have hardback covers and gilt lettering. Most likely, there are two versions because Anderson needed one to start his sales trip and was willing to accept the complete version later. So, he had printed a 151-page *Life* bound in blue cloth and then, later in 1892, began selling the 192-page *Life* bound in red. For Anderson, the version did not really matter since the whole point was to have an attractive book to *show*. Anderson would continue to show—and profit by—his book for the next ten years. In that time, he would completely rewrite his autobiography so he could continue selling to the "friends" who had made him one of the most successful self-published authors of the nineteenth century.

The Rise of Robert B. Anderson

As Anderson writes in the preface to *The Anderson Surpriser*, the fifth edition of his autobiography was a "continuation of the first, but is complete in itself."[40] Anderson's statement aside, the *Surpriser* is not really complete since it does not include reprintings of earlier versions of *The Life*. The *Surpriser* offers readers no information about Anderson's life in slavery, his religious conversion, his work as a religious leader and his experience as a father. Gone too are the remedies for smallpox, the description of the "brother in white," and Anderson's prophesies about Christ's return to earth. Instead, the book begins *in media res* with a description of Anderson's 1893 bookselling trip through Georgia and Florida, a journey that he begins on his seventy-fourth birthday. The rest of the *Surpriser* details Anderson's experiences as he sold the fourth edition of his *Life* (i.e., the two versions with the "nice attractive cover") up and down the Eastern Seaboard. At the same time, the *Surpriser* does tell a complete story, one that takes Anderson from Macon, Georgia, to Boston, Massachusetts, and back again. And, because Anderson journeys beyond the limited geographies he traversed for most of his career as a bookseller, the *Surpriser* becomes something more than the monotonous travelogue that occupies so much of the third and fourth editions of *The Life*.

In the *Surpriser*, Anderson paints a startling portrait of a country struggling to overcome the trauma of slavery and civil war, and he describes the lingering effects of that trauma for whites and Blacks alike. Like W. E. B. Du Bois in *The Souls of Black Folk*, or the unnamed narrator in James Weldon Johnson's *Autobiography of an Ex-Colored Man*, Robert Anderson is a traveler in strange lands, and his autobiography attests to the enduring schism between North and South. The surprise in the *Surpriser* is that, unlike the displaced Northern protagonists of the more popular fin de siècle fiction and autobiography named above, Anderson is happy to return to the Southern side of the Mason-Dixon line, the place where his "friends" were always glad to support him through the book purchases he relied on since he was "too far advanced in years to be efficient in his life work, the ministry."[41] This statement seems quite suspicious given that Anderson's book describes his months of travel and his never-ending search for opportunities to preach to congregations around the country. Still, there may be a kernel of truth in his plea, for Anderson had already found that his work as an author and bookseller was far more remunerative than his old job.

Readers see this quite clearly at the beginning of the *Surpriser* when Anderson visits the annual Methodist Episcopal conference at Brunswick, Georgia, and finds that he received only twenty dollars from the fund for superannuated ministers. The small apportionment was no accident; Anderson's fellow ministers knew his history, and they knew he was making money by selling his book. None of this stopped Anderson from feeling slighted, though, and he notes that his apportionment from the church was the "least of all." Using this small apportionment as a pretext to continue selling books, Anderson decided to leave his support to the "hands of God," and he set out to find "kind-hearted friends," who would buy his book, many of whom materialized in Brunswick.[42] Anderson found friends who "published [him] in the paper" announcing his presence, friends at the Baptist Sabbath School, friends at the Methodist Episcopal Church, and "particularly . . . white friends." By the end of the conference, Anderson had "obtained about $30 by gift and by selling . . . books."[43] The twenty-dollar pittance apportioned by the church must have seemed nothing but an unpleasant memory by the time Anderson departed for Fernandina, Florida.

Even though Anderson could no longer rely on the financial support of the M.E. Church, his religious affiliations continued to make the work of bookselling easier. First, because he was a former minister hawking an ostensibly religious book, Anderson was usually allowed to sell in most towns without purchasing a peddling license and, as an aged, deferential, minister, he was almost always treated with respect by Black and white Southerners. Second, as Anderson explains, he capitalized on his status to move from town to town quite cheaply. At one point he reports that he was able to acquire a "minister's half-fare ticket" for railroad passage, and he frequently received carriage rides or other conveyances from friendly ministers eager to aid one of their brethren.[44] Finally, Anderson's contacts from his days as a minister helped him gain access to various congregations and Sunday schools, and his experience as a preacher helped him secure sales and donations. Though few of the members of the Black congregations could afford his two-dollar autobiography, at the conclusion of a sermon or a lesson, Anderson would ask the entire congregation to pool their money to "treat [the pastor] to a book of [his]." On many occasions they did so "with a great deal of pleasure"; congregations that could not muster two dollars simply offered Anderson a small donation.[45]

Anderson's success as a bookseller also depended on his maintenance of his "obliging" nature, especially with the "generous . . . white friends" he met in every town. As he explains, Anderson "always made it my first business whenever I went to a city or a town, to go and see the head authority," which usually involved an especially deferential conversation with the mayor.[46] Anderson benefited by bowing to authority, and smart mayors may have learned that they could benefit too, for whenever he met with a particularly generous public figure or a community of men and women willing to buy his book, Anderson would describe the town in glowing terms and encourage his readers to visit. For example, after his visit to St. Augustine, Florida, where he "did as well . . . as ever I did in any place of the same size," Anderson claims that the town is "heaven on earth," and he twice encourages his readers to "go and see it."[47]

When Anderson tried to sell his book to a white buyer, he could also highlight the kind words he used to describe whites and show that he, at least, was no critic of the Southern way of life. Anderson ingratiated himself with printers and editors and, through them, encouraged newspapers to announce his presence and drum up interest in his book. Advertisements for Anderson appear in many papers, and most of them suggest that Anderson was peddling a very particular kind of narrative. For example, the 1893 *Charlotte News* notes that his book was so "entirely free from such overdrawn pictures as Mrs. Stowe drew with her pen that it is a relief to read it."[48] It is amazing that Southern editors were still fuming over *Uncle Tom's Cabin* more than forty years after it was published, but this use of Stowe as a foil is telling. As he pursued an advertising campaign that leveraged favorable press notices, word of mouth, and church appearances, Anderson made sure he would meet "friends" and "do well" in the Southern towns he visited.

For Anderson, "doing well" meant more than just selling books, since he was happy to accept charity from those who declined to purchase. For example, on his successful trip to St. Augustine, he uses the "chance to speak to a great many about myself and the book" to obtain donations of twenty-five to seventy-five cents.[49] In this instance and many others like it, the fact that Anderson was *trying* to sell his book meant that he did not *need* to sell it to support himself. He constantly traversed the line between entrepreneurship and supplication, just as he did as a traveling missionary. Anderson understood, as did his "friends," that the work of authorship, publication, and bookselling were the things that carried value in the patronage-oriented embedded markets in which he peddled his wares. Those markets, which were defined by paternalism, recall the structures of deference and exchange that Leon Jackson describes in his research of George Moses Horton. As Jackson explains, "a paternalist ethos permeated every aspect" of the antebellum South, and this ethos was "cemented by regularized and ritualized acts of generosity in which masters bestowed their largesse upon" the enslaved.[50] In much of post-Reconstruction Georgia, moneyed whites hoped to reinstate the same "paternalist ethos," and Anderson took advantage. As he notes, "white friends [seemed] to like [his books] very much and to enjoy buying them because of their being the writing of a colored person, and an old one besides."[51] For Anderson's "friends," the book represented Anderson's industry and perhaps a reminder of an era they recalled with some fondness, but it seems unlikely the book was something they planned to read. Anderson preferred that his buyers also be readers, but he did not quibble when he saw the potential to make a sale.

In one sales anecdote from the 1892 *Life*, Anderson offers his prospectus and book to a train conductor: "He took [the prospectus] and read it, then handed me a dollar. I presented him with a copy of my book, but he kindly handed it back to me." Another railroad employee asks the conductor why he did not take a copy of the book, and the conductor explains that "[Anderson] was old and unable to do much. The book was given back to [him] that he might sell it and get another dollar." In turn, Anderson blesses the conductor as "one of the best and kindest men I have ever traveled with." The train conductor was not alone, either: Later, after Anderson boards a boat to Fernandina, Florida, Anderson shows his book to the captain and receives free passage as well as charitable donations from two crew members.[52] In the *Surpriser*, Anderson recalls a visit to Daytona, Florida, in which he meets a man and says, "I would be glad, sir, if you would look at my book, and carefully note its contents." The man replies, "I do not care so much about the book, but here is a dollar for it." Though the man "carelessly turned the leaves" of the book, Anderson accepts his dollar, and goes on to "bless that man for his deeds of goodness."[53]

In these anecdotes, the selling of his book provides an occasion for a ritual in which the white buyer proves his economic and social status (he does not care what he buys or even care to keep the book) while the African American salesman accepts the money and the diminished status that comes with it. This behavior is profitable in economic terms, but it is undoubtedly an instance of what Ann Fabian describes as "accept[ing] humility" by "defer[ring] to those who claimed a right to exercise social and cultural" control over Black

Southerners like Anderson.[54] And, indeed, Anderson blesses his benefactors and celebrates the larger social formation of which his "white friends" are a part. Anderson's acceptance of the Redemption-era social formations meant that his *Life* could function as a commodity, a symbol of his achievement, an implicit request for donations, and a passport granting him passage on public conveyances. Indeed, *The Life* is everything but a book to be read. Because his book was designed and sold as an object of exchange rather than an object for reading and consideration, Anderson expected he would find repeat buyers and was dismayed when he did not. During his 1894 visit to Gainesville, Florida, Anderson notes "those who had previously purchased my books were pleased with them, so well pleased, in fact, that they rendered their satisfaction as an excuse for not buying."[55] As Jackson explains in his analysis of Southern paternalism, the rules of the social game required Anderson to sell, but they also required wealthy whites to pay, even if they had paid before; repeat buyers helped Anderson sell "over two thousand copies of [his] books in the South" by 1894.[56]

The anecdotes in Anderson's books help us understand how he managed his bookselling performances and give some insight into where people bought his book (or at least offered him money for it). Anderson also gives us the identities of many of his purchasers by including a list of purchasers in the first pages of each book (fig. 6.1). These lists help us know what kinds of customers Anderson approached and from whom he received the most patronage. The lists I have examined appear in the fourth (1892) and sixth (1900) editions of *The Life* as well as the *Surpriser* (1895). The longest list of names (around 1,000) appears in the two versions of the fourth edition, but in total there are more than 1,700 names of "friends" who gave Anderson money for his books. Some of those names, like Reverdy Ransom, would become well-known; some names repeat (Baptist bishop Lucius Holsey purchased both the *Surpriser* and *The Life*); and, some "names" are corporate purchases ("The Troy Steam Laundry" "The Standard Wagon Co.," "Wide Awake Furniture Co.," "A.M.E. Sunday School").[57] This much is clear, though: of the 500 individuals in Anderson's books who can be positively identified via census records or city directories, 420 (84 percent) are white.[58] Caveats abound: the census is notoriously unreliable, especially for men and women of color; city directories and other resources are similarly unreliable; not every one of Anderson's buyers advertised their purchase by recording their name in his book; and Anderson's own recordkeeping may have privileged white purchasers over Black purchasers. Even so, Anderson obviously knew who held the money in the South, and he targeted those buyers with remarkable precision.

A Grand Report in the Way of Selling 191

When Anderson decided to sell *The Life* on his "first trip to the Northern States and cities," he would find that the rules of the social and economic games were different from those he had learned so well.[59] As a stranger in most of the towns he visited, he found it difficult to gain traction with local purchasers. Even in a town as close to home as Columbia, South Carolina, the "white people . . . say that money is scarce" and Anderson accuses one reluctant customer of "'[disdaining] the idea of buying a book written by'" a Black man.[60] By the time he gets to Baltimore, Anderson complains that he "would have been glad to have made a good report for this large city, if I could have sold any books," but purchasers proved hard to find.[61] Unfamiliar urban spaces seem not to agree with Anderson the salesman, for he had previously relied on word-of-mouth advertising, notices in local newspapers, and badgering townspeople, churchgoers, and resort guests. In the North, Anderson found that his old way of doing things did not work so well, and perhaps this spurred him to visit the A.M.E. book concern in Philadelphia and the Methodist Episcopal Church book concern in New York City. Though he does not explain his reasons for meeting with the book distributors, one would imagine that Anderson wanted to publish and/or sell his book to a much wider audience. This was not to be the case, though, and Anderson left both offices "very much disappointed."[62]

Anderson's books would remain self-published and self-distributed, but as the man behind this bookselling enterprise moved farther north, he found people and places increasingly unfamiliar and inhospitable. Philadelphia proved to be the "worst place for cursing and swearing," and Anderson was appalled at the "white women and colored men dancing together" at all hours.[63] Anderson records his increasing frustration in the pages of the *Surpriser* as he notes the carousing and foul language running rampant at midnight and then writes again later near "the hour of two o'clock" when the "cursing and swearing is still going on." He employs the present tense when he asks the reader to join him in his room and "Listen, if you please: 'God d—n such a one.'"[64] Anderson's request that we listen, with him, to the blasphemer outside his window and his repeated mentions of white female depravity suggest that Anderson knew he would not be coming north again. Finding his immortal soul endangered and his book sales dwindling, Anderson began to focus his writing on the next group of "white friends" who might enjoy tales of depravity from the North, which Anderson insists is "worse instead of better" than the South.[65]

After he leaves Philadelphia, Anderson becomes more willing to share his views on lynching and amalgamation, and he highlights his disagreements with Northern Blacks who seem not to understand life in the South. When he recalls an anti-lynching lecture he witnessed in a New York church, Anderson insists that if Blacks kept to their "own side; then there will be no lynchings." More than this, he "[glories] in the spunk of the virtuous white girls, who would not stoop so low as to be caught with a colored man. If the negroes have not sense enough, when they happen to meet white ladies, to let them pass with their virtue, they ought to be dealt with."[66] This is the language of white supremacy, the language of a man who believes (or says he believes) in the myth of white virtue and Black sexual aggression. Anderson recalls that his views proved especially problematic when he found an audience with the large and politically active African American population in Boston. He was evicted from one Boston boarding house because he "took sides with the whites of the South," and he later fears for his own safety because he is identified as a traitor to his race. Though he finds that whites in Boston "treated me with due respect, buying my books and giving me their money," he insists that "if the colored people in this section of the country had their way about things in general, I think that there would be any amount of blood shed."[67]

The Northern "way" would never be Anderson's way, for, irrespective of his true political feelings, the Northern way would not pay. Anderson makes this point for readers when he narrates his eviction from the Boston boarding house and recalls being forced to settle his $2.50 debt: "[The boarding-house keeper] thought that I being a poor old man, that I did not have any money, but she was badly disappointed. I said to her all right. I opened my satchel right before them all, which I did not wish to do, and paid her out of a roll of money that I had rolled up and put aside, but I unrolled it and paid her." Anderson's showiness seems to upset the boarding-house keeper even more, and she threatens to expose him by "publish[ing him] in the papers" Anderson invites her to do just that and cautions her as he leaves, "you better not come South with that spirit in you."[68] Though that "spirit" was easy enough to maintain in Boston, Anderson knew he had to face a different set of problems back home in Georgia. And, as his money roll indicates to both his Boston adversary and his Southern readers, he managed those problems quite well, at least from an economic standpoint.

Anderson left Boston by steamship and arrived in Savannah three days later; after returning to Macon, he prepared the *Surpriser* for publication and then began selling his paean to the Southern way of life around his home state and, eventually, as far away as Ohio and Illinois, but he never returned to the inhospitable climate of New England.[69] Though he seems to have sold his books for most of the next five years, Anderson did not print a new edition of his life story until 1900. When it came time to produce the new edition, Anderson chose to print his book at Foote & Davies in Atlanta rather than with J. W. Burke in Macon. Anderson does not explain the reason for this change, but there is little doubt that Foote & Davies—which was one of the leading printers in Georgia—helped Anderson produce copies of his book with speed and economy.[70] Indeed, Foote & Davies printed 1,000 copies of *The Life* in only eleven days.[71]

By the time Anderson left Atlanta, he used sixty-five dollars he had accumulated by preselling copies of *The Life* in Atlanta to pay down his bill with Foote & Davies. These sales indicate that Anderson had indeed won for himself the kind of esteem he may have been seeking, at least from the upper-class whites to whom he sold his books. In the short note preceding the sixth edition, the printers note the "high character" of the men who have endorsed Anderson over the years and add their own endorsement. They identify Anderson as a man of "rare personal merit" who enjoys the "unquestioning confidence of all who know him," and "commend this eminently worthy colored man to the public at large as richly deserving all the success" he might meet.[72] As with the earlier editions of *The Life*, these commendations precede a lengthy list of book buyers from places like Miami, Chattanooga, Cincinnati, and Chicago and newspaper clippings about Anderson's life and book.

The final edition of *The Life* reprints the entirety of the fourth edition but appends a new preface titled "The Anderson Trumpet" in which Anderson showcases all the things that make him such a remarkable writer. The "Trumpet" contains a lengthy travelogue, most of which focuses on Miami and Chicago, and, like Anderson's other books, it also includes bizarre non sequiturs and brief flights into ribaldry. For example, Anderson explains that "circumcision is a good thing so far as the flesh is concerned, that is, it destroys to some extent the strength of the devil in the flesh," but he is glad that the devil is not completely out of his flesh since he had "a younger wife than myself . . . and to have all the devil out of me would not be very profitable."[73]

As always, what was most profitable for Anderson was pleasing the well-to-do whites who might benefit him: Like the "rich men or companies that will spend their money in building railroads," companies that were also willing to give Anderson "tickets at half rates so that I can travel all over their roads."[74] Or, like the capitalist Henry Flagler, who permitted Anderson to sell to the rich guests at his palatial resort hotels in Miami, Ormond, and Palm Beach and who—the author notes—employed numerous Black men and women at his establishments.[75] At one of Flagler's hotels, Anderson "would tell some of slavery, and that would appear to surprise [the guests] very much, and for that they would give or buy of me. I saw that it pleased them very much."[76] It is not hard to imagine what Anderson must have been saying about slavery that pleased his wealthy benefactors.

Though Anderson had long been willing to trade quiescence and historical whitewashing for cash, in the "Trumpet" he seems to have become more and more of a huckster willing to advertise whoever helps him. In addition to his paeans to Henry Flagler and other "rich men," he also celebrates the "noble-hearted" owner of the St. John's Hotel in Florida ("he has always been my friend by letting me sell my book"), the boarding-house keepers in Chattanooga ("all that wish to come to this boarding house will be made happy"), and the printers in Atlanta ("if any friends wish to have printing done, well that can have it done in Atlanta by Messrs. Foote and Davies, East Alabama Street"). In the "Trumpet," the book becomes a skeleton key that unlocks the transportation, lodging, and dining services Anderson requires for his travels. Those travels likely brought him numerous psychological rewards, but they were, first and foremost, opportunities to sell. And, in this respect, his repeated journeys were extraordinarily successful. Indeed, so lucrative was Anderson's work that he seemed never to tire of it, and he sustained his authorial brand into the twentieth century when he was more than eighty years old. In 1900, he was selling books in Augusta, Georgia; two years later, he claimed to be raising money for a church as he traveled through Indiana and Kentucky; and in September of 1902, Anderson preached at the A.M.E. Church in Grand Rapids, Michigan.[77] As the 1900 *Augusta Chronicle* story indicates, "age seem[ed] to sit lightly upon him."[78] And, indeed, it was not age that would kill him. Only a month after he preached in Michigan, Anderson visited Columbus, Georgia, where he was struck and killed by a runaway mule.[79] While the short newspaper story announcing his death does not explain why Anderson was in Columbus, one imagines that he was looking for "friends" on his never-ending sales trip around the United States.

Robert Anderson's life story is, at turns, astounding, humorous, and deeply troubling. There is simply no avoiding the fact that Anderson was an opportunist who capitalized on white supremacy and did so to the detriment of Black Americans. At the same time, Anderson was a remarkably savvy man who understood the intersecting social, religious, and economic communities around him and learned how to profit within them. While it is true that Anderson profited off white supremacy, it is also true that he mostly profited off white buyers who supported him. In this way, we might say that he sought to rebalance the economic scales in the South, though that rebalancing seemed only to have benefited him and no one else.

Coda
The Walking Book

One of the central arguments of this book is that Black men and women capitalized on the possibilities of self-publication by producing texts suited for the moment and the market. For Black author-publishers working outside of the mainstream print market, the ability to make money often depended on finding purchasers across a wide geographic range, and this required travel. Whether it was the desire to travel and meet others that preceded the decision to publish or the necessity of bookselling that drove authors to start traveling, there is no doubt that many of the writers in this study became purveyors of what might be called the walking book. The walking book moved with its author and enabled that author to meet new people, spread his or her message, and reap the psychological and economic rewards concomitant with both.

The phrase "the walking book" signifies on Henry Louis Gates Jr.'s theorization of the "trope of the talking book," which he defines as "the Ur-trope of the Anglo-African tradition."[1] Gates outlines several authors' use of the trope of the talking book in eighteenth- and nineteenth-century African American narratives and argues that use of that trope demonstrates the desire of a "black slave narrator . . . to transform himself . . . from silent object to speaking subject, in the form of a life containable in autobiography."[2] I offer the idea of the walking book not as a replacement for Gates's figuration, but as another way of thinking about the African American literary tradition in the nineteenth century, a century marked by significant legal, political, and economic changes for Black Americans. As Gates argues, literacy and writing were crucial tools that Black people used to encourage those changes, but, over the course of the century, Black movement and mobility helped cement those changes by transforming the places in which Americans lived. Writing in *Black Atlas*, Judith Madera argues that "places are generated through processes of participation," and it is this kind of active participation I have in mind when I consider the significance of the walking book.[3] As Madera's words suggest, Black participation in a space could help generate new understandings of that space. So, though it may seem pedestrian, walking is a potentially transgressive act that demonstrates both subjectivity and citizenship.

Even today, Black Americans cannot be confident they will be permitted to walk safely on public streets and sidewalks, and the situation in the nineteenth century was far worse. Obviously, enslaved men and women were closely surveilled and were only rarely allowed to travel; free Black Americans faced racist laws restricting or forbidding their passage on streetcars, trains, and boats, and many had to deal with social conventions that limited their ability to so much as walk down the street. Indeed, as many of the authors in this book note, walking through a new town or seeking refuge in a stranger's barn could engender hostility or violence. For these reasons, unfettered mobility was not something a Black American could take for granted, which leads Cheryl Fish to argue that we can understand the fact of Black mobility, "even if incomplete or compromised," as an assertion of "agency" that "reflects a desire for empowerment."[4] Building on Fish's work, Eric Gardner argues that mobility, while fraught with potential dangers, could also enable "racial elevation, citizenship, and broader participation" in community-oriented work and could create interpersonal ties that helped connect Black Americans to the "multiracial nation" of which they are a part.[5] When they moved into new geographic spaces and wrote their stories in those spaces, Black men and women expanded the map of places in which they "belonged" and thereby "defin[ed] themselves as residents, citizens, and members of the United States."[6] Self-publication is a crucial piece of this story, for the "act of making something publicly known" granted Black authors both a reason and a method for engaging with the wider world and representing themselves within various communities.[7] As they moved from house to house or town to town, author-publishers bridged gaps and created connections between regions and people; and they created new spaces (both physical and intellectual) in which their stories might be valued. Furthermore, by recording and preserving their stories in printed form, those authors enabled connections between past and present.

Perhaps there is no one who embodies these various forms of connection more than the indomitable James Mars, who started selling his pamphlet at age seventy-four in 1864 and continued for fifteen years. Mars had been enslaved in Connecticut until 1815, and his pamphlet served notice of that. In an 1870 photograph of Mars, we see an aged but still hearty man whose cane sits in his right hand (fig. C.1). Mars clearly wanted the cane in the photo, perhaps to remind those who looked at it that he "had a fall and uncapped my knee, that laid me by ten months, so that I was unable to travel or do anything to help myself, but by the help of Him that does all things well, I have got so as to be able to walk with a staff."[8] Mars's staff is a symbol of the

FIGURE C.1 Portrait of James Mars, taken in Winstead, Connecticut, in 1870. Note the cane in Mars's right hand. Courtesy of the Connecticut Historical Society.

obstacles he faced and his dogged determination to surmount them. Walking a desultory path around Connecticut, New York, and Massachusetts, Mars used his bookselling to transform the spaces through which he traveled in at least two ways. First, Mars reminded the Connecticut residents he met that he intended to "act like a man, and vote like a man," but that he could not do so in his "native State." Instead, he had to "remove to the old Bay State for the right to be a man."[9] That would change after Mars had been selling his book for five years and Connecticut ratified the Fifteenth Amendment to the Constitution, which granted full political citizenship to all men regardless of race. Second, Mars's story countered the historical amnesia and the bad faith of those he met who "did not know that slavery was ever allowed in Connecticut, and [those who] affirm that it never did exist in the State."[10] As he wrote about and traversed the places he had lived, he helped generate a revised sense of history for his fellow citizens. Connecticut residents had to confront the fact that the legacy of slavery was their legacy as well, and James Mars reminded them that their state was his state too. The walking book was both a passport that gave Mars a reason to travel and a tool that helped him generate change.

Stories of the walking book are important because they illustrate the agency and action of everyday Black Americans who worked with their minds and their bodies to remake the world around them. Purveyors of those books did not just write their stories, but they sought—and sometimes demanded—an audience. Printing and selling a book did not guarantee monetary gain, the righting of judicial wrongs, or widespread acceptance of alternate viewpoints. But it did offer determined authors a route to pursue all those things. Publication granted women like Harriet Wilson a way to earn rather than beg; it granted men like Jacob Stroyer the opportunity to celebrate a lifetime of education, personal achievement, and community service; it granted men like Norvel Blair the chance to fight back against powerful and designing men and protect the fortune he had earned. When we look to these and so many other writers, we come to understand that what Derrick Spires calls the "work of citizenship" is deeply indebted to the self-publishers who told and sold their stories and thereby nurtured a tradition of critique and creativity separate from white gatekeepers and political leaders.[11] For these authors and those we have yet to discover, self-publication was yet another way that they could insist that their stories—like their lives—mattered.

Notes

Introduction

1. Bellinger and Myers, *Stray Leaves from the Port-Folio of a Methodist Local Preacher*; Lewis, *Eight Nights with a Reading Club*.

2. Anderson, *Life* (1892), 145.

3. The meeting took place in Macon, Georgia, from January 29 to February 2, 1891. See *Minutes of the Savannah Annual Conference of the Methodist Episcopal Church*.

4. Anderson tabulates his earnings in the 1892 edition of his *Life*, 145–48. The entirety of his publishing career is treated in chapter 6.

5. McHenry, "'Out of the Business,'" 408.

6. Black Self-Publishing, https://www.americanantiquarian.org/black-self-pub lishing. The AAS site catalogs all self-published texts written by authors born before 1851 or published before 1876, so some late-century texts are not included among this number. Also, some of the earliest self-published texts predate the nineteenth century, so those texts *are* included.

7. Though the development of this system was by no means linear, the royalty system did come to dominate American publishing over the nineteenth century. On the rise of that system, and on the nineteenth-century literary marketplace(s) more generally, see Casper et al., eds., *The Industrial Book*; Charvat and Bruccoli, *The Profession of Authorship in America*; Gross and Kelley, eds., *An Extensive Republic*; Kaestle and Radway, eds., *Print in Motion*; Loughran, *The Republic in Print*, and Zboray, *A Fictive People*.

8. On royalties, see Tebbel, *Between the Covers*. Tebbel notes that most houses offered authors 10 percent of the retail price for all copies sold beyond the first 1,000 or more.

9. As Tebbel explains, even in the late nineteenth century, authors often had to pay part of the costs for producing their books with "mainstream publishers." Thus, self-publishers and authors working with commercial presses were often financially involved in the bookmaking process. See Tebbel, *Between the Covers*, 172.

10. Zboray, *A Fictive People*, chapter 4.

11. Into the 1850s, newspapers could be sent across state lines for only $0.01, whereas letters cost $0.03. This meant that papers published in one place had a much wider circulation than the city of their origin. See Zboray and Zboray, "The Dissemination of Reading Material during the American Civil War."

12. Gardner, *Black Print Unbound*, 10. In addition to Gardner's outstanding work on the *Christian Recorder* and other periodicals like the *San Francisco Elevator*, authors like Penelope Bullock, Benjamin Fagan, Kim Gallon, I. Garland Penn, Derrick Spires, and Andréa Williams have illuminated the reach and influence of nineteenth-century Black newspapers and periodicals.

13. Roy, *Fugitive Texts*, 50.

14. Foster, *Written by Herself*, 107.

15. Stepto, *From Behind the Veil*, 3.

16. Witness, for example, the first-person narratives included in the *Norton Anthology of African American Literature* (3rd edition): Frederick Douglass, Olaudah Equiano, Harriet Jacobs, Solomon Northup, Venture Smith, and Booker T. Washington. Or, consider the authors of the most frequently accessed narratives in the library of North American Slave Narratives hosted on Documenting the American South: Frederick Douglass (1845), Olaudah Equiano, Harriet Jacobs, and Solomon Northup. By contrast, Robert Anderson's 1892 *Life* is not among the one hundred most frequently accessed narratives on Documenting the American South between 2014 and 2019. Thanks to William L. Andrews for sharing these statistics with me.

17. Goddu, "The Slave Narrative as Material Text," 150.

18. Roy, *Fugitive Texts*, 133.

19. Anderson, *The Anderson Surpriser*, 25.

20. Roy, *Fugitive Texts*, 50. I have used the term "the walking book" to describe this kind of narrative, and I elaborate on that concept and the rewards it could bring in the coda.

21. Weyler, *Empowering Words*, 2.

22. Laquintano, *Mass Authorship*, 14–15.

23. Laquintano, *Mass Authorship*, 15.

24. Anderson, *Life* (1892), 79.

25. Anderson, *The Anderson Surpriser*, 22.

26. Fish, *Black and White Women's Travel Narratives*, 6–7.

27. Laquintano, *Mass Authorship*, 12.

28. McGann, *The Textual Condition*, 13.

29. For a helpful summary of this strain of African Americanist criticism, see Barrett, "African-American Slave Narratives: Literacy, the Body, Authority." More recently, Christopher Hager has highlighted the significance of literacy for nineteenth-century African Americans in *Word by Word: Emancipation and the Act of Writing*.

30. See especially Andrews, *To Tell a Free Story*; Baker, *Blues, Ideology, and Afro-American Literature*; Foster, *Witnessing Slavery*; Gates, *Figures in Black* and *The Signifying Monkey*; and Stepto, *From Behind the Veil*.

31. Here I am following in the footsteps of Teresa Goddu and Michaël Roy, both of whom argue that we must account for the materiality of the slave narrative to write a complete and accurate history of the genre.

32. Goldsby and McGill, "What is 'Black' about Black Bibliography?," 177.

33. The AAS's Black Self-Publishing project is a collaborative project under the editorial stewardship of Elizabeth Pope.

34. The bibliographies I used to develop my list of self-published narratives were William L. Andrews's bibliography hosted on Documenting the American South, Russell C. Brignano's *Black Americans in Autobiography*, and Dorothy Porter's "Early American Negro Writings: A Bibliographical Study."

35. Print histories of four such publications are included in tables 1–4.

36. McGill, "Format," 673–74.

37. McKenzie, *Bibliography and the Sociology of Texts*, 17.

38. McGill, "Literary History," 33. My efforts to author a fuller book history for African American literature were also encouraged by Leon Jackson's "The Talking Book and the Talking Book Historian."

39. Gibbs, *Shadow and Light*.

40. On the significance of paratexts in African American literature, see McCoy, "Race and the (Para)Textual Condition."

41. Rusert, "From Black Lit to Black Print," 994.

42. Whitman, "Song of Myself." *Leaves of Grass* (Brooklyn, 1855), 55.

43. Ernest, "Genealogies Beyond Modernities," 786.

44. US Bureau of the Census, *Manufactures* (Washington: Government Printing Office, 1905).

45. Account book of the *Salem Press*, 1871–72. On job printing and its relationship to the ways knowledge is shaped and organized, see Gitelman, Lisa. *Paper Knowledge*, chapter 1.

46. McHenry, "'Out of the Business,'" 410.

47. McHenry, *To Make Negro Literature*, 11.

48. When I use the term "self-publication" throughout this book, this is the very process I have in mind. In commercial publishing arrangements, the publisher is the person who pays for printing and handles the distribution of the printed pamphlet or book. The authors featured in this study do the same thing for their own work.

49. The records from the *Salem Press* show that 1,200 copies of the *Bulletin for Essex Institute* (a sixteen page, twenty-five-centimeter booklet) for September 1870 cost $52.65. The cost breakdowns are as follows: Paper = $18.00; Presswork = $10.00; Comp[osition] (17,454 ems @ $0.75/1,000) = $13.09; Folding ($0.13/100) = $1.56; Correcting = $2.00.

50. Johnson's *Narrative of the Fugitive Slave, William of Maryland* includes the phrase "Dictated by Himself" on the cover and title page; Veney's amanuensis identifies him/herself in the preface with the initials "M. W. G."

51. Black, *The Life and Sufferings of Leonard Black*, 2.

52. Lane, *The Narrative of Lunsford Lane*, iv.

53. On costs for composition, see Silver, *The American Printer, 1787–1825*, 81.

54. Grimes, *Life of William Grimes, the Runaway Slave*, 84.

55. "Multiple News Items," *New Haven Palladium*, August 22, 1865.

56. Winship, "'The Greatest Book of Its Kind,'" 325.

57. Both William Wells Brown (1847) and Harriet Jacobs (1861) paid to have their books stereotyped. See Roy, *Fugitive Texts*, 83, 151. On the costs of stereotyping, see Winship, *American Literary Publishing*, 104–6.

58. Newman, Rael, and Lapsansky, eds., *Pamphlets of Protest*, 2.

59. Records of the General Conference, thirteenth session, Paris, 1964: Resolutions, 145.

60. Rezek, "The Print Atlantic," 23.

61. Green, "Bound/Unbound," 615; Roy, "The Slave Narrative Unbound," 261–62.

62. On the ways that electronic editions have shaped our understanding of nineteenth-century texts, see also, Roy, "The Slave Narrative Unbound," 262–63;

Rusert, "New World: The Impact of Digitization on the Study of Slavery," 268; and Sinche, "The Walking Book," 282.

63. Hesse, "Books in Time," 26.

64. Brooks, "The Early American Public Sphere," 75. See also Warner, *The Letters of the Republic*.

65. On the relationship between format and function, see also Roy, "Cheap Editions, Little Books, and Handsome Duodecimos."

66. Newman, Rael, and Lapsansky, *Pamphlets of Protest*, 7.

67. G. W. Offley Papers, volume 1. Interestingly, Offley's 1859 book was not his first or last foray into self-publishing. In 1844, he published a pamphlet titled *Slavery in the South*, and in 1875 published *God's Immutable Declaration of His Own Moral and Assumed Natural Image, and Likeness in Man*.

68. Lee, *Religious Experience and Journal*, 79.

69. Lee, *Religious Experience and Journal*, 86 ff.

70. Offley, *A Narrative* (1860).

71. Offley's arrangement was not unique. In the preface to the second edition of his autobiography, *The Night of Affliction and the Morning of Recovery*, William Magee writes, "When I contemplated publishing I had not a dollar on hand to begin with . . . I went immediately to my publisher and told him my circumstances and my desires that I would pay him from ten to twenty dollars a week as my circumstances would allow if he would undertake my work. He undertook it for me as I believe through the help of God in answer to prayer and got out a fine edition which met a ready sale and a hearty approval" (i–ii).

72. See, for example, Foster, *Witnessing Slavery*, chapter 1, and Rohrbach, *Truth Stranger than Fiction*, chapter 2.

73. Michaël Roy deserves enormous credit for clarifying our understanding of the slave narrative's popularity. See *Fugitive Texts*, 158–60.

74. Jackson, *The Business of Letters*, 2.

75. Weyler, *Empowering Words*, 5.

76. Jackson, *The Business of Letters*, 2.

77. Jackson, *The Business of Letters*, 3.

78. Jackson, *The Business of Letters*, 3.

79. Peterson, *Doers of the Word*, 13.

80. Peterson, *Doers of the Word*, 13. Peterson's work intersects with important books by Houston Baker and Dwight McBride, both of whom view the market for abolitionist print as an opportunity for African American writers and, simultaneously, a limiting factor in the development of an authentic African American literature. See Baker, *Blues, Ideology, and African American Literature*, and McBride, *Impossible Witnesses*.

81. Bruce, *Black American Writing from the Nadir*, 13. Charles W. Chesnutt is perhaps the best-known example of the phenomenon Bruce describes in his book. Working with editor Walter Hines Page, Chesnutt shaped his work in order to publish in elite magazines like the *Atlantic Monthly* and with commercial publishers like Houghton Mifflin.

82. As Michaël Roy notes, commercial publishers did support Black-authored texts in the 1850s (in the wake of *Uncle Tom's Cabin*), but those publications were

certainly shaped by white readers' demands and expectations. See Roy, *Fugitive Texts*, chapter 3.

83. McGill, *American Literature and the Culture of Reprinting*, 19.

84. This proverb—which is biblical in origin—has been used by numerous African American speakers and writers through the years (from Dr. Martin Luther King Jr. to Senator Raphael Warnock).

85. Peterson, *Doers of the Word*, 13.

86. See the introduction to Sanda, *Appointed: An American Novel*. This specific point emerged from Gardner's research into the lives and careers of Anderson and Stowers.

87. See, for example, "Literary Review," *The Congregationalist*, September 17, 1879, and "Rev. Robert Anderson," *The Milledgeville Union Recorder*, May 19, 1896.

88. See Kelly, "Edmund Kelly's Appeal to Lovers of Freedom, Righteous Progress, and Christianity" (1876); and Wilkerson, *The Midnight Cry* (1859).

89. As Ronald Zboray notes in *A Fictive People*, antebellum bookstores were almost always in urban spaces. Rural readers would have acquired reading material through the mail, at local print shops/newspapers, and from book peddlers.

90. On David Ruggles's career as an editor, author, and bookseller, see Hodges, *David Ruggles*. Also see Michaël Roy's *Fugitive Texts* on the limited commercial venues in which readers could purchase antislavery literature.

91. Wilson, *Our Nig*, 140.

92. Parker, *Autobiography*, 1, 8.

93. Manchester, *The History of Colebrook*, 170.

94. Ernest, *Chaotic Justice*, 4.

95. Moody and Rambsy. "Guest Editors' Introduction," 2.

96. Andrews, *To Tell a Free Story*, 5.

97. Roy, "The Slave Narrative Unbound," 271. Mining a similar vein, Eric Gardner writes that "nineteenth-century African American literature has often been reduced to southern stories told in bound books that were written by blacks in the urban Northeast and published books in . . . New York, Philadelphia, and Boston" (*Unexpected Places*, 12). My work is deeply indebted to Gardner's call to expand the scholarly map of nineteenth-century African American literature; as such, only one of the authors I treat in this book might be said to fit the narrow definition of "African American literature" Gardner laments.

98. Mars, *Life*, 3.

99. Foster, "A Narrative," 720.

100. Spires, *The Practice of Citizenship*, 13.

101. See coloredconventions.org and Foreman, Casey, and Patterson, *The Colored Conventions Movement*.

102. Foreman, "Black Organizing," 24.

103. Ernest, "Life Beyond Biography."

104. McHenry, *To Make Negro Literature*, 11.

105. McHenry, *To Make Negro Literature*, 20.

106. Nishikawa, "The Archive on Its Own," 178, 180. Another history of (much earlier) lost books is Brooks, "The Unfortunates."

107. I treat this phenomenon in more detail in chapter 1, but the best source on such publications by white authors is Fabian, *The Unvarnished Truth*.

108. Zafar, *We Wear the Mask*, 13. On the formal and generic overlaps between white and African American self-publishers, also see Fabian, *The Unvarnished Truth*; and Weyler, *Empowering Words*.

109. See Carretta, "'Property of Author.'"

110. McCarthy, "To Plead Our Own Cause," 133.

111. On this, see (among others) Dinius, "'Look!! Look!!! At This!!!!'"; Hinks, "Introduction."

112. See Painter, *Sojourner Truth*; Rohrbach, *Thinking Outside the Book*, chapter 2; and Roy, *Fugitive Texts*, chapter 2.

113. Here I am thinking especially of Ernest, *Liberation Historiography*; Foreman, *Activist Sentiments*; and, Hall, *A Faithful Account of the Race*.

Chapter One

1. Davis, *A Narrative of the Life*, 71.

2. Wilson, *Our Nig*, 140.

3. This form has, in some places, been described as "mendicant literature." I have coined the term "supplicant text," though, because it captures the combination of personal supplication and bookselling that typified the form for former slaves. Moreover, a supplicant is not necessarily a mendicant (as in the cases of Noah Davis and Edmond Kelley, among others). On impoverished booksellers, see Cumming, "Mendicant Pieces," and Fabian, "Beggars and Books."

4. Fabian, *The Unvarnished Truth*, 11.

5. Prince, *A Narrative* (1850), 3.

6. Prince, *A Narrative* (1853), 23.

7. Jones, *The Experience* (1885), 83.

8. Cohen, "Notes from the State of Saint Domingue," 374–75. On the form of the canonical slave narrative, see Andrews, *To Tell a Free Story*; Baker, "Autobiographical Acts"; and Olney, "'I Was Born.'"

9. Garvey, *Writing with Scissors*, 26. On the commonplace book, also see Gross, "Reading for an Extensive Republic," 536–38; and Thomas, "Reading and Writing the Renaissance Commonplace Book."

10. Aaron, *The Light and the Truth* (1840s?), 1.

11. Aaron, *The Light and the Truth* (1845), 6.

12. On Offley, see Doughton and McCarthy, eds., *From Bondage to Belonging*, 160–64; and Offley, *A Narrative of the Life* (1859) and *A Narrative of the Life* (1860).

13. Aaron, *The Light and the Truth of Slavery* (1840s?), 1.

14. Aaron, *The Light and the Truth*, (1840s?), 1.

15. As William Gilmore explains, peddlers were quite common in New England, especially in rural areas, well into the 1860s. There would have been nothing remarkable about a man selling books door-to-door. See Gilmore, "Peddlers and the Dissemination of Printed Material." Also see Zboray, *A Fictive People*, chapter 3.

16. Aaron, *The Light and the Truth* (1840s?), 4.

17. Aaron, *The Light and the Truth* (1840s?), 1.
18. Aaron, *The Light and the Truth* (1840s?), 5.
19. Aaron, *The Light and the Truth* (1840s?), 7.
20. Aaron, *The Light and the Truth* (1840s?), 19.
21. Aaron, *The Light and Truth* (1845), 43. Cossington is listed as a Malden resident in both marriage and death records from the period.
22. Aaron, *The Light and the Truth* (1840s?), 41.
23. One exception to the anonymity that pervades the narrative is Aaron's mention of "Mr. Ludlow" on two occasions. Given that he locates Ludlow in New Haven (and later mentions that he moved to Poughkeepsie), this is almost certainly Henry G. Ludlow, a minister and abolitionist who formed part of the Amistad Committee in 1840.
24. There is no obvious logic of citation in *The Light and Truth of Slavery*, but it may be that attributions in Aaron's book reflect their presence in the original clippings. This is the case with a piece of writing by Elizur Wright or "Dr. Channing." In other places, though (as in the case of Cowper or Isaac Watts), borrowed material is presented without attribution.
25. Aaron, *The Light and the Truth* (1840s?), 29–30.
26. Grandy, *Narrative of the Life*, 72.
27. On the market for slave narratives, see, among others, Fabian, *The Unvarnished Truth*, 79–116; and Augusta Rohrbach, *Truth Stranger than Fiction*, 29–50. Relatedly, Michaël Roy argues that the 1840s were the heyday of what he calls the "itinerant text," which is a text peddled or sold by its author. See *Fugitive Texts*, chapter 2.
28. On this idea, see especially Hack, *The Material Interests*, 101–46.
29. Stanley, "Beggars Can't Be Choosers," 1265. On begging, also see Schweik, *The Ugly Laws*.
30. Aaron, *The Light and Truth* (1845), 45.
31. Aaron, *The Light and Truth* (1845), 44.
32. Aaron, *The Light and Truth* (1845), 45.
33. Prince, *A Narrative* (1853), 3.
34. Jackson, *The Story of Mattie J. Jackson*, 2.
35. Adams, *Narrative*, 3.
36. On these publications, see Fabian, *The Unvarnished Truth*, chapter 4.
37. Parker, *Autobiography*, 5.
38. Parker, *Autobiography*, 1, 8.
39. Parker, *Autobiography*, 4.
40. Parker, *Autobiography*, 7.
41. Parker, *Autobiography*, 7.
42. "Colored Persons Riding in Omnibuses," *Cleveland Herald*, April 27, 1865. On Storer, see Reed, Randall, and Greve, *Bench and Bar of Ohio*, 113–14.
43. Leon Jackson's excellent work on this moment in Horton's literary career appears in *The Business of Letters*, chapter 2; on Grandy, see Williams, "Introduction" in *North Carolina Slave Narratives*, 133–51; on Henson, see Fabian, *The Unvarnished Truth*; Rohrbach, *Truth Stranger than Fiction*; and Roy, "Cheap Editions"; on Roper, see Andrews, *To Tell a Free Story*; and Finseth, "Introduction" in *North Carolina Slave Narratives*, 23–34.

44. Joseph, *Life*, 3.
45. Kelley, *A Family Redeemed*, 3.
46. Kelley, *A Family Redeemed*, 3.
47. Kelley, *A Family Redeemed*, 3.
48. Kelley, *A Family Redeemed*, 3.
49. Kelley, *A Family Redeemed*, 5.
50. Douglass, Frederick. *Narrative of the Life* (1845), in *The Oxford Frederick Douglass Reader*, edited by William L. Andrews, 89. New York: Oxford University Press, 1996.
51. Keckley, *Behind the Scenes*, 56–62.
52. Kelley, *A Family Redeemed*, 7.
53. See Grover, *The Fugitive's Gibraltar*; and Mulderink, *New Bedford's Civil War*.
54. Kelley, *A Family Redeemed*, 9.
55. Kelley, *A Family Redeemed*, 10.
56. Kelley, *A Family Redeemed*, 10.
57. Kelley, *A Family Redeemed*, 11.
58. Johnson, *Soul by Soul*, 112.
59. Kelley, *A Family Redeemed*, 11.
60. Brooks, "The Unfortunates," 51.
61. See *Africa's Quotoa [sic] to the American Nation Must Be Equally Diffused among the Whole*; *Edmund Kelly's Appeal to Lovers of Freedom, Righteous Progress, and Christianity*; *The Great Exodus of the Colored People from the South to the West. Its Cause and Probable Results. The Duty of the Plighted Nation to Them in the Premises*; and, *Important Questions Adapted to the Use of Sabbath Schools, Bible Classes, and Private Families*.
62. Barbara White discovered a trove of information about the Bellmont family and helped connect Wilson's novel to her life. P. Gabrielle Foreman and Reginald Pitts discovered that Wilson was both a peddler of hair tonic (before she published her book) and a medium (after). Finally, Eric Gardner has done extensive work on the purchasers and readers of Wilson's book. See Foreman, "Recovered Autobiographies"; Foreman and Pitts, "Introduction"; Gardner, "'This Attempt of Their Sister'" and "Of Bottles and Books"; and White, "'Our Nig' and the She-Devil."
63. Wilson, *Our Nig*, 3, 130.
64. Eric Gardner's work on Wilson's book sales is highly detailed and proves that Wilson's work sold within a narrow geographic and temporal range. See "'This Attempt of Their Sister'" and "Of Bottles and Books."
65. Pratofiorito, "'To Demand Your Sympathy and Aid,'" 32.
66. Dowling, *Capital Letters*, 29.
67. See Henry Louis Gates Jr. and R. J. Ellis, "Introduction," lix; Ernest, "Economics of Identity"; and Holloway, "Economies of Space."
68. See Gardner, "'This Attempt of Their Sister,'" 232. Gardner also notes that the book itself was an inexpensive or "plain" edition that—while more expensive to produce than a pamphlet—would have cost very little to print and bind.
69. Gardner, "'This Attempt of Their Sister,'" 238.
70. Gardner, "'This Attempt of Their Sister,'" 244.

71. Roy, *Fugitive Texts*, chapter 3. As Roy notes, antislavery novels sold well in the 1850s, but Wilson's book is something of an anomaly in that regard, so it may not have been attractive to a trade publisher.

72. Wilson, *Our Nig*, 140.

Chapter Two

1. Sinha, *The Slave's Cause*, 421.
2. Roy, *Fugitive Texts*, 9.
3. See Rohrbach, *Truth Stranger than Fiction*; and Roy, *Fugitive Texts*, chapter 2.
4. On the connections between abolition and England, see especially Fisch, *American Slaves in Victorian England*; and Tamarkin, *Anglophilia*. Formerly enslaved narrators to publish books in England include (among others) William and Ellen Crafts, Frederick Douglass, Moses Grandy, Moses Roper, and James Watkins.
5. Sekora, "Black Message/White Envelope."
6. Peabody, "Narratives of Fugitive Slaves," 19.
7. McBride, *Impossible Witnesses*, 5.
8. Fanuzzi, *Abolition's Public Sphere*, xxi.
9. See Ernest, *Liberation Historiography*; Hall, *A Faithful Account of the Race*; Litwack, *North of Slavery*; and Quarles, *Black Abolitionists*.
10. McBride, *Impossible Witnesses*, 82.
11. On white influences/limitations and these Black writers' struggles against them, see especially Greenspan, *William Wells Brown*; McFeely, *Frederick Douglass*; Painter, *Sojourner Truth*; and Yellin, *Harriet Jacobs: A Life*.
12. See the bibliography section on self-published narratives for a full listing of Black's publications.
13. Johnson, *Narrative*, 16.
14. Offley, *A Narrative of the Life* (1860), 22.
15. Foreman, "Black Organizing," 29 [italics in original].
16. In this respect, several of the narratives in this chapter bring to mind Robert Stepto's analysis of William Wells Brown's "collection of disparate texts" in the autobiographical sketch preceding *Clotel* and the relationship between that collection of texts and Brown's ability to "authenticate himself." Stepto, *From Behind the Veil*, 28–29.
17. Tilmon, *Brief Miscellaneous Narrative*, 15.
18. Tilmon, *Brief Miscellaneous Narrative*, 27. For a full biographical sketch of Tilmon's life and career, see Jared Hickman, "Tilmon, Levin."
19. Information on the *Sentinel* is scarce, but its editorial outlook is clear in the pages of the more popular Jersey City *Telegraph*, which was a Whig paper that criticized the Know-Nothing politics of the *Sentinel*.
20. James L. Smith—another autobiographer who self-published his book in 1881—recalled Tilmon visiting Norwich, Connecticut, to set up a church. Smith writes, "Rev. Leaven Tilman came to Norwich to aid us in organizing a Methodist Church, as it was his business to organize churches wherever they were needed. He went around to solicit funds for that purpose, and was very zealous in the work.

Myself and others, with his aid, solicited funds for purchasing the ground, and for the building." See Smith, *Autobiography of James L. Smith*, 72.

21. Tilmon, *Brief Miscellaneous Narrative*, 76–77.

22. Tilmon, *Brief Miscellaneous Narrative*, 25. On Tilmon's ordination and work with the church, see Handy, *Scraps of African Methodist Episcopal History*, 173, 179.

23. On one manifestation of this community—the relationship between William Julius Wilson and James McCune Smith—see Spires, *The Practice of Citizenship*, 121–60.

24. See, for example, *Remarks on the Character and Exertions of Elias Hicks on the Abolition of Slavery: Being an Address Delivered Before the African Benevolent Societies in Zion's Chapel, New-York, March 15, 1830*.

25. Tilmon, *The Consequences*, 33–36.

26. Tilmon, *The Consequences*, 31.

27. "Letter from the Editor." *Frederick Douglass's Paper*, May 27, 1853.

28. "Literary Exhibitions in New York City," *Frederick Douglass's Paper*, November 3, 1854.

29. "Communipaw" [James McCune Smith], "New York Literary and Productive Union," *Frederick Douglass's Paper*, February 9, 1855.

30. Spires, *The Practice of Citizenship*, 4.

31. DeLombard, "African American Cultures of Print," 362.

32. On Brown's biography, see Dinius, *The Textual Effects*, chapter 6; and Weaver, "Brown, Paola."

33. Brown, *Address Intended to Be Delivered in the City Hall*.

34. "Lecture of Paola Brown, Esq., on Slavery," *Weekly Spectator*, February 13, 1851.

35. On the rise of Black Canadian communities and Black Canadian writing in the nineteenth century, see Clarke, *Odysseys Home*; Dinius, *The Textual Effects*; and Winks, *The Blacks in Canada*.

36. On abolition movements in Ontario, see Dinius, *The Textual Effects*; and Stouffer, *The Light of Nature and the Law of God*. Stouffer notes that the Anti-Slavery Society of Canada (ASC) enjoyed a major surge in significance in the early 1850s and welcomed Frederick Douglass to speak in Canada on several occasions. As Stouffer notes, the ASC held a weeklong convention in Toronto in April of 1851 (around the time Smallwood published his book) featuring speeches by Douglass, Samuel May, and George Thompson. A few months later, the North American Convention of Colored People in Toronto featured Smallwood as a delegate.

37. The best source on Smallwood is, unsurprisingly, his *Narrative*, which was printed for Smallwood by James Stephens of Toronto in 1851. On Smallwood's life in Canada after the publication of his book, the best source is Richard Almonte's "Introduction" in *A Narrative of Thomas Smallwood*.

38. On the life of Charles Torrey, see Torrey, *The Martyrdom of Abolitionist Charles Torrey*; and Harrold, *Subversives*, 64–93. Harrold is the only scholar to have pursued the Samivel Weller/Thomas Smallwood connection, though his focus is entirely historical.

39. On Gerrit Smith's career as an abolitionist, see Stauffer, *The Black Hearts of Men*. In his book, Stauffer highlights the successes born of interracial antislavery collaboration but notes that—for various reasons—such collaborations did not survive long.

40. Harrold, *Subversives*, 70–71.

41. Smallwood, *A Narrative*, x. In *Textual Effects*, Marcy J. Dinius argues persuasively that, while Smallwood may have been justified in decrying Brown's borrowings of Walker's words, Brown did not simply copy all of Walker's *Appeal* but made a series of changes intended to shape Walker's message for a Canadian audience.

42. Smallwood's publication straddles the line between book and pamphlet. It is a stitched octavo volume sixteen centimeters wide and sixty-four pages long, but it is wrapped in yellow paper covers. I have described it as a pamphlet because Smallwood himself does so.

43. Smallwood, *Narrative*, iii, ix.

44. Jones, *The Experience of Thomas H. Jones* (1862), 3.

45. Dinius's interpretation of Smallwood's preface aligns with mine almost entirely, though I read Smallwood's use of other authors as an example of what Robert Stepto might call the "authenticating narrative," in which a formerly enslaved author exerts complete control over the white voices in his text. See Dinius, *The Textual Effects*, 203–7; Stepto, *From Behind the Veil*, 26–31.

46. Smallwood, *Narrative*, ix.

47. Smallwood, *Narrative*, x.

48. Stouffer, *The Light of Nature*, 113–17. On the September convention, see "North American Convention" in *Voice of the Fugitive*, September 21, 1851.

49. Smallwood, *Narrative*, 14.

50. Smallwood, *Narrative*, 15.

51. Smallwood, *Narrative*, 20.

52. Smallwood, *Narrative*, 20.

53. Smallwood, *Narrative*, 25.

54. Smallwood, *Narrative*, 28.

55. Smallwood, *Narrative*, 24.

56. See Almonte, "Introduction," as well as scattered newspaper notices from the Toronto *Globe* and other papers. Smallwood owned a saw-sharpening shop that he worked at until 1872, and the April 10, 1880, issue of the *Globe* includes a notice of a farm "in a high state of cultivation" that was sold from Thomas Smallwood to T. H. McCaul.

57. Samivel Weller is the name of a character in Dickens's *Pickwick Papers*. There may have been reasons particular to the character that led Smallwood to adopt this name, but he may also have enjoyed the alliterative connection between "Sam Weller" and "Small Wood."

58. Smallwood, *Narrative*, 56.

59. Smallwood, *Narrative*, 61.

60. Smallwood's first column as Weller appears in the July 27, 1842, issue of the *Tocsin of Liberty*. The entire run of papers in which Smallwood published is held at the Boston Public Library.

61. Smallwood, *Narrative*, 56.

62. McBride, *Impossible Witnesses*, 5. McBride's ideas find an echo in John Ernest's *Liberation Historiography*, wherein Ernest describes "the theater of antislavery culture" in which Black activists spoke and wrote. See Ernest, *Liberation Historiography*, 187.

63. McBride, *Impossible Witnesses*, 3.

64. Anderson, *Life and Narrative*, 3rd ed., 38.

65. Anderson's obituary explains that the M. E. church "asked Anderson to stop his overt Underground Railroad activities," which recalls something of Frederick Douglass's critique of the *"overground railroad"* in his 1845 *Narrative*. See "William Anderson, Colored Preacher, Died Here, Buried in Springdale," *Madison Courier*, March 17, 1867.

66. 1850 Federal Census, Indiana, Jefferson County.

67. *Terre Haute Wabash Express*, January 16, 1856, p. 3.

68. "'O Shame, Where is Thy Blush?'" and "Sambo Jubilant—Negrophiliacs in Ecstasy," *Goshen Democrat*, July 16, 1856, p. 3.

69. "Tremendous Gathering," *Goshen Democrat*, October 1, 1856, p. 3.

70. *Vevay Weekly Reveille*, August 6, 1856, p. 3.

71. "DISUNION," *Weekly Indiana State Sentinel*, November 13, 1856, p. 6.

72. Spires, *The Practice of Citizenship*, 3.

73. Anderson, *Life and Narrative*, 53.

74. "From the New York Times. MORE OF THE NEGRO INSURRECTION IN TENNESSEE," *The Liberator*, December 19, 1856, p. 3. Other versions of this story appeared in papers around the country. This, in turn, led to Anderson's arrest being mentioned on the floor of Congress amid a debate between William Hayden English and William Cumback. English insisted that "the lowest and most God forsaken Negro-stealers in the country were to be found side by side with . . . the Republican party" and accused Cumback of having Anderson campaign and make speeches for him in 1856. Cumback denied the charge. Indiana congressman Schuyler Colfax even insisted that Anderson was a paid operative of the Democratic Party meant to scare white people into voting against Republicans. For a transcript of the congressional debate, see "THIRTY-FOURTH CONGRESS. THIRD SESSION," *National Era*, December 25, 1856, p. 1.

75. Records of Anderson's arrest and arraignment have been lost. The only legal records related to Anderson's case are those connected with Elijah Anderson's subsequent conviction. It was Elijah Anderson who was eventually convicted of the very crime for which William Anderson was first arrested. Even so, William J. Anderson's name is not mentioned in the records of Elijah Anderson's trial. See "Commonwealth of Kentucky vs. Elijah Anderson, free person of color," Trimble County Circuit Court Records, Bedford, Kentucky. Order Book 3, 1855–1865.

76. Anderson, *Life and Narrative*, 55.

77. Anderson, *Life and Narrative*, 3.

78. Anderson did not copy all of Nell's work, but several of his anecdotes (including his first entry on Crispus Attucks) were clearly taken from *The Colored Patriots*.

79. Andrews, *To Tell a Free Story*, 184.

80. Dinius, "'Look!! Look!!! At This,'" 56.

81. Anderson, *Life and Narrative*, 4.

82. Anderson, *Life and Narrative*, 4.

83. Orr's work appears in many children's books of the antebellum period including popular editions by Jacob Abbot and Susan Warner.

84. A very similar portrait (not signed by Orr) appears in *Experience and Personal Narrative of Uncle Tom Jones, who was for Forty Years a Slave; also, the Surprising Adventures of Wild Tom, of the Island Retreat, a Fugitive Negro from South Carolina*. This pamphlet, which combines a part of Jones's self-published *Narrative* and a part of Richard Hildreth's novel *Archy Moore*, was first published in New York in 1854 and reprinted in Boston in 1858.

85. As Marcus Wood explains, Black authors were attuned to "the snares and pitfalls surrounding the representation of the black body within a white Northern publishing environment" and usually sought images that "obey the rules of the European portrait tradition." Wood, *Black Milk*, 113, 112.

86. Casmier-Paz, "Slave Narratives," 92.

87. Anderson, *Life and Narrative*, 3rd ed., 29.

88. Anderson, *Life and Narrative*, 3rd. ed., 14, 21, 27.

89. My analysis here is deeply indebted to Saidiya Hartman's *Scenes of Subjection*.

90. See, for example, *New Albany* (IN) *Daily Ledger*, January 3, 1857; *Seymour* (IN) *Times*, September 4, 1857; and *Minnesota Weekly Pioneer and Democrat*, July 11, 1862.

91. "AN APPEAL TO THE FRIENDS OF HUMANITY," *Christian Recorder*, December 23, 1865; "A VOICE FROM MICHIGAN," *Christian Recorder*, December 30, 1865.

92. "State Items [from the *Indianapolis Herald*]," *Cincinnati Enquirer*, March 22, 1867, p. 2.

93. "William Anderson, Colored Preacher, Died Here, Buried in Springdale," *Madison Courier*, March 18, 1867.

Chapter Three

1. Bethel, *The Roots of African American Identity*, 168. Bethel's book is an excellent source for the relationship between historical memory and the foundations of Black identity. Other authors who have evaluated nineteenth-century African American historical writing focus less on identity per se and more on political or social activism.

2. Pennington, *A Text Book of the Origin and History*, 3; Nell, *The Colored Patriots of the American Revolution*, 10.

3. On this idea, excellent but quite different treatments include Hall, *A Faithful Account of the Race*, which focuses on both the Black public sphere in the nineteenth century and the emergence of African American history as a profession, Quarles, "Black History's Antebellum Origins," which recovers and summarizes the work of antebellum Black historians, and Sweet, *Black Images of America*, which highlights the ways Black historians imagined the United States and their place within it.

4. Parfait, Le Dantec-Lowry, and Bourhis-Mariotti, introduction to *Writing History from the Margins*, 2.

5. Parfait, "'The Grandest Book Ever Written.'"

6. Smith, *Autobiography of James L. Smith*, 100.

7. Veney, *Narrative*, 43.

8. Ernest, *Liberation Historiography*, 159.

9. On Anderson's relationship with Shadd-Cary, see Rhodes, *Mary Ann Shadd Cary*, 118; and Ripley, *The Black Abolitionist Papers*, vol. 2, 428.

10. Rhodes, *Mary Ann Shadd Cary*, 131.

11. Goutier, S. "Letter from Toronto." *Weekly Anglo-African*, April 28, 1860.

12. "News About Boston," *Weekly Anglo-African*, January 12, 1861.

13. W[illiam] C. N[ell], "Meeting of Colored Citizens in Boston," *The Liberator*, January 11, 1861.

14. Nell, "Meeting."

15. Nell, "Meeting."

16. These are the very qualities celebrated in the January 4, 1861, review of Perry's narrative. See "Rev. of *A Voice from Harper's Ferry*," *The Liberator*, January 4, 1861.

17. "New Publications," *Douglass' Monthly Magazine*, February 1861, p. 411.

18. "At Home," *The Liberator*, November 8, 1861, p. 2.

19. In the 1873 edition of *A Voice from Harper's Ferry*, J. D. Enos indicates that, because he feared for his life, Anderson refused to visit the United States until after the war. Contemporary newspaper evidence indicates that Anderson did visit the United States, but it seems likely that his visits were brief and focused on book promotion and book selling. See Anderson and Enos, *A Voice from Harper's Ferry*, 4.

20. Anderson, *A Voice from Harper's Ferry*, 3.

21. Anderson, *A Voice from Harper's Ferry*, 8.

22. Anderson, *A Voice from Harper's Ferry*, 8.

23. Anderson, *A Voice from Harper's Ferry*, 14.

24. Anderson, *A Voice from Harper's Ferry*, 23.

25. Anderson, *A Voice from Harper's Ferry*, 24.

26. Anderson, *A Voice from Harper's Ferry*, 27.

27. Anderson, *A Voice from Harper's Ferry*, 59.

28. Anderson, *A Voice from Harper's Ferry*, 60.

29. Anderson, *A Voice from Harper's Ferry*, 61–62.

30. Though census records and city directories indicate that a J. D. Enos was appointed as a postmaster after the Civil War, I have not been able to identify Enos with any certainty, nor have I been able to locate any definitive information on him or his connection to Anderson.

31. Enos, preface to *A Voice from Harper's Ferry*, 3.

32. Enos, preface, 3.

33. See Chester County Poorhouse Records; US Census 1870.

34. Roy, *Fugitive Texts*, 84.

35. On the Connecticut law, see Menschel, "Abolition without Deliverance."

36. "Supreme Court of Errors," *Connecticut Times*, June 17, 1837; "Convention of Colored People," *The Liberator*, June 19, 1840.

37. In addition to his published pamphlet, the best source on Mars is David White's "The Real Life of James Mars."

38. *Proceedings of the National Convention of Colored People and Their Friends*, 18.

39. *Proceedings of the National Convention of Colored People and Their Friends*, 19.

40. Mars, *Life of James Mars* (1866), 36.

41. Mars, *Life of James Mars* (1866), 36–37.

42. Of the fifteen copies of Mars's *Life* that I have examined, only one—the twelfth edition housed at the American Antiquarian Society—includes a purchaser's name. Floyd Hamblin (perhaps of upstate New York) purchased a copy of Mars's book on October 11, 1875, in Norfolk, Connecticut. Hamblin penned the following note at the end of the book: "The writer of this book is still alive hail [sic] and hearty. I have made his acquaintance."

43. "New England Notes," *Lowell Daily Citizen*, June 28, 1879.

44. See, for example, "Pointers," *Daily Inter Ocean*, August 23, 1879; "A Connecticut Slave," *New Orleans Times-Picayune*, September 13, 1879; "Pensioning Connecticut's Slaves," *Daily Evening Bulletin*, August 28, 1879.

45. "A Connecticut Slave," *New Haven Evening Register*, August 21, 1879.

46. On this unfortunate phenomenon, see Sinche, "Self-Publication, Self-Promotion."

47. A preaching license was issued by a board of elders after a potential minister delivered a trial sermon and passed examination by the board. The license would have allowed its bearer to preach within the denomination for a year. Whether or not James licensed Douglass is up for debate, but Douglass did recall James as one of many men who helped him find a home in the A. M. E. Zion Church in the late 1830s. See Hood, *One Hundred Years of the African Methodist Episcopal Zion Church*, 541.

48. James appears in the call for the convention that was published in both the June 18, 1840, *National Anti-Slavery Standard* and the June 6 and June 13, 1840, *Colored American*. His contributions to the convention are noted in *Convention of the Colored Inhabitants of the State of New York 1840*.

49. "Rev. Thomas James," *Frederick Douglass's Paper*, January 28, 1859.

50. "Rev. Thomas James," *Frederick Douglass's Paper*, April 15, 1859.

51. James, *Life*, 17.

52. When General John Palmer ran for governor of Illinois in 1868 as a Republican, he recalled his support for Thomas James's authority during the war and thereby affirmed his bona fides as a civil rights champion. See "General Palmer. His Speech at Carlinville, Ills," *Louisville Daily Courier*, September 29, 1868. Palmer won the election and served one term.

53. James, *Life*, 18.

54. James, *Life*, 22.

55. "AN AGED COLORED LECTURER," *New York Times*, July 25, 1884.

56. Ernest, *Liberation Historiography*, 187; McBride, *Impossible Witnesses*, 5.

57. According to its own corporate history, the *Rochester Post-Express* boasted "one of the largest" job printing establishments "to be found in any but the chief cities of the country." See Devoy, *Rochester and the Post-Express*, 275.

58. "An Anti-Slavery Veteran," *New York Freeman*, June 26, 1886.

59. "Black Diamond City," *Cleveland Gazette*, July 17, 1886.

60. "Rochester, N.Y.," *Cleveland Gazette*, October 9, 1886.

61. Jeffrey, *Abolitionists Remember*, 62.

62. James, *Life*, 23.

63. James, *Wonderful Eventful Life*, 24.

64. "Personal and Pertinent," *New York Age*, July 4, 1891.

65. See, for example, "Rochester Ripples," *New York Age*, April 25, 1891; "Telegraphic Notes," *Evening Bulletin*, April 20, 1891; and "An Interesting Career," *Washington Post*, April 20, 1891.

66. "Obituary," *New York Tribune*, April 19, 1891.

67. Public documents allow us to track Stroyer with some accuracy: According to the 1871 *Worcester City Directory*, Stroyer was working as a laborer; by 1875, he is listed as a student in the English Department in the Worcester Academy yearbook. In 1878, the *Worcester City Directory* lists him as a clergyman, and in 1879, he is listed as the pastor of the Salem A.M.E. church in the Salem Directory published by Sampson, Davenport, and Co. (though his name also appears in the Worcester directory). Interestingly, the 1880 census lists Stroyer as a Worcester resident and "book agent." Stroyer eventually moved to Salem full time since his death appears as one of the "Historical Events of Salem" in the 1911 Naumkeag Salem City Directory, suggesting he had attained some notoriety (or even fame) in his adopted hometown.

68. The 1898 records for Newcomb and Gauss have been lost, but in 1901 James B. Giffords paid $112 to print 200 copies of his book *Crankisms: Random Thoughts Written in Verse*. His payment included $18 for binding of 100 copies. The book is somewhat longer than Stroyer's and is bound in red cloth with gold-stamped letters; it also has much larger margins and heavier paper. Based on Giffords's book, I would estimate that Stroyer's printing costs were around $100–$120 for 200 bound copies. If Stroyer printed more copies, the price per copy would have been somewhat lower. Day Book, Newcomb and Gauss, 1899–1905.

69. One of the few twentieth-century scholars to showcase Stroyer's work was Marhsall Fishwick, who included his sketch "The Custom of Christmas" in the edited collection *Remus, Rastus, Revolution*. Stroyer's 1879 narrative also appears (prefaced by an informative introduction) in McCarthy and Doughton, eds., *From Bondage to Belonging*, 174–206.

70. Stroyer, *My Life in the South* (1885), 8.

71. Stroyer, *My Life in the South* (1885), 83.

72. See Washington, *Up from Slavery*; and Blight, *Race and Reunion*.

73. Faulkner, *Requiem for a Nun*, 80.

74. Stroyer, *My Life in the South* (1885), 4–7.

75. Stroyer, *My Life in the South* (1885), 7.

76. Stroyer, *My Life in the South* (1885), 4.

77. Stroyer, *My Life in the South* (1885), 6.

78. Stroyer, *My Life in the South* (1885), 7.

79. Foreman, "'Reading Aright,'" 330.

80. Ernest, *Liberation Historiography*, 157.

81. Ernest, *Liberation Historiography*, 209.

82. Gardner, "Slave Narratives and Archival Research," 44–45.

83. Irwin Russell's "Christmas in the Quarters," Thomas Nelson Page's *In Old Virginia*, and Joel Chandler Harris's "Uncle Remus" stories are representative here. Though these texts are not without their moments of critique, they evince what Lucinda Mackethan

calls "a sentimental rather than a critical vision of life in the Old South." See "Plantation Fiction," 209-18.

84. Stroyer, *My Life in the South* (1885), 10.
85. Stroyer, *My Life in the South* (1885), 11.
86. Stroyer, *My Life in the South* (1885), 14.
87. Stroyer, *My Life in the South* (1885), 15.
88. Stroyer, *My Life in the South* (1885), 39.
89. Stroyer, *My Life in the South* (1885), 43.
90. Stroyer, *My Life in the South* (1885), 44.
91. Stroyer, *My Life in the South* (1885), 49, 51, 54, 63-64.
92. Stroyer, *My Life in the South* (1885), 40.
93. On these aspects of *My Southern Home*, see Ernest, "William Wells Brown Maps the South."
94. In addition to those papers from which quotations are drawn, advertisements for Stroyer's book or notices of his bookselling visits appear in the *New Hampshire Sentinel*, the *New Haven Evening Register*, the *Springfield Republican*, and the *St. Albans Messenger*.
95. *Worcester Daily Spy*, September 27, 1879. Gager's inscribed copy of *My Life in the South* resides at the New York Historical Society. Gager's only writing on the book is on the title page and includes his name, the date of purchase, and the price. Gager was the longtime town clerk in Norwich, Connecticut (see *National Leader*, June 22, 1889).
96. *Cleveland Gazette*, December 24, 1887.
97. Stroyer, *My Life in the South* (1898), 85-86.

Chapter Four

1. Marx, "Mr. Eliot," 428.
2. Marx, "Mr. Eliot," 428.
3. Evidence of these critical responses focusing on Jim's plight might be found in Arac, *Huckleberry Finn as Idol and Target*; Graff and Phelan, eds. *The Adventures of Huckleberry Finn: A Case Study in Critical Controversy*; and Leonard, Tenney, and Davis, eds., *Satire or Evasion?*.
4. On the 1880s contexts for Twain's novel, see (among others) Arac, *Huckleberry Finn as Idol and Target*; and Sundquist, *To Wake the Nations: Race in the Making of American Literature*, chapter 3.
5. Ernest, *Chaotic Justice*; Hannah-Jones, "America Wasn't a Democracy;" Franklin, *From Slavery to Freedom*; Huggins, *Black Odyssey*; Litwack, *Been in the Storm So Long*.
6. On the history of racial injustice in the United States, see Berry, *Black Resistance/White Law*; Blackmon, *Slavery by Another Name*; Higginbotham, *In the Matter of Color* and *Shades of Freedom*; Jones, *Birthright Citizens*; Luxenberg, *Separate: The Story of Plessy v. Ferguson*; Gordon-Reed, ed. *Race on Trial*; Smith, *Civic Ideals*.
7. Cover, "Violence and the Word," 1604.
8. Wagner, *Disturbing the Peace*, 153.
9. Smith, *A Narrative*, 30.

10. Brinch, *The Blind African Slave*, 177.
11. See Eldridge, *Memoirs of Elleanor Eldridge* and Lane, *The Narrative of Lunsford Lane*.
12. Eldridge, *Memoirs of Elleanor Eldridge*, 87 [italics in original].
13. Eldridge, *Memoirs of Elleanor Eldridge*, 90.
14. DeLombard, *Slavery on Trial*, 7.
15. McCarthy, "To Plead Our Own Cause," 137.
16. DeLombard, *Slavery on Trial*, 3.
17. DeLombard, "Slave Narratives and US Legal History," 70.
18. McPherson, *Christ's Millennium*, 5.
19. McPherson, *Christ's Millennium*, 6. McPherson wrote to Adams six times in 1799–1800, though Adams never responded. In 1813, Adams wrote to Thomas Jefferson and asked about McPherson, whom Jefferson knew and had employed as a messenger. Interestingly, McPherson also knew James Madison and had dined with him in 1800 (after delivering the letter from Jefferson). Madison obviously trusted McPherson since he loaned him horses after the dinner. See Berkeley, "Prophet Without Honor," 180–90.
20. McPherson, *Christ's Millennium*, 11.
21. Richmond City Legislative Petition, December 10, 1810, Virginia State Library.
22. McPherson, *Christ's Millennium*, 17–18
23. See Berkeley, "Prophet Without Honor"; Robert, "William Wirt, Virginian"; and Van Schreeven, "William Waller Hening."
24. McPherson, *Christ's Millennium*, 20.
25. McPherson, *Christ's Millennium*, 15.
26. McPherson, *Christ's Millennium*, 11.
27. McPherson, *Christ's Millennium*, 6. See also "Richmond City Legislative Petition."
28. McPherson, *Christ's Millennium*, 7.
29. McPherson, *Christ's Millennium*, 7.
30. McPherson, *Christ's Millennium*, 8.
31. This may have come as a surprise to Thomas Jefferson, who wrote in 1812 that he had known McPherson for twenty years and that he was "was too honest to be molested by any body, & too inoffensive to be a subject for the Mad-house." See "Thomas Jefferson to John Adams, 20 April 1812," in Jefferson et al., *The Papers of Thomas Jefferson*, Retirement Series, vol. 4, 626–28. Jefferson's comment came in a letter to John Adams after the latter received a letter from McPherson in February of 1812.
32. McPherson, *Christ's Millennium*, 11.
33. McPherson, *Christ's Millennium*, 11.
34. "Notice," *Virginia Argus*, October 21, 1815, p. 1.
35. Berkeley, "Prophet Without Honor," 189.
36. See *Richmond Commercial Compiler*, June 12, 1818, and August 6, 1818.
37. Smith, *A Short History of the Life of Christopher McPherson*.
38. Randolph, *Sketches of Slave Life*, 3. On Haskill, see Randolph, *Sketches of Slave Life*, 37.
39. Randolph, *Sketches of Slave Life*, 37.
40. Randolph, *Sketches of Slave Life*, 5–10.

41. Randolph, *Sketches of Slave Life*, 12.

42. Randolph, *Sketches of Slave Life*, 34.

43. Randolph, *Sketches of Slave Life*, 9.

44. Bassard, introduction to *Sketches of Slave Life*, 11. Bassard's edition of Randolph's book is one of several editions of self-published African American texts that have been reprinted in the Regenerations series with West Virginia University Press. This series, under the editorial leadership of Joycelyn Moody and John Ernest, has done a great deal to bring understudied texts to new readers.

45. Randolph, *Sketches of Slave Life*, 21–22.

46. Katherine Clay Bassard's excellent research confirms that Harriet Barber was the mother of Edloe's children. See Bassard, introduction to *Sketches of Slave Life*, 16–19.

47. Randolph, *Sketches of Slave Life*, 26–27.

48. The best sources on Burns are Charles Emery Stevens, *Anthony Burns: A History*, and, much more recently, Gordon S. Barker, *The Imperfect Revolution*.

49. On this campaign, see Barker, *The Imperfect Revolution*, chapter 4.

50. Clarke, *The Rendition of Anthony Burns*, 9.

51. Randolph, *Sketches of Slave Life*, 26.

52. Randolph, *Sketches of Slave Life*, 27.

53. The distinction between status and contract relationships in antebellum slave narratives is treated in detail in DeLombard, "Slave Narratives and US Legal History," 72–74.

54. On the court case, see Bassard, introduction to *Sketches of Slave Life*, 23–24. In the decades after he published *Sketches of Slave Life*, Peter Randolph occasionally worked as a waiter and laborer, but he always identified himself as a clergyman, and he served as the pastor to churches in New York, Connecticut, and Massachusetts. After the Civil War, Randolph relocated to Virginia to aid in Reconstruction efforts among emancipated Blacks, but he would return to Boston in the 1870s and live there until his death in 1897.

55. In the first (and only extant) issue of the *Joliet Record*, published on June 7, 1880, the editors of the *Record* describe it as a "live, uncompromising Democratic . . . paper."

56. Perhaps because his pamphlet is so atypical, Blair has been almost entirely ignored by critics except for brief mentions in Gardner, "Slave Narratives and Archival Research," and Andrews, "Slave Narratives, 1865–1900."

57. Ninth Census of the United States, 1870, National Archives, Washington, DC.

58. Tenth Census of the United States, 1880, Records of the Bureau of the Census, Record Group 29, National Archives, Washington, DC.

59. Blair, *Book for the People!*, 11.

60. Blair, *Book for the People!*, 6. Reading was the county judge and Ray the county treasurer. Both served from 1864 until 1878 (except for a two-year hiatus by Ray from 1876 to 1878). See *The History of Grundy County Illinois*.

61. Blair, *Book for the People!*, 7.

62. See case file #586, *Blair vs. Ray, Reading, and Schroder*, found in box 70 of the Grundy County Circuit Court Case Files, 1846–1963, which I located with the generous assistance of Chamere Poole-Warren of Illinois State University.

63. Blair, *Book for the People!*, 11–12.
64. Weyler, *Empowering Words*, 5.
65. Blair, *Book for the People!*, 13, 19.
66. DeLombard, "Slave Narratives and US Legal History," 79.
67. DeLombard, "Slave Narratives and US Legal History," 81; Blair, *Book for the People!*, 16, 23, 28, 29.
68. Blair, *Book for the People!*, 28.
69. Blair, *Book for the People!*, 22–23.
70. Blair, *Book for the People!*, 25.
71. Blair, *Book for the People!*, 25.
72. Gardner, *Unexpected Places*, 43.
73. Blair, *Book for the People!*, 4–5.
74. Blair, *Book for the People!*, 16, 15.
75. Blair, *Book for the People!*, 31.
76. Blair, *Book for the People!*, 13.
77. Blair, *Book for the People!*, 31.
78. See South Dakota, State Census, 1905 and US Indexed County Land Ownership Maps, 1860–1918 (Roll 102, Sully, 1916).
79. "Dakota Colored Rancher Dies at Age of 101 Years," *Forest City* (SD) *Press*, October 18, 1916; "One Hundred Years Old, Former Slave, Dead," *Omaha* (NE) *Daily Bee*, October 14, 1916. These exaggerations in age are quite typical for obituaries. Also see *100 Years of Proud People*.
80. Delaney, *From the Darkness Cometh the Light*, vii.
81. See Gardner, "'Face to Face.'"
82. Carby, *Reconstructing Womanhood*; Foreman, *Activist Sentiments*; Foster, *Written by Herself*.
83. Foreman, *Activist Sentiments*, 99.
84. Barrett, "Self-Knowledge, Law, and African American Autobiography," 115.
85. Gardner, "'You Have No Business to Whip Me'"; VanderVelde, *Redemption Songs*, 143–58.
86. Gardner, "'Face to Face,'" 61.
87. My own research on J. T. Smith merely duplicates Eric Gardner's work, which shows that John T. Smith's "publishing house" produced very few books and all of them were religious in nature. Smith was, like most of the printers mentioned in this book, a job printer who occasionally printed books. See Gardner, "Face to Face," 54.
88. Foreman, "Reading-Aright," 351–52.
89. Delaney, *From the Darkness Cometh the Light*, 40.
90. Delaney, *From the Darkness Cometh the Light*, 41.
91. Barrett, "Self-Knowledge, Law, and African American Autobiography," 119.
92. Delaney, *From the Darkness Cometh the Light*, 47.
93. Barrett, "Self-Knowledge, Law, and African American Autobiography," 115.
94. In terms of African American autobiography, this is a point made by Houston Baker, Dwight McBride, and Robert Stepto (among others).
95. VanderVelde, *Redemption Songs*, 145.
96. Gardner, "'You Have No Business,'" 45.

97. Delaney, *From the Darkness Cometh the Light*, 63.

98. As Carby, Foreman, and Foster all note, this aspect of Delaney's personality is certainly comparable to Harper's Iola Leroy.

99. Delaney, *From the Darkness Cometh the Light*, 63.

100. This is a point made most directly by Mary Frances Berry in *Black Resistance/White Law*.

101. Delaney, *From the Darkness Cometh the Light*, v.

102. "Their Outraged Dead," *Boston Daily Advertiser*, June 1, 1892. According to the report, Randolph attended the meeting and gave the invocation.

103. Wagner, *Disturbing the Peace*, 153.

Chapter Five

1. White, *A Brief Account*, 11.
2. Andrews, *To Tell a Free Story*, 55.
3. On White's post-narrative career, see Hodges, "Introduction," in *Black Itinerant Ministers of the Gospel*, 1–49.
4. Glaude, *Exodus!*, 21; Ernest, *A Nation within a Nation*, 59.
5. Glaude, *Exodus!*, 21.
6. Bassard, *Spiritual Interrogations*, 20.
7. This is a point made with especial force by Frances Smith Foster in "A Narrative."
8. Allen, *The Life, Experience and Gospel Labors*.
9. Asher, *An Autobiography*, iii.
10. Thompson, *Biography of a Slave*, iii.
11. Foote, *A Brand Plucked from the Fire*. On Doty, see *Christian Harvester*, vol. 4, no. 4 (April 1876): 316.
12. Amanda Smith, *An Autobiography*. On Thoburn, see Brackney, "Thoburn, James Mills (1836–1922), Methodist missionary and bishop," *American National Biography*.
13. Andrews, "The Politics of African-American Ministerial Autobiography," 117.
14. Peterson, *The Looking Glass*, 58 ff.
15. Henry, *Autobiography of Rev. Thomas W. Henry*, 3.
16. Henry, *Autobiography*, 3.
17. Gardner, *Unexpected Places*, 18.
18. Smith, *Biography*, 7.
19. Smith, *Biography*, 11.
20. Smith, *Biography*, 15.
21. Smith, *Biography*, 96–97.
22. Smith, *Biography*, 6.
23. Smith, *Biography*, 7.
24. "Father David Smith," *Christian Recorder*, May 5, 1881, p. 2.
25. "Notice," *Christian Recorder*, January 5, 1882. Advertisements ran (off and on) until October of 1882.
26. Gardner, *Black Print Unbound*, 71–80.
27. Smith, *Biography*, 7.
28. Smith, *Biography*, 38.

29. Smith, *Biography*, 52–53. The church Smith founded was the Israel A.M.E. Church, which lasted into the 1870s. Moreover, as of 1915, eight extant churches could "directly and indirectly trace their origin to Israel." See John W. Cromwell, "News of Churches: Israel A.M.E. Church," *Washington Sun*, February 26, 1915, p. 3.

30. Smith, *Biography*, 42.
31. Smith, *Biography*, 50.
32. Smith, *Biography*, 96.
33. Marrs, *Life and History*, x.
34. Marrs, *Life and History*, 15.
35. Marrs, *Life and History*, 17.
36. Marrs, *Life and History*, 23.
37. Marrs, *Life and History*, 76.
38. Marrs, *Life and History*, 61.
39. Marrs, *Life and History*, 137.
40. Marrs, *Life and History*, 126.
41. Marrs, *Life and History*, 101.
42. Marrs, *Life and History*, 105.
43. Marrs, *Life and History*, 106.

44. See Parrish, ed., *Golden Jubilee*, 107. Beargrass Baptist Church celebrated its 140th anniversary in 2020.

45. Simmons, *Men of Mark*, 581. As president of the Kentucky Normal and Theological Institute, Simmons would have known Marrs, so we can assume this information came from Marrs himself. In his discussion of Marrs, Simmons also notes that Marrs "has amassed some worldly goods, in value to the extent of $3,500."

46. Butcher appears in census records in 1860, 1870, and 1880 and in city directory listings throughout the period. Based on my searches of all men and women working at printers' offices in 1881, Butcher was the only Black employee of any printing shop in Louisville at the time. See *Caron's Directory*, vol. 11.

47. Gibson, *History of the United Brothers of Friendship*, 29.

48. I base this claim on my reading of various city directories published between 1873 and 1908.

49. Lee, *Journal*, 40.
50. Lee, *Journal*, 5.
51. Lee, *Journal*, 6, 12, 13, 16.
52. Lee, *Journal*, 10.
53. Foster, *Written by Herself*, 74.
54. Elrod, *Piety and Dissent*, 136.

55. In this respect, Lee is one of the nineteenth-century Black women for whom, as Joycelyn Moody writes, "both the personal and the *spiritual* are political." See Moody, *Sentimental Confessions*, 17.

56. Lee, *Journal*, 11.
57. Lee, *Journal*, 11.
58. Lee, *Journal*, 77.
59. Lee, *Life*, 24.
60. Payne, *History of the African Methodist Episcopal Church*, 190.

61. Foster, *Written by Herself*, 74.
62. Payne, *History of the African Methodist Episcopal Church*, 192.
63. Lee, *Journal*, 79.
64. Lee, *Journal*, 88.
65. Wilkerson, *The Midnight Cry* (1859). By referencing the general who served with Gates at Saratoga, Wilkerson links himself to James Wilkinson, the Revolutionary War general.
66. Roosevelt, *The Winning of the West*, vol. 3, 124.
67. Wilkerson, *Midnight Cry* (1859). A portion of Wilkerson's broadside is the basis for a story retold in Anna-Lisa Cox, *The Bone and Sinew of the Land*, 105.
68. Wilkerson, *The Midnight Cry* (1859).
69. Wilkerson, *History*, 4.
70. Tanner, *An Apology for African Methodism*, 314.
71. Langston, *From the Virginia Plantation to the National Capitol*, 64. For a speculative version of Wilkerson's role in the riots, see Cox, *The Bone and Sinew of the Land*, 102–8.
72. Payne, *Recollections of Seventy Years*, 225; Payne, *History of the African Methodist Episcopal Church*, 186.
73. Wilkerson, *History*, 10.
74. Wilkerson, *History*, 14.
75. Wilkerson, *History*, 21.
76. Wilkerson, *History*, 26.
77. Wilkerson, *History*, 32.
78. "Various Churches," *Western Christian Advocate*, July 17, 1850.
79. *Minutes of the Ohio Annual Conference of the African Methodist Episcopal Church* (1850), 15, 19.
80. Wilkerson, *History*, 38.
81. "Various Churches," *Western Christian Advocate*, October 30, 1850; "Religious Notice," *Madison Daily Banner*, May 30, 1851.
82. "Religious Notice," *Madison Daily Banner*, May 30, 1851.
83. *Minutes of the Ohio Annual Conference of the African Methodist Episcopal Church* (1852), 11–12.
84. These claims appear in Wilkerson's self-published *Preamble*, 9–10. There is no mention of the Educational Orphan Institute in the extant proceedings of the A.M.E. Church.
85. Wilkerson, *History*, 40.
86. Wilkerson, *History*, 40.
87. Though there was an A.M.E. minister and elder named William P. Quinn whom Wilkerson knew and admired, he is not the printer of the broadside. William Quinn appears as a job printer in several Philadelphia city directories of the period and printed several broadsides for other clients. See, for example, the broadside published by the Burns Club of Philadelphia: Celebration of the Centennial Anniversary of the Birth of Robert Burns, by the Burns Club, of Philadelphia, January 25th, 1859. See also *McElroy's Philadelphia City Directory*.
88. Wilkerson, *History*, 40.

89. Wilkerson, The Midnight Cry.

90. *Twelfth General Conference of the African M.E. Church* (1860), 16.

91. *Twelfth General Conference*, 33.

92. Wilkerson, *History*, 8.

93. Wilkerson, *History*, 2.

94. *Thirteenth General Conference of the African M.E. Church* (1864): 9–10.

95. *Thirteenth General Conference of the African M.E. Church* (1864): 10. Revels's pronouncement notwithstanding, I have not located any condemnations of Wilkerson in either the *Christian Recorder* or the *Anglo-African*.

96. Wilkerson, *The Midnight Cry & Millennium Dawn*.

97. "Rev. James Wilkerson," *Alexandria Gazette*, January 11, 1867, p. 1.

98. *Times-Picayune*, March 6, 1867, p. 1.

99. M., "Indianapolis Correspondence," *Christian Recorder*, November 16, 1867, and November 30, 1867.

100. H[enry] M[cNeal] Turner, "Letter from Savannah," *Christian Recorder*, March 12, 1874.

101. Julia W. Roberts, "Biographical," *Christian Recorder*, December 29, 1881.

102. For example, James Handy's *Scraps of African Methodist Episcopal History* (1902), Alexander Payne's *History of the African Methodist Episcopal Church* (1891), David Smith's *Biography* (1881), and Alexander Wayman's *My Recollections of African M.E. Ministers, or Forty Years' Experience in the African Methodist Episcopal Church* (1881).

Chapter Six

1. Fabian, *The Unvarnished Truth*, 3.

2. On Roper, see Finseth, "Introduction," in *North Carolina Slave Narratives*.

3. Price, "Moses Roper," *The Patriot*, November 16, 1840.

4. Brooks, *Bodies in Dissent*, 130. On Brown, also see Fisch, *American Slaves in Victorian England*; and Ruggles, *The Unboxing of Henry Brown*.

5. See Parker, *Recollections of Slavery Times*; O'Neil, *Life and History of William O'neil*; and Smith, *Fifty Years of Slavery in the United States of America*.

6. Charlton and Brown, *Sketch of the Life of Mr. Lewis Charlton*, 8. See also "A Colored Imposter," *Westminster Democratic Advocate*, December 9, 1882, p. 3.

7. See "Order of Publication," *Westminster Democratic Advocate*, September 18, 1886, p. 4. Thanks to William L. Andrews for sharing this information with me.

8. On this history, see Blight, *Race and Reunion*, 300–37.

9. Washington, *Up from Slavery*; and Norrell, *Up from History*. William Monroe Trotter, W. E. B. Du Bois, and (later) Ida B. Wells criticized Washington for his willingness to compromise with white supremacists, but—as Robert Norrell notes in his biography of Washington—few of those critics had to live and work in the South.

10. Anderson, *The Life of Rev. Robert Anderson* (1892), 55.

11. John W. Burke was a white Methodist Episcopal minister who was, for a time, the pastor of Anderson's church in Macon; he also owned a major print shop in Macon and did the printing for the Georgia Conference of the M.E. Church South, a church that was notably quiescent (or retrograde) on matters of race and civil rights.

It seems that Burke and Anderson were friendly, and Burke may well have been happy to help his fellow minister.

12. "BY THE PUBLISHERS," in Anderson, *The Life of Rev. Robert Anderson* (1900), 5.

13. Anderson was a traveling minister, and he moved around quite a bit, but the 1870 census places Anderson in Macon (Bibb County) and the 1900 census places him in Sandersville (Washington County). Macon was his earliest residence, and he lived in Sandersville after 1885 and into the twentieth century. The two cities are about sixty miles apart.

14. See Andrews, "The Representation of Slavery."

15. Anderson, *The Life* (1892), 62.

16. Anderson, *The Life* (1892), 62.

17. Anderson, *The Life* (1892), 58.

18. Anderson, *The Life* (1892), 60. See also "News from the Churches," *Christian Recorder*, October 30, 1873, p. 4.

19. Andrews, *Slavery and Class in the American South*, 164.

20. Anderson, *The Life* (1892), 36.

21. Anderson, *The Life* (1892), 36.

22. Anderson, *The Life* (1892), 17.

23. Anderson, *The Life* (1892), 131.

24. "Caution," *Christian Recorder*, January 17, 1884.

25. Anderson, *The Life* (1892), 46.

26. Anderson, *The Life* (1892), 46.

27. Anderson, *The Life* (1892), 49–50.

28. Anderson, *The Life* (1892), 47.

29. Anderson, *The Life* (1892), 126.

30. Anderson, *The Life* (1892), 123.

31. Anderson, *The Life* (1892), 145.

32. *Minutes of the Savannah Annual Conference*, 22.

33. A superannuated minister was deemed too old to preach but was still supported by the church. Anderson, *The Life* (1892), 21.

34. According to the convention minutes, Anderson was paid thirty dollars, but he took that money out of the funds he had already collected. So, Anderson was not supported by the conference but rather allowed to keep the money he had raised. *Minutes*, 21.

35. Anderson, *The Life* (1892), 145.

36. "Rev. Robert Anderson," *Macon Telegraph*, May 22, 1891.

37. Anderson, *The Life* (1892), 145.

38. Anderson published a note of thanks to local buyers in the *Savannah Morning News* on May 9, 1891, in which he offers prayers on behalf of the mayor and other purchasers "until [he would] return next winter."

39. Anderson, *The Life* (1892), 191.

40. Anderson, *The Anderson Surpriser*, ii.

41. Anderson, *The Anderson Surpriser*, ii.

42. Anderson, *The Anderson Surpriser*, 18.

43. Anderson, *The Anderson Surpriser*, 18.

44. Anderson, *The Anderson Surpriser*, 19.
45. Anderson, *The Anderson Surpriser*, 26.
46. Anderson, *The Anderson Surpriser*, 34.
47. Anderson, *The Anderson Surpriser*, 22–23.
48. "A Noted Negro Preacher," *Charlotte News*, November 9, 1893, p. 2. Similar descriptions of Anderson's book might be found in several other newspaper pieces including "An Aged Colored Preacher and His Book," *Columbus Enquirer-Sun*, June 30, 1893, p. 4; "Rev. Robert Anderson in Town," *Augusta Chronicle*, September 16, 1900, p. 2.
49. Anderson, *The Anderson Surpriser*, 32.
50. Jackson, *The Business of Letters*, 59.
51. Anderson, *The Anderson Surpriser*, 37.
52. Anderson, *The Life* (1892), 178, 184.
53. Anderson, *The Anderson Surpriser*, 38.
54. Fabian, *The Unvarnished Truth*, 7. On the links between charitable giving and racial condescension in an antebellum context, also see Ryan, *The Grammar of Good Intentions*, 2–5.
55. Anderson, *The Anderson Surpriser*, 45.
56. Anderson, *The Anderson Surpriser*, 49.
57. Though Ransom would have only been thirty years old and a young A.M.E. minister when he bought Anderson's book, he went on to become a member of the Niagara Movement, the editor of the *A.M.E. Church Review*, and a bishop in the church. See Luker, "Reverdy Cassius Ransom," in *American National Biography*.
58. For the purposes of this analysis, I only "counted" a purchaser when a single individual from one of Anderson's lists could be positively identified via city directories or via census, tax, and vital records. Though there were many speculative matches that might have been made, I eschewed speculation in order to reduce the possibility for error.
59. Anderson, *The Anderson Surpriser*, 50.
60. Anderson, *The Anderson Surpriser*, 52, 56.
61. Anderson, *The Anderson Surpriser*, 63.
62. Anderson, *The Anderson Surpriser*, 73.
63. Anderson, *The Anderson Surpriser*, 68.
64. Anderson, *The Anderson Surpriser*, 70.
65. Anderson, *The Anderson Surpriser*, 70.
66. Anderson, *The Anderson Surpriser*, 77.
67. Anderson, *The Anderson Surpriser*, 105, 104.
68. Anderson, *The Anderson Surpriser*, 102.
69. On Anderson's travels after the publication of *The Anderson Surpriser*, see "A Lecture," *Thomasville Daily Times Enterprise*, March 25, 1896; and "A Negro Preacher Wants the President to Help Build a Church," *Statesville Landmark*, July 20, 1897.
70. There is no printed history of the Foote & Davies company (which still exists today), but the printers produced hundreds of editions of Southern history, fiction, and memoir along with the kinds of government documents (legal codes, budget documents) that were highly remunerative. For self-serving praise of the print shop, see Severance, *Official Guide*, 125.

71. Anderson, *The Life* (1900), 13. It seems odd that Anderson included a note on the printing of his book *in* the same book he was having printed, but Anderson almost certainly produced two different versions of the sixth edition and the second version included the description of the publication process. This theory seems likely given that the last line of Anderson's preface (supposedly written in July of 1900) is, "I intend on having a thousand more printed by them if the Lord will help me as he has done." The edition in which this line appears was printed in December 1900.

72. Anderson, *The Life* (1900), 5.

73. Anderson, *The Life* (1900), 12–13.

74. Anderson, *The Life* (1900), 16.

75. With John D. Rockefeller and Samuel Andrews, Henry Morrison Flagler was one of three partners in the firm that became Standard Oil. After accruing a massive fortune in the 1870s and 1880s, Flagler moved to Florida, built numerous luxury hotels, and became president of the Jacksonville, St. Augustine & Indian River Railway. It was at Flagler's hotels (in the "Newport of the South") that Anderson found fertile ground for selling his book. See Graham, *Mr. Flagler's St. Augustine*; and Stover, "Flagler, Henry Morrison."

76. Anderson, *The Life* (1900), 21

77. "Rev. Robert Anderson in Town," *Augusta Chronicle*, September 16, 1900, p. 2.; "Were Joined in Wedlock," *Indianapolis Freeman*, February 15, 1902; "Talked in the Town," *Grand Rapids Press*, September 5, 1902.

78. "Rev. Robert Anderson in Town." *Augusta Chronicle*, September 16, 1900, p. 2.

79. "Budget from Capital City," *Columbus Enquirer-Sun*, October 19, 1902, p. 15.

Coda

1. Gates, *The Signifying Monkey*, 131.
2. Gates, *The Signifying Monkey*, 165.
3. Madera, *Black Atlas*, 3.
4. Fish, *Black and White Women's Travel Narratives*, 7.
5. Gardner, *Unexpected Places*, 20.
6. Gardner, *Unexpected Places*, 13.
7. *Oxford English Dictionary*, 2nd ed., s.v. "Publication."
8. Mars, *Life* (1868), 37.
9. Mars, *Life* (1868), 38.
10. Mars, *Life* (1868), 37.
11. Spires, *The Practice of Citizenship*, 13.

Bibliography

Archival Sources/Government Documents

Account book of the Salem Press, 1871-72. MSS 1376. Phillips Library, Peabody Essex Museum.
Bourbon (KY) County Court of Common Pleas. Kentucky Historical Society.
Chester (PA) County Poorhouse Records.
Day Book, Newcomb and Gauss. MSS 1265.1. Phillips Library, Peabody Essex Museum.
Grundy (IL) County Circuit Court Case Files, 1846-1963. Illinois State University.
G. W. Offley Papers. American Antiquarian Society.
Richmond (VA) City Legislative Petition, December 10, 1810, Virginia State Library.
South Dakota State Census.
Trimble (KY) County Circuit Court Records. Order Book 3, 1855-1865. Kentucky Historical Society.
United Nations Educational, Scientific, and Cultural Organization (UNESCO) Records of the General Conference, Thirteenth Session, 1964.
US Bureau of the Census, *Manufactures*, 1905.
US Federal Census: 1830, 1840, 1850, 1860, 1870, 1880, 1890, 1900.
US Indexed County Land Ownership Maps, 1860-1918.

Newspapers

Albany (NY) *Weekly Patriot-Tocsin of Liberty*
Alexandria (VA) *Gazette*
American Baptist (Louisville, KY)
American Citizen (Lexington, KY)
Augusta (GA) *Chronicle*
Boston Daily Advertiser
Carlisle (PA) *Mercury*
Charlotte (NC) *News*
Christian Harvester (Cleveland, Ohio)
Christian Recorder (Philadelphia)
Cincinnati Enquirer
Cleveland Gazette
Cleveland Herald
Colored American (New York, 1837-1842)
Colored Citizen (Cincinnati, Ohio)
Columbus (GA) *Enquirer-Sun*
Congregationalist (Boston)
Connecticut Courant (Hartford)
Connecticut Times (Hartford)
Daily Colonist (Victoria, BC)
Daily Evening Bulletin (San Francisco)
The Daily Inter Ocean (Chicago)
Douglass' Monthly Magazine (New York)
Evening Bulletin (San Francisco)
Fells Point News-Letter and Mercantile Advertiser (Baltimore)
Forest City (SD) *Press*
Frederick Douglass's Paper (Rochester, NY)
Goshen (IN) *Democrat*
Grand Rapids (MI) *Press*
Hamilton (ON) *Spectator*
Indianapolis Freeman
Joliet (IL) *Record*
Kansas City (MO) *Star*
Kansas City (MO) *Times*

Liberator (Boston)
Little Rock (AR) *Daily Republican*
Louisville (KY) *Commercial*
Louisville (KY) *Daily Courier*
Lowell (MA) *Daily Citizen*
Macon (GA) *Telegraph*
Madison (IN) *Courier*
Madison (IN) *Daily Banner*
Milledgeville (GA) *Union Recorder*
Minnesota Weekly Pioneer and Democrat (St. Paul)
National Anti-Slavery Standard (New York)
National Era (New York)
National Leader (Washington, DC)
New Albany (IN) *Daily Ledger*
New Hampshire Sentinel (Keene)
New Haven (CT) *Evening Register*
New Haven (CT) *Palladium*
New Orleans Times-Picayune
New York Age
New York Freeman
New York Herald
New York Times
New York Tribune
New York Weekly Witness
Omaha (NE) *Daily Bee*
Oxford (NC) *Torchlight*
The Patriot (London)
Provincial Freeman (Windsor, ON)
Raleigh (NC) *News and Observer*
Richmond (VA) *Commercial Compiler*
Rock Island (IL) *Argus*
St. Albans (VT) *Messenger*
Salem (MA) *Observer*
Salem (MA) *Press*
Savannah (GA) *Morning News*
Seymour (IN) *Times*
Springfield (MA) *Republican*
Star of Zion (Charlotte, NC)
Statesville (GA) *Landmark*
Terre Haute (IN) *Wabash Express*
Thomasville (GA) *Daily Times Enterprise*
Toronto Globe
True Union (Baltimore)
Vevay (IN) *Weekly Reveille*
Virginia Argus (Richmond)
Voice of the Fugitive (Windsor, ON)
Washington (DC) *Post*
Washington (DC) *Sun*
Weekly Anglo-African (Boston)
Weekly Indiana State Sentinel (Indianapolis)
Weekly Spectator (Hamilton, ON)
Western Christian Advocate (Cincinnati)
Westminster (MD) *Democratic Advocate*
Worcester (MA) *Daily Spy*
Xenia (OH) *Gazette*

City Directories

Caron's Directory of the City of Louisville
McElroy's Philadelphia City Directory (A. McElroy & Co., 1859)
The Naumkeag Directory for Salem (MA)
Rochester (NY) *City Directory* (Drew, Allis, and Company)
Salem Directory (Sampson, Davenport, and Company)
Sholes' Macon (GA) *City Directory*
Worcester City Directory (Drew, Allis, and Company)

Conference Proceedings/Minutes

Convention of the Colored Inhabitants of the State of New York 1840, Held at Albany
General Conference of the African Methodist Episcopal Zion Church, of 1864
Golden Jubilee of the General Association of Colored Baptists in Kentucky: The Story of 50 Years' Work from 1865–1915

Journal of the General Conference of the African Methodist Episcopal Zion Church
Journal of the General Conference of the Colored Methodist Episcopal Church
Journal of Proceedings of the Annual Conference of the African Methodist Episcopal Church for the District of Indiana
Minutes of the Baltimore, Philadelphia, New-York, and New England Annual Conferences, of the African Methodist Episcopal Zion Church, in America
Minutes of the New-York and New-England Annual Conferences of the African Methodist Episcopal Zion Church in America.
Minutes of the New York Annual Conference of the African Methodist Episcopal Zion Church
Minutes of the North Carolina Annual Conference of the African Methodist Episcopal Zion Church in America, 1865
Minutes of the Ohio Annual Conference of the African Methodist Episcopal Church
Minutes of the Savannah Annual Conference of the Methodist Episcopal Church
Minutes of the Several Annual Conferences of the African Methodist Episcopal Church in America
Proceedings of the National Convention of Colored People and Their Friends Held in Troy, N.Y. on the 6th, 7th, 8th, and 9th of October, 1847
Thirteenth General Conference of the African M.E. Church: Held in Philadelphia, Pa. May 2, 1864
Twelfth General Conference of the African M.E. Church: Held in Pittsburgh, Pa., May 7, 1860

Self-Published Narratives

[Aaron]. *The Light and [the] Truth of Slavery: Aaron's History*. Worcester: Printed at Worcester, MA, for Aaron [1840s?].
———. *The Light and the Truth of Slavery*. Springfield, MA: s.n., 1845.
———. *The Light and Truth of Slavery*. Springfield, MA: s.n., 1845.
Adams, John Quincy. *Narrative of the Life of John Quincy Adams, When in Slavery, and Now as a Freeman*. Harrisburg, PA: Sieg, printer, 1872.
Anderson, Osborne P. *A Voice from Harper's Ferry: A Narrative of Events at Harper's Ferry: With Incidents Prior and Subsequent to Its Capture by Captain Brown and His Men*. Boston: Printed for the author, 1861.
Anderson, Osborne P., and J. D. Enos. *A Voice from Harper's Ferry: Life and Death of the Last John Brown Hero: A Narrative of Events at Harper's Ferry, with Incidents Prior and Subsequent to Its Capture by Captain Brown and His Men*. Washington, DC: J. D. Enos, 1873.
Anderson, Robert. *The Anderson Surpriser*. Macon, GA: Printed for the author, 1895.
———. *The Life of Rev. Robert Anderson: Born on the 22d Day of February, in the Year of Our Lord 1819, and Joined the Methodist Episcopal Church in 1839: This Book Shall Be Called the Young Men's Guide, or, the Brother in White: Besides Containing a History of the Leading Events in the Life of Rev. Robert Anderson, This Book Has a Remedy for the Cure of Small Pox, Millennium Story of Christ, the Reason Why God Does Not Kill the Devil, and a Series of Questions Alphabetically Arranged*. Macon, GA: J. W. Burke & Co., printers, stationers, and binders, 1891.

———. *The Life of Rev. Robert Anderson*. Macon, GA: Printed for the author, 1892.

———. *The Life of Rev. Robert Anderson: Born the 22d of February, in the Year of Our Lord 1819, and Joined the Methodist Episcopal Church in 1839*. Atlanta: Foote & Davies, 1900.

Anderson William J. *Life and Narrative of William J. Anderson, Twenty-Four Years a Slave: Also, a Simple and Easy Plan to Abolish Slavery in the United States: Together with an Account of the Services of Colored Men in the Revolutionary War*. Chicago: Daily Tribune Book and Job Printing Office, 1857.

———. *Life and Narrative of William J. Anderson, Twenty-Four Years a Slave; Sold Eight Times! In Jail Sixty Times!! Whipped Three Hundred Times!!! or The Dark Deeds of American Slavery Revealed: Containing Scriptural Views of the Origin of the Black and of the White Man : Also, a Simple and Easy Plan to Abolish Slavery in the United States: Together with an Account of the Services of Colored Men in the Revolutionary War — Day and Date, and Interesting Facts*. 3rd ed. Chicago: Daily Tribune Book and Job Printing Office, 1857.

Asher, Jeremiah. *An Autobiography, with Details of a Visit to England: And Some Account of the History of the Meeting Street Baptist Church, Providence, R.I., and of the Shiloh Baptist Church, Philadelphia, Pa*. Philadelphia: The author, 1862.

Black, Leonard. *The Life and Sufferings of Leonard Black, a Fugitive from Slavery*. Providence, RI: s.n., 1847.

———. *Sketch of the Life of Rev. Leonard Black*. Brooklyn: Printed for the author, 1851.

Blair, Norvel. *Book for the People! To Be Read by All Voters, Black and White, with Thrilling Events of the Life of Norvel Blair, of Grundy County, State of Illinois. Written and Published by Him, and with the Money He Earned by His Own Labor, and Is Sent Out with the Sincere Hope that if Carefully Read, It Will Tend to Put a Stop to Northern Bull-Dozing and Will Give to All a Free Ballot, without Fear, Favor or Affection and Respect*. Joliet, IL: Jolliet Daily Record Steam Print, 1880.

Brinch, Boyrereau. *The Blind African Slave, or Memoirs of Boyrereau Brinch, Nicknamed Jeffrey Brace*. Edited by Kari J. Winter. Madison: University of Wisconsin Press, 2004.

Brown, Paola. *Address Intended to Be Delivered in the City Hall, Hamilton, February 7, 1851, on the Subject of Slavery*. Hamilton, ON: Printed for the author, 1851.

Brown, William J. *The Life of William J. Brown, of Providence, R.I.: With Personal Recollections of Incidents in Rhode Island*. Providence, RI: Angell & Co., printers, 1883.

Campbell, Israel. *Bond and Free: Or, Yearnings for Freedom, from My Green Brier House: Being the Story of My Life in Bondage, and My Life in Freedom*. Philadelphia: Published by the author, C. E. P. Brinckloe & Co., printers, 1861.

Charlton, Lewis. *The Life of Lewis Charlton: A Poor Old Slave, Who, for Twenty-Eight Years, Suffered in American Bondage*. Fredericton, NB: Printed by Pitts and Crockett, 1880.

Charlton, Lewis, and Edward Everett Brown. *Sketch of the Life of Mr. Lewis Charlton, and Reminiscences of Slavery*. Portland, ME: Daily Press Print, 1879.

Davis, Noah. *A Narrative of the Life of Rev. Noah Davis, a Colored Man. Written by Himself, at the Age of Fifty-Four*. Baltimore: Jno. Weishampel, 1859.

Delaney, Lucy A. *From the Darkness Cometh the Light, or, Struggles for Freedom*. St. Louis: J. T. Smith, [1891?].

Dorr, David F. *A Colored Man Round the World*. Cleveland: Printed for the author, 1858.
Drumgoold, Kate. *A Slave Girl's Story: Being an Autobiography of Kate Drumgoold*. Brooklyn: The author, 1897.
Eldridge, Elleanor, and Frances H. Green. *Elleanor's Second Book*. Providence, RI: Printed by B. T. Albro, 1842.
———. *Memoirs of Elleanor Eldridge*. Providence, RI: B. T. Albro, 1838.
Ferebee, L. R. *A Brief History of the Slave Life of Rev. L. R. Ferebee: And the Battles of Life, and Four Years of His Ministerial Life: Written from Memory, to 1882*. Raleigh, NC: Edwards, Broughton & Co., 1882.
Foote, Julia A. J. *A Brand Plucked from the Fire. An Autobiographical Sketch*. Cleveland: Printed for the author by W. F. Schneider, 1879.
Frederick, Francis. *Autobiography of Rev. Francis Frederick, of Virginia*. Baltimore: J. W. Woods, printer, 1869.
Gibbs, Mifflin Wistar. *Shadow and Light: An Autobiography with Reminiscences of the Last and Present Century*. Washington, DC: s.n., 1902.
Green, Elisha Winfield. *Life of the Rev. Elisha W. Green, One of the Founders of the Kentucky Normal and Theological Institute*. Maysville, KY: The Republican Printing Office, 1888.
Grimes, William. *Life of William Grimes, the Runaway Slave*. Edited by William L. Andrews and Regina Mason. New York: Oxford University Press, 2008.
Hayden, William. *Narrative of William Hayden Containing a Faithful Account of His Travels for a Number of Years, Whilst a Slave, in the South*. Cincinnati: Published for the author, 1846.
Henry, Thomas W. *The Autobiography of Rev. Thomas W. Henry of the A. M. E. Church*. s.l.: s.n., 1872.
Hughes, Louis. *Thirty Years a Slave: From Bondage to Freedom: The Institution of Slavery as Seen on the Plantation and in the Home of the Planter*. Milwaukee, WI: South Side Printing, 1897.
Jackson, Mattie J. *The Story of Mattie J. Jackson: Her Parentage, Experience of Eighteen Years in Slavery, Incidents During the War, Her Escape from Slavery: A True Story*. Lawrence, MA: Sentinel Office, 1866.
[Jacobs, Harriet.] *Incidents in the Life of a Slave Girl*. Edited by Jean Fagan Yellin. Cambridge, MA: Harvard University Press, 2000.
James, Thomas. *Life of Rev. Thomas James, by Himself*. Rochester, NY: Post-Express Print Co., 1886.
———. *Wonderful Eventful Life of Rev. Thomas James*. Rochester, NY: Post-Express Printing Co., 1887.
Johnson, William H. *Narrative of the Fugitive Slave, William, of Maryland*. Worcester [sic], MA: Printed for Wm. H. Johnson, 1847.
Jones, Friday. *Days of Bondage: Autobiography of Friday Jones Being a Brief Narrative of His Trials and Tribulations in Slavery*. Washington, DC: Commercial Publishing Company, 1883.
Jones, Thomas H. *The Experience of Thomas Jones, Who Was a Slave for Forty-Three Years*. Boston: Printed by D. Laing, Jr., 1850.

———. *The Experience of Thomas Jones, Who Was a Slave for Forty-Three Years.* Springfield, MA: Printed by H. S. Taylor, 1854.

———. *The Experience of Thomas H. Jones: Who Was a Slave for Forty-Three Years.* Worcester, MA: Printed by Henry J. Howland, 1857.

———. *The Experience of Thomas H. Jones: Who Was a Slave for Forty-Three Years.* Boston, MA: Printed by Bazin and Chandler, 1862.

———. *The Experience of Thomas H. Jones, Who Was a Slave for Forty-Three Years.* New Bedford, MA: E. Anthony, 1885.

Joseph, John. *The Life and Sufferings of John Joseph, a Native of Ashantee, in Western Africa: Who Was Stolen from His Parents at the Age of 3 Years, and Sold to Mr. Johnstone, a Cotton Planter, in New Orleans, South America.* Wellington: Printed for John Joseph by J. Greedy, 1848.

Kelley, Edmond. *A Family Redeemed from Bondage; Being Rev. Edmond Kelley, (the Author,) His Wife, and Four Children.* New Bedford, MA: Published by the author, 1851.

Lane, Lunsford. *The Narrative of Lunsford Lane, Formerly of Raleigh, N.C.: Embracing an Account of His Early Life, the Redemption by Purchase of Himself and Family from Slavery, and His Banishment from the Place of His Birth for the Crime of Wearing a Colored Skin.* Boston: Printed for the publisher, J. G. Torrey, printer, 1842.

Lee, Jarena. *The Life and Religious Experience of Jarena Lee.* Philadelphia: Published for the author, 1836.

———. *The Life and Religious Experience of Jarena Lee, a Colored Lady: Giving an Account of the Call to Preach the Gospel. Revised and Corrected from the Original Mss.* 2nd ed. Cincinnati: Printed and published for the author, 1839.

———. *Religious Experience and Journal of Mrs. Jarena Lee, Giving an Account of Her Call to Preach the Gospel, Revised and Corrected from the Original Manuscript Written by Herself.* Philadelphia: Published for the author, 1849.

Magee, James H. *The Night of Affliction and Morning of Recovery: An Autobiography.* 2nd ed. Cincinnati, OH: The author, 1873.

Marrs, Elijah P. *Life and History of the Rev. Elijah P. Marrs.* Louisville, KY: Bradley & Gilbert Company, 1885.

Mars, James. *Life of James Mars, a Slave; Born and Sold in Connecticut.* Hartford, CT: Press of Case, Lockwood & Co., 1864–78.

McPherson, Christopher. *Christ's Millennium, of One Thousand Years Commenced and the Downfall of Kings, &C. before the Throne of Justice, the Word Particularly Sent to Them as Noted Herin. Also, the Restoration of the Jews to New Zion, as Foretold by the Prophets.* Richmond, VA: Printed for the author, 1811.

Offley, Greensbury Washington. *A Narrative of the Life and Labors of the Rev. G. W. Offley: A Colored Man, Local Preacher and Missionary.* Hartford, CT: s.n., 1859.

———. *A Narrative of the Life and Labors of the Rev. G. W. Offley, a Colored Man and Local Preacher.* Hartford, CT: s.n., 1860.

———. *Slavery in the South.* Hartford, CT: s.n., 1844.

O'Neil, William. *Life and History of William O'Neil, or, the Man Who Sold His Wife.* St. Louis: A. R. Fleming, 1896.

Parker, Allen. *Recollections of Slavery Times.* Worcester, MA: Chas. W. Burbank & Co., 1895.

Parker, Henry. *Autobiography of Henry Parker*. s.l: s.n., 1870.
Peterson, Daniel H. *The Looking Glass: Being a True Report and Narrative of the Life, Travels, and Labors of the Rev. Daniel H. Peterson, a Colored Clergyman; Embracing a Period of Time from the Year 1812 to 1854, and Including His Visit to Western Africa. With Engravings*. New York: Wright: Printer, 1854.
Prince, Nancy. *A Narrative of the Life and Travels of Mrs. Nancy Prince*. Boston: Published by the author, 1850.
Prince, Nancy. *A Narrative of the Life and Travels of Mrs. Nancy Prince*. 2nd ed. Boston: Published by the author, 1853.
———. *A Narrative of the Life and Travels of Mrs. Nancy Prince*. 3rd ed. Boston: Published by the author, 1856.
Randolph, Peter. *Sketches of Slave Life and From Slave Cabin to the Pulpit*. Edited by Katherine Clay Bassard. Morgantown: West Virginia University Press, 2016.
Roberts, James. *The Narrative of James Roberts: A Soldier under Gen. Washington in the Revolutionary War, and under Gen. Jackson at the Battle of New Orleans, in the War of 1812: "A Battle Which Cost Me a Limb, Some Blood, and Almost My Life."* Chicago: Printed for the author, 1858.
Smallwood, Thomas. *A Narrative of Thomas Smallwood (Coloured Man)*. Edited by Richard Almonte. Toronto: Mercury Press, 2000.
Smith, Amanda. *An Autobiography: the Story of the Lord's Dealings with Mrs. Amanda Smith, the Colored Evangelist: Containing an Account of Her Life Work of Faith, and Her Travels in America, England, Ireland, Scotland, India, and Africa, as an Independent Missionary*. Chicago: Meyer & Brother, 1893.
Smith, Christopher McPherson. *A Short History of the Life of Christopher McPherson, Alias Pherson, Son of Christ . . .* Lynchburg, VA: Published by Christopher McPherson Smith, printed at the Virginian Job Office, 1855.
Smith, David. *Biography of Rev. David Smith of the A.M.E. Church; Being a Complete History, Embracing over Sixty Years' Labor in the Advancement of the Redeemer's Kingdom on Earth*. Xenia, OH: Printed at the Xenia Gazette Office, 1881.
———. *A Brief Account of the Awakening and Conversion of David Smith, Preacher of the Gospel, in the African Methodist Episcopal Church*. Washington, DC: Printed by D. Rapine, 1822.
Smith, Harry. *Fifty Years of Slavery in the United States of America*. Grand Rapids, MI: West Michigan Print Co., 1891
Smith, James L. *Autobiography of James L. Smith: Including Also, Reminiscences of Slave Life, Recollections of the War, Education of Freedmen, Causes of the Exodus, Etc.* Norwich, CT: Press of the Bulletin Co., 1881.
Smith, Venture. *A Narrative of the Life and Adventures of Venture, a Native of Africa: But Resident above Sixty Years in the United States of America. Related by Himself*. New London, CT: Printed at the Bee Office, 1798.
Still, James. *Early Recollections and Life of Dr. James Still*. Philadelphia: Printed for the author by J. B. Lippincott & Co., 1877.
Stroyer, Jacob. *My Life in the South*. New and enl. ed. Salem, MA: Salem Observer Book and Job Print, 1885.
———. *My Life in the South*. New and enl. ed. Salem, MA: Newcomb & Gauss, 1898.

———. *Sketches of My Life in the South. Part I*. Salem, MA: Salem Press, 1879.
Thompson, Charles. *Biography of a Slave; Being the Experiences of Rev. Charles Thompson, a Preacher of the United Brethren Church, While a Slave in the South*. Dayton, OH: United Brethren Pub. House, 1875.
Thompson, John. *The Life of John Thompson, a Fugitive Slave: Containing His History of 25 Years in Bondage, and His Providential Escape / Written by Himself*. Worcester, MA: Published by John Thompson, 1856.
Tilmon, Levin. *Brief Miscellaneous Narrative of the More Early Part of the Life of L. Tilmon*. Jersey City, NJ: W. W. & L. A. Pratt, printers, 1853.
———. *The Consequences of One Important Misstep in Life*. New York: Mitchell, 1853.
Truth, Sojourner. *Narrative of Sojourner Truth: A Northern Slave, Emancipated from Bodily Servitude by the State of New York, in 1828*. Boston: Printed for the author, 1850.
Veney, Bethany. *The Narrative of Bethany Veney, a Slave Woman*. Worcester, MA: s.n., 1889.
Webb, William. *The History of William Webb*. Detroit: E. Hoekstra, 1873.
White, George. *A Brief Account of the Life, Experience, Travels, and Gospel Labours of George White, an African*. New York: Printed by John C. Totten, 1810.
Wilkerson, Major James. *The Midnight Cry: The Parable of the Great Supper—Luke, 14th Chapter, Verses 16, 17, 18, 19, 20, 21, and 22. New Orleans, Louisiana, 8th of First Month, A.D. 1859. To the Church of Christ:—the Undersigned, Thy Servant for Christ's Sake, Has Here Thought Fit to Spread before You, for Your Consideration, His Candid and Impartial Views in Regard to the Subject Set Forth above, of the Great Epoch That Seems to Be Fast Dawning on This Our World*. Philadelphia: Quinn, card and job printer, southwest corner of Third and Market Streets, 1859.
———. *The Midnight Cry & Millennium Dawn: A Cry from the Forest or Wilderness—Prepare to Meet Thy God, O Israel!* [New Orleans?]: 1865.
———. *Preamble and Constitution of the Educational Orphan Institute and Daughters of Salem Both under the Patronage of the A.M.E. Church*. Pittsburgh: Printed by J. McMillan, 1853.
———. *Wilkerson's History of His Travels and Labors, in the United States, as a Missionary, in Particular, That of the Union Seminary, Located in Franklin Co., Ohio, since He Purchased His Liberty in New Orleans, La., &C*. Columbus, OH: s.n., 1861.
Wilson, Harriet. *Our Nig: Or, Sketches in the Life of a Free Black*. Edited by Henry Louis Gates Jr. New York: Vintage, 1983.

Works Cited

Allen, Richard. *The Life, Experience and Gospel Labors of the Rt. Rev. Richard Allen. . . .* Nashville: A.M.E. Sunday School Union, 1833.
Almonte, Richard. "Introduction." In *A Narrative of Thomas Smallwood (Coloured Man)*, edited by Richard Almonte, 9–22. Toronto: Mercury Press, 2000.
Anderson, William H., and Walter Stowers. *Appointed: An American Novel*. Edited by Eric Gardner and Bryan Sinche. Morganton: West Virginia University Press, 2019.

Andrews, William L. "The Politics of African-American Ministerial Autobiography from Reconstruction to the 1920s." In *African-American Christianity: Essays in History*, edited by Paul E. Johnson, 111-33. Berkeley: University of California Press, 1994.

———. "The Representation of Slavery and the Rise of Afro-American Literary Realism, 1865-1920." In *Slavery and the Literary Imagination*, edited by Deborah E. McDowell and Arnold Rampersad, 62-80. Baltimore: Johns Hopkins University Press, 1989.

———. "Slave Narratives, 1865-1900." In *The Oxford Handbook of the African American Slave Narrative*, edited by John Ernest, 219-34. New York: Oxford University Press, 2014.

———. *Slavery and Class in the American South: A Generation of Slave Narrative Testimony, 1840-1865*. New York: Oxford University Press, 2019.

———. *To Tell a Free Story: The First Century of Afro-American Autobiography, 1760-1865*. Urbana: University of Illinois Press, 1986.

Arac, Jonathan. *Huckleberry Finn as Idol and Target: The Functions of Criticism in Our Time*. Madison: University of Wisconsin Press, 1997.

Baker, Houston A. "Autobiographical Acts and the Voice of the Southern Slave." In *The Slave's Narrative*, edited by Henry Louis Gates Jr., and Charles Davis, 242-61. New York: Oxford University Press, 1986.

———. *Blues, Ideology, and Afro-American Literature: A Vernacular Theory*. Chicago: University of Chicago Press, 1984.

Barker, Gordon S. *The Imperfect Revolution: Anthony Burns and the Landscape of Race in Antebellum America*. Kent, OH: Kent State University Press, 2010.

Barrett, Lindon. "African-American Slave Narratives: Literacy, the Body, Authority." *American Literary History* 7 (1995): 415-42.

———. "Self-Knowledge, Law, and African American Autobiography: Lucy A. Delaney's 'from the Darkness Cometh Light'." In *The Culture of Autobiography: Constructions of Self-Representation*, edited by Robert Folkenflik, 104-24. Stanford, CA: Stanford University Press, 1993.

Bassard, Katherine Clay. Introduction to *Sketches of Slave Life and from Slave Cabin to the Pulpit*. Morgantown: West Virginia University Press, 2016.

———. *Spiritual Interrogations: Culture, Gender, and Community in Early African American Women's Writing*. Princeton, NJ: Princeton University Press, 1999.

Bates, Barnabas. *Remarks on the Character and Exertions of Elias Hicks on the Abolition of Slavery: Being an Address Delivered Before the African Benevolent Societies in Zion's Chapel New-York March 15 1830*. New York: Printed by Mitchell and Davis, 1830.

Bellinger, Lucius. *Stray Leaves from the Port-Folio of a Methodist Local Preacher*. Macon, GA: Printed for the author, 1870.

Berkeley, Edmund, Jr. "Prophet Without Honor: Christopher McPherson, Free Person of Color." *Virginia Magazine of History and Biography* 77, no. 2 (April 1999): 180-90.

Berry, Mary Frances. *Black Resistance/White Law: A History of Constitutional Racism in America*. New York: Penguin, 1994.

Bethel, Elizabeth Rauh. *The Roots of African American Identity: Memory and History in Free Antebellum Communities*. New York: St. Martin's Press, 1997.

Blackmon, Douglas A. *Slavery by Another Name: The Re-Enslavement of Black People in America from the Civil War to World War II*. New York: Doubleday, 2008.

Blight, David. *Race and Reunion: The Civil War in American Memory*. Cambridge, MA: Harvard University Press, 2001.

Brackney, William H. "Thoburn, James Mills." In *American National Biography*. Edited by John A. Garraty and Mark C. Carnes. New York: Oxford University Press, 1999.

Brignano, Russell C. *Black Americans in Autobiography: An Annotated Bibliography of Autobiographies and Autobiographical Books Written since the Civil War*. Durham, NC: Duke University Press, 1974.

Brooks, Daphne. *Bodies in Dissent: Spectacular Performances of Race and Freedom, 1850-1910*. Durham: Duke University Press, 2006.

Brooks, Joanna. "The Early American Public Sphere and the Emergence of a Black Print Counterpublic." *William & Mary Quarterly* 62, no. 1 (Jan. 2005): 67-92.

———. "The Unfortunates: What the Life Spans of Early Black Books Tell Us About Book History." In *Early African American Print Culture*, edited by Lara Langer Cohen and Jordan Alexander Stein, 40-52. Philadelphia: University of Pennsylvania Press, 2012.

Bruce, Dickson D., Jr. *Black American Writing from the Nadir: The Evolution of a Literary Tradition 1877-1915*. Baton Rouge: Louisiana State University Press, 1992.

———. *The Origins of African American Literature, 1680-1865*. Charlottesville: University Press of Virginia, 2001.

Carby, Hazel V. *Reconstructing Womanhood: The Emergence of the Afro-American Woman Novelist*. New York: Oxford University Press, 1987.

Carretta, Vincent. "'Property of Author': Olaudah Equiano's Place in the History of the Book." In *Genius in Bondage: Literature of the Early Black Atlantic*, edited by Vincent Carretta and Philip Gould, 130-51. Lexington: University Press of Kentucky, 2001.

Casmier-Paz, Lynn A. "Slave Narratives and the Rhetoric of Author Portraiture." *New Literary History* 34, no. 1 (Winter 2003): 91-116.

Casper, Scott E., Jeffrey D. Groves, Stephen W. Nissenbaum, and Michael Winship, eds. *The Industrial Book, 1840-1880*. Vol. 3 of *A History of the Book in America*. Chapel Hill: University of North Carolina Press, 2007.

Charvat, William and Matthew Bruccoli. *The Profession of Authorship in America*. New York: Columbia University Press, 1992.

Clarke, George Elliott. *Odysseys Home: Mapping African-Canadian Literature*. Toronto: University of Toronto Press, 2002.

Clarke, James Freeman. *The Rendition of Anthony Burns. Its Causes and Consequences. A Discourse on Christian Politics, Delivered in Williams Hall, Boston, on Whitsunday, June 4, 1854*. Boston: Crosby and Nichols, 1854.

Cohen, Lara Langer. "Notes from the State of Saint Domingue: The Practice of Citation in *Clotel*." In *Early African American Print Culture*, 161-77. Philadelphia: University of Pennsylvania Press, 2012.

Cover, Robert M. "Violence and the Word." *Yale Law Journal* 95, no. 8 (July 1986): 1601–30.

Cox, Anna-Lisa. *The Bone and Sinew of the Land: America's Forgotten Black Pioneers and the Struggle for Equality*. New York: Public Affairs, 2018.

Cumming, John. "Mendicant Pieces." *American Book Collector* 16 (1965): 17–19.

DeLombard, Jeannine Marie. "African American Cultures of Print." In *The Industrial Book, 1840–1880*. Vol. 3 of *A History of the Book in America*, edited by Scott E. Casper, Jeffrey D. Groves, Stephen W. Nissenbaum, and Michael Winship. 360–73. Chapel Hill: University of North Carolina Press, 2007.

———. "Slave Narratives and US Legal History." In *The Oxford Handbook of the African American Slave Narrative*, edited by John Ernest, 67–88. New York: Oxford University Press, 2014.

———. *Slavery on Trial: Law, Abolitionism, and Print Culture*. Chapel Hill: University of North Carolina Press, 2007.

Devoy, John, ed. *Rochester and the Post Express: A History of the City of Rochester from the Earliest Times: The Pioneers and Their Predecessors, Frontier Life in the Genesee Country, Biographical Sketches: with a Record of the Post Express*. Rochester, NY: Post Express Printing Co., 1895.

Dinius, Marcy J. "'Look!! Look!!! At This!!!!': The Radical Typography of David Walker's Appeal." *PMLA* 126, no. 1 (2011): 55–72.

———. *The Textual Effects of David Walker's Appeal: Print-Based Activism Against Slavery, Racism, and Discrimination, 1829–1851*. Philadelphia: University of Pennsylvania Press, 2022.

Douglass, Frederick. *The Oxford Frederick Douglass Reader*. Edited by William L. Andrews. New York: Oxford University Press, 1996.

Dowling, David. *Capital Letters: Authorship in the Antebellum Literary Market*. Iowa City: University of Iowa Press, 2009.

Elrod, Eileen Razzari. *Piety and Dissent: Race, Gender, and Biblical Rhetoric in Early American Autobiography*. Amherst: University of Massachusetts Press, 2008.

Ernest, John. *Chaotic Justice: Rethinking African American Literary History*. Chapel Hill: University of North Carolina Press, 2009.

———. "Economics of Identity: Harriet E. Wilson's Our Nig." *PMLA* 109, no. 3 (1994): 424–38.

———. "Genealogies Beyond Modernities." *American Literary History* 32, no. 4 (October 2020): 781–88.

———. *Liberation Historiography: African American Writers and the Challenge of History, 1794–1861*. Chapel Hill: University of North Carolina Press, 2004.

———. "Life Beyond Biography: Black Lives and Biographical Research." *Commonplace: The Journal of Early American life*, May 4, 2021. http://commonplace.online/article/life-beyond-biography/.

———. *A Nation within a Nation: Organizing African-American Communities before the Civil War*. The American Ways Series. Chicago: Ivan R. Dee, Inc., 2011.

———. "William Wells Brown Maps the South in *My Southern Home: Or, the South and Its People*." *Southern Quarterly* 45, no. 3 (2008): 88–107.

Fabian, Ann. "Beggars and Books." *Proceedings of the American Antiquarian Society* 108, no. 1 (1998): 67–112.

———. *The Unvarnished Truth: Personal Narratives in Nineteenth-Century America*. Berkeley: University of California Press, 2000.

Fagan, Benjamin. *The Black Newspaper and the Chosen Nation*. Athens: University of Georgia Press, 2016.

Fanuzzi, Robert. *Abolition's Public Sphere*. Minneapolis: University of Minnesota Press, 2003.

Faulkner, William. *Requiem for a Nun*. New York: Vintage, 1975.

Fielder, Brigitte, and Jonathan Senchyne, ed. *Against a Sharp White Background*. Madison: University of Wisconsin Press, 2019.

Finseth, Ian. "Introduction to *The Narrative of the Escape and Adventures of Moses Roper*." In *North Carolina Slave Narratives*, edited by William L. Andrews, 23–34. Chapel Hill: University of North Carolina Press, 2003.

Fisch, Audrey A. *American Slaves in Victorian England: Abolitionist Politics in Popular Literature and Culture*. Cambridge: Cambridge University Press, 2000.

Fish, Cheryl. *Black and White Women's Travel Narratives: Antebellum Explorations*. Gainesville: University Press of Florida, 2005.

Foreman, P. Gabrielle. *Activist Sentiments: Reading Black Women in the Nineteenth Century*. Urbana: University of Illinois Press, 2009.

———. "Black Organizing, Print Advocacy, and Collective Authorship: The Long History of the Colored Conventions Movement." In *The Colored Conventions Movement*, edited by P. Gabrielle Foreman et al., 21–71. Chapel Hill: University of North Carolina Press, 2021.

———. "'Reading-Aright': White Slavery, Black Referents, and the Strategy of Histotextuality in 'Iola Leroy'." *Yale Journal of Criticism* 10, no. 2 (1997): 327–54.

———. "Recovered Autobiographies and the Marketplace: *Our Nig's* Generic Genealogies and Harriet Wilson's Entrepreneurial Enterprise." In *Harriet Wilson's New England*, edited by JerriAnne Boggis et al., 123–38. Durham: University of New Hampshire Press, 2007.

Foreman, P. Gabrielle, Jim Casey, and Sarah Lynn Patterson, eds. *The Colored Conventions Movement: Black Organizing in the Nineteenth Century*. Chapel Hill: University of North Carolina Press, 2021.

Foreman, P. Gabrielle, and Reginald Pitts. "Introduction." In *Our Nig: Or, Sketches from the Life of a Free Black*, vii–l. New York: Penguin, 2005.

Foster, Frances Smith. "A Narrative of the Interesting Origins and (Somewhat) Surprising Developments of African-American Print Culture." *American Literary History* 17, no. 4 (2005): 714–40.

———. *Witnessing Slavery: The Development of Ante-Bellum Slave Narratives*. 2nd ed. Madison: University of Wisconsin Press, 1994.

———. *Written by Herself: Literary Production by African American Women, 1746–1892*. Bloomington: Indiana University Press, 1993.

Franklin, John Hope. From Slavery to Freedom: A History of African Americans. Ninth Edition. New York: McGraw-Hill, 2009.

Gardner, Eric. *Black Print Unbound: The Christian Recorder, African American Literature, and Periodical Culture.* New York: Oxford University Press, 2015.

———. "Of Bottles and Books: Reconsidering the Readers of Harriet Wilson's *Our Nig.*" In *Harriet Wilson's New England*, edited by JerriAnne Boggis et al., 3–26. Durham: University of New Hampshire Press, 2007.

———. "Slave Narratives and Archival Research." In *The Oxford Handbook of the African American Slave Narrative*, edited by John Ernest, 36–53. New York: Oxford University Press, 2014.

———. "'This Attempt of Their Sister': Harriet Wilson's Our Nig from Printer to Readers." *New England Quarterly: A Historical Review of New England Life and Letters* 66, no. 2 (1993): 226–46.

———. *Unexpected Places: Relocating Nineteenth-Century African American Literature.* Jackson: University Press of Mississippi, 2009.

———. "'You Have No Business to Whip Me': The Freedom Suits of Polly Wash and Lucy Ann Delaney." *African American Review* 41, no. 1 (2007): 33–50.

Garvey, Ellen Gruber. *Writing With Scissors: American Scrapbooks from the Civil War to the Harlem Renaissance.* New York: Oxford University Press, 2013.

Gates, Henry Louis. *Figures in Black: Words, Signs, and the "Racial" Self.* New York: Oxford University Press, 1987.

———. *The Signifying Monkey: A Theory of Afro-American Literary Criticism.* New York: Oxford University Press, 1988.

Gates, Henry Louis, Jr., and R. J. Ellis. "Introduction." In *Our Nig: Or, Sketches from the Life of a Free Black . . .* , edited by Henry Louis Gates Jr. and Richard J. Ellis, xiii–lxvii. New York: Vintage, 2011.

Gates, Henry Louis, Jr., and Evelyn Brooks Higginbotham, eds. *The African American National Biography.* Oxford University Press, 2008.

Gibson, William H. *History of the United Brothers of Friendship and Sisters of the Mysterious Ten: In Two Parts; a Negro Order; Organized August 1, 1861, in the City of Louisville, Ky.* Louisville, KY: Bradley & Gilbert Company, 1897.

Gilmore, William J. "Peddlers and the Dissemination of Printed Material in Northern New England." In Benes, Peter and Jane Montague Benes, eds. Dublin Seminar for New England Folklife. *Itinerancy in New England and New York*, 84–88. Boston: Boston University, 1986.

Gitelman, Lisa. *Paper Knowledge: Toward a Media History of Documents.* Durham, NH: Duke University Press, 2014.

Glaude, Eddie S., Jr. *Exodus!: Religion, Race, and Nation in Early Nineteenth-Century Black America.* Chicago: University of Chicago Press, 2000.

Goddu, Teresa A. "The Slave Narrative as Material Text." In *The Oxford Handbook of the African American Slave Narrative*, edited by John Ernest, 149–64. New York: Oxford University Press, 2014.

Goldsby, Jacqueline, and Meredith McGill. "What is 'Black' about Black Bibliography?" *Publications of the Bibliographic Society of America* 116, no. 2 (June 2022): 161–89.

Gordon-Reed, Annette, ed. *Race on Trial: Law and Justice in American History*. New York: Oxford University Press, 2002.

Graff, Gerald, and James Phelan, eds. *The Adventures of Huckleberry Finn: A Case Study in Critical Controversy*. Boston: Bedford/St. Martin's, 1995.

Graham, Thomas. *Mr. Flagler's St. Augustine*. Gainesville: University Press of Florida, 2014.

Grandy, Moses. *Narrative of the Life of Moses Grandy, Late a Slave in the United States of America*. London: Gilpin, 1843.

Green, James. "Bound/Unbound." *Early American Studies* 16, no. 4 (2018): 614–20.

Greenspan, Ezra. *William Wells Brown: An African American Life*. New York: W. W. Norton, 2014.

Gross, Robert. "Reading for an Extensive Republic." In *An Extensive Republic: Print, Culture, and Society in the New Nation, 1790-1840*. Vol. 2 of *A History of the Book in America*, edited by Robert Gross and Mary Kelley, 516–44. Chapel Hill: University of North Carolina Press, 2010.

Gross, Robert A., and Mary Kelley, eds. *An Extensive Republic: Print, Culture, and Society in the New Nation, 1790-1840*. Vol. 2 of *A History of the Book in America*. Chapel Hill: University of North Carolina Press, 2010.

Grover, Kathryn. *The Fugitive's Gibraltar: Escaping Slaves and Abolitionism in New Bedford, Massachusetts*. Amherst: University Massachusetts Press, 2001.

Hack, Daniel. *The Material Interests of the Victorian Novel*. Charlottesville: University of Virginia Press, 2005.

Hager, Christopher. *Word by Word: Emancipation and the Act of Writing*. Cambridge, MA: Harvard University Press, 2013.

Hall, Stephen G. *A Faithful Account of the Race: African American Historical Writing in Nineteenth-Century America*. Chapel Hill: University of North Carolina Press, 2009.

Handy, James. *Scraps of African Methodist Episcopal History*. Philadelphia: A.M.E. Book Concern, 1902.

Hannah-Jones, Nikole. "America Wasn't a Democracy, until Black Americans Made It One: The 1619 Project." *New York Times Magazine*, August 14, 2019.

Harrold, Stanley. *Subversives: Antislavery Community in Washington, D.C., 1828–1865*. Baton Rouge: Louisiana State University Press, 2003.

Hartman, Saidiya. *Scenes of Subjection. Terror, Slavery, and Self-Making in Nineteenth-Century America*. New York: Oxford University Press, 1997.

Hesse, Carla. "Books in Time." In *The Future of the Book*, edited by Geoffrey Nunberg, 21–36. Berkeley: University of California Press, 1997.

Hickman, Jared Winston. "Tilmon, Levin." *African American Studies Center*. Oxford University Press. https://doi.org/10.1093/acref/9780195301731.013.38043.

Higginbotham, A. Leon. *In the Matter of Color: Race and the American Legal Process: The Colonial Period*. New York: Oxford University Press, 1978.

———. *Shades of Freedom: Racial Politics and Presumptions of the American Legal Process*. New York: Oxford University Press, 1996.

Hinks, Peter. "Introduction." In *David Walker's Appeal to the Coloured Citizens of the World*, edited by Peter Hinks, xi–xliv. University Park, PA: Pennsylvania State University Press, 2000.

The History of Grundy County Illinois. Chicago: O.L. Baskin & Co. Historical Publishers, 1882.

Hodges, Graham Russell, ed. *Black Itinerants of the Gospel: The Narratives of John Jea and George White*. Madison, WI: Madison House, 1993.

———. *David Ruggles: A Radical Black Abolitionist and the Underground Railroad in New York City*. Chapel Hill: University of North Carolina Press, 2010.

Holloway, Karla F. C. "Economies of Space: Markets and Marketability in *Our Nig* and *Iola Leroy*." In *The (Other) American Traditions: Nineteenth-Century Women Writers*, edited by Joyce W. Warren, 126–40. New Brunswick, NJ: Rutgers University Press, 1993.

Hood, J. W. *One Hundred Years of the African Methodist Episcopal Zion Church, or, the Centennial of African Methodism*. New York: A.M.E. Zion Book Concern, 1895.

Huggins, Nathan Irvin. *Black Odyssey: The Afro-American Ordeal in Slavery*. New York: Pantheon Books, 1977.

Jackson, Leon. *The Business of Letters: Authorial Economies in Antebellum America*. Palo Alto, CA: Stanford University Press, 2008.

———. "The Talking Book and the Talking Book Historian: African American Cultures of Print-the State of the Discipline." *Book History* 13 (2010): 252–308.

Jefferson, Thomas, Julian P. Boyd, Mina R. Bryan, L. H. Butterfield, Charles T. Cullen, John Catanzariti, Barbara Oberg, James P. McClure, Martha J. King, and Tom Downey. *The Papers of Thomas Jefferson*. Princeton, NJ: Princeton University Press, 1950–present.

Jeffrey, Julie Roy. *Abolitionists Remember: Antislavery Autobiographies & the Unfinished Work of Emancipation*. Chapel Hill: University of North Carolina Press, 2008.

Johnson, Walter. *Soul by Soul: Life Inside the Antebellum Slave Market*. Cambridge, MA: Harvard University Press, 2001.

Jones, Martha S. *Birthright Citizens: A History of Race and Rights in Antebellum America*. Studies in Legal History. New York: Cambridge University Press, 2018.

Jones, Thomas H., and Richard Hildreth. *Experience and personal narrative of Uncle Tom Jones, who was for forty years a slave; also, The surprising adventures of Wild Tom, of the island retreat, a fugitive negro from South Carolina*. Boston: J.E. Farwell and Co, 1854.

Kaestle, Carl F., and Janice A. Radway, eds. *Print in Motion: The Expansion of Publishing and Reading in the United States, 1880–1940*. Chapel Hill: University of North Carolina Press, 2009.

Keckley, Elizabeth. *Behind the Scenes, or Thirty Years a Slave and Four Years in the White House*. New York: G.W. Carleton and Co., 1868.

Kelly, Edmund. *Africa's Quotoa [sic] to the American Nation, Must Be Equally Diffused among the Whole*. Washington, DC: Argus, 1979.

———. *Edmund Kelly's Appeal to Lovers of Freedom, Righteous Progress, and Christianity. Friends, Labor, Watch, Pray and Vote Right*. [New Bedford, Mass.]: s.n., 1876.

———. *The Great Exodus of the Colored People from the South to the West: Its Cause and Probable Results. The Duty of the Plighted Nation to Them in the Premises*. Washington, DC: s.n., 1879.

———. *Important Questions Adapted to the Use of Sabbath Schools, Bible Classes, and Private Families : Including Many Testimonials North and South*. New Bedford [Mass.]: The author, 1864.

Langston, John Mercer. *From the Virginia Plantation to the National Capitol: Or, the First and Only Negro Representative in Congress from the Old Dominion*. Hartford, CT: American Publishing Company, 1894.

Laquintano, Timothy. *Mass Authorship and the Rise of Self-Publishing*. Iowa City: University of Iowa Press, 2016.

Leonard, James S., Thomas A. Tenney, and Thadious M. Davis, eds. *Satire or Evasion? Black Perspectives on Huckleberry Finn*. Durham, NC: Duke University Press, 1992.

Lewis, Sid. *Eight Nights With a Reading Club*. Macon, GA: J.W. Burke & Co, 1871.

Litwack, Leon F. *Been in the Storm So Long: The Aftermath of Slavery*. New York: Vintage, 1979.

———. *North of Slavery; the Negro in the Free States, 1790–1860*. Chicago: University of Chicago Press, 1961.

Loughran, Trish. *The Republic in Print: Print Culture in the Age of US Nation Building, 1770–1870*. New York: Columbia University Press, 2007.

Luker, Ralph. "Reverdy Cassius Ransom." In *American National Biography*. Edited by John A. Garraty and Mark C. Carnes. New York: Oxford University Press, 1999.

Luxenberg, Steve. *Separate: The Story of Plessy v. Ferguson, and America's Journey from Slavery to Segregation*. New York: W. W. Norton, 2019.

MacKethan, Lucinda. "Plantation Fiction." In *The History of Southern Literature*, edited by Louis Rubin, 209–18. Baton Rouge: Louisiana State University Press, 1985.

Madera, Judith. *Black Atlas: Geography and Flow in Nineteenth-Century African American Literature*. Durham, NC: Duke University Press, 2015.

Manchester, Irving. *The History of Colebrook*. Winstead, CT: Citizen Print Co., 1935.

Marx, Leo. "Mr. Eliot, Mr. Trilling, and *Huckleberry Finn*." *American Scholar* 22, no. 4 (Autumn 1953): 423–40.

McBride, Dwight A. *Impossible Witnesses: Truth, Abolitionism, and Slave Testimony*. New York: New York University Press, 2001.

McCarthy, B. Eugene, and Thomas L. Doughton, eds. *From Bondage to Belonging: The Worcester Slave Narratives*. Amherst: University of Massachusetts Press, 2007.

McCarthy, Timothy Patrick. "To Plead Our Own Cause." In *Prophets of Protest: Reconsidering the History of American Abolitionism*, edited by Timothy Patrick McCarthy and John Stauffer, 114–46. New York: The New Press, 2012.

McCoy, Beth A. "Race and the (Para)Textual Condition." *PMLA* 121 (January 2006): 156–69.

McFeely, William S. *Frederick Douglass*. New York: W. W. Norton, 1991.

McGann, Jerome. *The Textual Condition*. Princeton, NJ: Princeton University Press, 1990.

McGill, Meredith L. *American Literature and the Culture of Reprinting, 1834–1853*. Philadelphia: University of Pennsylvania Press, 2003.

———. "Format." *Early American Studies* 16, no. 4 (2018): 671–77.

———. "Literary History, Book History, and Media Studies." In *Turns of Event: Nineteenth-Century American Literary Studies in Motion*, edited by Hester Blum, 23–40. Philadelphia: University Pennsylvania Press, 2016.

McHenry, Elizabeth. "'Out of the Business Once Established Could Grow Various Enterprises': W. E. B. Du Bois and the Ed. L. Simon & Co. Printers." *Book History* 24, no. 2 (2021): 405–50.

———. *To Make Negro Literature: Writing, Literary Practice, and African American Authorship*. Durham, NC: Duke University Press, 2021.

McKenzie, D. F. *Bibliography and the Sociology of Texts*. Cambridge: Cambridge University Press, 1999.

Menschel, David. "Abolition without Deliverance: The Law of Connecticut Slavery 1784–1848." *Yale Law Journal* 111 (2001): 183–222.

Moody, Joycelyn. *Sentimental Confessions: Spiritual Narratives of Nineteenth-Century African American Women*. Athens: University of Georgia Press, 2001.

Moody, Joycelyn, and Howard Rambsy. "Guest Editors' Introduction: African American Print Cultures." *MELUS: Multi-Ethnic Literature of the United States* 40, no. 3 (2015): 1–11.

Mulderink, Earl F. *New Bedford's Civil War*. New York: Fordham University Press, 2012.

Nell, William Cooper. *The Colored Patriots of the American Revolution: With Sketches of Several Distinguished Colored Persons* . . . Boston: Robert F. Walcutt, 1855.

Newman, Richard, Patrick Rael, and Phillip Lapsansky, eds. *Pamphlets of Protest: An Anthology of Early African-American Protest Literature, 1790–1860*. London: Routledge, 2001.

Nishikawa, Kinohi. "The Archive on Its Own: Black Politics, Independent Publishing, and 'The *Negotiations*'." *MELUS: Multi-Ethnic Literature of the United States* 40, no. 3, (2015): 176–201.

Norrell, Robert. *Up from History: The Life of Booker T. Washington*. Cambridge, MA: Harvard University Press, 2009.

Olney, James. "'I Was Born': Slave Narratives, Their Status as Autobiography, and as Literature." In *The Slave's Narrative*, edited by Charles T. Davis and Henry Louis Gates Jr., 148–75. New York: Oxford University Press, 1985.

Painter, Nell Irvin. *Sojourner Truth: A Life, a Symbol*. New York: W. W. Norton, 1996.

Parfait, Claire. "The Grandest Book Ever Written: Advertising Joseph T. Wilson's *Black Phalanx*." In *Writing History from the Margins*, edited by Claire Parfait, Hélène Le Dantec-Lowry, and Claire Bourhis-Mariotti, 13–25. New York: Routledge, 2017.

Parfait, Claire, Hélène Le Dantec-Lowry, and Claire Bourhis-Mariotti, eds. *Writing History from the Margins: African Americans and the Quest for Freedom*. New York: Routledge, 2017.

Parrish, C. H., ed. *Golden Jubilee of the General Association of Colored Baptists in Kentucky: The Story of 50 Years' Work from 1865–1915*. Louisville, KY: Mayes Printing Co., 1915.

Payne, Daniel Alexander. *Recollections of Seventy Years*. Nashville: Publishing House of the A. M. E. Sunday School Union, 1888.

Payne, Daniel Alexander. *History of the African Methodist Episcopal Church*. Edited by C. S. Smith. Nashville: Publishing House of the A.M.E. Sunday School Union, 1891.

Peabody, Ephraim. "Narratives of Fugitive Slaves." In *The Slave's Narrative*, edited by Charles Davis and Henry Louis Gates Jr., 19-28. New York: Oxford University Press, 1985.

Pennington, James W. C. *A Text Book of the Origin and History, &c. &c. of the Colored People*. Hartford, CT: s.n., 1841.

Peterson, Carla L. *Doers of the Word: African-American Women Speakers and Writers in the North, 1830-1880*. New York: Oxford University Press, 1995.

Porter, Dorothy. "Early American Negro Writings: A Bibliographical Study." *Papers of the Bibliographical Society of America* 39, no. 3 (1945), 181-270.

———. *The Negro in the United States; a Selected Bibliography*. Washington, DC: Library of Congress, 1970.

Pratofiorito, Ellen. "'To Demand Your Sympathy and Aid': *Our Nig* and the Problem of No Audience." *Journal of American & Comparative Cultures* 24, no. 1/2 (Spring 2001): 31-48.

Quarles, Benjamin. *Black Abolitionists*. New York: Oxford University Press, 1969.

———. "Black History's Antebellum Origins." *Proceedings of the American Antiquarian Society* 89, no. 1 (April 1979): 89-122.

Reed, George Irving, E. O. Randall, and Charles Theodore Greve. *Bench and Bar of Ohio: A Compendium of History and Biography*. Chicago: Century Pub. and Engraving Co, 1897.

Rezek, Joseph. "The Print Atlantic: Phillis Wheatley, Ignatius Sancho, and the Cultural Significance of the Book." In *Early African American Print Culture*, edited by Lara Langer Cohen and Jordan Alexander Stein, 19-39. Philadelphia: University of Pennsylvania Press, 2012.

Rhodes, Jane. *Mary Ann Shadd Cary: The Black Press and Protest in the Nineteenth Century*. Bloomington: Indiana University Press, 1998.

Ripley, C. P. *The Black Abolitionist Papers*. Chapel Hill: University of North Carolina Press, 1985-92.

Robert, Joseph C. "William Wirt, Virginian." *Virginia Magazine of History and Biography* 80, no. 4 (1972): 387-441.

Rohrbach, Augusta. *Thinking Outside the Book*. Amherst: University of Massachusetts Press, 2014.

———. *Truth Stranger than Fiction: Race, Realism, and the US Literary Marketplace*. New York: Palgrave, 2002.

Roosevelt, Theodore. *The Winning of the West*. 5 vols. New York: G. P. Putnam's Sons, 1889.

Roy, Michaël. "Cheap Editions, Little Books, and Handsome Duodecimos: A Book History Approach to Antebellum Slave Narratives." *MELUS: Multi-Ethnic Literature of the United States* 40, no. 3 (2015): 69-93.

———. *Fugitive Texts: Slave Narratives in Antebellum Print Culture*. Translated by Susan Pickford. Madison: University of Wisconsin Press, 2022.

———. "The Slave Narrative Unbound." In *Against a Sharp White Background*, edited by Brigette Fielder and Jonathan Senchyne, 259–76. Madison: University of Wisconsin Press, 2019.

Ruggles, Jeffrey. *The Unboxing of Henry Brown*. Richmond: Library of Virginia, 2002.

Rusert. Britt. "From Black Lit to Black Print: The Return to the Archive in African American Literary Studies." *American Quarterly* 68, no. 4 (2016): 993–1005.

———. "New World: The Impact of Digitization on the Study of Slavery." *American Literary History* 29, no. 2 (2017): 267–86.

Ryan, Susan. *The Grammar of Good Intentions: Race and the Antebellum Culture of Benevolence*. Ithaca, NY: Cornell University Press, 2003.

Schweik, Susan M. *The Ugly Laws: Disability in Public*. New York: New York University Press, 2009.

Sekora, John. "Black Message/White Envelope: Genre, Authenticity, and Authority in the Antebellum Slave Narrative." *Callaloo: A Journal of African American and African Arts and Letters* 10, no. 3 (1987): 482–515.

Severance, Margaret. *Official Guide to Atlanta: Including Information of the Cotton States and International Exposition*. Atlanta: Foote & Davies Co., 1895.

Silver, Rollo G. *The American Printer, 1787-1825*. Charlottesville: University Press of Virginia, 1967.

Simmons, William J. *Men of Mark: Eminent, Progressive and Rising*. Cleveland: Geo. M. Rewell & Co., 1887.

Sinche, Bryan. "Self-Publication, Self-Promotion, and the *Life of William Grimes, the Runaway Slave*." *Biography* 42, no. 4 (2019): 825–45.

———. "The Walking Book." In *Against a Sharp White Background: Infrastructures of African American Print*, edited by Brigette Fielder and Jonathan Senchyne, 279–97. Madison: University of Wisconsin Press, 2019.

Sinha, Manisha. *The Slave's Cause: A New History of Abolition*. New Haven, CT: Yale University Press, 2016.

Smith, Rogers M. *Civic Ideals: Conflicting Visions of Citizenship in US History*. New Haven, CT: Yale University Press, 1997.

Spires, Derrick. *The Practice of Citizenship: Black Politics and Print Culture in the Early United States*. Philadelphia: University of Pennsylvania Press, 2019.

Stanley, Amy Dru. "Beggars Can't Be Choosers: Compulsion and Contract in Postbellum America." *Journal of American History* 78, no. 4 (1992): 1265–93.

Stauffer, John. *The Black Hearts of Men: Radical Abolitionists and the Transformation of Race*. Cambridge, MA: Harvard University Press, 2000.

Stepto, Robert B. *From Behind the Veil: A Study of Afro-American Narrative*. Revised edition. Urbana: University of Illinois Press, 1991.

Stevens, Charles Emery. *Anthony Burns: A History*. Boston: John P. Jewett, 1856.

Stouffer, Allen P. *The Light of Nature and the Law of God: Antislavery in Ontario, 1833-1877*. Baton Rouge: Louisiana State University Press, 1992.

Stover, John F. "Flagler, Henry Morrison." In *American National Biography*, v. 8. General editors John A. Garraty, Mark C. Carnes. New York: Oxford University Press, 1999.

Sweet, Leonard I. *Black Images of America: 1784–1870*. New York: W. W. Norton, 1976.
Sully County Centennial History Book Committee. *100 Years of Proud People, 1883–1983: A History of Sully County*. Onida, SD: Sully County Centennial History Book Committee, 1983.
Sundquist, Eric. *To Wake the Nations: Race in the Making of American Literature*. Cambridge, MA: Harvard University Press, 1993.
Tamarkin, Elisa. *Anglophilia: Deference, Devotion, and Antebellum America*. Chicago: University of Chicago Press, 2008.
Tanner, Benjamin T. *An Apology for African Methodism*. Baltimore: s.n., 1867.
Tebbel, John. *Between the Covers: The Rise and Transformation of Book Publishing in America*. New York: Oxford University Press, 1987.
Thomas, Max. "Reading and Writing the Renaissance Commonplace Book: A Question of Authorship?" In *The Construction of Authorship: Textual Appropriation in Law and Literature*, edited by Martha Woodmansee and Peter Jaszi, 401–16. Durham, NC: Duke University Press, 1994.
Torrey, Edwin F. *The Martyrdom of Abolitionist Charles Torrey*. Baton Rouge: Louisiana State University Press, 2013.
VanderVelde, Lea. *Redemption Songs: Suing for Freedom before Dred Scott*. New York: Oxford University Press, 2014.
Van Schreeven, William J. "William Waller Hening." *The William and Mary Quarterly* 22, no. 2 (1942): 161–64.
Wagner, Bryan. *Disturbing the Peace: Black Culture and the Police Power After Slavery*. Cambridge, MA: Harvard University Press, 2009.
Walker, David. *David Walker's Appeal to the Coloured Citizens of the World*. Edited by Peter Hinks. University Park: Pennsylvania State University Press, 2000.
Warner, Michael. *The Letters of the Republic: Publication and the Public Sphere in Eighteenth-Century America*. Cambridge, MA: Harvard University Press, 1990.
Washington, Booker T. *Up from Slavery*. Edited by William L. Andrews. New York: W. W. Norton, 1995.
Wayman, Alexander W. *My Recollections of African M. E. Ministers, or Forty Years' Experience in the African Methodist Episcopal Church*. Philadelphia: A. M. E. Book Rooms, 1881
Weaver, John C. "Brown, Paola." In *Dictionary of Canadian Biography*, vol. 8. Toronto: University of Toronto/Université Laval, 2003.
Weyler, Karen. *Empowering Words: Outsiders and Authorship in Early America*. Athens: University of Georgia Press, 2013.
White, Barbara A. "'Our Nig' and the She-Devil: New Information about Harriet Wilson and the 'Bellmont' Family." American Literature 65, no. 1 (1993): 19–52.
White, David. "The Real Life of James Mars." *Connecticut History* 43, no. 1 (2004): 28–46.
Williams, Andreá. "Introduction to *Narrative of the Life of Moses Grandy*." In *North Carolina Slave Narratives*, edited by William L. Andrews, 133–51. Chapel Hill: University of North Carolina Press, 2003.
Winks, Robin W. *The Blacks in Canada: A History*. Montreal: McGill-Queen's University Press, 1971.

Winship, Michael. *American Literary Publishing in the Mid-Nineteenth Century: The Business of Ticknor and Fields*. Cambridge University Press, 1995.

———. "'The Greatest Book of Its Kind': A Publishing History of *Uncle Tom's Cabin*." *Proceedings of the American Antiquarian Society* 109, no. 2 (October 1999): 309–32.

Wood Marcus. *Black Milk: Imagining Slavery in the Visual Cultures of Brazil and America*. Oxford: Oxford University Press, 2013.

Yellin, Jean Fagan. *Harriet Jacobs: A Life*. New York: Basic Civitas, 2004.

Zafar, Rafia. *We Wear the Mask: African Americans Write American Literature, 1760–1870*. New York: Columbia University Press, 1997.

Zboray, Ronald. *A Fictive People*. New York: Oxford University Press, 1993.

Zboray, Ronald J., and Mary Saracino Zboray. "The Dissemination of Reading Material during the American Civil War." In *Print Culture Beyond the Metropolis*, edited by James J. Connolly, Patrick Collier, Frank Felsenstein, Kenneth R. Hall, and Robert G. Hall, 123–49. Toronto: University of Toronto Press, 2016.

Index

Aaron, 34, 40–50, 52–53, 59, 62
abolitionism, 4, 34, 47, 56, 62, 65–66; and Charles Torrey, 74–75; Democratic Party opposed to, 81–82; and James Mars, 98; and legal system, 120; and Levin Tilmon, 67, 71, 73, 173; organizations participating in, 10, 64–66, 80, 89, 173; and Osborne P. Anderson, 94–95; and Peter Randolph, 133; relationship to print culture, 29, 70, 79, 93, 121; religious groups participating in, 49, 59; relationship to self-publication, 64, 70, 93; "theater of," 79–80, 85, 106; and Thomas James, 92, 103–5, 107, 109; and Thomas Smallwood, 73–75, 77–79, 80; and William Anderson, 84, 88; *See also* antislavery
Adams, John, 122, 125
Adams, John Quincy, 50
African Methodist Episcopal Church (A.M.E. Church), 20, 45, 67–69, 71, 145–46, 148–49; and David Smith, 150, 152–54; in Indiana, 166; and Jacob Stroyer, 109; and Major James Wilkerson, 163–65, 168, 170–72; and Jarena Lee, 162, 172; leadership, 175; and Robert B. Anderson, 82, 89, 176, 179–81, 183, 186, 188–89, 192–93, 195; Wilberforce University, 167
African Methodist Episcopal Zion Church (A.M.E. Zion), 71, 104–6, 146
A.M.E. Church Review, 4
American Anti-Slavery Society, 74
American South, 109; and Aaron, 45; antebellum, 190; and anti-Black legislation, 174, 193; cross-racial alliances in, 5, 179–82; and Jacob Stroyer, 113, 116–17; and laws, 133; and Lucy Delaney, 122; and race, 178, 192; during Reconstruction, 144, 178; and slavery, 163
Anderson, Osborne P., 31, 34, 92, 93–98; death of, 97; Harpers Ferry Raid, role in, 97; published work, 97–98, 103
Anderson, Robert B., 1, 5–8, 35, 173–95; advertisements by, 27, 189; and A.M.E. Church, 183, 195; autobiographies by, 1, 175–78, 193, 195; in Chicago, 36; John W. Burke, relationship with 1, 186, 193–94; and M.E. Church, 185, 188; in Philadelphia, 192; as preacher, 36; as public speaker, 185; as self-publisher, 4, 9, 12, 36, 172, 174–75, 178–81, 183–84, 189–93; and slavery, 1, 195; and *The Anderson Surpriser*, 187–93; and *The Life of Rev. Robert Anderson* (1892), 5–6, 8, 32, 179–83, 186–87, 191, 194; and whitewashing, 179
Anderson, Vincent, 98
Anderson, William J., 25, 34, 67, 80; and *Christian Recorder*, 89; and *Indianapolis Herald*, 89; and M.E. Church, 81; *Narrative*, 87–89; political work, 83; as public speaker, 82–83; published work, 83–86, 88
Andrews, William L., 10–11, 28, 29, 85, 145, 148, 180
antebellum era, 172, 190; and abolitionism, 85, 95, 106; Black activism in, 70, 89, 146; and freedom suits, 141; and John Brown, 95; literary markets in, 24, 37; and print culture, 23; and slave narratives, 107, 140; and writing, 24, 34, 50, 61, 104, 121

251

antislavery movement, 38–39, 47, 64, 66, 73, 75, 79–82, 93–96, 107; linked to churches, 53; linked to Civil War, 13; labor, 34, 78, 88; and Levin Tilmon, 34, 89; in New Bedford, 53; and newspapers, 74; and Thomas Smallwood, 13, 34, 77–78; and William J. Anderson, 34, 81, 84–85, 89; and writing, 30, 34, 48–49, 61, 66–67, 71–73, 104–6, 110, 112–14
Anti-Slavery Almanac (1839), 48
Anti-Slavery office (Boston), 26
Anti-Slavery Record (1835), 47–48
Anti-Slavery Society of Canada, 77, 210n36
autobiographies, 5; by Amanda Smith, 147; Black, 10–11, 15, 29, 65, 70, 98, 112, 131–32, 146, 157; by Booker T. Washington, 131; by David Smith, 150–52; by Elijah Marrs, 154; by Elleanor Eldridge, 120; by G. W. Offley, 66; by George White, 145; by Henry Parker, 50–51; by Jacob Stroyer, 109–11, 113–14, 117; by James Mars, 93, 100–1, 103; by Major James Wilkerson, 165, 167–68, 172; by Jarena Lee, 159–62; by Jerimiah Asher, 147; by Julia Foote, 147; by Levin Tilmon, 67–68, 70, 73, 80, 89; by Lucy Delaney, 122, 140–42; by M. W. Gibbs, 13, 18, 141; by Norvel Blair, 135; by Olaudah Equiano, 19; by Peter Randolph, 131; by Robert B. Anderson, 1, 5, 8, 175–76, 178, 181, 187–88; by Thomas James, 107, 109; by Thomas Jones, 39, 86; by Thomas Smallwood, 67, 77, 80, 89; by Thomas W. Henry, 149; and self-publication, 11, 15, 149, 157; by Venture Smith, 119; by Willian J. Anderson, 84

Baptist churches, 37, 53, 56–58, 93–94, 146–47, 149, 155, 157–58, 188, 191
Black, Leonard, 15, 52, 66, 70

Black Americans, as activists, 20, 67, 83, 211n62; and agency, 92, 199; and American life, 35, 90; and American Revolution, 84; autobiographies by, 10–11, 23, 64–65, 81, 98, 112–13, 132, 148, 157, 204n80; and books, 3, 24–25, 28; in Boston, 133, 193; and community-building, 31, 56, 75, 99, 114, 181; discrimination experienced by, 33, 144, 174, 179, 195, 197; and economics, 177–79, 196; and freedom, 34, 128, 132; and identity, 213n1; in Kentucky, 155, 157; and labor, 66, 174, 194; and the law, 134–35; and literacy, 10, 17; and literature, 17, 19, 24, 28–33, 36, 40, 60–61, 70, 76, 140, 190, 203n38, 205n97; in Maryland, 66; and middle class, 140, 174; as ministers, 32, 35, 46, 71, 104, 145–72, 184–85; in New England, 45; and perspective, 35; and press, 4, 15, 25, 28, 106, 159, 201n12; and print shops, 15, 99, 222n46; and readership, 4, 24, 73, 95–96, 106, 134, 192; and slavery, 96–97, 175; in the South, 188, 191; and violence, 80, 164, 197; and voting rights, 83; and women, 142, 151, 163, 172, 179, 194, 222n55
Blair, Norvel, 13, 35, 135–139; *Book for the People!*, 135–39; family, 136; in Illinois, 135, 139; legal fights, 136–38; use of pamphlets, 135, 137–38; self-publication, 30, 199; in South Dakota, 139; in Tennessee, 136
Boston, Massachusetts: and Anthony Burns, 133; anti-slavery, movement 95; book sales in, 26, 36, 205n97; Black population, 193; Edmond Kelley in, 54, 56, 58; Osborne P. Anderson in, 93–94; and Peter Randolph, 130, 132, 144, 235, 219n54; Robert B. Anderson in, 187; and William Hayden in, 25
Brown, Abel, 75

Brown, Henry Box, 173
Brown, Jane, 66
Brown, John, 37, 93–98
Brown, John Mifflin, 165, 170
Brown, Paola, 73–77, 79
Brown, William Wells, 64, 70, 88, 90, 116
Burke, John W., 1–2, 175, 178, 186, 194
Butcher, William, 159

Channing, William Ellery, 48
Christian Recorder, 4, 89, 149, 151–52, 171–72, 183
churches, 54–55, 70–71; linked to antislavery, 53, 74, 81; in Baltimore, 150; Baptist, 147, 149, 156–58; Bethel Church, Pennsylvania, 106; Black, 21, 68, 144–50, 153, 181; and education, 73, 152; hierarchies, 145, 148–49; histories, 1, 104, 148–49, 153, 184; leadership, 150, 159–61; preachers, 104, 107, 185; records, 11; and Thomas James, 106–7
civil rights, 24, 34, 71, 98, 103, 106–7
Civil War: African Americans in, 145; Confederate Army, 117; and David Smith, 151; and Elijah Marrs, 154–55; experiences of, 32, 50; and General John Palmer, 107; history of, 35; Jacob Stroyer in, 110, 112, 117; and John Brown, 94, 96, 98; and Lucy Delaney, 140; and Osborne P. Anderson, 93–94, 98; and Robert B. Anderson, 179–80, 187; and soldiers, 50–51, 103; and Thomas James, 13, 105, 109; and William J. Anderson, 88
Connecticut, 26–27, 47, 98–103, 120, 153, 197–99
Cooper, James Fenimore, 3
Cowper, William, 47, 49, 76

Davis, Noah, 37–38, 52, 146
Delaney, Lucy, 35, 140–44; agency, 142–43; autobiography, 122, 140–41, 144; freedom lawsuit, 141–42; and M.E. Church, 143–44; and narrative, 35, 122, 140–43; and self-publication, 30; and slavery, 140
Detroit Law Printing Co., 25
Douglass, Frederick, 7, 19, 137; as abolitionist, 67; as A.M.E. Zion preacher, 104; referenced by Edmond Kelley, 55; and Levin Tilmon, 68, 70; *Narrative of the Life* (1845), 19, 64; as public speaker, 77; as self-publisher, 33, 64; and Thomas James, 105, 107; and Young Men's Literary Productive Society, 71–72

Eastern New York Antislavery Society (ENYAS), 75
economic citizenship, 92
economic inequality, 61, 125, 158
economic interests, 20, 23, 186
economic motivations, 77, 85, 173
economic need, 7, 32, 34, 38, 98
economic position, 69, 183
economic productivity, 71
economic ritual, 23, 49–50, 55, 190
economic status, 13, 33, 39, 53, 81, 90, 110, 190
economic success, 5, 8–9, 25, 80, 89–91, 120, 122, 145, 162, 174–75
economic sustainability, 152
economic system, 9, 12, 33, 59, 175, 179
economic venture, 167
Edloe, Carter: children, 132; Christianity, 132; death of, 133–34; "Edloe Slaves," 131, 133, 135; plantation, 132, 134–35
Eight Nights with a Reading Club, 1
Enos, J. D., 97–98, 214n30
enslaved African Americans: Aaron, 43, 45; and abolitionist movement, 53, 65, 80; and Booker T. Washington, 158; and Carter Edloe, 133–35; Christopher McPherson, 122, 125; and Civil War, 91, 117; and Connecticut, 103; David Smith, 150; Edmond Kelley, 55–56; Elijah Marrs, 155; and escapes, 75; and freedom, 113; and

Index 253

enslaved African Americans (cont.)
Fugitive Slave Act, 65, 74, 133; George White, 145; and Harpers Ferry, 96; Jacob Stroyer, 114, 131; James Mars, 98, 197; and James Walker, 57; Major James Wilkerson, 163; and John Brown, 96; Lucy Delaney, 140; and ministers, 32; and narratives, 5, 29, 64, 66; Noah Davis, 37; and Osborne P. Anderson, 93; Peter Randolph, 130–34; Robert Anderson, 1, 81, 175–76, 178–81; and self-publication, 29–30, 66; and surveillance, 197; Thomas James, 104; Thomas Smallwood, 75, 77–78; white abolitionists, relationships with, 20; William J. Anderson, 84. See also slavery

enslavers, 13, 75, 80, 92, 114, 122, 136, 181; and Betheny Veney, 91; Charles Suttle, 133; and David Smith, 150; and Elijah Marrs, 155; and escapes from, 68, 173; and Jacob Stroyer, 109, 117; and James Mars, 98; James Walker, 57–59; and Robert B. Anderson, 179

Ernest, John, 14, 28, 31, 65, 91, 113–14, 118, 146

first-person narratives, 3, 10–11, 13–14, 23, 50, 91, 93

Foreman, P. Gabrielle, 28, 30–31, 60, 66, 113, 140

Foster, Frances Smith, 5, 10, 28, 30, 140, 160

Fugitive Slave Law, 83

Gardner, Eric, 4, 60, 62, 114, 138, 140–41, 143, 149–50, 152, 197

Garrison, William Lloyd, 64, 74

Gates, Henry Louis, Jr., 10, 28, 60, 196

Gibson, William H., 159

Grimes, Leonard, 133

Grimes, William, 15–18, 26

Hallock, William, 42

Harlem Renaissance, 3

Harper Brothers, 3

Harpers Ferry raid, 37, 92–97

Harrison, William B., 134

Hayden, William, 25

Indiana, 80–84, 89, 166, 171, 195

injustice, 30, 53, 120

Irving, Washington, 3

Jackson, Leon, 23, 190–91

Johnson, James Weldon, 187

Johnson, Samuel, 76, 103

Johnson, Walter, 58

Johnson, William H., 15, 66

justice, 35, 52, 117–18, 120–21, 128–29, 131, 134, 139–40, 144

justice system, 119, 122, 135, 143

Kelley, Edmond, 26, 34, 39, 52–60; *A Family Redeemed from Bondage* (1851), 39, 53, 55, 59; family, 56–58; and finances, 54–55, 58–59; freedom, 58; as fugitive, 56, 60; and James Walker, 57; in Massachusetts, 56, 60; as minister, 56; in New Bedford, 60, 173; and newspapers, 26; self-publication, 54–55, 60, 173; and slavery, 13, 53, 56–60, 146

law, 35, 119, 137, 141; and Black citizens, 33, 49, 71, 119, 133, 144; and Christopher McPherson, 125, 128; equal treatment under, 71, 119, 143–44; and freedom, 133; and language of, 57, 142; and "law still to come," 119–21, 139; and lawyers, 133, 136, 138; and lawsuits, 120, 123, 130, 136; and Lucy Delaney, 140–44; and Peter Randolph, 134–35; and racism, 197; in Virginia, 133–35; and white supremacy, 131

Lee, Jarena, 20, 26, 35, 148, 159–63; as preacher in A.M.E. Church, 148,

161–62; and autobiographies, 159–62; pamphlets, use of, 149; relationship with Richard Allen, 161; and self-publication, 20–21, 149, 162, 172

The Light and the Truth of Slavery (1840s, Aaron), 39–45, 47–49, 62

Macon, Georgia, 1–2, 175–80, 184, 186–87, 193–94

Marrs, Elijah, 35, 154–59; as minister in Baptist Church, 158; and Civil War, 154–56; and David Smith, 147–48; as historian, 148; and *Life and History*, 155–56, 158–59; and Loyal League, 157; and self-publication, 147, 155

Mars, James, 18, 27, 30–31, 34–35, 98–103, 197–98; and book sales, 100, 103, 199; in Connecticut, 27, 98–99, 103; and pamphlets, 92, 197; and self-publication, 92, 98, 100, 197; and slavery, 98, 103

Massachusetts Anti-Slavery Society (MASS), 64

McPherson, Christopher, 35, 121–130; audience, 123; birth, 122; family, 128, 130; and John Adams, 218n19; and legal system, 128–29; use of pamphlets, 141; in New York, 130; and self-publication, 123, 129; and Thomas Jefferson, 218n31; in Virginia, 122, 126, 128; and writing, 121–22

Methodist Episcopal Church (M.E. Church), 1, 81, 143, 145, 150, 153, 159, 185, 188

Michigan, 44, 50–51, 82, 89, 150, 165, 195

The Midnight Cry (1859), 13, 168–71

The Mirror of Slavery, 173

Mitchell, William, 70

My Life in the South (1898), 109–12, 114–16

National Convention of Colored People, 99

Nell, William C., 70, 84, 90, 94

New Orleans, 81, 163, 166, 168

newspapers, 1, 3–5, 11, 13, 135, 168; and abolition, 71, 80, 88; advertisements, 3–4, 27, 128, 149; antislavery, 74; Black, 25, 66, 106, 121; editors, 103; and Elijah Marrs, 148, 154–55, 157; *Frederick Douglass's Paper*, 68, 71–2, 104–5; in Indiana, 80; and Jacob Stroyer, 116; and James Mars, 103; and Levin Tilmon, 68, 89; and Paola Brown, 73; as printing shops, 14; and Robert B. Anderson, 189, 192, 194–95; and Thomas James, 104; and Thomas Smallwood, 79–80, 89, 211n56; and William J. Anderson, 25, 89; *Xenia Gazette*, 151

New York City: African Americans in, 70; antislavery activity in, 75, 95; and bookstores, 26; and Christopher McPherson, 130; churches in, 192–93; and Harper Brothers, 3; and Levin Tilmon, 67–71, 173; and literary conferences, 72; and Osborne P. Anderson, 94; publishing houses in, 4; and Thomas James, 106

New York Tribune, 69, 109

New York Witness, 157

novels: antislavery, 209n71; by Harriet Wilson, 60–63, 208n62; by Herman Gilbert, 32; by Mark Twain, 118, 217n4; by Richard Hildreth, 213n84; and self-publication, 25

Oberlin College, 110, 133

Offley, Greensbury Washington, 20–22, 27, 43, 45, 48, 66, 99

Ohio, 13, 20, 47, 51–52, 81, 110, 150–53, 164–67, 193

Ohio River, 83, 105

O'Neill, William, 174

pamphlets, 1; by Aaron, 40, 45–49, 62; and activism, 20, 89; by African-American writers, 3–5, 8, 13, 20, 42–43, 121; and A.M.E. Church, 183; and audiences, 10; by Charles

Index 255

pamphlets (cont.)
Thompson, 146–47; and Charles T. Torrey, 75; by Christopher McPherson, 123–25, 128–29, 141; and cost of production, 4; by Edmond Kelley, 53–55, 58, 60; by Greensbury Washington Offley, 21–22, 27, 45, 66, 99; by Henry Parker, 13, 17–18, 27, 39, 50–51; by Jacob Stroyer, 109–10; by James Mars, 20, 92, 99–101, 103, 106, 197; by Major James Wilkerson, 149, 167–68; by Jarena Lee, 160–62; by Levin Tilmon, 67–71; by Norvel Blair, 13, 135–38, 141; by Osborne P. Anderson, 31, 92–93, 95, 97; by Paola Brown, 79; by Peter Randolph, 130–31; printing process for, 15, 18–19; and readership, 18–19, 32; by Robert B. Anderson, 7–8, 175–81; by Thomas James, 105–7, 109; by Thomas Smallwood, 76–77, 79; sale of, 20–21, 26; self-publication of, 8, 11–12, 14, 23, 42; and sermons, 13; and supplicant texts, 47; by William Grimes, 17–18; by William J. Anderson, 84, 86, 88
Parker, Henry, 13, 17, 27, 34, 39, 50–52
Pennington, James W. C., 64, 70, 90, 98
Plessy v. Ferguson (1896), 117
Prince, Nancy, 39, 50
Prince George County, Virginia, 132
print culture, 20, 29, 65; Black, 11–12, 15, 28, 30–31, 33, 60, 121
printers, 2–3, 11, 15, 18, 26, 68, 159, 178, 189, 194–95
print market, 3, 170, 196
print shops, 15, 17, 26, 70, 86, 110, 112, 130
public sphere, 20, 139

Randolph, Peter, 35, 130–135; and Anthony Burns, 133; in Boston, 25, 144; and Carter Edloe, 133–35; and readership, 122; and Samuel May Jr., 131; and self-publication, 25, 130–32, 135; and *Sketches of a Slave Life*, 131; and slavery, 121, 134
Reminiscences of Slavery, 174
Republican National Convention, 157
Revels, William, 171
Roy, Michaël, 4–5, 7–8, 19, 29, 62, 64, 98, 162

Saratoga Street Baptist Church, 37
Second Baptist Church, 53, 56
Second Congregational Church, 99
self-publication, 3–4; and activism, 20, 31, 34, 67; as alternate testimony, 118; and collectivity, 30; and David Smith, 148, 151; and economies, 33; and judicial system, 119; by Leonard Black, 66; linked to abolitionism, 65; and religion, 36, 172; and sales, 12, 21, 28, 61, 159; and supplicant texts, 52; and W. E. B. DuBois, 14
self-published narratives, 1, 7, 11, 14, 17, 34, 55, 58, 90, 117, 120, 146–47
sermons: by David Smith, 147–48, 154; by Elijah Marrs, 147–48; by Jacob Stroyer, 110; by Jarena Lee, 26; by Leonard Black, 66; by Levin Tilmon, 13, 68, 89; and Noah Davis, 37; and Richard Allen, 160; by Robert B. Anderson, 188; and self-publication, 5, 34, 89
Shakespeare, William, 76
slave narratives, 5, 19, 35, 114, 121, 139, 181; by Aaron, 40; and abolition, 64–65; antebellum, 107, 140; and author portraiture, 86; in Canada, 76; diversity of, 29; by James Mars, 30; and legal history, 133; by Moses Grandy, 48; by Noah Davis, 37; by Peter Randolph, 132; and self-publication, 1; and supplication, 52; and white abolitionists, 20; by William J. Anderson, 86, 88
slavery: and abolition, 64, 89, 104, 121–22, 180; in Connecticut, 100, 103; linked to Democratic Party, 82; and

economics, 59; in *A Family Redeemed from Bondage*, 55–59; and J. B. Ferguson, 74; in *From the Darkness Cometh the Light* 140–41, 143; and racism, 95; and self-publication, 52; and Robert B. Anderson, 187, 194–95; in *Sketches of Slave Life*, 131–134; and Thomas Smallwood, 74, 77, 80; violence within, 80, 175, 181; and writing, 23, 29, 35, 48–49, 53, 65, 96–97, 100, 146, 184

Smallwood, Thomas, 13, 73–80; and Abel Brown, 75; work in abolitionist movement, 34, 73–74, 77–79, 96; and *A Narrative of Thomas Smallwood (Coloured Man)*, 75–78, 89; relationship with Charles Torrey, 74–75, 78; as columnist Samivel Weller, 79–80; and Maryland, 74; and self-publication, 76–77, 80, 89;

Smith, Amanda, 147
Smith, Christopher McPherson, 130
Smith, David, 35, 147–48, 150–54, 164
Smith, Gerrit, 75
Smith, Harry, 174
Smith, James Lindsay, 91, 92
Smith, James McCune, 67, 71
Smith, J. T., 141
Smith, Venture, 119–20, 140
Spires, Derrick, 28, 30–31, 71, 83, 199
Stray Leaves from the Portfolio of a Methodist Local Preacher, 1
Stroyer, Jacob, 109–17; autobiography, 113; book sales, 113; Civil War, service in, 117; education, 110, 199; family history, 114–15; use of histotextuality, 113; and self-publication, 25, 27, 93, 113, 173, 199; and *Sketches of My Life in the South*, 110–12, 114–16
supplicant texts, 34, 38, 206n3; by Aaron, 39, 49–50, 52, 62; and abolitionism, 59; and buyers, 38; by Edmond Kelley, 53–54, 59; by Harriet Wilson, 38, 40, 62–63; by Henry Parker, 52; and J. D. Enos, 97; by Mattie J. Jackson, 50; by Moses Grandy, 48; by Nancy Prince, 39, 50; and Osborne P. Anderson, 97; sales of, 40, 59; self-publication, 37, 50; *The Light and Truth of Slavery* as, 39–40, 49

Talcott Street Congregational Church, 98
Terauley Street Baptist Church (Toronto), 93
Thoburn, William, 147
Tilmon, Levin, 13, 68–73; activism, 71, 73, 173; in A.M.E. Church, 69, 71; autobiography, 69, 73; bibliography by, 68, 70; and First Colored Congregational Church, 69; Frederick Douglass, relationship with, 68, 70; narratives by, 68–69; in Philadelphia, 67; use of self-publication, 34, 67–68, 70–71; and storytelling, 70
Torrey, Charles, 74–75

Union Seminary, 164–65, 167, 170–71
United Brethren Church, 147

Virginia: and Carter Edloe, 133; Christopher McPherson in, 121–23, 125–26, 128–30; Henry Parker in, 50; Major James Wilkerson in, 163, 171; Osborne P. Anderson in, 93; and Peter Randolph in, 131–35; and slavery, 37, 96, 125–26, 135; and William J. Anderson in, 81

Walker, David, 33–34, 75–77
Walker, James, 56–59
Washington, Booker T., 13, 131, 158, 175
Washington DC, 74–75, 78–79, 97, 150, 153–54, 180
white ministers, 151, 158
Wilkerson, Major James, 26, 35, 148, 163–172; and A.M.E. Church, 163–64, 166–67, 171–72; in Albany, 165; in Boston, 165; connection to David Smith, 151; health, 165–66; *History*

Wilkerson (cont.)
(1861), 168, 171; as preacher, 164; press coverage of, 26, 166; *The Midnight Cry* (1859), 13, 168–71; writings, 13, 35, 149, 165, 167

Wilson, Harriet, 38, 40, 60–63, 199

women: in abolitionist movement, 49, 66, 80, 85, 107; as activists, 36, 90; in Black churches, 145–46, 151, 159, 179; and Carter Edloe, 132–33; and Civil War, 119, 155; enslaved, 45, 48, 53, 66, 80, 85, 88, 96, 132, 135; and literacy, 10; in Missouri, 140; and print culture, 4

Wordsworth, William, 76

Xenia, Ohio, 151–54, 167

Young Men's Catholic Temperance Society, 14

Young Men's Literary Productive Society, 70–72

www.ingramcontent.com/pod-product-compliance
Lightning Source LLC
Chambersburg PA
CBHW030532230426
43665CB00010B/864